SAP R/3 Reporting Tools

SAP R/3 Reporting Tools

Danielle Larocca

McGraw-Hill

New York • San Francisco • Washington, D.C. • Auckland • Bogotá • Caracas
Lisbon • London • Madrid • Mexico City • Milan • Montreal • New Delhi
San Juan • Singapore • Sydney • Tokyo • Toronto

McGraw-Hill

A Division of The McGraw-Hill Companies

"SAP" is a registered trademark of SAP Aktiengesellschaft, Systems, Applications, and Products in Data Processing, Neurottstrasse 16, 69190 Walldorf, Germany. The publisher gratefully acknowledges SAP's kind permission to use its trademark in this publication. SAP AG is not the publisher of this book and is not responsible for it under any aspect of press law.

1 2 3 4 5 6 7 8 9 0 AGM/AGM 9 0 4 3 2 1 0 9

ISBN 0-07-212342-7

The sponsoring editor for this book was Simon Yates and the production supervisor was Clare Stanley. It was set in Sabon by D&G Limited, LLC.

Printed and bound by Quebecor/Martinsburg.

McGraw-Hill books are available at special quantity discounts to use as premiums and sales promotions, or for use in corporate training programs. For more information, please write to Director of Special Sales, McGraw-Hill, 11 West 19th Street, New York, NY 10011. Or contact your local bookstore.

To my best friend, Jimmy

Contents

Acknowledgments

A moment of thanks to my family, who have asked to be named individually this time, so here goes: Dad, Mom, Patricia, Cathy, Grandpa, Grandma, and not to forget Wellesley, Fu, and regretfully Alex. Many thanks to the newest members of my family for their support: Mary, Janeen, Joe and Pat, and the little guys that make me smile, Timothy ande Michael. Warm thanks to Nicole Kaupp, Kathi Workman, Jeanette Williams, and Kristen Garra for their encouragement and friendship. And a special thanks for the support, companionship, and love of the man I cannot wait to walk down the aisle to, James Signorile.

Introduction

Consider yourself lucky. You now have this massive SAP R/3 system that is capable of accomplishing almost any task you request, according to some people. This statement might or might not be true. We will maintain, however, that the resources available to assist you with getting data out of your SAP system are limited at best. Essentially, this process is what reporting is all about—getting data out of your system and into a format that is beneficial to you.

Did you know that your SAP system (Version 4.0B and higher) contains a selection of more than 3,000 standard reports? This number seems large, considering that most reports used within an SAP organization are custom reports created by programmers using the ABAP language. One would think that a selection of 3,000 reports would be sufficient, but in the real world, that is not always the case. The main reason is poor change management. Frequently, when a company migrates to SAP, it imposes its current thinking and business practices onto its

SAP system, instead of embracing the new (and in some cases, advanced) functionality available within SAP R/3. The company often tries to continue its business practices and workflow as performed prior to SAP, without utilizing the value inherent in SAP to improve and re-engineer those business practices to create a more efficient work output. Despite the obvious commitment to change made evident by the decision to use SAP, many customers still try to mold their SAP reports to their old reports, rather than considering new reports and functionalities that would improve the old.

Consider the following example of a Human Resources/ Payroll implementation at Company X. In Company X's old legacy system, a report was created listing the names and Social Security numbers of all employees to be used as a reference. Simple, single-employee inquiries in the legacy system were not timely and required legacy system skills. This report was printed on a weekly basis in order to keep current with turnover and new hires. This bulky, 60 plus-page report was distributed to five employees in the human resources department each week. Now, Company X works in SAP and has the availability—at any time—to access a user's information quickly and easily. Unfortunately, Company X still decides to create, copy, and distribute the report weekly. So, despite the 3,000-plus standard reports and the reports that can be created by users (which we discuss in this book), ABAP programmers still create many custom reports.

What is the big deal, you say? The answer is as follows: The old method limits the capabilities of the employees and places a heavy reliance on the skills of the programmer. In many cases, this programmer is a consultant, and as we all know, the consultant's time means money. In addition, once you create a custom report, the report requires periodic maintenance—especially if the SAP system undergoes any release or version changes. These custom reports written in code can become a huge hassle. But many people felt that these custom reports were their only option.

Clearly, a big misconception exists about the reporting capabilities within SAP R/3. Many believe that the only options available are the standard reports or the custom reports written by ABAP programmers. This idea is not true. SAP contains report-writing tools designed for users who do not require any technical or programming skills. The main tool is called the ABAP Query, and we discuss this tool in great detail throughout the book. We introduce and discuss other tools, as well. Users who are empowered with the skills to create their own reports without reliance on others can become savvy R/3 users, can be more productive in their work, and can better communicate and comprehend their SAP data.

This book is a tool to teach you how to effectively retrieve the data you want from your R/3 system using the tools SAP provides. The most exciting part is that anyone can do these tasks. You do not need to be a system administrator, an ABAP programmer, or even a computer geek. SAP has the tools and resources that you can easily use to help you get the output that you want and need from your SAP R/3 system. The skills you will learn in this book will empower you with the capability to manage and communicate your SAP information effectively.

Let's get started.

Introduction to Reporting in R/3

In *Systems Applications and Products in Data Processing* (SAP), you will learn that there are several different ways to accomplish the same task. There is no exception when it comes to reporting in R/3. SAP has several different tools available for reporting that we discuss in this book. But before we start creating our own reports, it is necessary to first take a look at these different tools and the basic reporting concepts associated with them.

Programs

The first concept to understand about R/3 reports is that reports are essentially programs in SAP. Programs are comprised of code and syntaxes that are executed behind the scenes to perform a function. In reporting, this function is to retrieve and output data. The technical way of explaining this concept is to say that programs use *Advanced Business-Application Programming* (ABAP) Open *Structured Query Language* (SQL) to read data from the R/3 database. Although this description sounds extremely technical, we will gain a better understanding of this process in Section 3, where we learn in detail about the origin of the data that we include in our reports. As we mentioned at the start of this chapter, in SAP, there are several ways to do the same function. For example, you can use R/3 menu paths to navigate through the system, or you can jump directly to screens using transaction codes in the command field. This same rule applies to reporting. A few tools exist that are used for reporting in SAP, and we examine these tools in the following section.

Reporting Tools in SAP R/3

Reporting tools in R/3 can be separated into two categories: viewing reports and creating reports.

- Viewing reports
  - Executive Information System
  - R/3 General Report Selection Tree
- Creating reports
  - R/3 ABAP Query
  - R/3 Ad-Hoc Query (Human Resources module only)
  - Report Painter and Report Writer
  - Structural graphics
  - ABAP list processing (ABAP programming)
  - Web reporting

Executive Information System

Using this function, executives can retrieve their own custom report portfolio specifically prepared for their use. Think of this report portfolio as being similar to the inbox on your boss's desk. Everything is painstakingly put together by others and is neatly prepared and placed in the inbox. The Executive Information System report portfolio works in a similar manner. The portfolio can be put together in a hierarchy graphic, reporting tree, or custom reporting tree. The Executive Information System provides information about all the factors that influence the business activities within the company by combining relevant data from external and internal sources into one easy and efficient assembly. The Executive Information System is a useful tool for viewing existing SAP reports. We provide a peek at the Executive Information System in Figure 1-1.

R/3 General Report Selection Tree

The R/3 General Report Selection Tree is a conglomeration of all the canned reports in your SAP system in a single location for easy access. We will take a look at the R/3 General Report Selection Tree later in this chapter. We discuss the R/3 General Report Selection

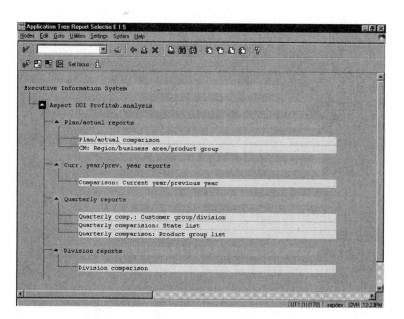

Figure 1-1 *The Executive Information System can be configured for the user's personal preferences.*

Tree in greater detail in Chapter 7, "R/3 General Report Selection Tree." In addition, we will discuss how to create your own custom reporting trees (just like the executives) in Chapter 22, "Customizing Report Trees in R/3." The reporting tree is perhaps the most popular tool used to execute reports in your R/3 system. The reports that are included in the General Report Selection Tree come delivered with your system, and in many cases, they can satisfy some of your company's reporting needs. You can see a preview of the R/3 General Report Selection Tree in Figure 1-2.

R/3 ABAP Query

The ABAP query is a powerful tool that you can use to create your own SAP reports without any programming experience whatsoever. ABAP queries pull data from tables or logical databases in the R/3 system. Logical databases are explained later in Chapter 3, "Reporting Database Concepts." Using these logical databases in conjunction with application and functional areas,

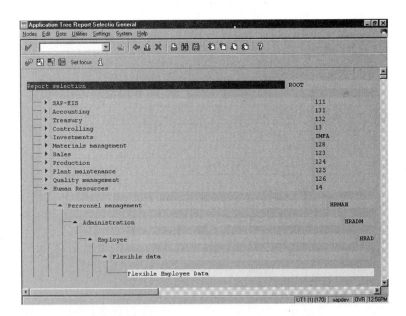

Figure 1-2 *The SAP R/3 General Report Selection Tree is a central location housing many of the canned reports provided in your R/3 system.*

language comparisons, and user groups, you can create your own custom reports. In-depth coverage of the creation and use of functional areas and user groups can be found in Chapter 9, "ABAP Queries Behind the Scenes." Chapter 10, "ABAP Query Reporting Basics," introduces ABAP query reporting and includes instructions on how to create your own R/3 reports. These reports include lists of data in your R/3 system, as well as calculated fields performing manipulations on that data. A large portion of this book discusses the use of this tool, because it is the most superior user tool offered in the R/3 system. The main advantage of using the ABAP query is that you can access data from any table in the R/3 system, unlike other tools that are restricted to certain tables. Figure 1-3 displays a sample of the R/3 ABAP query.

R/3 Ad-Hoc Query (Human Resources Module Only)

Similar to the ABAP query tool, the Ad-Hoc Query is based on logical databases, language comparisons, functional areas, and

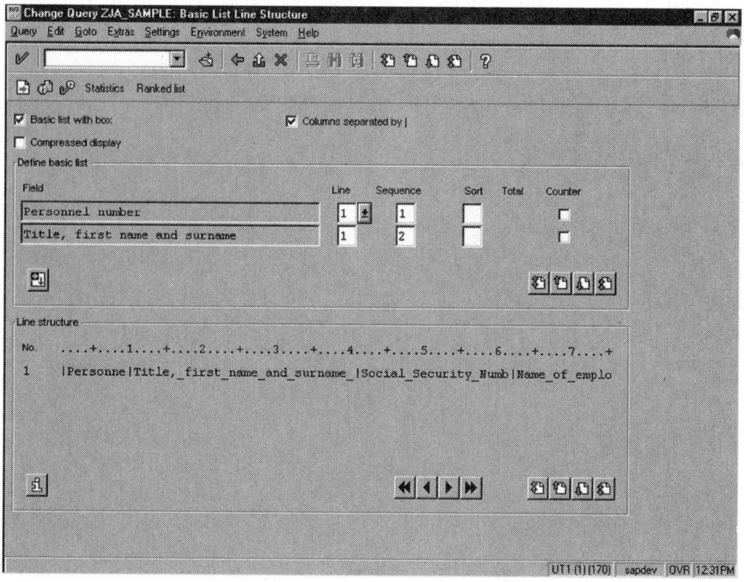

Figure 1-3 *The R/3 ABAP query is a flexible tool designed to be utilized by users of all levels to produce reports.*

user groups. Unlike the ABAP query, this tool is used only for reporting in the Human Resources module. The ABAP query tool can also be used for reporting in Human Resources. This additional tool enables simpler, more detailed selection criteria and is primarily used as a one-time reference for posing queries to your SAP database with regards to your human resources data. For example, if a Human Resources Administrator wanted to find the number of active employees who are female, who are older than 50, and who are located in the Jacksonville office, an Ad-Hoc Query can be used to retrieve the answer. The Ad-Hoc Query tool is discussed in detail in Chapter 16, "The Ad-Hoc Query Reporting Tool (Human Resources Module)," and a preview is shown in Figure 1-4.

Report Painter and Report Writer

Report Writer has been available for some time in R/3, and Report Painter was developed based on the Report Writer interface in order to provide more functionality. The Report Painter

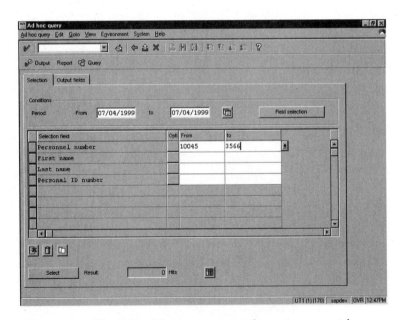

Figure 1-4 *The R/3 ad-hoc query provides assistance with posing one-time questions to your system.*

works as an advanced, add-on graphical interface to support the functionality of Report Writer. The advantages of Report Painter and Report Writer are that they enable you to report from multiple applications. These tools, however, are only used to display numeric fields (such as quantities or currencies) and do not display text fields (with the exception of column headings). Report Writer and Report Painter do enable the complex grouping of data usually found in financial statements and the like. These tools are popular for creating standard numeric reports in the financial and controlling modules, including month-end and budget-analysis reports. Use the transaction code FGRP or the menu path Information systems→Ad hoc reports→Report painter to take a look at these tools.

Structural Graphics

Structural graphics are used for the creation and maintenance of organizational plans in the organization and planning component of the human resources module. Structural graphics enable you to view and work with objects in a graphical format, similar to a pictorial organizational chart with boxes. This graphical presentation makes it easier to distinguish the inter-relationships and hierarchies that exist between objects. Within structural graphics, you can display and edit the structures and objects within your company's organizational plan.

ABAP List Processing (ABAP Programming)

OK, here comes the technical stuff. ABAP List Processing uses the ABAP language to retrieve data. These are the types of reports created by SAP ABAP programmers. This type of reporting requires the skills of an ABAP programmer and cannot be performed by the standard SAP end user. These programmers write code and syntaxes that select the data from the database, and then outputs the data in a desired format. This job is no easy task, and for this reason, ABAP programmers make big bucks. When you hear people talk about custom reports in SAP, they are generally referring to reports written in ABAP code. Because there is not a lot of information available (before this book) on the other reporting tools in SAP, customers have had to rely heavily

```
ABAP Editor: Display Program RPLGEB30
Program  Edit  Goto  Utilities  Block/buffer  Settings  System  Help

Markers   Mark line

78   data: begin of store,
79         pernr    like p0001-pernr,
80         orgeh    like p0001-orgeh,
81         name     like name,
82         hiredate like hiredate,
83         firedate like firedate,
84         gbdat    like p0002-gbdat,
85         alter    like alter,
86      end of store.
87   **************************************************
88   *    Field-Groups                                *
89   **************************************************
90   field-groups: header, record.    "Sort-area fuer Insert,...
91   insert p0001-orgeh p0001-pernr into header.
92   * Einfuegen eines oder mehrerer Felder in die Feldgruppe sort-area
93   insert

                                    Line   78 — 93  of  387

                                        UT1 (1) (170)  sapdev   OVR  12:50PM
```

Figure 1-5 *ABAP List Processing is code written in the ABAP language by skilled SAP programmers.*

on these types of custom reports. For a sample of what this ABAP language looks like in the behind-the-scenes view of a SAP report, see Figure 1-5.

Web Reporting

Your SAP system can be configured to enable Web reporting. Web reporting enables executing, viewing, and printing reports from the Internet or intranet. You are probably familiar with the term *Uniform Resource Locator* (URL), which represents an address of a file (resource) that is accessible on the Internet. Selecting a URL on a Web page will bring you to the selected item. When looking at Web reporting from its most basic level, you will find that Web reporting is based on that URL concept. Web pages contains URLs that access (via *Remote Function Calls*, or RFCs) reports from your R/3 system. Reports can be executed with or without selection screens, depending on the code embedded in the URL command. Web reporting is the wave of the future in terms of managing your R/3 data.

Four Essential Concepts for R/3 Reporting

Now that we are familiar with the tools, we can move on to the basics of reporting in R/3. In other applications, reports are easy to conceptualize. You think about the data stored in the database as simply organized into standard columns and rows of output. On the surface, this concept is similar in SAP, except that there are four general, fundamental basics that need to be understood about R/3 reporting:

- Reports are programs in SAP.

- Reporting database concepts (i.e., where is the data coming from?)

- Selection screens

- Reports and lists

Reports are Programs in SAP

The first concept is that reports are essentially programs in SAP, and this idea was mentioned early in the chapter. In other words, there is an important distinction between the report name and the program name. The report name is the title of the report that we would use to distinguish the report. The "Birthday List" report would be the name of the report, for example. All reports in SAP have a program name as well, however. Usually, this name is absolutely meaningless to the user and is not a good indicator of what the program does. For example, RPLGEB30 is the program name for the "Birthday List" report in your Human Resources module. The distinction here is that the *report name* is what is recognized by the user, and the *program name* is what is used by the system to execute the report. Although the program names might not appear familiar, there are naming conventions used to classify reports. For example, customer reports begin with RFD, and accounting reports begin with RGC. Reports are not the only kinds of programs in SAP. There are also programs that perform other functions besides producing output. The SAP R/3 system is driven by programs that perform processing and administrative functions and generally serve as the core of your SAP system. Many different kinds of programs in SAP can be called from the ABAP Editor in the ABAP Workbench—including reports.

Program Names

To obtain a better idea of how these concepts all fit together, let's take a look at some program names of reports in the SAP R/3 General Report Selection Tree. To get started, navigate to the SAP R/3 General Report Selection Tree using the menu path Information systems→General report selection. The screen should appear similar to the one shown in Figure 1-6.

Note   Take a look at the title bar of the screen capture in Figure 1-6. Does anything look strange to you? The word "Selection" is misspelled. We point out this mistake because we want you to understand that SAP is not perfect. There are many mistakes similar to this one, and we want to make it clear right now that you can question what you see in your R/3 system. As the picture shows, SAP is not always correct.

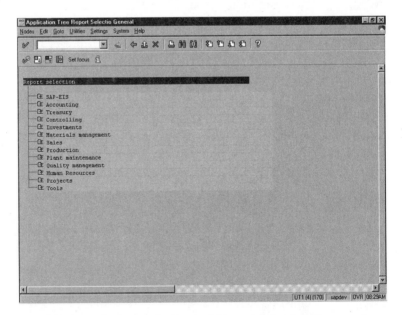

Figure 1-6 *The SAP R/3 General Report Selection Tree can be used to execute standard reports in SAP.*

General Report Selection is a list of many of the standard reports that come delivered in your SAP system. You can navigate to and execute the different reports directly from the report tree. We will take a detailed look at the SAP R/3 General Report Selection Tree later in Chapter 7, "R/3 General Report Selection Tree." For starters, let's become familiar with the application toolbar for the General Report Selection Tree screen. Table 1.1 shows how the application toolbar for the SAP R/3 General Report Selection Tree appears on screen.

Use the Expand subtree button from the application toolbar to open the Human resources node of the General Report Selection Tree. Continue to use the Expand subtree button to expand to the Administration→Employee→Birthday→Birthday List, as shown in Figure 1-7.

The "Birthday List" refers to the report name in SAP that we discussed earlier. The default view of the report tree lists only the report names and does not list the program names for the different

Table 1.1 *The application toolbar for the SAP R/3 General Report Selection Tree screen*

	The Execute button is used to execute the report.
	The Expand subtree button is used to expand the subnodes of the selected tree.
	The Collapse subtree button is used to collapse the subnodes of the selected tree.
	The Node Attributes button is used to view the attributes of the selected node, including node type, destination, and authorization group.
Set focus	The Set focus button is used to center the focus on a particular node in the tree.
	The Online manual button is used to display the hypertext help for the General Report Tree functions.

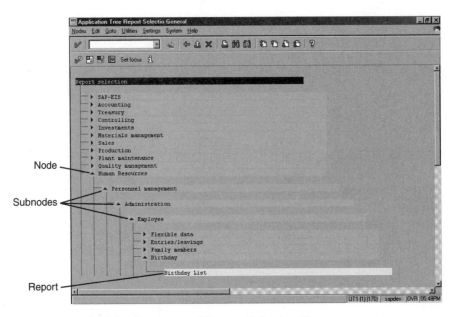

Figure 1-7 *The SAP R/3 General Report Selection Tree segregates reports by the different application modules.*

reports. This setting can be turned off and on. Take the following steps to view program names of the reports:

1. Place your cursor on a node in the tree (i.e., Human resources).

2. Make sure that the tree is expanded so that the report names are showing by following the menu path Edit→Expand subtree or by selecting the Expand subtree button from the application toolbar.

3. Follow the menu path Settings→Technical names on/off.

4. The program names for reports in the tree will be displayed on the right-hand side of the screen (see Figure 1-8).

Note   Looking closely at Figure 1-8, you can see that in addition to the reports, the nodes and subnodes have technical names, as well. In SAP, everything has an identifying technical name behind the scenes. When we work with customizing report trees later in Chapter 22, "Customizing Report Trees in R/3," these node names will become important.

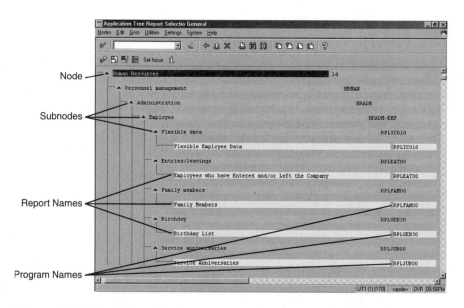

Figure 1-8 *The technical program names for the SAP R/3 General Report Selection Tree reports can usually be executed through the ABAP Editor.*

Database Concepts (i.e., "Where is the Data Coming From?")

We are confident that you are now familiar with the first essential component of reporting in R/3. The next important piece of knowledge is how you comprehend the relationship between the data you view on your R/3 selection screens and the output you retrieve in your reports. Databases are essentially large warehouses of information. The data entered in your SAP selection screens is stored in fields, which are contained in tables. These tables are connected through extensive relationships. If you are familiar with the concepts of databases, then you have an advantage here. In Chapter 3, however, "Reporting Database Concepts," we take an in-depth look at how the relationship between the data on your R/3 screens and the output on your reports is associated.

Selection Screens

The third essential concept of reporting in R/3 is selection screens. Selection screens are the key to producing the desired output with your reports. They also provide you with flexibility in reporting. A selection screen comes up each time you execute a report in R/3, giving you the opportunity to specify exactly what data you would like to see in your output. This concept is extremely important. A selection screen will be displayed any time a report is executed before you see your output (with the exception of background processing, which is discussed later in Chapter 11, "ABAP Query Maintenance and Variants"). We can think of an example of a selection screen using a concept from the Financials module as an example. Let's say that you create a report listing all purchase orders in your R/3 system and their relevant details. When you execute the report, a selection screen will appear, giving you an opportunity to be more specific with your report. What if you only want to see open purchase orders? Using your selection screen, you can specify precisely the output you desire. Or, you can specify only open purchase orders created in December for a particular vendor. Suddenly, your single purchase-order report has multiple purposes. Every time you execute this report, you can specify exactly what output you want to see using the selection screen. In Chapter 4, "Selection Screens," we examine R/3 selection screens to see how they are an essential part of reporting in R/3 and how you can use them to your advantage.

Reports and Lists

Finally, the last essential concept of reporting in R/3 is the distinction between reports and lists in R/3. Reports in SAP are the executable function that produces the output. (Remember the term "program"? We are referring to it here.) The list is essentially the output, or the final result. The distinction between the two is important. The report can be run at any time to produce real-time, live data results from your R/3 system. A list is the output from a report generation that displays the output of data at a frozen point in time and does not reflect real-time, active R/3 data. For example, if we execute the "Open Invoices" report Monday and save the output as a list, then that list—if opened Tuesday—will contain only Monday's data. Although, if the report is executed again on Tuesday, it will contain real-time Tuesday data. This confusing concept is difficult to grasp, but it is an important idea. The concepts of reports and lists is discussed again in greater detail in Chapter 5, "Executing and Maintaining SAP R/3 Reports." The focus of Chapter 5 is to not only explain how to execute reports, but also to describe how to effectively manage your lists in your R/3 system.

Chapter Wrap-Up

Now that we have been introduced to the different reporting tools and the four essential reporting concepts, we will make sure that we are familiar with the basic concepts of R/3. Chapter 2, "SAP R/3 Basics Review," will review basic navigational and functional concepts of R/3 that are required skills for the remainder of the book. This review is intended to substantiate familiarity with SAP and the terms, ideas, and navigational concepts used in this book. After we pace our way through a handful of chapters, discussing some important concepts in reporting, we will dive right in to creating our own custom reports in SAP.

SAP R/3 Basics Review

This chapter will help ensure that you are familiar with the basics of your SAP system and will help substantiate that you know how to navigate and function within R/3. Many of the concepts and terms discussed in this chapter are used throughout the book. Even if you are an experienced SAPper, you might find it helpful to review this chapter.

Getting Started

Getting started in SAP requires three basic steps:

1. Installing the SAP software (known as the SAPGUI)

2. Providing a connection to the database and application servers for your R/3 system

3. Providing a client number, username, and password to log on to the R/3 system

Once these three basics are out of the way, you are ready to get started with R/3.

Logging On to SAP

Each time you connect or "log on" to SAP, you create a "session." A session is a separate operating environment in which you can process tasks in R/3. For example, you can have one session open where you are creating an invoice in the Financials module, while a second session can display a list of other users who are currently on the R/3 system—and a third session can display your SAPoffice inbox. Only your initial session requires the entry of a name and password. The third basic requirement for connecting to R/3 is the client number. The client in R/3 refers to the number designated for a specific operating environment. For example, your SAP installation might contain a creative (development) client, where the system is configured and a production (live-data) environment is available for the processing of actual data. Each of these clients would have a different number assigned to it that would be entered when you log on to SAP (see Figure 2-1).

In the example in Figure 2-1, the client number 095 will ensure that you connect to the correct server. This number will provide access to a particular SAP environment and database. If you logged in with client number 100, for example, you would be connected to your live production system. Most regular end users work only within their productive environment. After logging in, you will be presented with the main R/3 window, which will list your client and session number in the bottom-right system tray (as shown in Figure 2-2).

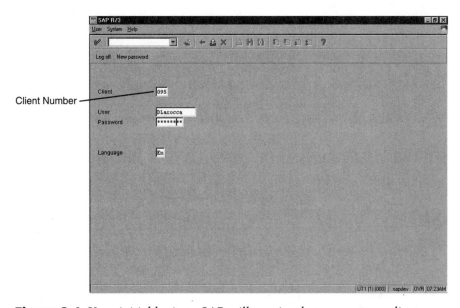

Figure 2-1 *Your initial login to SAP will require that you enter a client number, username, and password.*

Session Basics

Your current session number is also listed in the system tray. Each session provides you with a new environment. You can perform completely different tasks within these different sessions, and you can have a maximum of nine sessions open at any given time. Your company can restrict that number to fewer sessions. Keep in mind that each open session utilizes some of your computer's resources and might affect performance. As a rule, it is always a good idea to have at least two sessions open each time you log on to SAP.

Creating a New Session

Creating a new session in R/3 from any screen in the system is easy if you follow the menu path System→Create session. Data in other sessions will not be lost when you navigate from session to session. You can navigate between sessions using the Alt+Tab keys on your keyboard or by selecting the different sessions from your Microsoft Windows taskbar (see Figure 2-3).

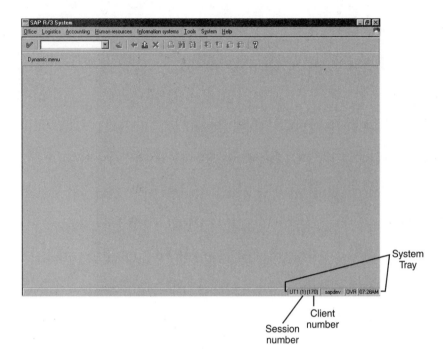

Figure 2-2 *The R/3 system tray will provide you with useful information regarding your R/3 connection.*

You can also create a new session using the R/3 Command Field from the Standard toolbar. The Command Field can be used to enter transaction codes that enable you to navigate through the system without using menu paths. We will talk more about this concept shortly.

Ending a Session

Ending a session is just as easy as creating one. You should note that you need to save any work in the session before ending the session. To end a session in R/3, follow the menu path System→End session. You can also use the X Close Window button on the top right-hand side of the window to end the session.

R/3 Window Basics

The R/3 window, sometimes referred to as the SAPGUI (with GUI standing for Graphical User Interface), has seven main ele-

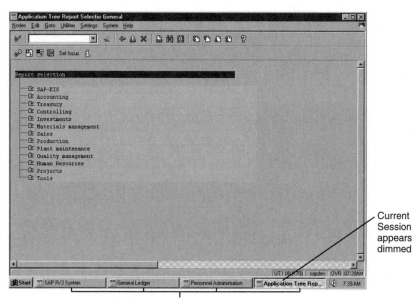

Figure 2-3 *Screen descriptions of your different R/3 sessions are shown in the taskbar.*

ments. These elements include the Title bar, Menu Bar, Standard toolbar, Application toolbar, Display, Status bar, and System Tray. These elements are shown in Figure 2-4.

Seven main elements might sound like a lot, but it's actually pretty simple. For example, we have already discussed the System Tray.

System Tray

The System Tray, shown earlier in Figure 2-2, provides some information about your system. This feature shows a display of your database name, session number, client number, host name, write mode, and system time. The database and host names describe the database to which you are connected. We are already familiar with the session and client numbers, which leaves only the write mode. The write mode refers to whether or not your SAP system is in insert or overwrite mode. This feature is similar

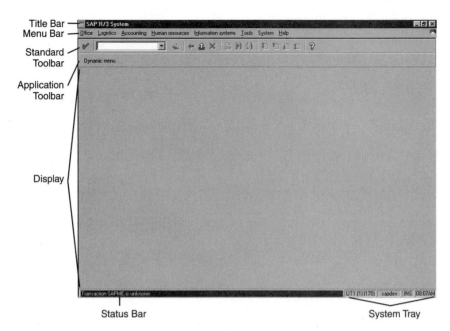

Figure 2-4 *The R/3 window's standard components are accessible on almost all SAP screens.*

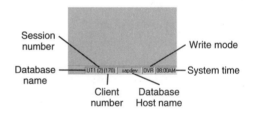

Figure 2-5 *The System Tray is present on all SAP screens in the bottom right-hand side of the window.*

to many word-processing applications. Insert mode enables you to insert new text without replacing the existing text. Overwrite mode does exactly what the name implies: it overwrites the text. This personal preference can be toggled on and off using the Insert key on the right side of your keyboard. By default, the setting is overwrite mode. Figure 2-5 displays the R/3 System Tray.

Title Bar

The Title bar is the top portion of the R/3 window. In many PC applications, the term Title bar is pretty standard, and it is always presented on the top, uppermost, left-hand portion of the window. The Title bar provides a description of the current screen or transaction. If you take a look at some of your other PC applications, such as Microsoft Word or Microsoft Windows Explorer, you will find that a Title bar is always present.

The Menu Bar

The Menu bar provides all of the navigational options available for the screen and is displayed directly under the Title bar. Similar to the Title bar, the Menu bar is a common item in PC applications. The Menu bar in SAP will vary, depending on the screen and transaction that you are processing within R/3. Transaction-specific menu items will be available to you. For example, if you are in a General Ledger screen, document and account-entry menu options will be available for use (as opposed to a Human Resources screen, where employee and applicant menu paths are available). There are two consistent items that exist on almost all SAP screens, however. These two menus appear at the far right of the Menu bar and are titled "System" and "Help." These menus provide you with assistance and functionality that is consistent across all R/3 applications.

The Standard Toolbar

You will use options from the Standard toolbar on almost all of your SAP screens when processing. Again, similar to the Title and Menu bars, the Standard toolbar is available in many PC applications. Think of the Save and Open buttons from your word processing and spreadsheet applications. This concept is the same in SAP. The core functions for processing your SAP data, including saving, printing, and navigating, are all available from the Standard toolbar. For descriptions of each of the items on the Standard toolbar, please refer to Table 2.1.

The Save button on the R/3 Standard toolbar appears identical to the Open button used in most Microsoft applications.   **Warning**

Table 2.1 *The SAP R/3 Standard toolbar*

	Enter button	The Enter button works like the Enter key on your keyboard. In most cases, this button is used to validate an entry on the screen. For example, if you enter your login information on the main screen when connecting, you can select the Enter button to process the data and complete your login.
	Command field	The Command field is used for quick navigation in R/3. Instead of navigating using the menu paths, you can enter transaction codes into the Command field and jump right to the transaction. (This feature is discussed in more detail later in the chapter.)
	Save button	The Save button saves your work and updates the database with any information entered on the screen. The Save function can also be performed using the F11 key.
	Back button	The Back button is used to return to the previous screen within a transaction. Using this button will return you to the previous screen without saving your data.
	Exit button	The Exit button is used to leave the current application. The system returns to the previous application or to the main menu screen.

	Cancel button	The Cancel button is used to exit the current task without saving your data. The Cancel function can also be performed by selecting Cancel from the Edit menu.
	Print button	The Print button is used to print data from the R/3 screen.
	Find button	The Find button is used to perform a search for data on the screen.
	Find Next button	The Find Next button is used to perform an extended search for data on the screen.
	First Page button	The First Page button is used to travel to the top of a screen (or page) if the information on the screen is too long to fit on a single screen.
	Previous Page (Page Up) button	The Previous Page button is used to travel up one screen (or page) if the information on the screen is too long to fit on a single screen. This button is equivalent to using the Page Up key on your keyboard.
	Next Page (Page Down) button	The Next Page button is used to travel down one screen when the information on the screen is too long to fit on a single screen. This button is equivalent to using the Page Down key on your keyboard.
	Last Page button	The Last Page button is used to travel to the end of a screen (or page) when the

Table 2.1 *The SAP R/3 Standard toolbar (Continued)*

[icon]		information on the screen is too long to fit on a single screen.
[icon]	Help button	The Help button is used for selection-sensitive, specific help. Placing your cursor into a field on an R/3 screen and selecting this button will launch field-specific help.

The Application Toolbar

Just below the Standard toolbar lies the Application toolbar. This toolbar is specific to the screen. In other words, the toolbar provides additional processing functionality that is specific to the screen in which you are processing. Similar to the Menu bar, the Application toolbar varies from screen to screen. For example, if you are in the General Report Selection Tree, there are buttons for executing and navigating between reports. If you are on the ABAP Workbench screen, the Application toolbar would display buttons for accessing different ABAP tools (such as ABAP Editor or Screen Painter).

Status Bar

The Status bar will provide you with system messages as you work in R/3. For example, the bar will present you with informational-type messages such as, "Your Report Has Been Sent To the Printer," or "You Do Not Have Access To The Selected Transaction." The Status bar will also contain error messages. You can configure your system to have these messages appear in pop-up dialog boxes (using the R/3 Options menu), but many find these pop-up dialog boxes to be annoying and unnecessary nuisances.

Navigation Using the Command Field

As introduced earlier, the Command field can be used to navigate automatically to a screen in R/3, bypassing the need for menu paths. Transaction codes are comprised of a four-digit character code. These codes are entered directly into the Command field. Samples of R/3 transaction codes are shown in Table 2.2.

The four-digit transaction codes can be entered in any SAP R/3 screen. From any R/3 screen other than the main window, you need to preface the transaction code with a /N. This /N (where *n* stands for new), plus the four-digit transaction code, will bring you to the new screen. For example, entering /NSQ01 into the Command field on the main SAP screen will bring you directly to the ABAP query main screen. From the ABAP query main screen, you can enter the transaction code /NS000 to return to the main SAP screen. The transaction codes are not case sensitive, which means that they can be entered in upper or lower case.

A neat trick that you can do using the Command field is creating a new session and navigating to a new transaction by adding a /0 (where *o* stands for open) before the four-digit transaction code. See the examples in Table 2.3.

Locating the Transaction Code

You might be thinking that using the Command field seems like a great idea, but how do you know what the transaction codes are? You can obtain the transaction code for any screen by following the menu path System→Status. A display window will

Table 2.2 *R/3 transaction code samples*

Transaction Code	Transaction Description
S000	Main SAP Screen
SQ01	ABAP Query Main Screen
PA00	Human Resources, Personnel Administration
ME00	Logistics, Purchasing
FSMN	Financials, General Ledger
KCCF	Executive Information System

Table 2.3 *A R/3 transaction code navigation example*

Entered into the Command Field	SAP Processing Result
/NSQ01	Will discontinue what is currently displayed on your screen and will navigate you to the ABAP query main screen
/OSQ01	Will leave your current screen as is and create a new session displaying the ABAP query main screen

emerge, listing the transaction code for the screen that you are viewing (or for the transaction in which you are processing). Figure 2-6 shows the Status window.

In some cases, several screens that are part of a transaction can all have the same transaction code. An example would be the creation of a purchase order. Let's say that there are three screens into which data has to be entered in order to create a purchase order. You cannot use a transaction code to jump to the last screen of that process, because the three screens are required in order for the creation to be completed. In cases such as these, a single transaction code is used for all of the screens within the transaction.

The History List

The Command field stores a history of all the transaction codes that you entered during your connection. This history is called the history list. You can use the Possible Entries Help button to display the entries in the history list to quickly navigate to previous screens, as shown in Figure 2-7.

Session Overview

You can obtain an overview of all of your open sessions by placing a /0 (where *o* stands for open) into the Command field, as shown in Figure 2-8.

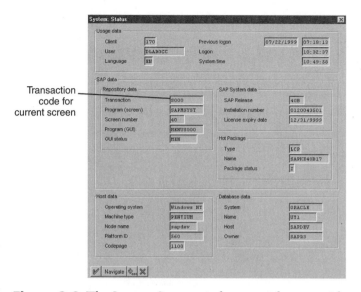

Figure 2-6 *The System: Status window provides you with useful information about your SAP system and about the transaction in which you are currently processing.*

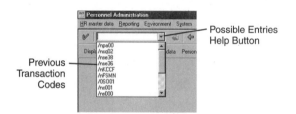

Figure 2-7 *The history list will save all of the transactions entered during your SAP connection.*

R/3 Screen Basics

In order to grasp the "big picture" of SAP, so to speak, it is important to understand that the fields you see on your R/3 screens are connected to your database. We will go into greater detail about this concept in the next chapter. There are two different types of fields on your screen: those that display data, called Display fields, and those in which you enter data, called Input

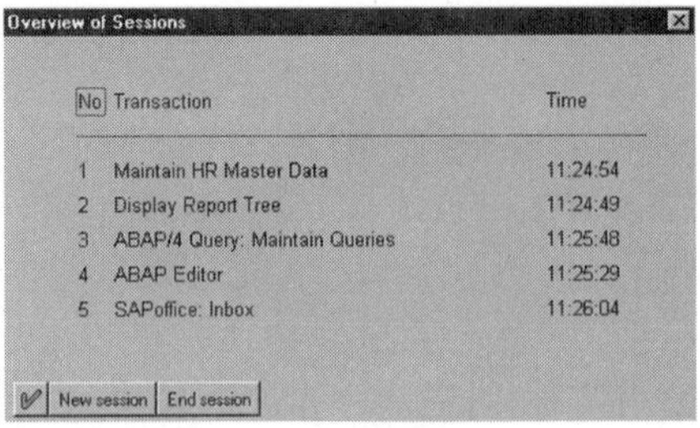

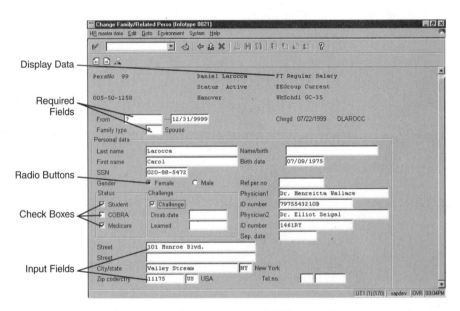

Figure 2-8 *From this overview box, you can navigate to, create, or end your different sessions.*

Figure 2-9 *SAP screens can have a series of different objects arranged in the Display window.*

fields. In addition to these two types of fields, there are other types of objects that can appear on your R/3 screens. See Figure 2-9 for an example.

Input Fields

Input fields function just like their name indicates. They are fields in which you input data. The screen displayed in Figure 2-9 is part of the Human Resources module. This particular screen is used to enter information about employees' dependents. In Figure 2-9, the Last name and First name fields where we have entered the name Carol Larocca are considered Input fields. Their white background indicates that they can accept the entry of data. These Input fields are connected to tables in the database. For example, the Last name field is linked to the P0021 table in the R/3 database. This particular field will accept the entry of characters up to 40 text characters in length. The Birth date field located on the right side of the screen is also linked to the P0021 table but will accept the input of an eight-digit numeric date. We talk more about database concepts such as these in Chapter 3, "Reporting Database Concepts." For now, it is enough to understand that Input fields are where you input data.

Required Fields

Some Input fields require that you enter data. These fields, as shown in Figure 2-9, display a question mark (?). The R/3 system will not permit you to proceed from a screen without inputting values into the required fields.

Remember how we mentioned earlier that SAP sometimes makes mistakes? Here is another area where SAP falters. Sometimes there are required fields in R/3 that do not display a question mark. If you leave a field blank and try to proceed, you will be presented with an error asking you to fill in the required field.

Warning

Display Data/Fields

Display fields will only display data and will not accept the input of data. Display fields appear with a shaded background. Displayed data can appear floating on the screen, as shown in Figure 2-9, or within a field, as shown in Figure 2-10.

Radio Buttons

Radio buttons are used when you need to make a choice between alternatives where only one selection is appropriate. For example, in Figure 2-9, two radio buttons are presented where

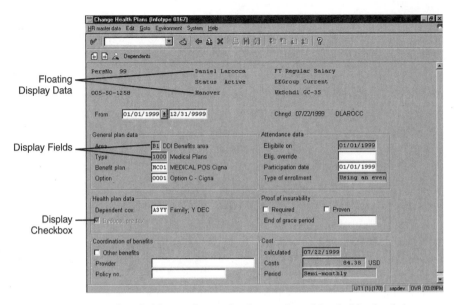

Figure 2-10 *Display fields can be in the form of a table, field, check box, or radio button.*

you can select the gender. You can only select one gender—male or female—and selecting both is not an option. Radio buttons are fields that are connected to the database, as well. For example, if you fill in the circle for the female gender, that value will be stored in the Q0021 table in the database.

Check Boxes

Check boxes are used when you want to make multiple selections between alternatives where possibly more than one selection is appropriate. For example, in Figure 2-9, check boxes can be used to indicate whether the person is a student, whether they are on Medicare, and whether they are challenged. A person can fit all three of these criteria, so it is possible to mark more than one check box. Similar to radio buttons, check boxes store a value in the database depending on the entry.

R/3 Trees

SAP is notorious for its use of trees in the R/3 system. An SAP salesperson once explained that "SAP is a German product, and

Germans are very logical thinkers . . . the development of report trees in SAP follows that logic." R/3 trees do work in a logical flow. They are set up similar to the Microsoft Windows Explorer (File Manager) in your computer, where there is a hierarchical structure with folders, subfolders, and files. In SAP, a tree is segregated by hierarchical, logical levels called nodes, subnodes, and programs. The salespersons' explanation does make some sense; however, it takes some time to get used to this idea. A report tree is displayed in Figure 2-11.

Table Controls

The last type of screen object is a table control. Table controls are used to display data in a spreadsheet format. Most of the configuration of the R/3 system performed during implementation is done through SAP data presented in table controls. A sample table control is shown in Figure 2-12.

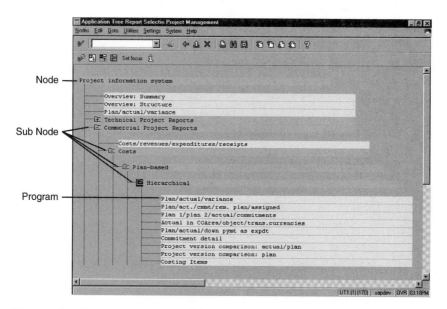

Figure 2-11 *Many screens and functions in R/3 contain tree-like structures.*

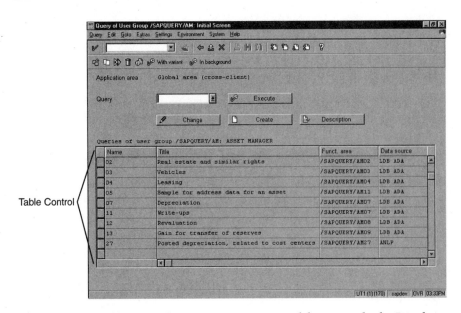

Table Control

Figure 2-12 *Table controls appear as mini-spreadsheets inside the Display portion of the SAP R/3 window.*

R/3 Functional Basics

Some functional tips will be helpful as you work with the R/3 system. These functional basics will provide you with a "short-cut" way of performing simple tasks in SAP.

Possible Entries Help

Possible Entries Help appears on many SAP screens in the form of a down arrow when the field is active (the cursor is placed in the field). In some instances, the Possible Entries Help provides you with a list of valid entries for the field (see Figure 2-13).

In other cases, this feature can be used to select data. For example, if you want to release a pending purchase order, you can go to the purchase order screen and use the Possible Entries Help button in the purchase order field to select the purchase order. Another use is for date fields. Using the Possible Entries Help button in a date field will provide you with a calendar display to assist you in the entry of a date (see Figure 2-14).

You must keep in mind that the Possible Entries Help button will only be visible if your cursor is placed in the field. Possible

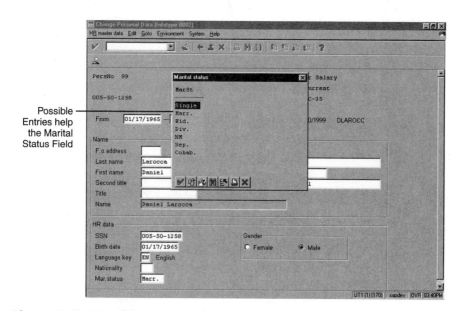

Figure 2-13 *Possible Entries Help speeds up the entry of data in R/3 and enables field-entry validation.*

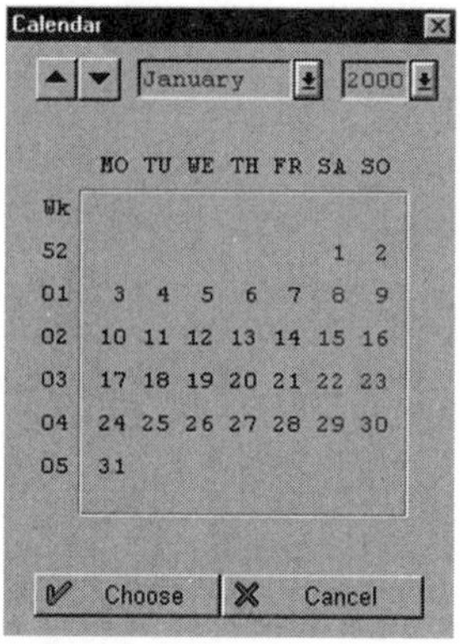

Figure 2-14 *Calendar Display Controls are used on almost all SAP date fields.*

Entries Help can also be retrieved for a field by selecting the F4 key from the top of your keyboard.

Chapter Wrap-Up

Throughout this chapter, you have learned the basic terms and functions of your R/3 system. Many of the terms and concepts will be used throughout the book. For example, in later chapters, you will be referred to buttons on the Application toolbar or will be asked to save your SAP data. You will need to know which items are being referred to and how to use them. The concepts learned in this chapter will arm you with necessary skills as you progress in this book. Now that you have the basics under your belt, it is time to move on to one of the four essential concepts in reporting: database concepts.

Reporting Database Concepts

To comprehend how reporting works in SAP, you should understand the workings of the R/3 database. The SAP system is built upon a large database. This database houses all of the information that you will be using on your reports.

Database Structure

A database is a container that can store, organize, retrieve, and present information. This electronic filing system is used to organize information. At the simplest level, a database is composed of four essential elements: tables, fields, data, and relationships. Tables house the data in columns (called fields) and rows (called records, or data). One way to think about a table is to think of your personal phone book. Your phone book would be the table containing fields (i.e., name, phone number, and birthday), and the data would be the actual information (i.e., John Smith, 555-555-1212, 1/14/65). An example of this concept is displayed in Figure 3-1.

In Figure 3-1, the table shown looks similar to a Microsoft Excel worksheet, with its use of columns and rows. They are similar in many ways, but there is one major difference. A database can have multiple tables that are connected via relationships. These relationships make it possible for the data within the database to be related. Here is an example. Consider a personal phone

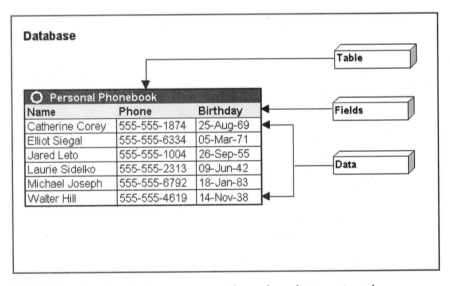

Figure 3-1 *Standard reference materials, such as dictionaries, phone books, and account records, can all be thought of in terms of a database of information.*

book that stores all of your friends' names, phone numbers, and birthdays, as we saw in Figure 3-1. Let's say that you want a list of all of their names, birthdays, and addresses. Your personal phone book table does not have their address information listed. You can obtain their addresses from another source (i.e., the Yellow Pages), but you still do not know their birthdays (see Figure 3-2).

What you can do is create a relationship between these two sources (based on a common field), and you will have all the data that you need. Take a look at Figure 3-3.

Relational Database Management System (RDBMS)

These relationships enable us to create detailed reports in our R/3 system. The technical term for this connection of multiple tables through relationships is known as Relational Database Management, and the actual database is called a *Relational Database Management System* (RDBMS).

O Personal Phonebook		
Name	**Phone**	**Birthday**
Catherine Corey	555-555-1874	25-Aug-69
Elliot Siegal	555-555-6334	05-Mar-71
Jared Leto	555-555-1004	26-Sep-55
Laurie Sidelko	555-555-2313	09-Jun-42
Michael Joseph	555-555-6792	18-Jan-83
Walter Hill	555-555-4619	14-Nov-38

O Yellow Pages	
Name	**Address**
Catherine Corey	101 Maple Ave Wantagh NY 11793
Elliot Siegal	501 Broadway Clearview FL 07865
Jared Leto	30 Munroe Avenue Hewlett NY 11234
Laurie Sidelko	905 Agate Street Sunnydale CA 89665
Michael Joseph	95 101st Street New York NY 10101
Walter Hill	PO Box 1100 Massapequa NY 11758

From the **Personal Phonebook Table** I Can Create A Report of Names, Phone Numbers and Birthdays

From the **YellowPages Table** I Can Create A Report of Names and Addresses

Name	Phone	Birthday
Catherine Corey	555-555-1874	25-Aug-69
Elliot Siegal	555-555-6334	05-Mar-71
Jared Leto	555-555-1004	26-Sep-55
Laurie Sidelko	555-555-2313	09-Jun-42
Michael Joseph	555-555-6792	18-Jan-83
Walter Hill	555-555-4619	14-Nov-38

Name	Address
Catherine Corey	101 Maple Ave Wantagh NY 11793
Elliot Siegal	501 Broadway Clearview FL 07865
Jared Leto	30 Munroe Avenue Hewlett NY 11234
Laurie Sidelko	905 Agate Street Sunnydale CA 89665
Michael Joseph	95 101st Street New York NY 10101
Walter Hill	PO Box 1100 Massapequa NY 11758

Figure 3-2 *Two tables without relationships will only produce reports stored within their tables.*

Relationship

Personal Phonebook		
Name	**Phone**	**Birthday**
Catherine Corey	555-555-1874	25-Aug-69
Elliot Siegal	555-555-6334	05-Mar-71
Jared Leto	555-555-1004	26-Sep-55
Laurie Sidelko	555-555-2313	09-Jun-42
Michael Joseph	555-555-6792	18-Jan-83
Walter Hill	555-555-4619	14-Nov-38

Yellow Pages	
Name	**Address**
Catherine Corey	101 Maple Ave Wantagh NY 11793
Elliot Siegal	501 Broadway Clearview FL 07865
Jared Leto	30 Munroe Avenue Hewlett NY 11234
Laurie Sidelko	905 Agate Street Sunnydale CA 89665
Michael Joseph	95 101st Street New York NY 10101
Walter Hill	PO Box 1100 Massapequa NY 11758

Based On The **Relationship**, A Report Can Be
Generated Using Data From Both Tables

Name	Phone	Birthday	Address
Catherine Corey	555-555-1874	25-Aug-69	101 Maple Ave Wantagh NY 11793
Elliot Siegal	555-555-6334	05-Mar-71	501 Broadway Clearview FL 07865
Jared Leto	555-555-1004	26-Sep-55	30 Munroe Avenue Hewlett NY 11234
Laurie Sidelko	555-555-2313	09-Jun-42	905 Agate Street Sunnydale CA 89665
Michael Joseph	555-555-6792	18-Jan-83	95 101st Street New York NY 10101
Walter Hill	555-555-4619	14-Nov-38	PO Box 1100 Massapequa NY 11758

Figure 3-3 *A relationship between tables is based on a common field in both tables.*

As the personal phone book and Yellow Pages example shows, a RDBMS eliminates the redundancy of data. If we were not able to have this relationship, we would need to add all of the addresses from the Yellow Pages table to our personal phone book, and then we would have our friends' addresses in two different places. Now, what if these friends moved? We would need to change their addresses in our personal phone book and again in the Yellow Pages table. Using a RDBMS, we need to store each piece of data only once.

Primary Keys

As we saw in the personal phone book and Yellow Pages example, both tables had a field that stored the same information: the Name field. This common field was used as the link between the two tables. This common field is called the primary key. This primary key field has to be unique so that you can distinguish it from all other fields. An example of a primary key in SAP is the vendor number. Your company might have thousands of vendors, and the data for these vendors could be stored in multiple tables. One master table will store the vendor's basic data, including their vendor number, contact and address information, etc. If you want to create a report of all vendors and their addresses (from the vendor master table) and their open purchase orders (from the purchase order table), you can do so because both are linked to the vendor number (see Figure 3-4).

Foreign Keys

When the vendor number (the primary key in the vendor table) exists in another table, it is not the primary key of the other table. Rather, this number is now referred to as a foreign key. Take a look at the purchase order table in Figure 3-4. The purchase number is the primary key of the purchase order table. The field(s) used to link a primary key field in another table is a foreign key, as shown in Figure 3-5.

In Figure 3-5, the primary key in the vendor address table is the vendor number. The vendor number is the foreign key in the purchase order table, which has the purchase number as its primary key. Lastly, the salesperson table has salesperson as its primary key, and it exists as a foreign key in the purchase order table, as well.

Primary Key Field

O Vendor Address Table			
Vendor #	**Name**	**Telephone**	**Address**
16789	Aspro Mechanical	555-555-8975	67 Washington St Valley Stream NY 10101
16889	Amity Travel	555-555-4125	314 Concourcse Ln Stewart NJ 98876
16989	ITP, Inc.	555-555-8025	89 Heights Park Brooklyn NY 11208
17089	Cinamon Industries	555-555-0044	12 Cinamon Way Newark NJ 11345
17189	Wellesley Corp.	555-555-3699	9 Walker Ct San Diego CA 91209
17289	Spencer Tires	555-555-7748	45A Ellen Circle Parker MD 34566

O Purchase Order Table		
Purchase #	**Order Date**	**Vendor #**
8874555	14-Nov-00	16789
8874655	25-May-00	16889
8874755	16-Dec-99	16989
8874855	04-Aug-01	16789
8874955	14-Jul-00	16789
8875055	06-Mar-99	17289

Based On The Relationship Using the Primary Key, A Report Can Be Generated Using Data From Both Tables

Vendor #	Name	Purchase Orders	Address
16789	Aspro Mechanical	8874555 8874855 8874955	67 Washington St Valley Stream NY 10101

Figure 3-4 *A primary key is composed of one more fields that make it unique.*

◯ Vendor Address Table			
Vendor #	Name	Telephone	Address
16789	Aspro Mechanical	555-555-8975	67 Washington St Valley Stream NY 10101
16889	Amity Travel	555-555-4125	314 Concourcse Ln Stewart NJ 98876
16989	ITP, Inc.	555-555-8025	89 Heights Park Brooklyn NY 11208
17089	Cinamon Industries	555-555-0044	12 Cinamon Way Newark NJ 11345
17189	Wellesley Corp.	555-555-3699	9 Walker Ct San Diego CA 91209
17289	Spencer Tires	555-555-7748	45A Ellen Circle Parker MD 34566

◯ Purchase Order Table			
Purchase #	Order Date	Vendor #	Salesperson
8874555	14-Nov-00	16789	KPG-0001645
8874655	25-May-00	16889	KPG-0001699
8874755	16-Dec-99	16989	MKT-0002322
8874855	04-Aug-01	16789	OPT-0000976
8874955	14-Jul-00	16789	KPG-0005542
8875055	06-Mar-99	17289	DWL-0001550

◯ Salesman Table		
Salesperson	Name	Territory
DWL-0001550	James Watterson	Montana
KPG-0001645	Kevin McCourt	Alabama
MKT-0002322	Sam Peterson	Colarado
OPT-0000976	Tracy Smith	Arizona

Figure 3-5 *Primary and foreign key concepts exist in all types of relational databases.*

Check Tables

Earlier in Chapter 2 (see Figure 2-13), we examined Input fields. Input fields sometimes contain a Possible Entries Help button that enables you to select from a list of possible entries for that field. In the example used in Figure 2-13, the Marital status field had seven possible entries. This field was connected to a Check table, where these seven entries were the only valid entries. For example, you could not enter a selection in the field that did not exist in the Check table. If the values in a field's Check table were New York and Florida, then the entry "California" would not be accepted. You would receive an error message. Check tables are used for entry verification and to ensure the accuracy and consistency of the data entered in your R/3 system.

Database Indexes

Some of your database tables will grow large in size. For example, think of the Human Resources module. A single table will store the employees' basic data (name, Social Security number, date of birth, etc.). Now, think of a large company that has hundreds of thousands of employees. That basic employee table will grow to be large. Now, imagine that you want to find a single employee from that table. This process might take a while, right? Not if that table has a database index (and most of them do). A database index is an efficiency mechanism for enhancing the retrieval of data from a table. In layman's terms, a database index is used to speed up the process of finding a row in a large table. An easy way to remember this concept is as follows: If you had put this book down and had forgotten your place, and you wanted to jump directly to this section, you would look up database indexes in the index. In R/3, the database index is used to jump directly to the row you want to retrieve from the database.

Database Objects Are Important in Reporting

Your R/3 system contains various types of objects and structures that are logically designed for the rapid storage, retrieval, and management of your data. The structure of some of the different objects in SAP is unique to SAP. Now that we are familiar with the structure of the basic elements, let's take a look at a database concept that is essential for R/3 reporting: logical databases.

Logical Databases

Logical databases are an important concept when it comes to reporting in SAP. Reports created using the ABAP and Ad-Hoc query tools might use logical databases for the source of their data. When creating reports, you will select fields from tables. These tables are arranged into logical groupings using relationships between the data. This concept is the essence of logical databases. When programmers write reports, they need to include the names of the different database tables that store the information they want to retrieve. In most cases, the data that the programmers want to output on their reports comes from multiple tables. As we saw earlier, tables in SAP are maintained through a series of relationships. What the programmer would need to do is include detailed instructions in his or her programming code that explain how these tables relate to each other. This task is not easy (and

again, for this reason, SAP programmers make big bucks). Lucky
for us, SAP realized how difficult this procedure would be and put
together logical databases for us to use that already have defined
relationships between multiple tables. For query reporting, a logical database is linked to an ABAP report program as one of the
program attributes. This database supplies the report program
with a set of hierarchically structured table entries derived from
different database tables. For example, in the Human Resources
Recruitment module, there are hundreds of tables. The global logical database /SAPQUERY/HR_APP (Human Resources Recruitment)
arranges these different tables into a single source of information
from which you can create reports (see Figure 3-6). This arrangement saves the developer from having to program the data
retrieval and enables non-technical SAP users to create their own
reports without programming. You will learn how to do this task
in Chapter 10, "ABAP Query Reporting Basics."

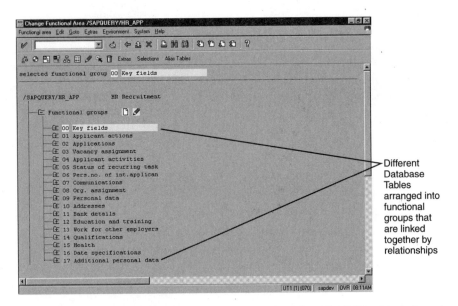

Figure 3-6 *Logical databases are maintained in the ABAP Workbench and
are usually maintained by the technical team.*

Logical databases will be examined in more detail when we introduce the concept of functional areas for ABAP query reporting later in Chapter 9, "ABAP Query Behind the Scenes."

Field Definition

When working with your SAP R/3 screens, you will find it helpful to obtain a definition about what data is needed for a field. As an example, we will use Create Cost Center: Initial screen, which is shown in Figure 3-7.

R/3 has a concept that is similar to many other applications, wherein you can place your cursor into a field and select the F1 button to retrieve field-sensitive help. Field-sensitive help will display a definition of the selected item. Using the Create Cost Center: Initial screen, we can retrieve the field-sensitive help for the Cost Center field by placing our cursor into the field and selecting the F1 key from the keyboard (see Figure 3-8).

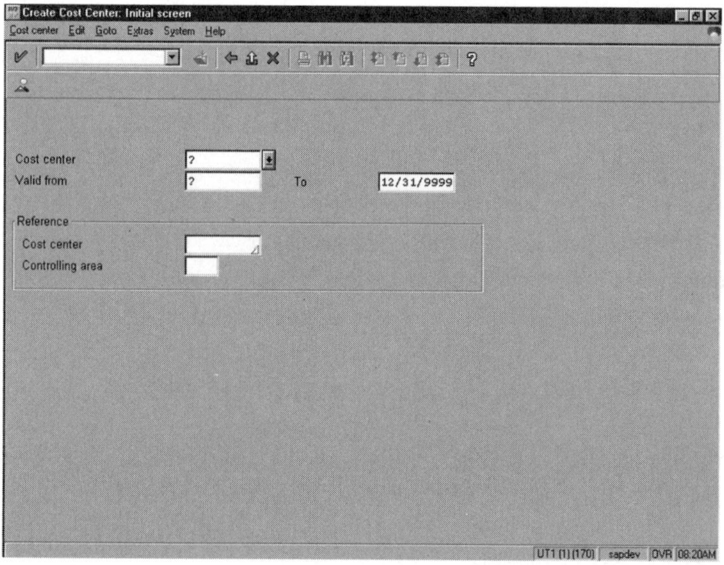

Figure 3-7 *The Create Cost Center: Initial screen is an example of a standard R/3 input screen that displays fields connected to the R/3 database.*

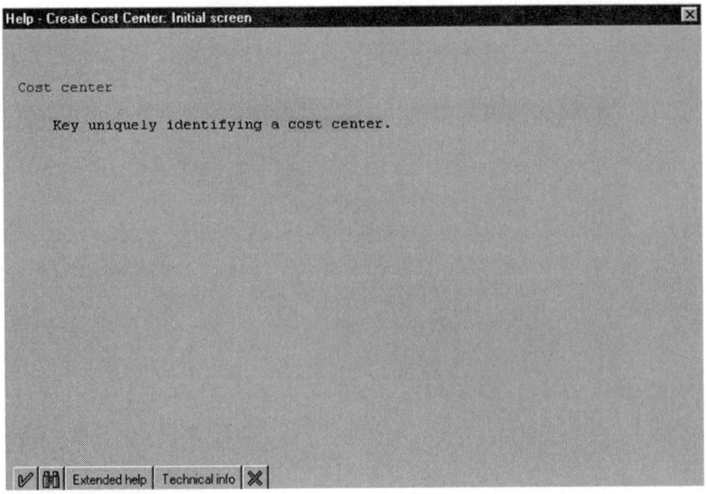

Figure 3-8 *The Field Sensitive Help dialog box provides you with a definition of the R/3 field.*

The definition might contain hypertext that when selected will bring you to an even more detailed definition of the item, as shown in Figure 3-9.

Field Extended Help

Sometimes the information provided in the field-sensitive help does not provide enough information about the field. In cases such as these, you can launch Extended Help, which will launch your R/3 help application (via a viewer or browser) that will launch to the area in need. This Extended Help can be retrieved by selecting the Extended help button from the Field Sensitive Help window (see Figure 3-8), or by placing your cursor into the Cost Center field and following the menu path Help→Extended help (see Figure 3-10).

Field R/3 Database Information

When you begin creating reports, you will need to be familiar with the particular tables and fields that are important for your output. In order to create a report, you will need to select fields

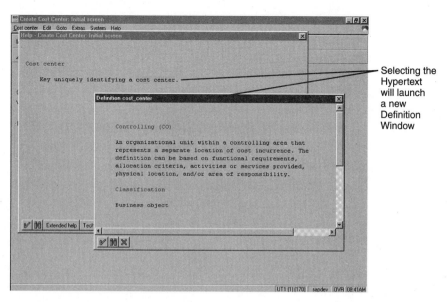

Figure 3-9 *Hypertext words are available within many field-sensitive help definitions.*

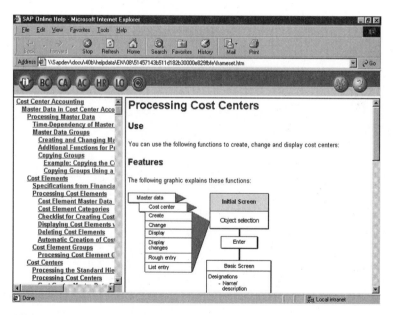

Figure 3-10 *Extended Help will launch your R/3 help application via a viewer or an Internet browser.*

from tables (arranged in the logical database) to be placed on your report. To get an idea of where the data that you work with on a day-to-day basis is stored in your R/3 database, you can use the R/3 field-sensitive help mentioned earlier. From within field-sensitive help, you can retrieve technical information (including the field and table names for any field displayed on a screen in your R/3 system). On the Field Sensitive Help display window (shown in Figure 3-8), a button appears for technical information. Selecting this box will launch a Technical Information dialog box displaying the R/3 database table and Field name for the selected field, as shown in Figure 3-11.

R/3 Data Dictionary

There are several types of tables and structures within the R/3 Data Dictionary. We are not going to take an advanced look at these different types of objects. The focus here is to present you with an elementary understanding of what the basic tables and fields look like in your R/3 database in order to assist you with reporting in R/3. The R/3 Data Dictionary is the tool used to look at database objects. The R/3 Data Dictionary is primarily used by your technical team. We will just take a look at the basics to get a fundamental understanding of how all the elements fit together.

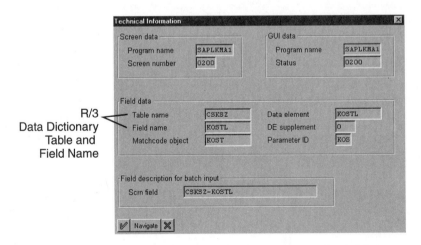

Figure 3-11 *The Technical Information dialog box contains the field data for the selected SAP field.*

Transaction code /nSE11 will take you to the R/3 Data Dictionary main screen, as shown in Figure 3-12. Depending on your SAP Authorization Profile, you may not be able to perform this transaction. If you are unable, just follow along in the text.

To take a look at a table in the R/3 Data Dictionary, enter the table's name on this screen and select the Display button. For this example, we will use the SPFLI table. The SPFLI table comes pre-delivered with your R/3 system as an instructional learning table. This table does not correspond to any real data that your company might be using, and it is designed only as a test table. The SPFLI table corresponds to a bogus airline scheduling system. After we enter the table name into the Object name box and hit the Display button, we see a Table/Structure view of the table (see Figure 3-13).

The left-hand side of the screen lists all of the field names in the table, and the right-hand side provides descriptions of the fields. For example, the CARRID field stores the airline carrier ID. This display is helpful; however, you might also want to view the table's contents (the actual data in the table). This task is

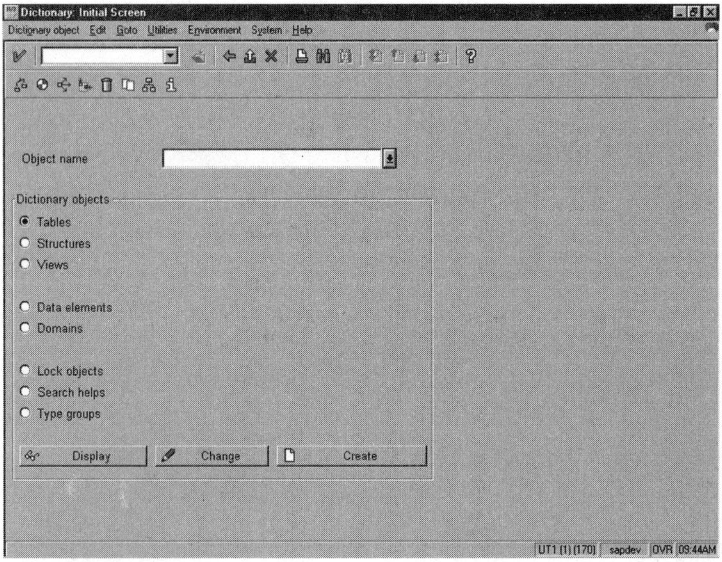

Figure 3-12 *Tables are defined in the R/3 Data Dictionary, independently of the database.*

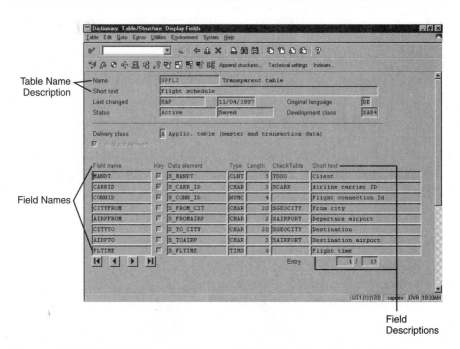

Table Name
Description

Field Names

Field
Descriptions

Figure 3-13 *The R/3 Data Dictionary Table/Structure: Display Fields screen lists all of the fields contained in the SPFLI table.*

possible for most R/3 tables by following the menu path Utilities→Table contents. A selection screen will appear, listing almost all fields in the table (see Figure 3-14).

On this selection screen (introduced in Chapter 1 and discussed in more detail in Chapter 4, "Selection Screens"), you can specify what data from the SPFLI table you would like to see. This feature is handy in case the table is large and unwieldy, because then we can specify only the data we want to see. For our purposes, we would like to see the entire table contents. We will not specify anything on this screen. Select the F8 button from the keyboard (or the Execute button on the Application toolbar) to execute the display of the table, as in Figure 3-15.

The contents of the SPFLI table should appear similar in format to the tables introduced earlier in the chapter, where the data is organized into columns (fields) and rows (data).

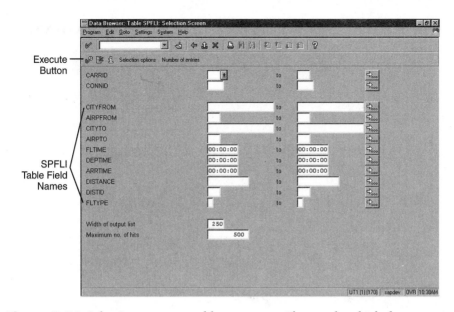

Figure 3-14 *Selection screens enable you to specify exactly which data you would like to see in your output.*

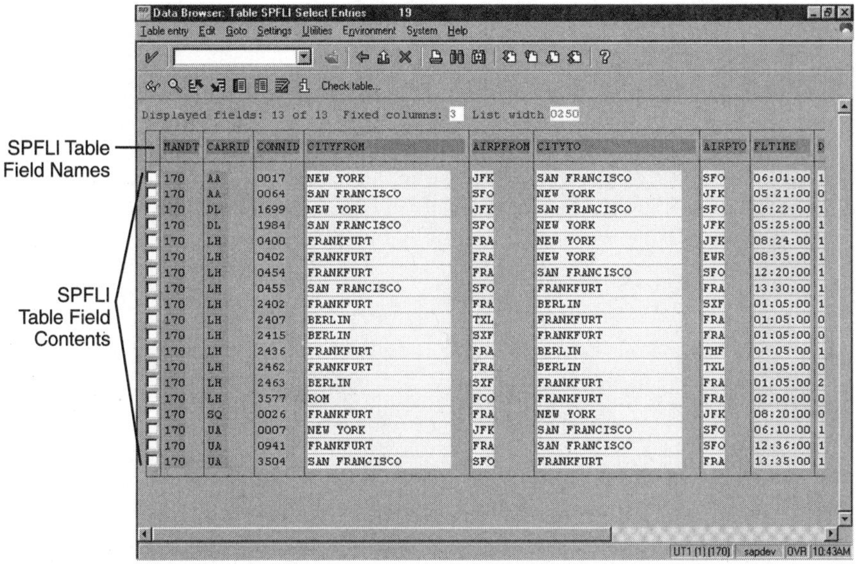

Figure 3-15 *The SPFLI table contents are displayed in rows and columns.*

Chapter Wrap-Up

In SAP reporting, knowing where the data can be found in the R/3 database is half the battle. Once you know which fields and tables you need to work with, all you need to decide is in what order and format you want them to appear in your report. Now that you have viewed this introduction to database concepts, you should feel more comfortable with determining where the data you want is located. The next important concept, discussed in the next chapter, is understanding how to specify only the data you want from tables. This task is done using selection screens.

Selection Screens

When executing a report in SAP, a program will run behind the scenes—retrieving all of the data for the report. After execution of a report, you will almost always be prompted with a selection screen. A selection screen enables you to specify exactly which data you want to see in your list. You will recall that a list in SAP is the final display of data or output.

Without specifications entered on a selection screen, the data that would be processed in a report might be so large that the report output would be meaningless. Specifications need to be entered on a selection screen to appropriately delimit precisely which output you are hoping to yield.

Our "Birthday List" Example

For our example, we will use the selection screen for the Birthday List report in the Human Resources module. To follow along on your SAP screen, navigate to the General Report Selection Screen by following the menu path Information systems→General report selection, and then follow these steps:

1. Place your cursor on the Human Resources node in the tree.

2. Select the Set focus button from the Application toolbar.

3. Expand the Personnel management node by selecting the plus sign (+) to the left of the node, or by selecting the node and then selecting the Expand sub-node button on the Application toolbar.

4. Expand the Administration node by selecting the plus sign to the left of the node, or by selecting the node and then selecting the Expand sub-node button on the Application toolbar.

5. Expand the Employee node by selecting the plus sign to the left of the node, or by selecting the node and then selecting the Expand sub-node button on the Application toolbar.

6. Expand the Birthday node by selecting the plus sign to the left of the node, or by selecting the node and then selecting the Expand sub-node button on the Application toolbar.

7. Execute the Birthday List report by double-clicking the report name, or by selecting the report and then selecting the Execute button from the Application toolbar.

8. You will be presented with a selection screen similar to the one shown in Figure 4-1.

Selection screens vary based on the type of report that you are running. Rarely do selection screens look alike, although the Application toolbar for selection screens remains relatively standard across reports (see Table 4.1).

Selection screens can become a user's best friend. They are infinitely helpful for providing you with the precise output that you need. If we left the selection screen blank for the Birthday List report and executed directly to the list, we would retrieve all

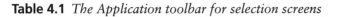

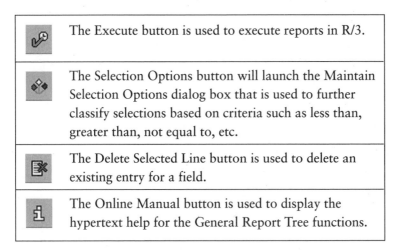

Figure 4-1 *Selection screens are used on almost all SAP reports to provide you with the flexibility for retrieving only the data in which you are interested.*

Table 4.1 *The Application toolbar for selection screens*

	The Execute button is used to execute reports in R/3.
	The Selection Options button will launch the Maintain Selection Options dialog box that is used to further classify selections based on criteria such as less than, greater than, not equal to, etc.
	The Delete Selected Line button is used to delete an existing entry for a field.
	The Online Manual button is used to display the hypertext help for the General Report Tree functions.

possible data from your SAP system regarding this report. To execute a report without specifying criteria, blank out all data on the selection screen, then select the Execute button from the Application toolbar. This action would yield, for example, a Birthday List for all employees in your system, regardless of whether they are retired, terminated, deceased, etc.

Warning In some cases, your selection screen will appear with data already completed. In some cases, the data is erroneous (dates, etc.), but in other scenarios, the data is useful for retrieving the appropriate output. Review the contents of the selections before modifying them.

Bypassing the selection screen might produce results that might not be too meaningful to the user. The report will probably take a long time to run (because it is retrieving all of the available records), and the data might be too cumbersome to provide any meaningful purpose. If you have been following along in your system, use the green Back arrow to return to the selection screen. This time, we will fill in the criteria on the selection screen to yield only the data that we want to see. On the selection screen, we will add a range of personnel numbers, and we will specify an Employment Status not equal to 0 (see Figure 4-2).

Entering this criteria and selecting the Execute button from the Application toolbar will produce the report with only the employees who meet the criteria entered on the selection screen, as in Figure 4-3.

Entering Criteria on a Selection Screen

The previous example illustrated how to fill in values on the selection screen to retrieve only the data necessary for your output. Basic field values can be entered to retrieve the relevant data.

Specifying a Period

The top of a selection screen almost always contains a section enabling you to segregate your data based on dates (see Figure 4-2). As you know, everything in SAP is date driven. The effectiveness of almost all items and objects in SAP depends on their date.

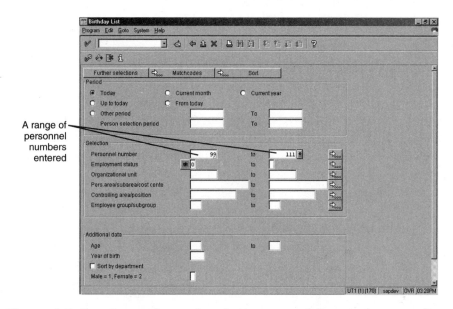

Figure 4-2 *Entering a value on the selection screen delineates the output list presented upon execution.*

Pers.no.	Name	Entry	Leaving da	D.o.b.	Age
00000099	Kathleen Zucker Workman	01/01/1999		01/17/1965	34
00000100	Patricia Roth Signorile	01/01/1999		01/11/1945	54
00000101	Carol Wulf	01/01/1999		05/18/1978	21
00000102	Jordan Catalano	01/01/1999		08/14/1972	27
00000103	Jared Leto	01/01/1999		03/17/1955	44
00000104	Carol Alice Hill	01/01/1999		05/21/1981	18
00000105	Thomas Losquadro	04/12/1999		06/17/1935	64
00000106	Nicole Kapp	02/15/1999		12/27/1967	32
00000107	Catherine Elizabeth Corey	01/01/1999		04/10/1945	54
00000108	Todd M Michaels	01/01/1999		10/19/1986	13
00000109	Patricia Alice Larocca	03/08/1999		09/17/1975	24
00000110	Terrance Gallagher	01/01/1999		11/08/1967	32
00000111	Anthony Michael Woods	01/01/1999		01/24/1947	52

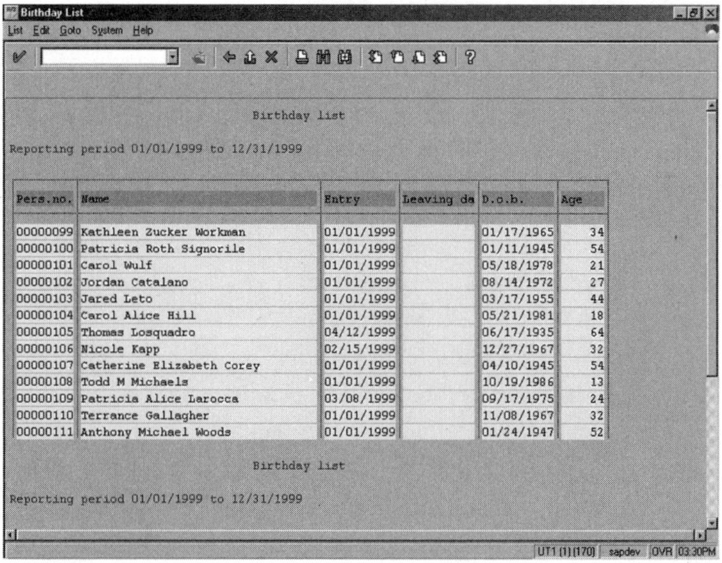

Figure 4-3 *The output list displays only the records that match the specifications entered on the selection screen—employees whose personnel numbers are between 99 and 111.*

You will sometimes hear this concept referred to as "true dating," "record dating," or "effective dating." Essentially, these terms mean that all of the data in your SAP system is date sensitive, and entering the date that you want your data to be valid for is crucial. To see how this action can have an effect on your output, we'll use sales orders as an example. Company X creates 10 sales orders a day. We also schedule future sales orders to be created two weeks in advance. If we ran a report of all open sales orders and did not specify a date on the selection screen, we would see all of the orders from the past, present, and future. The future orders truly should not be included in the report, because they have not yet been created. If we ran the same report and specified that we wanted to list all sales orders released as of today, then we would have an accurate representation of the orders in our list output. Try to keep this date concept in mind when running reports, in order to ensure that the correct output is retrieved.

Specifying Field Entries

Field-entry specification is defined just as it sounds. Looking back at Figure 4-2, you can see that we have entered a range of personnel numbers from 99 to 111 to be displayed in our results. This basic type of field entry can be used on many SAP selection screens. There are many instances where the fields contain possible entries that you can access using the Possible Entries Help button (discussed in Chapter 2). On the selection screen for the Birthday List, the Gender field has possible Entries Help available (see Figure 4-4).

Specifying Field Options for Your Fields

Entering basic data sometimes is not as easy as it looks. Sometimes you might want selection options for the data. For example, perhaps you want all employees whose personnel numbers are greater than 99 or less than 500, or you might want employees whose employment status is not equal to "terminated." For these types of specifications, you need to use the Maintain Selection Options dialog box. This dialog box can be opened by placing your cursor in a field and then selecting the Selection options button from the Application toolbar. A dialog box will appear that enables you to specify exactly what you want (see Figure 4-5).

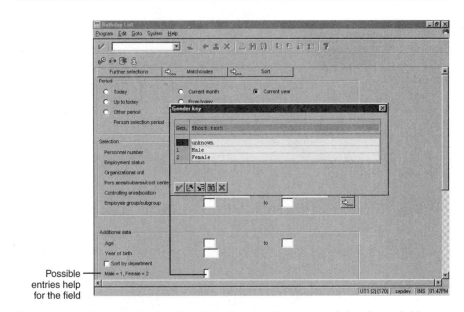

Figure 4-4 *To see whether Possible Entries Help is available for a field, place your cursor in the field to see whether a down arrow appears.*

Figure 4-5 *Selection options give you more freedom to specify criteria for your output.*

After selecting one of the options—for example, the Not equal to button—you will be returned to the selection screen. Immediately to the left of the field that contains the selection option will be a colored box indicating that the option will appear (see Figure 4-6).

To remove this selection, use the Delete Selected Line button from the Application toolbar. To select by an initial value, such as

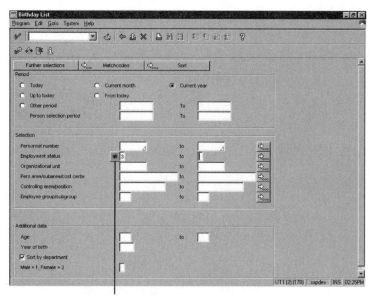

A Selection options box appears showing the selected
option: in this example, the not equal to sign

Figure 4-6 *The selected option will appear only if selected
options have been entered for the field.*

"all invoices greater than 0," you can double-click or choose
Selection options for a blank selection line. If initial entries are
canceled (overtyped with an initial value or canceled with '!'),
then the selection line is deleted.

Specifying a Range

Sometimes a basic entry is not enough. For example, in our
Birthday List report, we wanted to see all employees whose person-

Warning	If you use character fields in the starting and ending value selections, the selected set depends on the current character set. For example, a selection from DL0 to DL9 would not include the value DL91, because the character '1' is greater than the character ' ' in the ASCII character set. To include DL91, you need to specify DL0 to DL99.

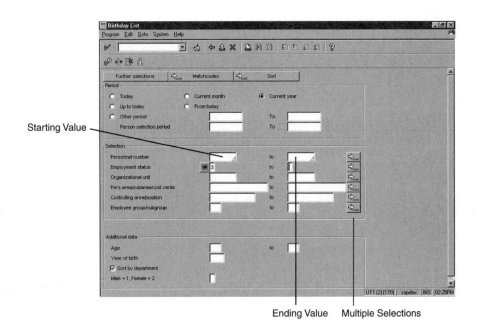

Starting Value

Ending Value   Multiple Selections

Figure 4-7 *A range is helpful when you want to include multiple employees who are logically grouped together in a sequence.*

nel numbers fell between 99 and 111. By entering a starting value in the first field and an ending value in the second field, we specified the range of employees we wanted in the output (see Figure 4-7).

Advanced Selection Criteria
Specifying Multiple Records That Do Not
Fall in a Range

Specifying a range is helpful, but what do you do when you want to specify multiple records that do not happen to be sequential? For example, what if you want to output all employees whose employee numbers are 31, 41, 67, and 1,005—plus personnel numbers between one and 100, 300 and 500, and 1,000 and 1,600—but not employees between 1,100 and 1,250? Does this task sound impossible? Well, you will find it easy if you use the Multiple Selections button. The Multiple Selections button is available on the selection screen and appears as a white arrow on the right side of your screen (see Figure 4-7).

Warning   On some selection screens, the Multiple Selection dialog box will not work unless a starting value (and, in some cases, an ending value) is filled in first.

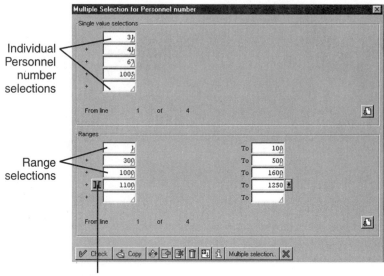

VSE of selection options to exclude
a range of personnel numbers

Figure 4-8 *Complicated selection criteria can be entered in a Multiple Selections dialog box.*

After entering the selection option in the Multiple Selection box, select the Check button to ensure that your selections are accurate. For example, if you mistakenly entered letters instead of numbers in one of the fields, you will be asked to check your entries. After you check your entries, select the Copy button to return to the selection screen. You will now notice that the selection options white arrow has turned green, indicating that multiple selections were entered for the field (see Figure 4-9).

Further Selections

Further selections are available on many report selection screens. For example, if you want to specify criteria for additional

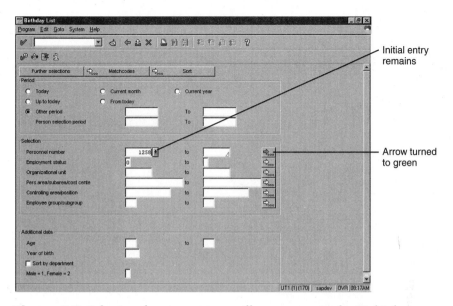

Initial entry remains

Arrow turned to green

Figure 4-9 *Selecting the green arrow will return you to the Multiple Selections box.*

fields that are not already included on the selection screen, you could use this function. When selecting the Further Selections button at the top of the selection screen, you will be prompted with a Standard Selection Criteria dialog box similar to the one shown in Figure 4-10.

From the Standard Selection Criteria dialog box, you can use the check boxes to select additional fields. You will notice that the check boxes are marked in the Choose column for fields that already appear on your selection screen. The Filled column of check boxes indicates selection fields where data is entered. Looking at the example in Figure 4-10, we see that the Personnel number, Employment status, Organizational unit, Personnel area, Personnel sub-area, Cost Center, Controlling area, Employee group, and Employee subgroup appear on our selection screen. Check Figure 4-9 for reference. In Figure 4-10, the Filled fields are Personnel number and Employment status. Again, take a look at Figure 4-9 and see that these two fields have filled-in values.

To add more fields, mark some additional Choose check boxes on your Standard Selection Criteria dialog box. For our example,

Further selections button   Standard selection Criteria dialog box

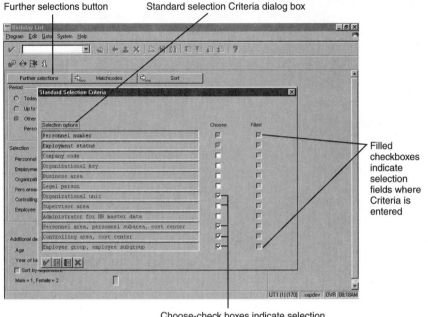

Filled
checkboxes
indicate
selection
fields where
Criteria is
entered

Choose-check boxes indicate selection
fields where Criteria is entered

Figure 4-10 *The Standard Selection Criteria dialog box enables you to specify additional criteria not shown on the selection screen by default.*

we will select the Company code and Organizational key fields, as in Figures 4-11 and 4-12.

When you return to the selection screen after the selection options have been entered in the Standard Selection Criteria dialog box, the Further Selections arrow button will now appear green, indicating that selections were made and that the new fields will be included.

Specifying Matchcodes

In addition to further selections on some selection screens, you can use matchcodes to specify output. The white arrow Matchcodes button appears on the top of many selection screens to the right of the Further Selections button. In SAP, a matchcode serves as a comparison key. Matchcodes enable you to locate the key of a particular database record (for example, the account number) by entering information contained in the record.

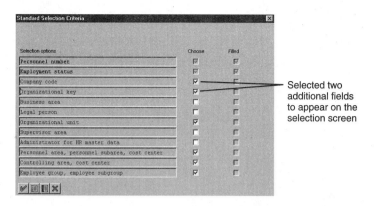

Figure 4-11 *The number of further selections available vary for each report.*

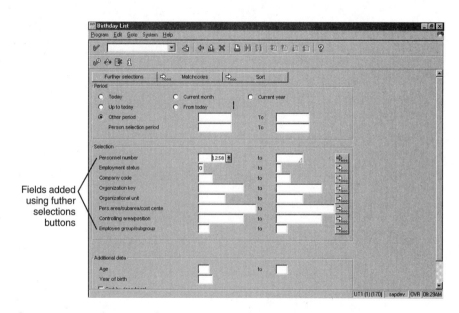

Figure 4-12 *The new selections now appear on the selection screen.*

Selecting the Matchcodes button from the selection screen is another means of retrieving the specific records for which you are searching. A Search Help selection screen will appear, asking you to select a field that you want to base the Matchcode on, as in Figure 4-13.

Search Help Selection dialog Box

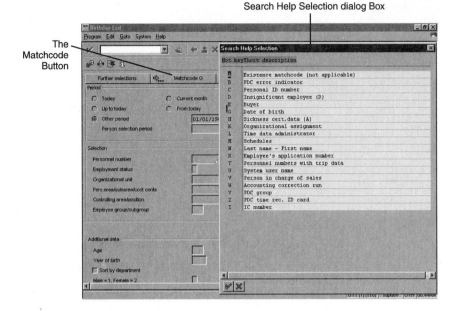

Figure 4-13 *Depending on the type of report, different fields will be available to you on the Search Help selection screen.*

Figure 4-14 *Depending on the field selected in the Search Help selection screen, a Restrict Value Range dialog box will appear with options based on that selection.*

Selecting a field to use as a matchcode will bring you to a Restrict Value Range dialog box for that field. In the following example, we will use the Date of Birth field as our matchcode. The Restrict Value Range dialog box will appear with options for specifying Date of Birth, as in Figure 4-14.

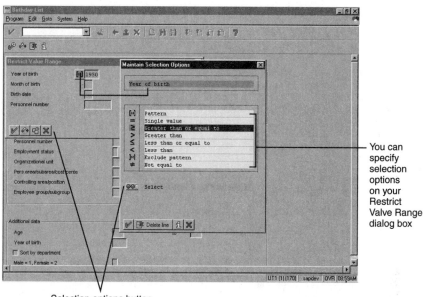

Selection options button

Figure 4-15 *Selection options can be used on multiple fields.*

The Restrict Value Range dialog box works according to the same functionality we have already used. For example, we could enter a year of birth in the Year of Birth field, and we would produce a report including only employees whose year of birth falls in that range. Or, we could use the Selection Options button (see Table 4.1 for reference) on the Restrict Value Range dialog box to specify additional options, as in Figure 4-15.

For example, using the Selection Options button on the Restrict Value Range dialog box, you can set your report to print only employees whose date of birth is equal to or greater than 1950. After the selection options have been entered on the Restrict Value Range dialog box, return to the selection screen, and the Matchcodes arrow button will now appear green (indicating that selections were made).

User Variables

An additional option, called user variables, is available for modifying your selection criteria. User variables can be accessed

from some report selection screens using the menu path
Goto→User variables. They can be customized for different users
within that user's parameters, which are stored on their master
record. This action affects the report output in accordance with
the user's customization.

Sort

These concepts give you an idea of how to retrieve the data
you want on your report. Now, we want to determine the order
or sequence in which the data is outputted. For example, if we
create a Birthday List report for all employees whose date of birth
is 1950 or greater, we might want to sort the output by employee
name. The white arrow Sort button appears at the top of many
selection screens to the right of the Matchcodes button. Selecting
the Sort button will bring up a Standard Selections dialog box
similar to the one shown in Figure 4-16.

The two columns on the Standard Selections dialog box represent the Sort options (fields available for sorting) and Sort
sequence (the order in which you want them to appear). By placing your cursor in a field on the left side in the Sort options column and then selecting the small, right, black arrow, it will then
appear in the right-hand Sort sequence column (you can also
double-click each line to move it) (see Figure 4-17).

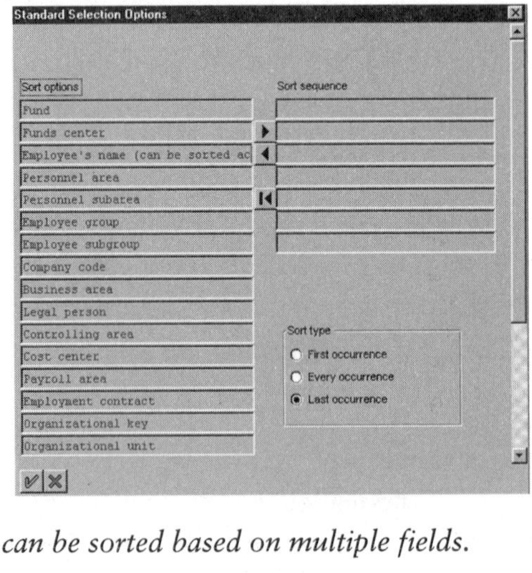

Figure 4-16 *Reports can be sorted based on multiple fields.*

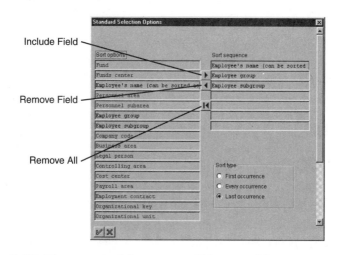

Include Field

Remove Field

Remove All

Figure 4-17 *The output of the report will be sorted by Employee name, then Employee group, then Employee subgroup.*

The Sort type box in the bottom of the Standard Selections dialog box window is used for various sort types available for time-period evaluations. For example, if an employee changes personnel areas in the middle of a month (for example, if they are assigned to personnel area 0001 in the first half of the month and to 0002 in the second half), then they will appear in the monthly valuation of the respective personnel area. The options for this selection are as follows:

- First occurrence once in personnel area 0001
- Last occurrence once in personnel area 0002
- Every occurrence once in personnel area 0001 and once in 0002

When you return to the selection screen after the sort criteria has been entered on the Standard Selections dialog box, the Sort arrow button will now appear green (indicating that selections were made).

Dynamic Selections

If the Application toolbar contains the push-button dynamic selections, you can use it to branch to a dialog where you define selections for other database fields that might occur in your current process. If dynamic selections are available for your selection screen, you could also navigate to them using the menu path Edit→Dynamic selections. These selections are passed directly to the database system.

All Selections

If the All selections function is active in the Edit menu (Edit→All selections), only the really relevant selection criteria and parameters appear on the selection screen. By selecting this function, you can display all of the other selections, as well. You can revert to the original state by following the menu path Edit→Chosen selections.

Chapter Wrap-Up

In the majority of reports, it will be beneficial to enter at least a minimum of criteria on the selection screen. Most importantly, a period should be entered (because all data in SAP is date driven). Selection screens also provide you with a great deal of flexibility. Perhaps you want to run an individual report for all open-shipping departures for your five warehouses. In traditional systems, you would create five individual reports. In SAP, it is the same report, only with different data entered in the selection screen. In the next chapter, we will learn how to save selection screen entries so that you do not need to fill them in each time you run a report. This feature also comes in handy because it enables you to schedule a report to run at a specified time (or after a specific event via workflow), with certain filled-in selection screen entries.

Executing and Maintaining SAP R/3 Reports

Reports in SAP can be executed from various places. The most common place from which reports can be executed is the R/3 General Report Selection Tree. We take an in-depth look at the General Report Selection Tree in Chapter 7, "R/3 General Report Selection Tree," and in Chapter 22, "Customizing Report Trees in R/3," we will examine the steps for creating our own R/3 reporting trees. The menu path to navigate to the R/3 General Reporting Tree from the main SAP screen is Information systems→ General report selection. The R/3 General Reporting Tree will appear similar to Figure 5-1.

71

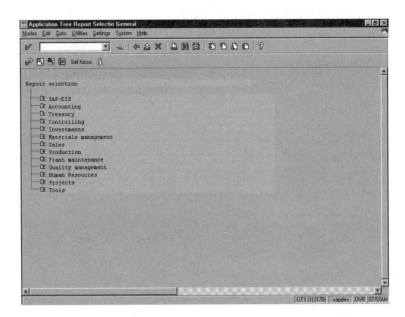

Figure 5-1 *The R/3 General Reporting Tree is a central location within your R/3 system from which you can execute reports from all the SAP modules.*

Note Like almost all SAP transactions, there is a transaction code associated with the R/3 General Reporting Tree (SART). Unfortunately, because of the significant size of the data that is displayed on the screen, sometimes the transaction code will be slow when accessing this screen. In some cases, the code will cause your system to produce an error. Using the menu path is your best bet for accessing the R/3 General Reporting Tree screen.

For starters, let's become familiar with the Application toolbar for the General Report Selection Tree (see Table 5.1).

Executing a Report

As discussed in Chapter 1, reports are essentially programs in SAP that need to be executed to produce output. These programs can be executed from various locations in SAP, including the R/3 General Reporting Tree. Let's navigate to a sample report in our

Table 5.1 *The Application toolbar for the R/3 General Reporting Tree*

![Execute button]	The Execute button is used to execute the report.
![Expand sub-tree button]	The Expand sub-tree button will expand the selected node of the tree.
![Collapse sub-tree button]	The Collapse sub-tree button will collapse the selected node of the tree.
![Node Attributes button]	The Node Attributes button will provide you with the basic attributes of the selected node.
Set focus	The Set Focus button will set the focus of the screen to the selected node and will move that node to the top of the screen.
![Information button]	The Information button displays the Report Tree Help Tree in your R/3 window.

tree. We will use the Payday Calendar Display report for our example, because it does not require you to have any SAP configuration in place in order for the report to be executed. In addition, this report can be used to make a basic annual calendar that you can print and use. Navigate to this report in your R/3 General Reporting Tree by expanding the subnodes Human Resources→Payroll accounting→Payroll accounting—USA→ Payday→Payday calendar→Payday Calendar Display. Your screen should appear similar to the one shown in Figure 5-2.

Reports can be executed from the R/3 General Reporting Tree by selecting the report and then selecting the Execute button from the Application toolbar, or by double-clicking the report name. To execute our sample report, double-click the Payday Calendar Display report. As we learned earlier in Chapter 4, upon execution of a report, we will almost always be presented with a selection screen. The selection screen for the Payday Calendar Display is shown in Figure 5-3.

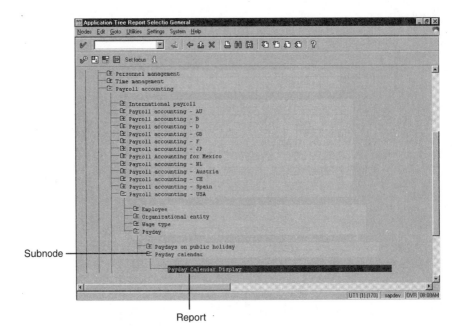

Subnode ———

Report ·

Figure 5-2 *Reports in the R/3 General Reporting Tree are the lowest level of a subtree that do not contain an Expand or Collapse subnode button.*

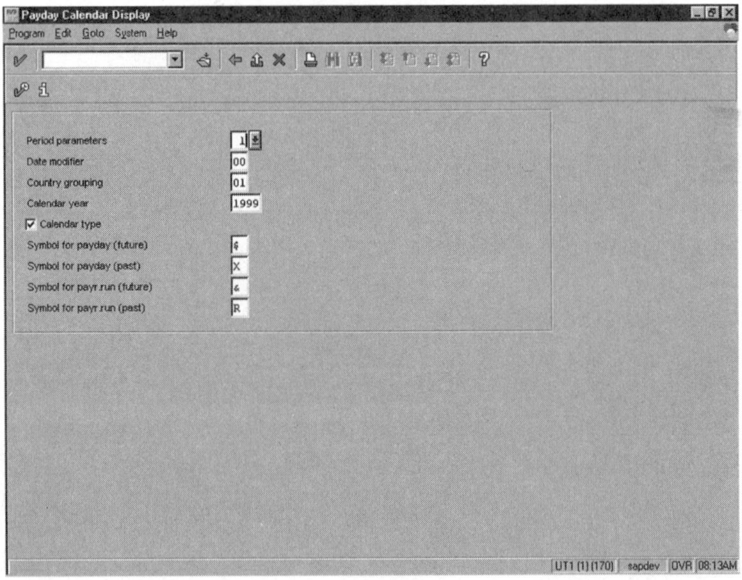

Figure 5-3 *Depending on the type of R/3 report, the selection screens and Application toolbars might appear slightly different.*

In Chapter 4, we discussed that selection screens enable us to specify exactly which data we would like to include in our output. The selection screen for the Payday Calendar Display report specifies which type of data we would like to see in our payday calendar. In this example, it is not the specification of data, but rather the specification of placeholders in the output. Do not be concerned if your selection screen contains different values from the one shown in Figure 5-3. Let's execute the report to get a better idea of what we are looking at on the selection screen. Select the Execute button from the Application toolbar on your selection screen. Your report output should appear similar to Figure 5-4.

Unlike the type of report we viewed in Chapter 4, the Payday Calendar Display report actually uses the values entered on the selection screen in its output. This report is a good example to use, because regardless of the data you have in your SAP system, this report gives you a good idea of how your entries on the selection screen affect your data. This example will also be helpful when we discuss variants later in this chapter. From looking at

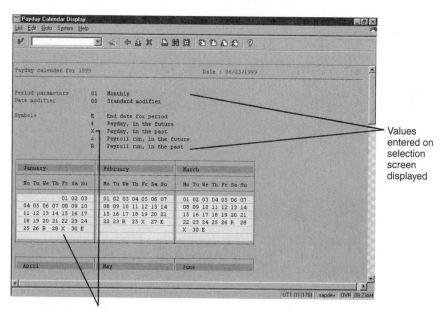

Values entered on selection screen displayed

Values appearing in the output

Figure 5-4 *This report is used to create a payday calendar for the payroll year.*

our report output, we can see that the actual values filled in on the selection screen affect the presentation of the data in the output. Use your green arrow Back button from the toolbar to return to the selection screen. On the selection screen, change the entries for some of the fields by selecting different values using the Possible Entries Help buttons for the fields (see Figure 5-5).

After making changes to the data entered on your selection screen, select the Execute button from the Application toolbar to see the effect it has on your output (see Figure 5-6).

Warning   If your company currently uses the Payday Calendar Display report and you are concerned with changing the settings, take a screen capture of the selection screen before making changes—so that you can return the settings to their original condition when the chapter is complete. Also, always seek the appropriate permissions before modifying any SAP data.

Possible entries for the field

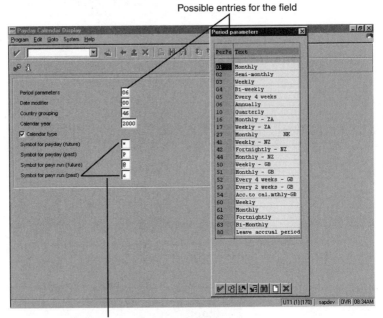

Some fields do not have Possible Entries Help

Figure 5-5   *Possible Entries Help buttons show you the valid entries that are available for the field.*

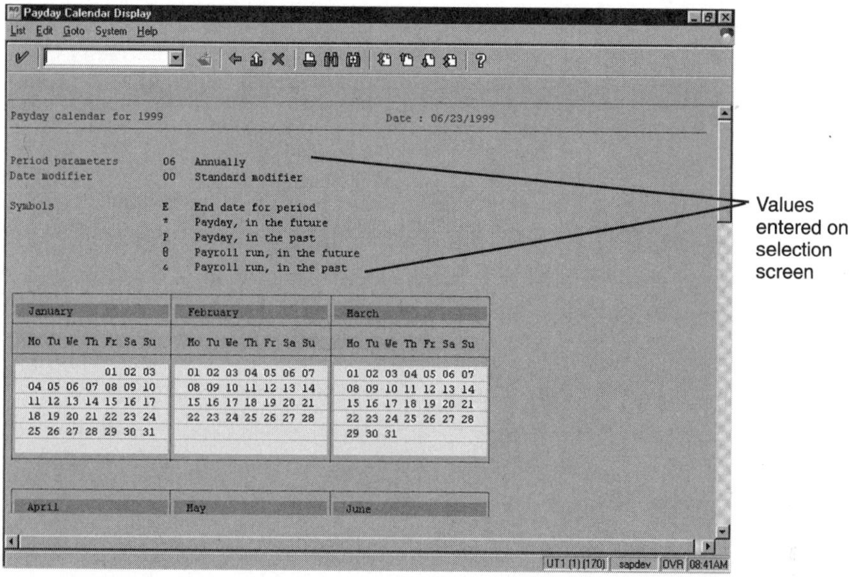

Figure 5-6 *Because no data exists in our system that is relevant to the entries made on our selection screen, our calendar display does not show any symbols in our chart, thus creating a plain calendar.*

The values that we changed on our selection screen (see Figure 5-5) appear at the top of our list output in Figure 5-6. Because the values on our selection screen do not correspond to any real data in our SAP system, these character markings do not appear within our calendar. For example, we used the calendar year 2000, when the year is still 1999. This one entry assures us that no data will be outputted on our calendar, because no payroll has been configured or run yet in the year 2000. So now we have learned how to make a calendar that we can hang in the office for the year 2000. This example will come in handy as we discuss variants.

Variants

When creating reports, the selection screen becomes an essential part of the output. As mentioned earlier, the same report can be used to yield all different types of data, depending on the selections entered on the selection screen. In managing your reports, you can save the data that you enter on the selection screen as a variant. Variants enable you to skip the process of manually entering all of your selections in the selection screen, because the variant will remember what values you want filled in.

When working with variants, there are two different ways you can use them with your reports. First, as mentioned earlier, you can create one report that includes all kinds of information and use that same report for multiple purposes by entering different data on the selection screen. In this example, you can save a bunch of different variants for a particular report, and when you run the report, you can pick the variant you want upon execution. The other method would be to save the variant with the report so that it automatically runs each time you run the report, thus bypassing the selection screen altogether and outputting the data. This second method is necessary if you want reports to run automatically—in the background or as part of workflow—without any intervention (data entry on the selection screen) by the user. Either way, variants are a useful tool. The way that you use them depends on your perspective of how you want to manage your reports.

Creating a Variant

As with everything in SAP, there are several ways to do the same task. We outline a single method in this section. For our example, we will use the Payday Calendar Display report.

1. From the R/3 General Report Selection Tree, we place our cursor on the report (Payday Calendar Display).

2. From there, we use the menu path Goto→Variants to display the ABAP: Variants initial screen, similar to the one shown in Figure 5-7.

3. On the initial screen, we enter a name for the variant that we want to create. For this example, we will use Zvariant_1.

4. Next, select the Create button. A Variants Change Screen Assignment dialog box will appear as shown in Figure 5-8.

5. This dialog box enables you to specify whether you want this variant to be available for all reports or for this report only.

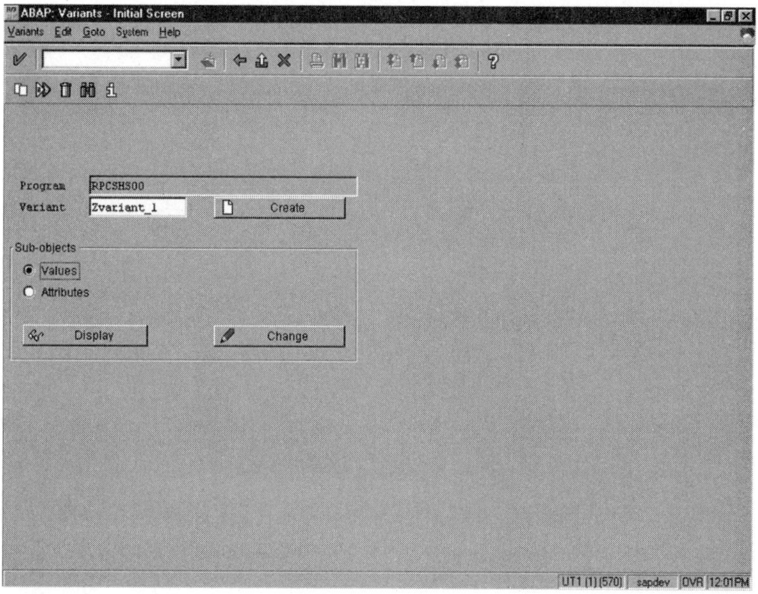

Figure 5-7 *Using variants in SAP enables you to save time when executing and managing your R/3 reports.*

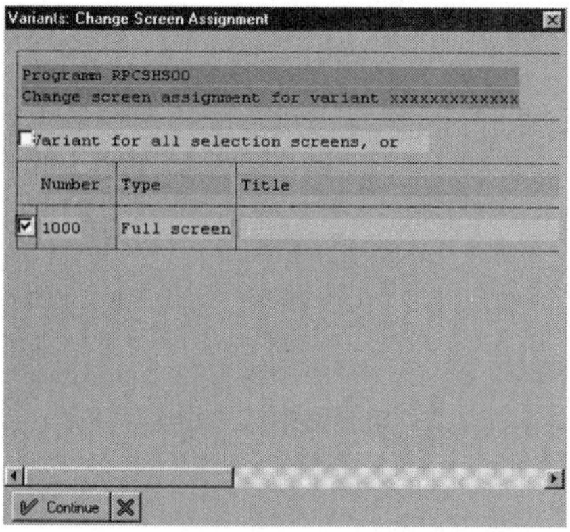

Figure 5-8 *A single variant can be made available for all of your R/3 reports.*

Unmark the Variant for all selection screens option and select the screen listed on the bottom of the box (in this case, screen number 1,000). Select the Continue button to proceed.

6. The selection screen for the selected report will appear next. Fill in all of the appropriate values, and select the Continue button to proceed to the ABAP: Save Attributes as Variant screen, similar to the one shown in Figure 5-9.

7. Enter a description for your variant, and select the open folder Save button to continue.

8. You will return to your selected reports selection screen, and a message will appear in the Status bar saying that your variant was saved.

9. Use the green arrow Back button two times to return to the R/3 General Report Selection Tree.

Once a variant has been created, additional menu options become available on your selection screen. You can use these options to retrieve, display, or delete variants.

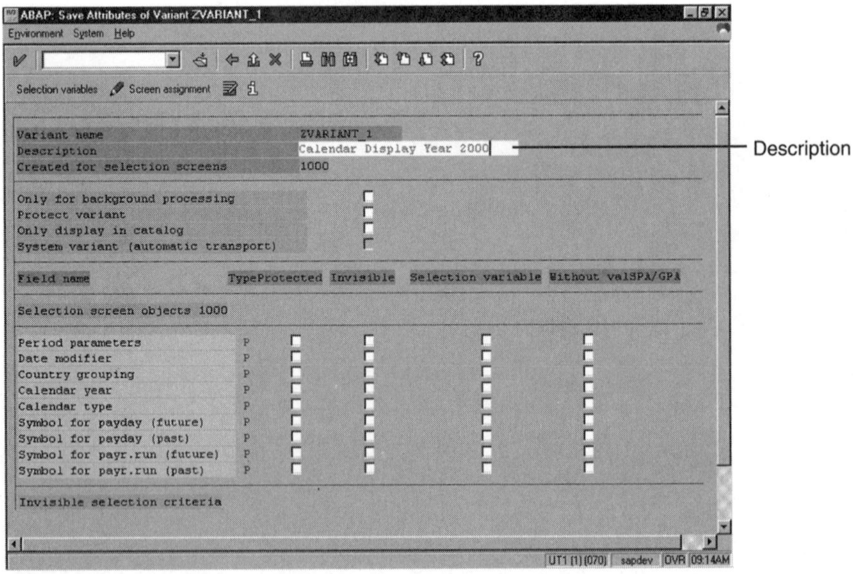

Figure 5-9 *Many technical settings can be entered on the Save Attributes of Variant screen.*

Executing Your Report Using a Variant

1. Once you return to the R/3 General Report Selection Tree, execute the Payday Calendar Display report.

2. When presented with the selection screen, you should use the menu path Goto→Variants→Get, and a Variant Directory dialog box will appear listing all available variants for this report (see Figure 5-10).

3. Select your variant, then select the Choose button to continue.

4. Your saved variant data will now appear in your selection screen, and your report is ready for execution.

Lists

The concept of lists was introduced in Chapter 1. The list is the output you have generated with your report. You can print the list, download it to a file, or save it for later reference. We mentioned that one of the four essential concepts in reporting is that there is an important distinction that needs to be made between lists and reports. The report is the execution of the data. This execution can be performed at any time and will contain "live data" in your system at the time of execution. A list is a saved execution of a report as of a given point in time. For example, we execute

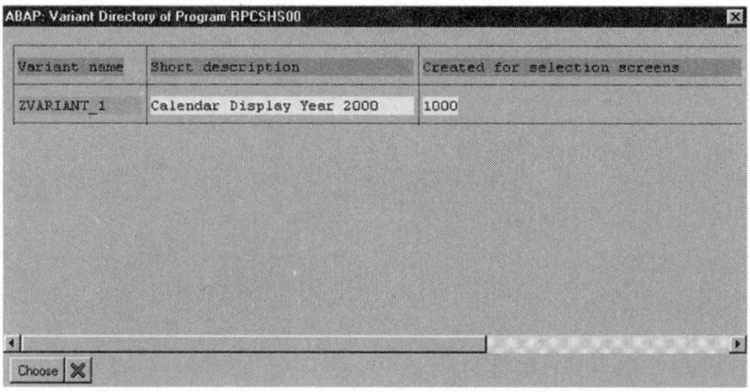

Figure 5-10 *All saved variants available in the directory are presented in the Variant Directory dialog box.*

an Invoice Listing report on Monday and save the list as file. If
we open that saved list on Thursday, it will still only contain the
data from Monday. If we executed the report again on Thursday,
the new list will contain data that is current in the system as of
Thursday.

Saving Lists

You can save lists to a local file or to an external file, or you
can transmit them via SAPoffice e-mail. Saving lists to SAPoffice
folders is discussed in Chapter 21, "List Management Using
SAPoffice." Some companies save lists and some do not, depending on how your company does business. Many companies feel
that saving the list is a moot point because of SAP's capability to
produce a report with a backdate. For example, you can create an
Invoice List report on March 1, 1999, and save it as a list. To
view that list at a later time, you can open the saved list, or you
could execute the report and fill in the March 1, 1999 period on
the selection screen.

Saving Lists to a Reporting Tree

Your lists can be saved directly to your reporting tree where
you have the capability to re-execute the list. Keep in mind that
the saved list is as of a certain point in time in your database.
Remember that if we execute this report on Monday and save the
list to our tree on Thursday, when we look at the list from our
reporting tree, it will contain data from our SAP system as of
Monday, not Thursday. You will need to execute the report on
Thursday to get Thursday's data. We can continue using the payday calendar as an example for this section. Follow these steps to
save a list to a reporting tree:

1. On your list screen (after the selection screen is executed and
   your final data is displayed), select the menu path List→
   Save→Reporting tree.

2. A Save List dialog box will appear, asking you to fill in the
   basic information (see Figure 5-11).

3. In the Save List dialog box, enter a name for your list in the
   Name of List box.

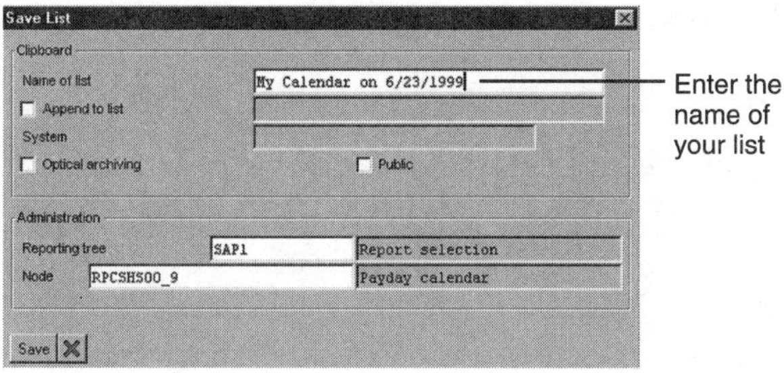

Figure 5-11 *The default reporting tree name that appears is the name of the tree from which the report was executed.*

| You should include the date of the output in the name of the report to help you distinguish the time for which the report was created. | **Note** |

4. The Administration portion of the screen defaults to the reporting tree name and node that you were on when you executed the report. We want to save our list in this node, so we will select the Save button to continue.

5. A confirmation message will appear in your Status bar, saying that the list has been added to the reporting tree (see Figure 5-12).

6. Use the green arrow Back button on the toolbar to return to the selection screen.

7. Use the green arrow Back button on the toolbar to return to the R/3 General Reporting Tree screen.

8. The Payday Calendar Display report will now contain an Expand sub-node button.

9. Expand the subnode to see your saved list, as in Figure 5-13.

10. Your saved list can be viewed from the R/3 General Reporting Tree by selecting the list and then selecting the Execute button from the Application toolbar (or by double-clicking the list name).

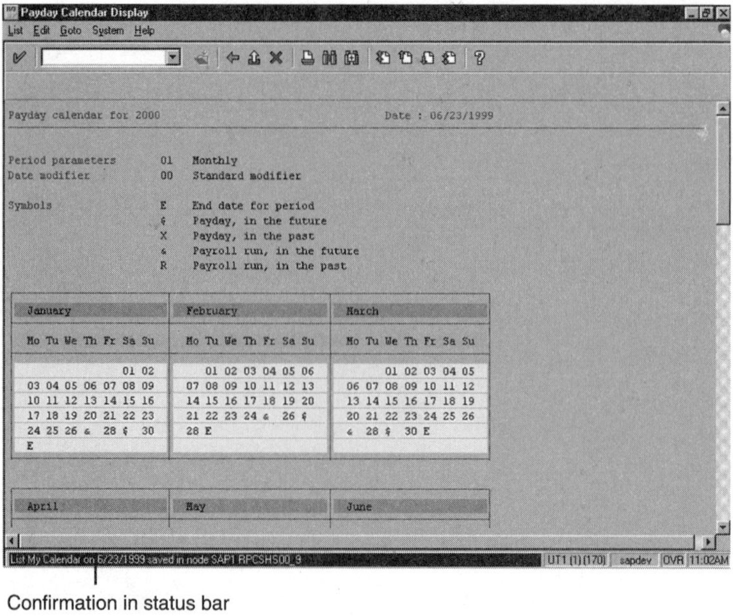

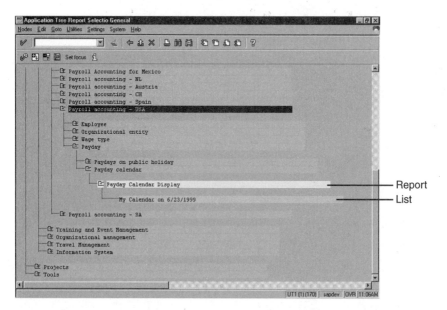

Confirmation in status bar

Figure 5-12 *If an error message appears in your Status bar, return to step one and try again.*

Figure 5-13 *The saved list can be added to the R/3 General Reporting Tree or to a custom report tree.*

> Be sure to note that when you execute a saved list from a reporting tree, no selection screen appears because the data is frozen in time and is not a real-time generation of the data.

Note

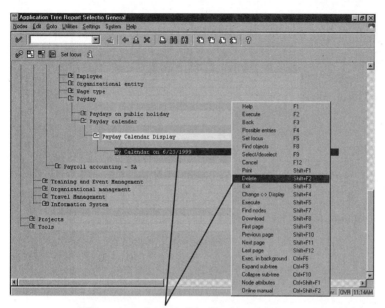

With cursor on list right click with mouse to select the delete option

Figure 5-14 *There is no undo option if you change your mind, so be certain before deleting any saved lists from your reporting tree.*

Deleting a List from a Report Tree

Lists added to the report tree can be easily deleted if necessary. From the R/3 General Reporting Tree screen, select your list and then right-click it with your mouse to display the Delete option, as in Figure 5-14.

Saving Lists to a File

Your list can also be saved to a file, where further manipulation of the data can take place if desired. Let's return to the R/3 General Report Selection Tree, and this time let's select a different report for the next example. Saving a list to a file involves displaying actual data output in your report. Depending on your company's installation and security configuration, only certain reports will have output. For example, if your SAP system is only used for the Financials package, you will not have output to generate in a Logistics or Human Resources module report. The example shown as follows can be used on any report in R/3 that displays data. For our example, we will use the Birthday List report that we used in earlier examples. As we begin this instruction, we are already at the list portion of the screen. We have already executed our report, filled in the selection screen, and produced the output list. If you would like to follow along, select and execute a report from any of the reports in the tree that correspond to a module that you have configured in your R/3 system. To save a list to a file, follow these steps:

1. From the List screen, select the menu path List→Save→File (see Figure 5-15).

   Depending on the report, one of two different dialog boxes will appear with options concerning the format you want your list in, as shown in Figure 5-16.

Figure 5-15 *The option to save your list as a file is available from almost all SAP report-output list screens.*

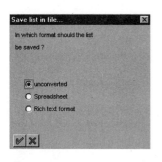

Figure 5-16 *Lists can be saved in different formats that are compatible with different applications on your PC.*

Table 5.2 *Download file formats*

Format	Description
Unconverted	Data will not be converted to a particular format.
Spreadsheet	Data will be formatted to be compatible with a spreadsheet application such as Microsoft Excel or Lotus.
Rich-text format	The data format will include formatting instructions that other programs, including compatible Microsoft programs, can read and interpret.

2. This dialog box enables you to specify a format. See Table 5.2 for additional information about the formats.

3. Select an appropriate format, then select the green check mark Enter key. For our example, we will select "unconverted."

4. You will be asked to provide a path and filename for the list, as shown in Figure 5-17.

5. Enter a path and filename for your file. The extension of your filename should be consistent with the application that you

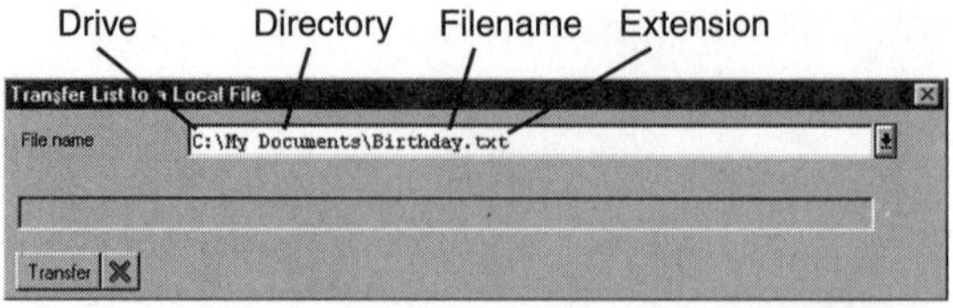

Drive   Directory   Filename   Extension

Figure 5-17 *The location will default to your SAP directory, so replace it with a location that is more familiar to you.*

will use to open the file. We will open this file using Windows Notepad, so we will give the file a .txt extension (text file).

6. Click the Transfer button. When the transfer is complete, a confirmation message will appear in your Status bar.

Now that the list is saved to a file, let's open the file using the PC application Windows Notepad. We selected to save the file in an unconverted format so that we could open the data using this application. Next, we will launch Windows Notepad (Start→ Run→Notepad) and open our SAP list, as shown in Figure 5-18. After selecting our file from the location that we entered in SAP, we can view our SAP data in a local file (see Figure 5-19).

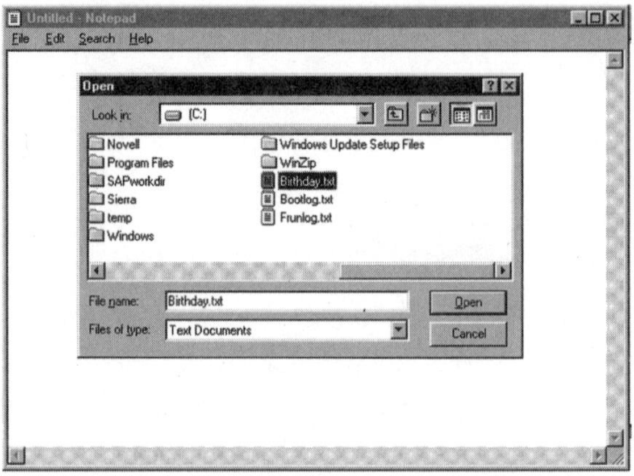

Figure 5-18 *We can use Windows Notepad to work with our downloaded SAP list.*

> Later chapters discuss how downloaded files can be used in Microsoft Access, Microsoft Excel, and Microsoft Word.

Note

```
Birthday.txt - Notepad
File  Edit  Search  Help
                            Birthday list
Reporting period 01/01/1999 to 12/31/1999

--------------------------------------------------------------------------
|Pers.no.|Name                         |Entry     |Leaving da|D.o.b.    |Age   |
--------------------------------------------------------------------------
| 00000500|Joseph Signorile            |01/01/1999|          |01/28/1968|  31|
| 00000501|Brett William Kirley        |01/01/1999|          |05/06/1974|  25|
| 00000502|Carol Wulf                  |05/17/1999|          |07/29/1980|  19|
| 00000503|Steven Litvak               |01/11/1999|          |09/09/1964|  35|
| 00000504|Jared Leto                  |05/24/1999|          |07/28/1980|  19|
| 00000505|Scott Speedman              |01/01/1999|          |03/08/1939|  60|
| 00000506|Patricia Roth               |01/01/1999|          |03/05/1963|  36|
| 00000507|Felicity Porter             |01/01/1999|          |06/04/1969|  30|
| 00000508|Ed Larocca                  |01/01/1999|          |03/09/1964|  35|
| 00000509|Albee Hill                  |01/01/1999|          |08/01/1974|  25|
| 00000510|Kevin C Witt                |01/18/1999|          |08/01/1976|  23|
                            Birthday list

Reporting period 01/01/1999 to 12/31/1999

--------------------------------------------------------------------------
|Pers.no.|Name                         |Entry     |Leaving da|D.o.b.    |Age   |
--------------------------------------------------------------------------


Reconciliation totals
--------------------------------------------------------------------------

      11 Persons selected by report RPLGEB30
```

Figure 5-19 *The format selected and the application used to view the file will affect the way the data is presented.*

Executing Reports in the Background

Executing reports in R/3 utilizes system resources. The amount of resources utilized varies, depending on the size of the report. Sometimes reports that are run immediately are processed in the foreground and are printed to your local printer. Other reports can be run in the background at prescheduled times, using a variant. For example, some companies schedule reports to run overnight while system activity is low, so users can have a printed hard copy waiting for them in the morning. To execute a report to run in the background, the report must have a variant saved for the report. When you think about this concept, it makes a lot of sense. Each time we execute a report, we are presented with a selection screen that we need to fill in (in order to generate the report). If a report is scheduled to run in the background, in the middle of the night, it must have a variant to fill in that selection screen data for you. Later in Chapter 11, "ABAP Query Maintenance and Variants," we discuss saving variants with reports so that they run automatically upon execution.

Chapter Wrap-Up

Executing reports in R/3 can be performed in several different ways. Through the use of report trees, background processing using variants, or custom reporting, the same concepts usually apply. You will always have selection screens where you need to enter data to specify your output. The use of variants will assist in the retrieval of desired data, and this desired output can be saved within SAP or to a local PC file.

Reporting Security Concepts

Your SAP system has a state-of-the-art security design. Security can be administered in several different ways in R/3; however, the basic security concepts remain the same. When you think about security at its most basic level, you think of protection from outside intrusion. In SAP, security needs to be administered not only from outside intrusion, but also from within the organization. For example, you do not want your sales team accessing confidential payroll records in the Human Resources module, just as you would not want a payroll clerk being able to create shipping orders in the Materials Management component. With this idea in mind, security should be addressed on several different levels.

User Authorizations

User authorizations are stored in the master record of each user. These authorizations enable you to perform certain tasks in R/3. The authorizations contained in your master record designate your access in R/3. Different users have different authorizations allotted to them, based on their role. For example, payroll clerks contain authorizations for running payroll and maintaining employee salary records but do not have authorizations for creating receiving documents in shipping. User authorizations are maintained by a systems or security administrator in R/3. That person has the responsibility to ensure that your master record contains all of the necessary authorizations that you need to perform your job functions in SAP. A sample user master record is shown in Figure 6-1.

On the six tabs of the master record, different pieces of information are stored about each user, including a list of authorization profiles to which they are entitled. Authorizations, objects, and fields that users are entitled to are bundled into a concept called an authorization profile.

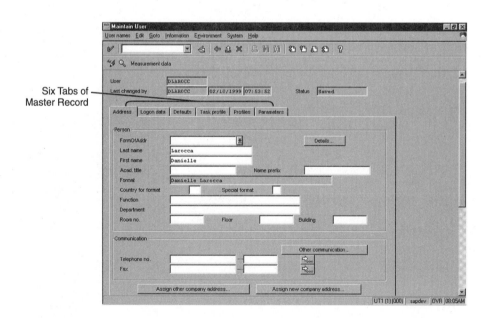

Figure 6-1 *You might not have access to view your own master record in R/3.*

Authorization Profiles

As a general rule, user authorizations are not directly assigned to a user master record. Instead, authorizations are assembled into collections called authorization profiles. To give you an idea of how many of these standard profiles are available in R/3, a table of some sample authorization profiles for all R/3 modules is shown in Table 6.1.

Table 6.1 *Sample authorization profiles in R/3*

Profile	Authorization Description
SAP_ALL	All authorizations in R/3
A_ALL	FI-AA Asset Accounting: Full Authorization
A_IMPR_00	Capital Investment Programs: Master Data, Budget, and Planning
A_IMPR_01	Capital Investment Programs, Budget, and Planning
A_IMPR_ALL	Capital Investment Programs: All Authorizations
A_IMPR_DIS	Capital Investment Programs: All Display Authorizations
A_IMPR_SYS	Capital Investment Programs: System Administrator
A_PROFIL_00	FI-AA Asset Accounting: Profile for System Administrator
A_PROFIL_01	FI-AA Asset Accounting: Profile for Asset Accountant
A_PROFIL_02	FI-AA Asset Accounting: Profile for Asset Accounting Clerk
A_PROFIL_03	FI-AA Asset Accounting: Profile for Buyer

Table 6.1 *Sample authorization profiles in R/3 (Continued)*

Profile	Authorization Description
A_PROFIL_04	FI-AA Asset Accounting: Profile for Technician
A_PROFIL_05	FI-AA Asset Accounting: Profile for a Warehouse Clerk
K_JOB_C_ACTU	CO: Order Customizing Actual Postings
K_JOB_C_BUDG	CO: Order Customizing Budget and Commitments
K_JOB_C_INFO	CO: Order Customizing Information System
K_JOB_C_MAST	CO: Order Customizing Master Data
K_JOB_C_PLAN	CO: Order Customizing Planning
K_JOB_CUST	CO: Orders Customizing
K_PCA_AL1	All Profit-Center Authorizations
K_PCA_ALL	All EC-PCA Authorizations
K_PCA_SD	All SD Authorizations for EC-PCA
K_PLAN_ALL	Maintenance Authorizations: CO-Om-Cca Planning
K_RCL_ADMI	Administration Authorizations: Co-Reconciliation Ledger
K_RCL_ALL	All Authorizations: Co-Reconciliation Ledger
K_RCL_USER	User Authorizations: Co-Reconciliation Ledger
K_REP_ALL	CO: All Authorizations for Interactive Drill-Down Reporting
K_RKC_ALL	All SAP-EIS Authorizations

Profile	Authorization Description
M_ALL	MM Materials Management: Universal Authorization
M_ANFR_ALL	MM Purchasing—Rfqs: Maintenance Authorization
M_ANFR_ANZ	MM Purchasing—Rfqs: Display Authorization
M_ANGE_ALL	MM Purchasing: Quotations: Maintenance Authorization
M_ANGE_ANZ	MM Purchasing: Quotations: Display Authorization
M_ANZ	MM Materials Management—Display Everything
M_BANF_ALL	MM Purchasing—Requisitions: Maintenance Authorization
M_BANF_ANZ	MM Purchasing—Requisitions: Display Authorization
M_BEFU_ALL	MM Inventory Management: Maintenance Authorization
M_BEFU_ANZ	MM Inventory Management: Display Authorization
M_BEST_ALL	MM Purchasing—Purchase Orders: Maintenance Authorization
M_BEST_ANZ	MM Purchasing—Purchase Orders: Display Authorization
M_BILA_ALL	MM Balance Sheet Valuation: Maintenance Authorization
M_BILA_ANZ	MM Balance Sheet Valuation: Display Authorization
M_DG_ALL	MM Dangerous Goods Management: All Authorizations at All GG Objects

Table 6.1 *Sample authorization profiles in R/3 (Continued)*

Profile	Authorization Description
M_DGM_ALL	MM Dangerous Goods Management: All Authorizations to GG-Mat and Text Display
M_DGM_MAIN	MM Dangerous Goods Management: Display and Chng GG-Mat. Records and Text Display
M_DGM_SHOW	MM Dangerous Goods Management: Display GG-Mat Records and GG Texts
P_ALL	HR: All Human Resources Authorizations
P_APL_ALL	HR: All Authorizations for Applicant Data in HR
P_BAS_ALL	HR: All Authorizations for Personal Data
P_BEN_ALL	HR: Employer Benefits Area
P_DISP_MC	HR: Display All Mathcodes Via HR Infotypes
P_PLAN	HR: Planning: All Authorizations
P_PLAN_ALL	All Authorizations for HR Planning
P_TAB_ALL	HR: System Administration (Control Tab, Archiving)
Q_ALL	All Authorizations in QM
Q_CAT_GRP	QM/PM: All Authorizations for Catalogs (Code Groups and Codes)
Q_CAT_SSET	QM: All Authorizations for Selected-Set Maintenance
Q_CATALOG	Catalog Processing

Profile	Authorization Description
Q_CERT_ALL	All Authorizations for Certificates
Q_CHAR_PRC	All Processing Steps for Characteristic Results
Q_GP_CODE	Catalog Application
Q_INSP_FIN	Authorization for Premature Inspection Completion
Q_INSP_TYPE	All Authorizations for Inspection Types
Q_MASTERD	All Authorizations for QM Master Data
Q_MATERIAL	All Material Groups
Q_QMEL	Process All Quality Notifications Completely
Q_ROUT_ALL	All Authorizations for Inspection Plans
Q_ROUT_STD	Maintain Reference Operation Set
S_A.ADMIN	Operator
S_A.CPIC	Special Profile for User SAPCPIC
S_A.CUSTOMIZ	Customizing (for All System-Setting Activities)
S_A.DEVELOP	Developer
S_A.DOKU	Technical Writer
S_A.SCON	SAPconnect: Send/Receive Process (RFC User)
S_A.SHOW	Basis: Display Authorizations Only
S_A.SYSTEM	System Administrator (Superuser)
S_A.TMSADM	Authorization for System User TMSADM
S_A.USER	Person in Charge (Basis Authorization)

Table 6.1 *Sample authorization profiles in R/3 (Continued)*

Profile	Authorization Description
S_ABAP_ALL	All Authorizations for ABAP/4
S_ABAP_ALL	All Authorizations for ABAP/4
S_ADDR_ALL	All Authorizations for the Central Address Management
S_ADMI_SAP	Administration Authorization (Apart from SPAD)
S_ADMI_SPO_	Spool: All Administration Authorizations
S_ADMI_SPO_	Spool: Device Administration
S_ADMI_SPO_	Spool: Extended Administration
S_ADMI_SPO_	Spool: Job Administration for All Clients
S_ADMI_SPO_	Spool: Device-Type Administration
S_DB2_ALLU	Authority Profile to Execute DB2/390 Commands ('ALLUSER')
S_DB2_COMM	Profile for Authorities to Change and Execute DB2 Commands
Z_CUSCO01	CO Customizing—Maintenance
Z_CUSCO02	CO Customizing—Display
Z_CUSFI01	FI Customizing—Maintenance
Z_CUSFI02	FI Customizing—Display
Z_CUSHR01	HR Customizing—Maintenance
Z_CUSHR02	HR Customizing—Display
Z_CUSMM01	MM Customizing—Maintenance
Z_CUSMM02	MM Customizing—Display
Z_CUSPM01	PM Customizing—Maintenance

Profile	Authorization Description
Z_CUSPM02	PM Customizing—Display
Z_CUSPP01	PP Customizing—Maintenance
Z_CUSPP02	PP Customizing—Display
Z_CUSPS01	PS Customizing—Maintenance
Z_CUSPS02	PS Customizing—Display
Z_CUSQM01	QM Customizing—Maintenance
Z_CUSQM02	QM Customizing—Display
Z_CUSRT01	Customizing Retail—Maintenance
Z_CUSRT02	Customizing Retail—Display
Z_CUSSD01	SD Customizing—Maintenance
Z_CUSSD02	SD Customizing—Display

Profile Generator

SAP has a tool called the Profile Generator, which can be used to create additional profiles in R/3. This tool became available in Version 3.1G in an effort to simplify the process of creating authorization profiles. The automatic maintenance offered by the Profile Generator has produced some skeptics among SAP users, who proclaim that it does not satisfy all requirements. Many companies begin with the Profile Generator to create the authorization profile and then tweak the profiles according to their individual needs.

Authorization Objects Relevant to Reporting

There are a handful of authorization objects that are relevant to ABAP query reporting in R/3. The administration of these objects will prove to be important for your company's reporting. Later in Chapter 9, "ABAP Query Behind the Scenes," we will discuss the concepts of user groups and functional areas that need to be created and maintained in order for ABAP query reporting to be available. These behind-the-scenes functions, as we describe them, are not usually performed by the same end users who are creating reports. These types of tasks should be delegated to system administration personnel. Also, end users should not have the capacity to modify user groups and functional areas in their R/3 system. The security authorization object managing this function is called S_QUERY.

Technical Information

The information in the next paragraph might get a little technical and is included here in case a system administrator needs assistance configuring access for users for the ABAP query. There are two authorizations for the S_QUERY authorization object that are relevant to the ABAP query: S_QUERY_ALL and S_QUERY_UPD. The default values enable more authorization than necessary for users who are assigned this authorization object. You should consider that the system administrators who will be performing the behind-the-scenes maintenance should have the authorization object S_QUERY with a value of "Maintain" (ACTVT), enabling them to modify these objects. Regular end users who will be creating reports in R/3 should only have the authorization object S_QUERY with a value of "Change" (ACTVT). Users with the authorization object S_QUERY with both values "Change" and "Maintain" can access all queries of all user groups without explicitly being a member of that group. If you are curious to see what this setup looks like from a system administration point of view, look at the comparison between an SAP System Administrator who has behind-the-scenes access— compared to a regular user's access (shown in Figure 6-2).

How Do These Ideas Affect Reporting in R/3?

There are several ways that security has an impact on reporting in R/3. In addition to the functionality permitted to you based on your ABAP query authorizations (S_QUERY), there are other factors to consider specifically (and your access to information in general).

Authorization Profile Security in Reporting

As mentioned earlier, based on your user master record and the authorization profiles it contains, only certain R/3 data is available

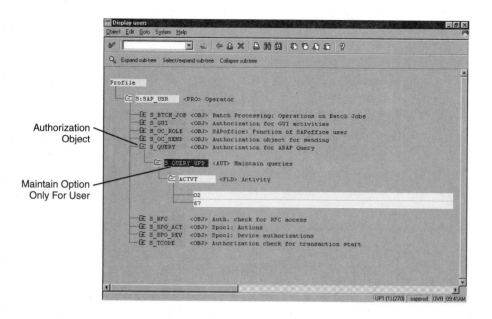

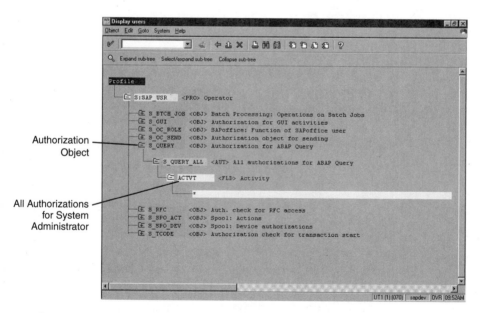

Figure 6-2 *The ABAP query authorization objects assigned to a user should be in direct relation to the function they perform in R/3.*

to you. To make this idea more clear, let's compare two different users in the R/3 Human Resources module. The first user is responsible for entering new employee information, including personal and salary information. The second user also works in the human resources department but has no interaction with employee salary information; however, the user can access employees' personal data. These two users would have different authorization objects within their authorization profiles to handle this task. But how does this idea affect reporting? Both users can run a report that lists employee names, addresses, and salaries. Guess what? The salary column for the second user appears blank. SAP has the capacity to determine which type of authorizations are available
to each user, and reports are generated accordingly.

User Group Security in Reporting

In Chapter 9, you will be introduced to the concept of user groups. R/3 users can belong to multiple user groups, depending on the functions they perform in SAP. For example, all shipping clerks will belong to a user group containing reports that are relevant to their position. Users only have access to reports that are available within their user group. Each member of a user group can execute any queries within that group. Only those user group members possessing the proper authorization, however, can maintain (make changes to) the queries within the group. In Chapter 10, "ABAP Query Reporting Basics," you will learn how to protect your queries from being changed by other users in your user group. In Chapter 9, we go into greater detail about user groups and how to create them in R/3.

Chapter Wrap-Up

Security concepts in R/3 are usually not a concern of end users; rather, security is maintained by your system administration team. The concepts detailed in this chapter provide you with an overview of how security concepts are administered in terms of reporting in R/3. You might also find it helpful to share this chapter with your system administrator to assist him or her with configuring the ABAP query authorization objects.

R/3 General Report Selection Tree

The R/3 General Report Selection Tree comes standard with your SAP system and contains most of the standard or "canned" reports in your R/3 system. The General Report Selection Tree is also sometimes referred to as the Information System, the Canned Reports, Report Selection, and the Report Tree. All reports displayed can be executed from the R/3 tree structure. The R/3 General Report Selection Tree can be modified to display only the nodes that are relevant to you and can be customized to include your own reports and lists. This customization in performed in the *Implementation Guide* (IMG). In Chapter 21, "List Management Using SAPoffice," we take a look at creating and modifying custom report trees.

103

Report Tree Basics

General Report Selection has a hierarchical structure of four levels. The top level contains the individual R/3 system applications (Accounting, Treasury, etc.). The second level contains the work areas of each application (Consolidation, General Ledger, Customers, etc.). The third level contains the objects within each work area (master data, financial reporting data, etc.). Reports and lists can be located and executed from the fourth level. The reports and lists are nodes of the tree. Earlier in Chapter 5, you were introduced to the basics of the report tree. As a review, let's take another look at the Application toolbar for the R/3 General Reporting Tree (see Table 7.1).

Basic Settings

There are some basic settings that can be used with the R/3 General Report Tree. For starters, let's expand the tree to view

Table 7.1 *The Application toolbar for the R/3 General Reporting Tree*

	The Execute button is used to execute R/3 reports.
	The Expand sub-tree button will expand the selected node of the tree.
	The Collapse sub-tree button will collapse the selected node of the tree.
	The Node attributes buttons will provide you with the basic attributes of the selected node.
Set focus	The Set Focus button will set the focus of the screen to the selected node and will move that node to the top of the screen.
	The Information button displays the Report Tree Help Tree in your R/3 window.

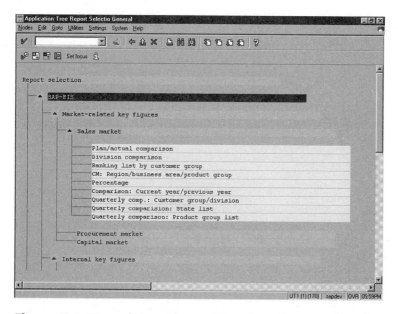

Figure 7-1 *Depending on the configuration of your system, the R/3 Report Tree might take a minute or two to expand all of its subnodes and may appear different from the one shown above.*

the subnodes. This action can be done by selecting the highest level of the tree and then selecting the Expand sub-node button from the Application toolbar, or by following the menu path Edit→Expand sub-tree. The R/3 General Reporting Tree, with its expanded subnodes, will appear similar to Figure 7-1.

Color Legend

To assist you with determining the difference between nodes and reports within the different levels and nodes of the tree, you can display a color legend. The color legend has three different colors distinguishing Structure nodes (the names of nodes, for example, EIS or Human Resources) from Executable nodes (for example, reports or saved lists). To display the color legend from the R/3 General Reporting Tree, follow the menu path Utilities→ Color legend. A sample of the color legend is shown in Figure 7-2.

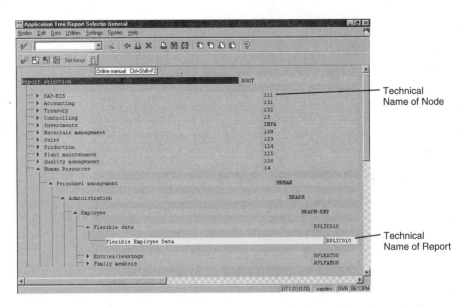

Figure 7-2 *The color legend is useful for distinguishing reports from saved lists.*

Figure 7-3 *When viewing the technical names of the reports, the color legend is useful in determining nodes from reports.*

Technical Names

As introduced in Chapter 1, you can choose whether to display the technical names of reports in the R/3 General Reporting Tree. To view the technical names, follow the menu path Settings→Technical names on/off. The technical names of nodes, subnodes, reports, and saved lists will appear to the right of each item, as shown in Figure 7-3.

Authorization Groups

You can also turn on the Authorization group names by following the menu path Settings→Authorization groups on/off. Every node can be assigned an authorization group. This group defines which user can work with this node. If no authorization group is specified for a node, then it inherits the group assigned to its predecessor in the report tree.

Reporting Tree Online Manual

If you require assistance while working on the R/3 General Reporting Tree, you can launch the online manual. The online manual is displayed within your R/3 window and does not launch your SAP Help Viewer. This online manual provides basic information about report trees and how to create, modify, delete, and customize them in your R/3 system. To access the online manual, follow the menu path Utilities→Online manual. This manual is displayed in a tree structure and functions in the same manner as all other R/3 tree structures. A sample of the online manual for the R/3 General Reporting Tree is shown in Figure 7-4.

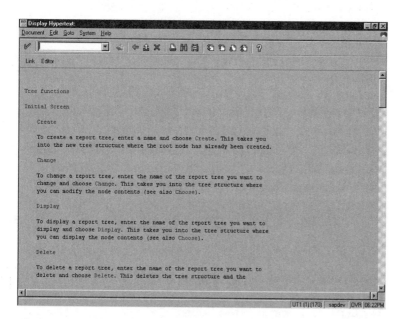

Figure 7-4 *The online manual is displayed in hypertext within your R/3 window and does not launch your SAP Help Viewer.*

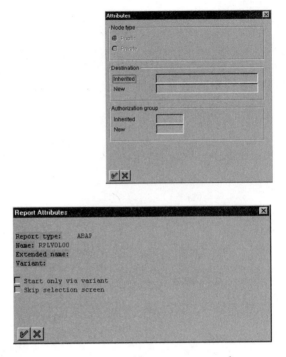

Figures 7-5 and 7-6 *The attributes of lists appear similar to the attributes of reports in the Node Attributes dialog box.*

Attributes

You can view the attributes of any node, subnode, report, or list in the report tree by selecting the item and following the menu path Edit→Node attributes. With this function, you can display and change the node characteristics (for example, whether the node is public or private). The objects of a public node are visible to all users. In a private node, the user can see all entries that they included in the node. You can distinguish between private and public nodes by their displayed color in the tree. You can also view and modify the authorization group for the selected node. The type of attributes that you will see displayed for nodes is shown in Figure 7-5, and for reports, see Figure 7-6.

R/3 General Reporting Tree Nodes

The R/3 General Report Selection Tree is divided into several nodes. Each node represents a different segregation of reports.

Each of these nodes contains subnodes, and the subnodes contain subnodes. They are logically arranged to assist you with finding reports quickly and easily. In Chapter 5, we discussed how to execute reports from the report tree. In this chapter, we will take a look at what standard reports are available. In the following sections, we will introduce the different nodes available in the R/3 General Reporting Tree and some of the sample work areas, objects, and reports contained within the node. This material does not provide an all-inclusive look at which reports are included in the R/3 General Reporting Tree, but the information should be helpful in giving you an idea of what is available.

SAP-EIS

The *Executive Information System* (EIS) was introduced in Chapter 1. From within the General Report Selection Tree, EIS contains subnodes for Market-related key figures, Internal key figures, and Short-term indicators. From within these nodes, Sales, Procurement, and Capital market-reporting capabilities are possible (in addition to Financial key figures and Personal reports). EIS is designed for the collection and evaluation of core data throughout your company's business. A sample display from the EIS in the General Report Selection Tree is shown in Figure 7-7.

Accounting

The Accounting node of the General Report Selection Tree contains subnodes for areas such as Consolidation, General ledger, Customers, Vendors, Assets, Special Purpose Ledger, and Funds management. Each of these subnodes contains its own objects, including Balance sheet/P+L, Cash flow, and Account information. Some reports in the Financials section of the General Report Selection Tree include Equity Holdings Adjustments for Associated Companies, Interactive Reporting in Consolidation, and Transaction Types for Consolidation. A sample display from the Accounting node in the General Report Selection Tree is shown in Figure 7-8.

Treasury

The treasury node of the General Report Selection Tree includes subnodes for Cash management and Cash budget management. Sample objects included in these nodes are Cash management and

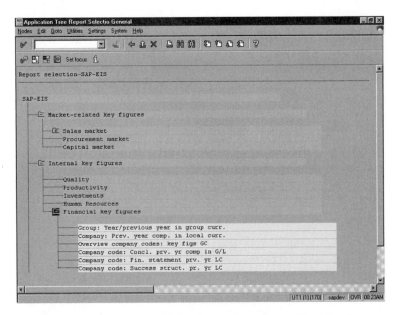

Figure 7-7 *An EIS provides information about all of the factors that influence the business activities of a company.*

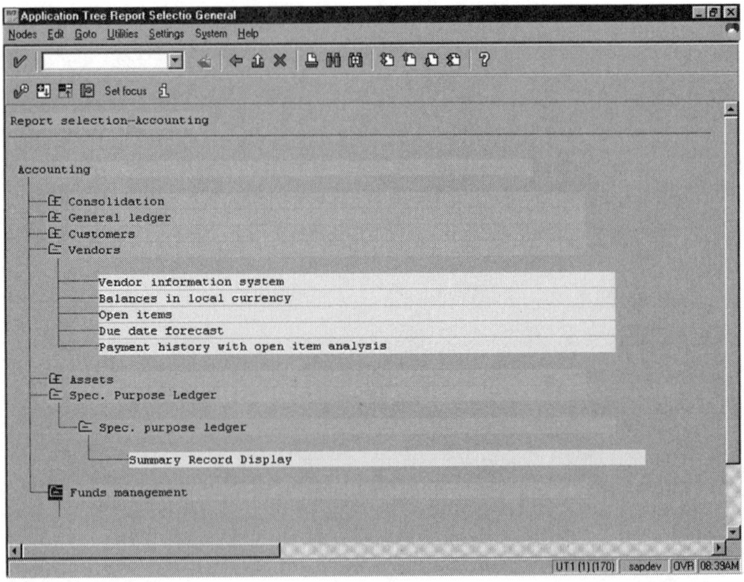

Figure 7-8 *The reports found in the Accounting node can be used to retrieve information about the data stored within your R/3 Financials module.*

forecast, Master data indexes, Totals records, and Line items. Some reports in this Treasury section include Cash Position, Liquidity forecast, Planned/actual comparison, and Commitment/ actual/inventory. A sample display from the Treasury node in the General Report Selection Tree is shown in Figure 7-9.

Controlling

In the General Report Selection Tree, the Controlling node contains subnodes for Cost-Element Accounting, Cost centers, Orders, Projects, Process costs, Product-Cost Controlling, and Profit-center accounting. These top-level objects contain subnodes for Overview, Reconciliation, Cost flow, Prices, Line items, Profitability reports, and Costs for Intangible Goods and Services. Sample objects included in these nodes are Basic data, Costs/Revenues, and Finances. Some reports in the Controlling section of the General Report Selection Tree include Reconciliation Ledger: CO Line Items, Cost Centers: Master Data Report, Master Data List Internal Orders, and Cost Elements: Master Data Report.

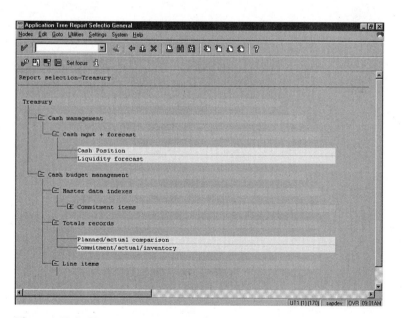

Figure 7-9 *Treasury comprises the components of Cash Management, Treasury Management, Loans, and Market-Risk Management.*

A sample display from the Controlling node in the General
Report Selection Tree is shown in Figure 7-10.

Investments

The Investments node of the General Report Selection Tree
contains the subnodes Programs, Projects, Orders, and Assets.
Sample objects within these nodes include Total depreciation
forecast, Proof of origin: Line items and summary, and Acquisi-
tions by invest. reason. Some sample order reports in the Investments section of the General Report Selection Tree include
Drilldown by Period, Actual/plan/price variance, and Actual/plan/
consumption, and sample List reports include Cost elements,
Account debits/credits, Planned debits/credits, and Budget/Actual/
Commitment. A sample display from the Investments node in the
General Report Selection Tree is shown in Figure 7-11.

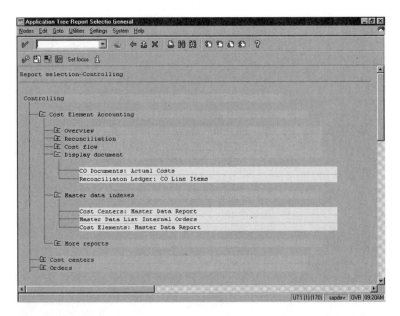

Figure 7-10 *The reports found in the Controlling node can be
used to retrieve information about the data stored within your
R/3 Financials module.*

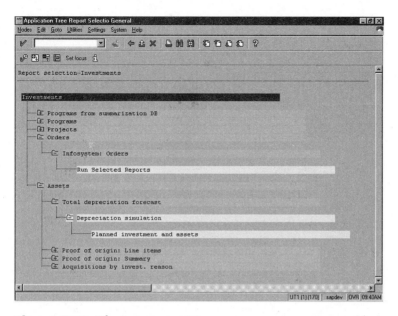

Figure 7-11 *The Investment Management component provides functions to support the planning, investment, and financing processes for capital investment measures in your enterprise.*

Materials Management

In the General Report Selection Tree, the Materials Management node is comprised of Inventory Management, Purchasing, and Warehouse management subnodes. These top-level objects house subnodes including Material, Vendor, Material and Purchasing groups, Stock placement/removal, Quantity flows, and Material placement/removal. Sample objects included in these nodes are Purchasing values, Purchasing quantities, Delivery reliability, Order price history, and Quotation price history. Some reports in the Materials Management section of the General Report Selection Tree include Analysis of Current Stock Values, Stock/Reqt Analysis Selection, Info Records Per Material, and Flow of Quantities Selection. A sample display from the Treasury node in the General Report Selection Tree is shown in Figure 7-12.

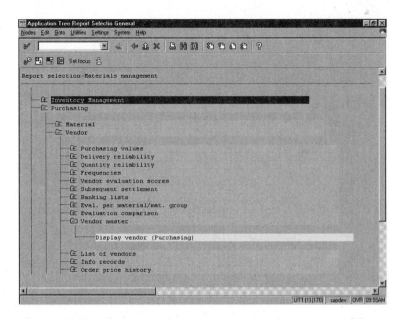

Figure 7-12 *The materials management application is widely used to support manufacturing, distribution, and service industries.*

Sales

The Sales node of the General Report Selection Tree contains several subnodes, including Customer, Material, Sales organization, Sales office, and Sales employee. Sample objects within these nodes include Incoming orders, Returns, Sales Credit memos, Material Master, Price list, and Price groups. Some sample reports in the Sales node of the General Report Selection Tree include List of Quotations, List of Sales Orders, and Exception Analysis: SIS and Sales Office Return. A sample display from the Sales node in the General Report Selection Tree is shown in Figure 7-13.

Production

In the General Report Selection Tree, the Production node is comprised of Product group, Material, Work center, Capacity Requirements Planning, Production resources and tools, Flexible analysis, and Exception analysis subnodes. These top-level objects contain subnodes including PRT routings, Material, Document, Lead times, Deadlines, Amounts, Lead times, and Deadlines

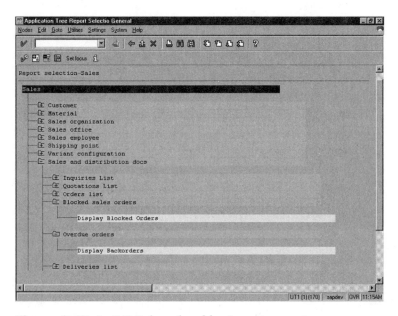

Figure 7-13 *In R/3 Sales related business transactions are recorded in the system as sales documents.*

Amounts. Sample reports from the Production section of the General Report Selection Tree include Sales and Operations Planning, Material Analysis Selection, Reporting Point Statistics, PRT Where Used Lists, and Execute Evaluation. A sample display from the Production node in the General Report Selection Tree is shown in Figure 7-14.

Plant Maintenance

The Plant Maintenance node of the General Report Selection Tree contains several subnodes, including Technical objects, Maintenance tasks, Regular maintenance, and Flexible analysis. Sample objects within these nodes include Object class, Manufacturer, Location, Object statistics, Equipment, and Preventive maintenance strategy. Some sample reports in the Plant Maintenance node of the General Report Selection Tree include Package Order, Graphical scheduling overview, Execute Evaluation, and Display PM Order Confirmation. A sample display from the Plant Maintenance node in the General Report Selection Tree is shown in Figure 7-15.

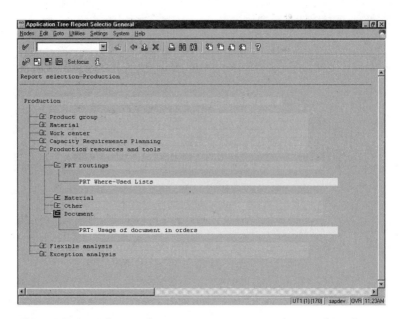

Figure 7-14 *The Production components are essential to the flow of materials and quality control within R/3.*

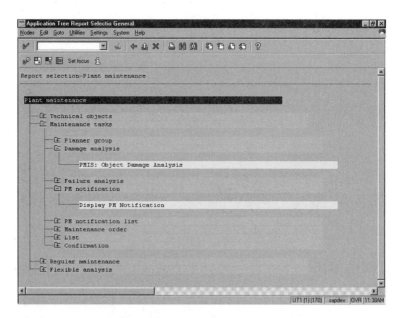

Figure 7-15 *The R/3 Plant Maintenance module is crucial to production industries and maintenance-service industries.*

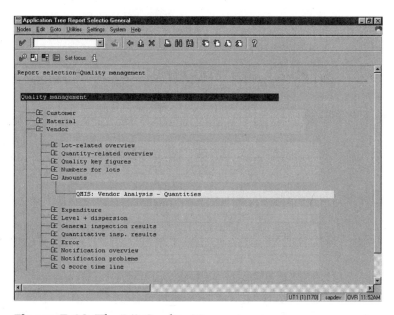

Figure 7-16 *The R/3 Quality Management component contains quality planning, inspection, and control.*

Quality Management

In the General Report Selection Tree, the Quality Management node contains subnodes for Customer, Material, Vendor, Flexible analysis, and Exception analysis. These top-level objects contain subnodes including Lot-related overview, Quantity-related overview, Quality key figures, Numbers for lots, Amounts, Expenditures, Notification overview, Notification problems, and Q score timeline. Sample reports in the Quality Management section of the General Report Selection Tree include Vendor Analysis Lot Overview, Vendor Analysis—Quality Overview, Vendor Analysis Quality Score, Vendor Analysis—Quantities, and General Results for Material. A sample display from the Quality Management node in the General Report Selection Tree is shown in Figure 7-16.

Human Resources

The Human Resources node of the General Report Selection Tree contains subnodes such as Personnel management, Time management, Payroll accounting, Training and Event Manage-

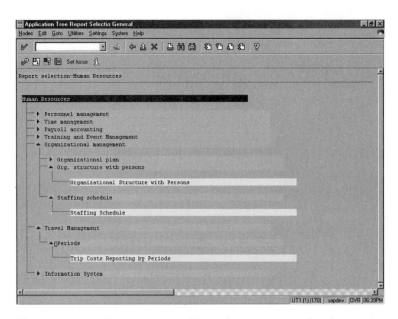

Figure 7-17 *Government and Regulatory reports for the Human Resources module come pre-delivered in Sap but are not listed in the report tree.*

ment, Organizational management, Travel Management, and Information System. Sample objects within these nodes include Administration, Recruitment, Personnel development, Benefits, Compensation management, and Payroll accounting—USA. Some sample reports in the Human Resources node of the General Report Selection Tree include Planned Labor Costs, Employee Demographics, Display attendance list, Plan Scenarios of Person-nel Cost Planning, Employee-flexible data reports, Payday Calen-dar Display, and Qualifications catalog. A sample display from the Human Resources node in the General Report Selection Tree is shown in Figure 7-17.

Projects

In the General Report Selection Tree, the Projects node is comprised of Structure, Deadlines, Costs, Revenues, Finances, and Resources subnodes. These top-level objects contain subnodes including Overview, Planning table, Progress, Reservation account assignment, Purchase order account assignment, Outline agreement account assignment, and Purchase order account assignment. Sample reports from the Projects section of the General Report Selection Tree include Funds overview, Requisitions by Account Assignment, Outline Agreements by Account Assignment, and Display project planning board. A sample display from the Projects node in the General Report Selection Tree is shown in Figure 7-18.

Tools

In the General Report Selection Tree, the Tools node contains only the Logistics Information System. The three objects within the logistics information system are Key figure search via information sets, Key figure search via text elem., and Key figure search via classification. The three reports available in the Tools node are Key Figure Retrieval via Classification, Key Figure Retrieval Using Text Strings, and Key Figure Retrieval via Information Sets. A sample display from the Tools node in the General Report Selection Tree is shown in Figure 7-19.

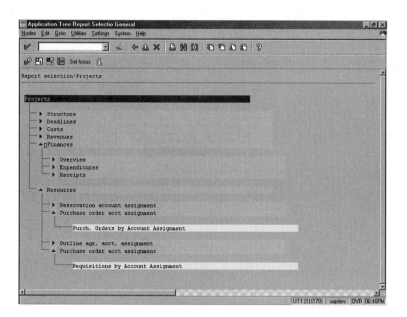

Figure 7-18 *The projects component is essential to the management of costs, structures, deadlines, and revenues.*

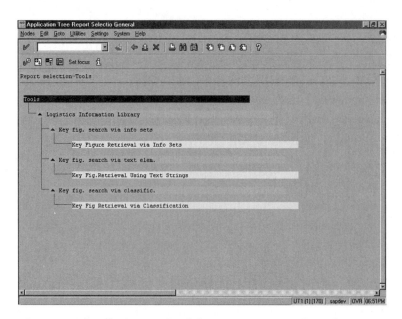

Figure 7-19 *The last node of the report tree, Tools, only contains the logistics information system.*

Searching for Reports

You can search for reports in the R/3 General Report Selection Tree. The trick to searching the tree is that the nodes must be expanded for the area that you are searching in order for the item to be found. For example, if the tree appears as it does in its initial position (with no subnodes expanded), and you search for a report contained in the subnodes, R/3 will not find the report. With that warning in mind, the first step for any search is to expand the subnodes of the tree. You do not have to expand the subnodes of the entire tree if you know the approximate area in which the report might exist. For example, if you wanted to search for the employee Birthday List report, you would only need to expand the Human Resources node. Nodes can expanded by selecting the highest level of the node, then selecting the Expand sub-node button from the Application toolbar or by following the path Edit→Expand sub-tree. Once all subnodes of the selected node have been expanded, select the Find button from

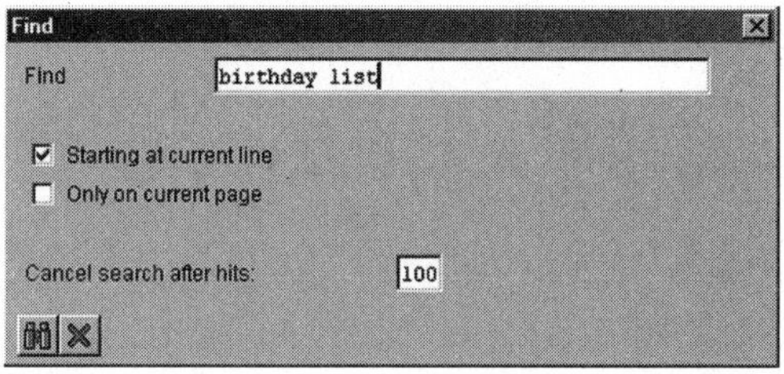

Figure 7-20 *You can search for reports in the report tree by entering a partial description into the Find dialog box.*

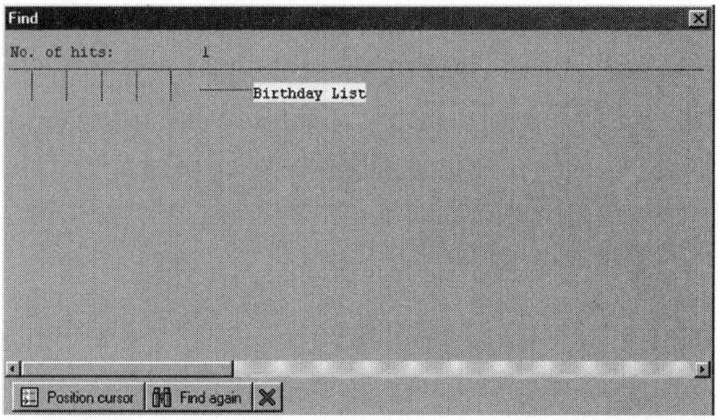

Figure 7-21 *Hypertext links appear with a shaded background and can be selected to automatically bring you to the selected location.*

the Standard toolbar. A Find dialog box will appear similar to the one shown in Figure 7-20.

After entering a partial description, select the Find (Enter) button on the Find Dialog box to proceed. A second dialog box will appear with the results of your search and a hypertext link to any items matching your search criteria (see Figure 7-21).

The top of the new Find box will display the number of hits, which translates to the number of reports that matched the search criteria. If multiple reports contained the words "Birthday List" in their report name, they would also appear as hypertext in the results.

Advanced Searches

You can use the menu path Edit→Find→Objects to perform a more advanced search for reports in the General Report Selection Tree. Again, the nodes and subnodes of the tree need to be expanded in order to conduct proper searching.

Viewing Report Documentation

You can view documentation for a report in the R/3 General Report Selection Tree if that report documentation is available in your login language. Many reports in the R/3 tree contain documentation that you can view to obtain a better understanding of the report and how the report is put together. Unfortunately, as of Version 4.0B, not all reports have this documentation available in English. To view documentation for a report, select the report and then follow the menu path Goto→Documentation. If no documentation is available, a message will appear in the R/3 Status bar indicating that the documentation is not available in English. If the information is available, it will appear within your R/3 window, as in Figure 7-22.

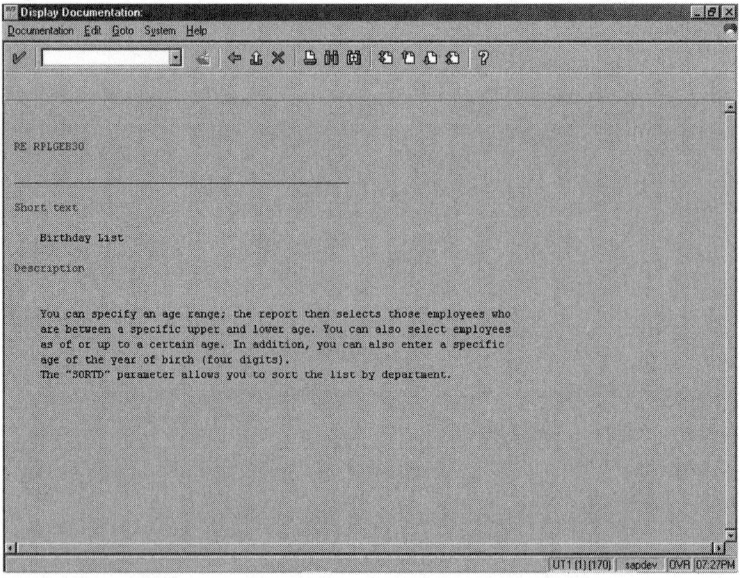

Figure 7-22 *The documentation provided for reports in R/3 varies from the brief to extremely detailed, depending on the report.*

Version 4.0B—3,000 Reports OSS Note

The General Report Selection Tree contains more than 3,000 reports and only comes standard in versions later than 4.0B; however, it is available for Version 4.0B through OSS Note #123601. This enhanced version of the report tree consists of several new structures, nodes, and reports. The standard report tree (not containing the 3,000 reports) is shown in Figure 7-23. Compare this figure to the enhanced report tree (containing the 3,000 reports) shown in Figure 7-24. If you are using Version 4.0B or later and do not have the enhanced report tree available, contact your system administrator and ask him or her to research OSS Note #123601.

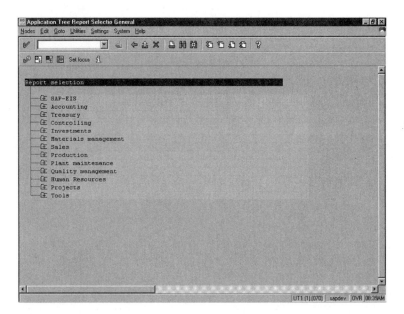

Figure 7-23 *The standard report tree for Version 4.0B does not include the new reports added to the later versions.*

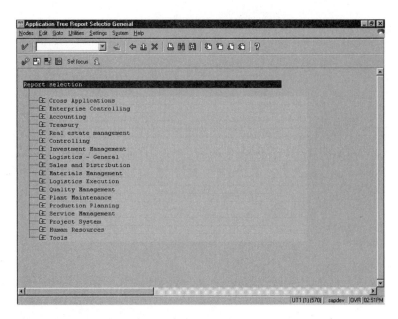

Figure 7-24 *The enhanced report tree contains more than 3,000 reports, including more than 100 additional human resources reports.*

Chapter Wrap-Up

Many reports are available in the R/3 General Report Selection Tree. The tree is a useful hub from which you can navigate to many reports that will provide you with relevant data in your SAP system. Unfortunately, the standard reports will probably not satisfy all of your reporting requirements, so you will have to create custom reports for your R/3 data. In the next section, we introduce the ABAP query tool that you can use to create your own reports without any programming skills.

Printing Reports in R/3

The ultimate goal in reporting is the output. Whether that output is displayed on the screen, saved in a folder, or e-mailed to a coworker, in many instances you will want that output on paper. Despite the fact that we are progressing more and more towards a paperless society that relies on electronic forms and reports, many people prefer to have an actual hard copy in hand. For this reason, printing your R/3 reports is important. For starters, in order to print in R/3, you need to be connected to a printer.

Printer Connections

Depending on the size of your SAP installation, you might be connected to a printer through your network or locally in your office. Contact your SAP administrator to ensure that you are connected to a printer. If you are still in the implementation phase and do not yet have a printer connected, you can follow along with the chapter and return to it once you are connected.

Printing Lists

Printing lists refer to the output of your report, known as the list. For our list examples, we will use a displayed list of the SPFLI table discussed earlier. The SPFLI table is part of SAP's instructional table structure and is not connected to your functioning, SAP R/3 live data pertinent to your organization. The SAP R/3 Print button is located on the Standard toolbar and appears on almost all SAP screens (see Figure 8-1).

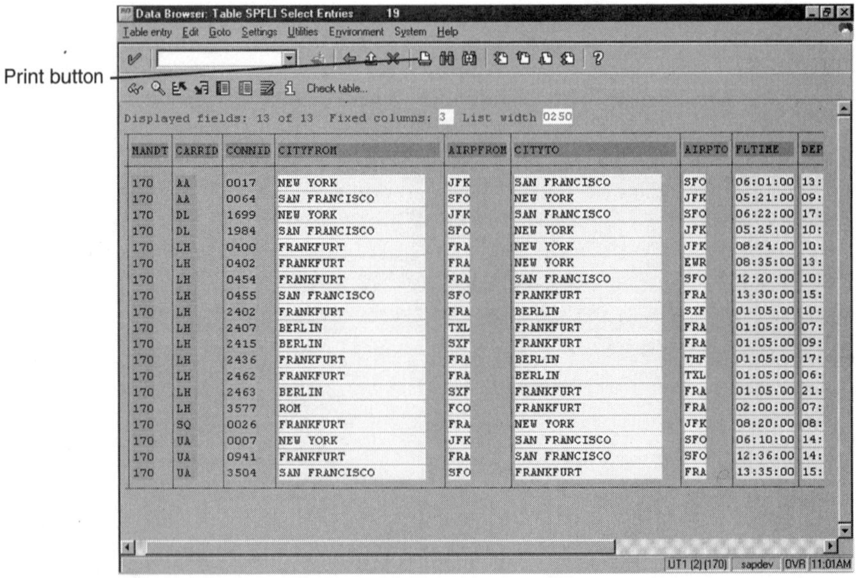

Print button

Figure 8-1 *A hard copy of your SAP output can be produced by selecting the Print button.*

Figure 8-1 shows a list of the SPFLI table. To print a list in R/3, select the Print button from the Standard toolbar.

Print List Screen

Upon selection of the Print button from any SAP screen, the R/3 Print List Screen window will appear (see Figure 8-2 for an example). All settings for the Print List Screen are detailed in Table 8.1.

Default Printer Settings

Each time the Print button is selected on an SAP screen, the Print List Screen, shown in Figure 8-2, will appear. You can pre-fill this screen with default settings that will appear each time the Print List Screen appears. In many cases, you can use these settings for many of the reports you print; in other cases, you can set default values for individual reports that will appear only for your particular report.

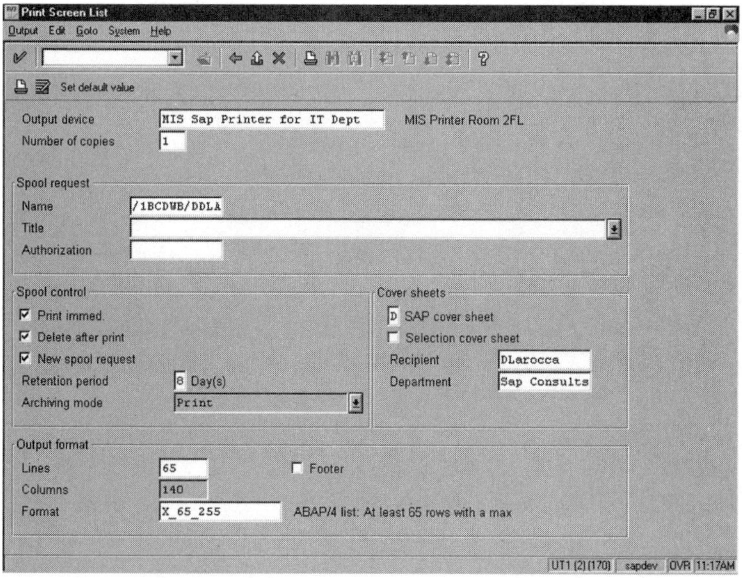

Figure 8-2 *The Print List Screen window includes your specified output device and printer settings.*

Table 8.1 *R/3 Print List Screen window settings*

Setting	Description
Output Device	The output device contains the name of the device where the output will be sent. This device could be a printer, fax machine, or any other type of output device connected to your R/3 system. To access a list of available output devices for your R/3 system, select the Possible Entries Help button or contact your system administrator.
Number of Copies	You can specify the number of copies that you would like to print in the Number of Copies field. Depending on the output, some reports in SAP can be extremely long. While the output is displayed on your screen, use the Page Up and Page Down buttons on the Standard toolbar to determine the report's length before printing.
Spool Request	
Name	By default, the Spool Request name is assigned by the SAP system. This name is comprised of letters, numbers, characters, and blanks. For reports, the name consists of the program name, a blank space, and the first three letters of your username.
Title	You can enter a description of your Spool Request into the Title field. This description will come in handy if you are searching for this spool

	request for page-print modifications or for inquiries. By default, the Title field is blank.
Authorization	The Spool Request Authorization field contains the authorization for the spool request. Only users with this authorization are permitted to display the contents of the spool request. As an example, if a purchasing manager prints a list of approved purchase requisitions and a spool request is created, only users with the appropriate authorizations to view purchase requisitions will be able to view the spool request.
Spool Control	
Print Immed	This field determines whether the spool request (that is, the report output) should be sent to the output device at once. The two permitted values are "yes" (for outputting immediately) or "no" (for "do not output immediately"). You will modify this setting based on the urgency of the output, on the available resources, and on the size of the report.
Delete after Print	This field determines whether to delete the spool request immediately after it has been sent to the output device, or only after the spool retention period has expired. The two permitted values are "yes" (for deleting after the expiration of the spool retention period) or "no" (for no

Table 8.1 *R/3 Print List Screen window settings (Continued)*

	deletion). You will modify this setting based on the urgency of the output, on the availability of resources, and on the size of the report. By default, this setting is blank so that the request is saved (a precautionary measure). You might send something to the printer, and if it never arrives, you can search for the spool request and determine what went wrong and print the data again. If the box was marked, the spool request would be immediately deleted, and you would be unable to recall it. For quick printing of screens and reports, it is a good idea to mark this box so you do not waste system resources by taking up system space for every saved item.
New Spool Request	This field determines whether to generate a new spool request or append the current spool request to an existing request with similar attributes. In order to append the current spool request to an existing spool request, the specifications for name, output device, number of copies, and format must be identical, and the existing spool request could not have been completed (released for output.) If no suitable spool request is found, then a new one is generated. The two permitted values are "yes" to generate a new spool

	request or "no" to locate and append to an existing spool request (if available).
Retention Period	This field determines how many days a spool request is to remain in the spool system before being deleted. Permissible selections include "delete after 1, 2, 3, 4, 5, 6, 7, or 8 days," or "do not delete."
Cover Sheets	
Cover Sheet	This field determines whether to include a cover sheet before your output. This cover sheet can include information such as recipient name (for faxes), department name (for delivery), format used, etc. The permitted values are "no cover sheet," "cover sheet," and the standard setting.
Selection Cover Sheet	This field determines whether the report output should include a cover sheet with the report selections. The two permitted values are "yes" for an output cover sheet or "no" for no cover sheet output.
Recipient	This field contains the spool request recipient's name that appears on the cover sheet of hard-copy printouts. By default, this field will contain the name of the current user.
Department	This field contains the name of the department from which the output originated. For hard-copy printouts, the name is displayed on the cover sheet.

Table 8.1 *R/3 Print List Screen window settings (Continued)*

Output Format	
Lines	The Output Format, Lines field determines the number of lines per list page. If this field contains a zero or is blank, the number of pages is unlimited (not permitted when printing). In this case, the length of the list is then determined by its content alone. Depending on the formatting you choose for your report, a maximum number of lines per page will be determined. To alter the number of lines, different formatting selections must be indicated for the report.
Columns	This field contains the current line width of the list. The maximum permitted column width is 255 characters. Depending on the formatting you choose for your report, a maximum line width will be determined. To alter line width, different formatting must be selected for the report.
Format	This field contains the spool request format for output. Available formats are defined by your selected output device. Essentially, the field defines the page format and will determine the maximum number of lines and columns per print page. Available format selections can be accessed from the Possible Entries Help button for this field.

Footer	This field determines whether the text extract is outputted at the end of each print page. The field-permissible values are "yes" for an output footer and "no" for "do not output footer."

R/3 General Default Printer Setting

For starters, enter the selections that you would like to be considered for your printing default settings in R/3. You might want to consult with your system administrator with regards to modifying the selections for the output device and the spool control. Follow these steps to set the default values for printing in R/3:

1. After entering your printing selections, select the Set Default Value button from the Application toolbar. A Print Screen List dialog box will appear, similar to the one shown in Figure 8-3.

2. Select the user-specific option, and then select the Continue button. Your general R/3 default printing options are saved for the client.

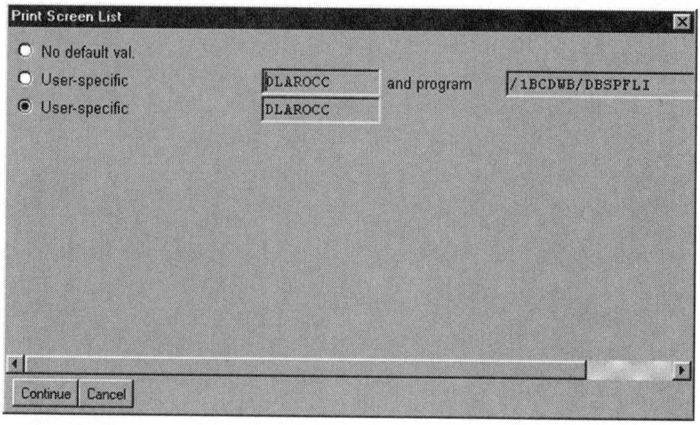

Figure 8-3 *Default values can be set for R/3 printing in general and for specific reports.*

Each time you select the Print button on an R/3 screen, you will be presented with the Print List Screen with your filled-in default options. This statement is true in all cases, except when you set an individual report or screen to use a different setting (see the information as follows).

Report-Specific Printer Setting

Depending on the report, you might want to modify the settings to fit the output in a different format than applied by the default. In cases such as these, execute the report, select the Print button, and enter the appropriate selections on the Print List screen. Next, select the Set Default Value button, and this time select the user-specific and program-specific option shown in Figure 8-4.

Each time you select the Print button for this report, you will be presented with the Print List screen with your report-specific default options completed.

Note   Keep in mind that even with default settings, you are still required to select the Print button from the Print List screen in order for your output to be sent to the printer (or to another output device).

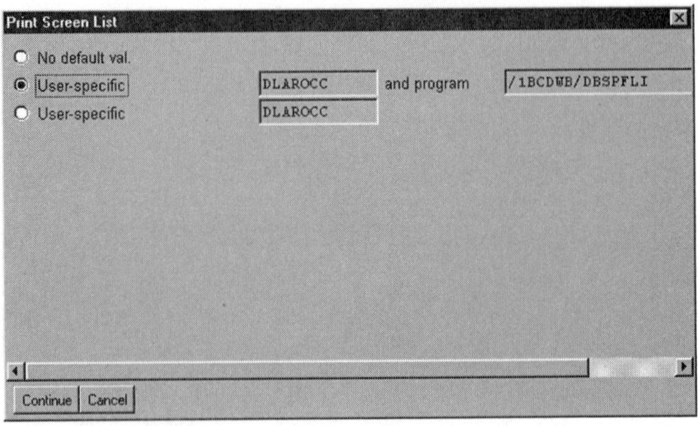

Figure 8-4 *Report-specific default printer settings are handy if you want to send the report to a different output device than normally used for R/3 reporting.*

Spool-Request Management

You can modify your spool request only if you did not mark the Print immed. and Delete after print check boxes on the Print List screen. Leaving these boxes unmarked ensures that your spool request is available in the system for you to modify the request. To view your spool request, follow the menu path System→Own spool requests to navigate to the Spool Requests screen. The screen will appear similar to the one shown in Figure 8-5.

You have several options in the management of your spool requests that can be accessed from the Application toolbar. The functions available on the toolbar are explained in Table 8.2.

Viewing Spool Request Attributes

From the Spool Request screen, you can select a spool request to view its attributes by selecting the request and then selecting the Attributes button from the Application toolbar. Or, you can double-click the request. The Spool: Attributes screen is shown in Figure 8-6.

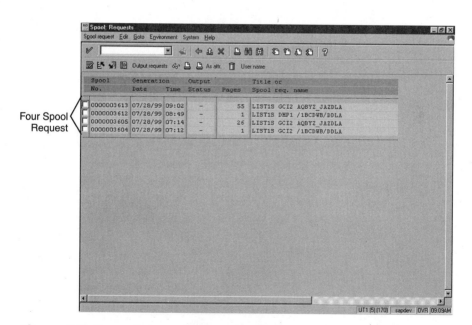

Figure 8-5 *Depending on your security privileges in R/3, you might have to request the availability of this transaction from your system administrator.*

Table 8.2 *Spool Requests Application toolbar*

Button	Function
	The Refresh button refreshes the screen's contents with the latest information available in your R/3 system.
	The Sort Ascending button is used to sort the contents of the display into ascending order.
	The Sort Descending button is used to sort the contents of the display into descending order.
	The Attribute button will display the attributes of a selected report (we show an example later in the chapter).
Output requests	The Output Requests button will display print requests or error logs for the selected spool request.
	The Display button will provide a screen preview of the spool request.
	The Print button will open the Spool: Output Request screen, which can be used to send the spool request to the printer.
As attr.	The Print As attr. button will automatically send the output to the printer.
	The Delete button will delete the selected spool request.
User name	The User Name button will toggle the display to show the username in place of the spool request date on the screen.
	The Date button will toggle the display to show the spool request date in place of the username on the screen.

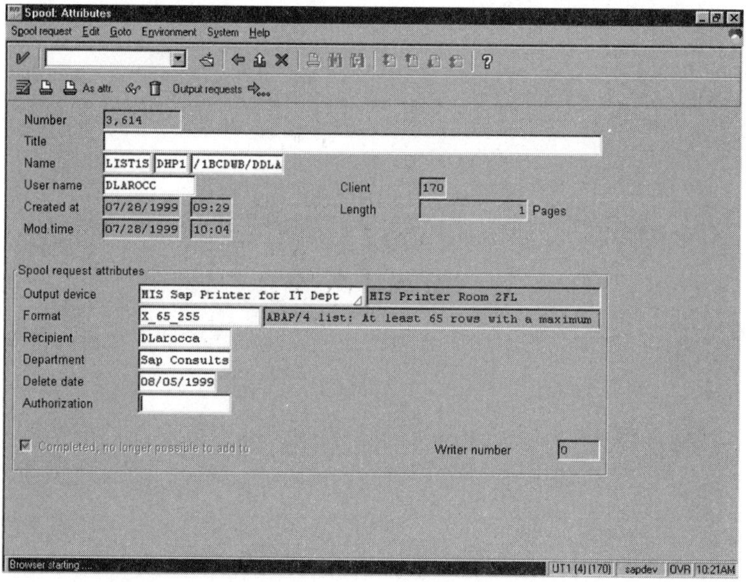

Figure 8-6 *The information displayed on the Attributes screen comes from the data entered on the Print List screen.*

Modifying the Number of Pages Printed

If you have a large report and only want to print the first 10 pages, you can modify your spool request. Remember that in order for you to modify your spool request, you need to unmark the Print immed. and the Delete after print check boxes. From the Spool Requests screen, select the Spool request and then the Print button from the Application toolbar. A Spool: Output Request screen will appear similar to the one shown in Figure 8-7.

On this screen, you can enter the number of copies and the starting and ending page numbers of the report that you would like to print.

Priority Level

You can also modify the priority level of your report from the Spool: Output Request screen. The spool system sends output requests to the printer, depending on the requests' priority levels. Priority levels apply to all output requests, and by default, all of them are set at a level of three. Acceptable values are between one and nine, with the lower number increasing the priority level.

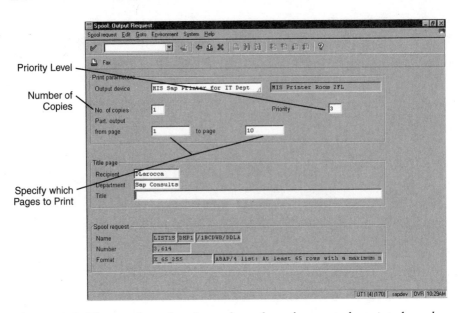

Figure 8-7 *The number of copies and number of pages to be printed can be modified for your R/3 reports.*

Deleting Spool Requests

Spool requests can be deleted from the Spool: Requests screen by selecting them and then selecting the Delete button from the Application toolbar. System administrators can also periodically clean out old spool requests using an ABAP report called RSPO0041. The report deletes old spool requests according to specified criteria.

Spool Request Evaluation

You can view the status of your spool requests on the Spool: requests screen at any time in R/3. A column called output status will display the status of your spool request. The different output statuses that are displayed are outlined in Table 8.3.

Viewing a Spool Error Log

If any errors occurred during the processing of an output request, these errors are reported in an error log. Error logs can be displayed by selecting the request, then selecting the Output

Table 8.3 *Spool requests output status*

Status	Description
– or =	The output has not yet been sent to the host system for printing (no output requests have been made).
+	The spool request is still being generated (stored in the spool system).
Wait	The output request is anticipating being processed by the spool system and has not yet been sent to the host system.
Process	The spooling process is formatting the output request for printing.
Print	The output request is being processed by the host system spooler. If the R/3 spool system cannot get status information from the host spooler, then this status appears for approximately one minute. After that time, the status is set to Complete or Error.
Compl	The output request has been successfully printed. In systems wherein the spool system is unable to retrieve information from the host spooler, the status becomes Complete as soon as the output request has been passed to the host spooler.
Error	This status indicates a technical problem, such as a network connectivity shortage or a disabled printer. In either case, the output request could not be printed. The spool system retains such requests until you delete them or until they age and are deleted by a reorganization.
Problem	This status indicates a mild technical problem, such as characters missing from a character set. The output request was printed, but it probably contains printing errors. The output should be verified.

Table 8.3 *Spool requests output status (Continued)*

Status	Description
Archive	This status applies to requests that were sent to an archiving device. The spool request has been processed by the spool system and is waiting for archiving.

Requests button from the Application toolbar. The error log reports messages from the R/3 spool work process or formatting process and from messages returned by the host spooler. The error log also includes a summary of the attributes of the output request. Detailed log information is also available.

Chapter Wrap-Up

Printing in your R/3 system is a necessity. Even as we move closer to a paperless and electronic business world, it is still necessary to produce hard copies of the output. This chapter was designed to familiarize you with how to customize your printer settings to maximize the output from your R/3 system.

ABAP Query Behind the Scenes

The ABAP query is sometimes referred to as SAP's query tool. Unlike true report writers, ABAP query is a tool for users requiring no programming skills whatsoever. The ABAP query enables you to select data from a series of tables that are logically grouped together and output them in reports in the format that you specify. In ABAP query, reports are referred to as queries.

The relevance of the information presented in this chapter will vary depending on your organization, on your phase of implementation, and on your role in the SAP team. In other words, we will present technical topics in this chapter which might (depending on your role) already be set up for you in your R/3 system. Most likely, you are an end user who will only be using the ABAP query tool to create reports. In that case, the information presented in this chapter might get a little technical for you. Despite that, it is a good idea to understand the basic concepts of how your ABAP queries (reports) are put together. The behind-the-scenes concepts discussed in this chapter, including user groups, functional areas, application areas, and language comparisons, may already be configured for your use in R/3 by your system-administration team. Check with the appropriate personnel to determine whether you have been assigned to a user group and whether the necessary functional areas have been configured. If they have been, make a note of this information. If they have not been configured, obtain the proper authorizations and use the guidelines outlined in this chapter to configure them (or provide this chapter to your systems administrator). Again, depending on your role in SAP, you might not have authorization access to the transactions necessary for this configuration, and be sure to request that your SAP administrator investigate the R/3 authorization object for the ABAP query. When getting started with the behind-the-scenes setup of the ABAP query, we need to become familiar with the four components that comprise the ABAP query. The four main components of the ABAP query are as follows:

- Application areas
- User groups
- Functional areas
- Language comparisons

Component 1—Application Areas

At the start of this book, we discussed how there are different clients available in your R/3 system. Depending on your role in SAP, you might only have access to the production (or live-data) client. Some users will have access to the development and quality-assurance clients, as well. These clients are individual operating areas within SAP. The production client contains real, live data and is used to run your business. The development client will most likely contain fictional data used primarily for testing, as will the quality-assurance client. You need to know about the client in which you will be creating your queries. Some companies create them in the development client, test them in the quality-assurance client, and then move (transport or import) them into the production client. Other companies enable users to create the queries in the production client. Be sure to check with your system administrator before creating any new queries. This question is relevant for application areas. When creating queries, you can specify whether you want to create them in the global or standard application areas. All query objects delivered by SAP (from Release 4.0) are located in the global area. Both the global and the standard application areas provide you with a full-range ABAP of query functions.

Global Application Area

The global application area designates that the query will appear in all clients (on a single database server). If you have your development and quality-assurance clients on a single database server, when you create the query in the development client, it will be available in the quality-assurance client as well. Objects created in the global application area are connected to the ABAP Workbench and can be transported to other clients that reside on different database servers.

Standard Application Area

Objects created in the standard application area are client specific. In other words, they will only be available in the client in which they were created. These clients, however, can be transported (or imported/exported) to other clients. The main difference is that they are not automatically available in all of the clients that reside on the same database server. Objects created in the standard application area are not connected to the ABAP Workbench. The decision of where to create your objects needs to made before you begin working with the ABAP query tool.

Changing Your Current Application Area

When you begin to access the different screens in the ABAP query, you will automatically be placed into one of the two application areas. To change application areas from one of the ABAP query configuration screens, you can use the menu path Environment→ Application areas and select the appropriate option from the dialog box. We will give this procedure a try in a few minutes.

Component 2—User Groups

You can think of the concept of user groups as departments within your organization. Depending on user roles and duties, employees are grouped into categories such as accounting department, human resources department, etc. User groups are based on that concept. You and the people who have jobs similar to yours will be logically grouped into a single user group. This group designation segregates you from other groups. All of the people within your group will create reports in a single area in SAP, called a user group. This concept of user groups is a way of organizing your reports in R/3. For example, all of the accountants will be in a user group containing all of the relevant accounting reports, and all human resources administrators will be in a separate group with their reports. A single user might belong to multiple user groups, although only users with the appropriate authorizations can modify or create new queries. Users who have the authority to create new reports can also specify that they do not want their reports to be modified. We will discuss this setting in the next chapter. For now, it is enough to understand that you need to be assigned to a user group before you can start creating queries.

Authorization Object for the ABAP Query

This small paragraph is relevant only for your R/3 security administrator. The concept of the authorization object for the use and configuration of the ABAP query was discussed in greater detail in Chapter 6, "Reporting Security Concepts." Feel free to pass this information along to them if security is not yet configured in your R/3 system for the ABAP query. There is an authorization object for the ABAP query called S_Query. This authorization object enables you to specify whether a selected user can create and change queries, maintain the environment for the ABAP query (functional areas and user groups), or translate query object texts. The default values of authorizations for the authorization object S_QUERY are S_QUERY_ALL, which enables users to change, maintain, and translate queries. S_QUERY_UPD enables users to only change and translate queries. Both of these authorizations can be found in the basis profiles supplied by SAP. Commonly, users will only have access to maintaining and creating queries and not user groups and functional areas (which are maintained by your technical team).

Create a New User Group

As mentioned at the beginning of this chapter, you will need the appropriate authorizations to create a new user group. The creation of user groups is usually performed by system administrators. Follow these steps to create a new user group in the standard application area:

1. Start at the User Groups: Initial screen, which you can navigate to using the transaction code /nSQ03 or the menu path Tools→ ABAP Workbench→Utilities→ABAP Query→User groups.

2. Make sure that you are in the standard application area by following the menu path Environment→Application areas and selecting the Standard option from the dialog box.

3. The User Groups: Initial screen will appear similar to the one displayed in Figure 9-1.

4. Your company might have its own naming convention for objects, which you might need to follow. In our example, we will call our user group Z_Flights. Enter the name for the user group that you would like to create into the User Group Input field, and select the Create button to proceed.

5. A dialog box will appear, asking you to fill in a description for your user group (see our example in Figure 9-2).

6. Select the green check mark Save button on the dialog box, and your user group is successfully created. Next, you need to add users to the group.

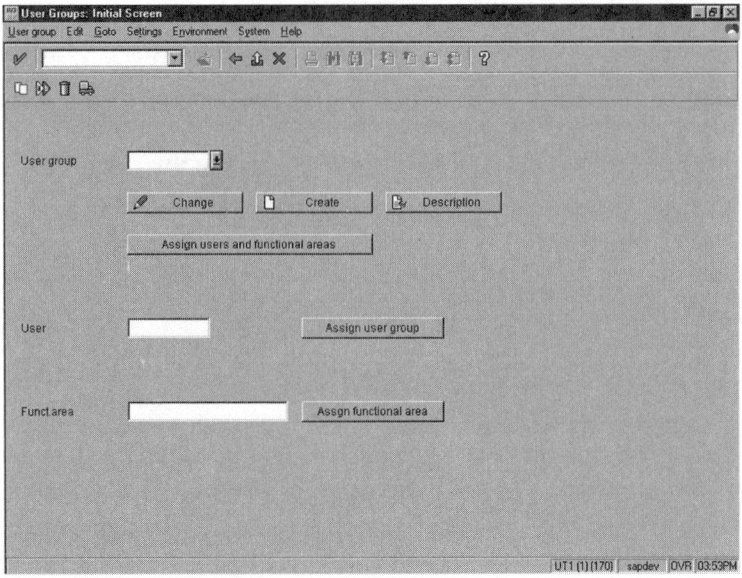

Figure 9-1 *Depending on your use of this screen, it might contain different values in the input fields.*

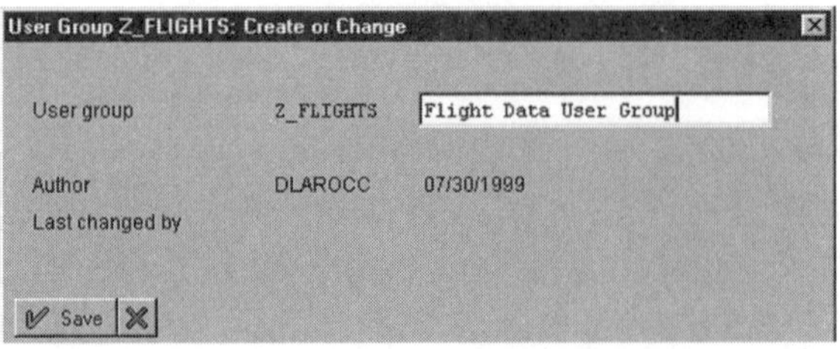

Figure 9-2 *The user group description is used to describe the task area for the user group.*

7. Your user group name will appear in the User Group field. Select the Assign Users and Functional Areas button.

8. A User Group: Assign Users screen will appear, where you can fill in all of the usernames of SAP users who will be grouped into this user group. For our example, we will only enter our own username (see Figure 9-3).

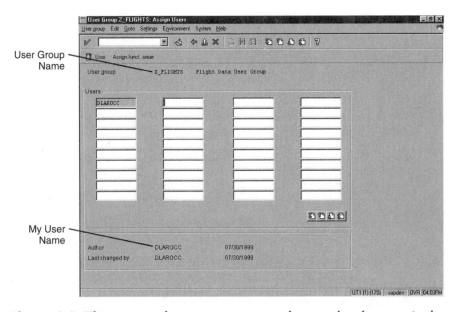

User Group
Name

My User
Name

Figure 9-3 *This screen only accepts usernames that are already set up in the SAP client.*

9. After entering your name, select the green check mark Enter key from the Standard toolbar. If the username was typed incorrectly, you will receive an error message in the Status bar. Your username appears at the bottom of the User Group: Assign Users screen.

10. After entering your username, select the Open Folder Save button from the Standard toolbar. A message will appear in the Status bar saying that the user group has been saved.

11. Use the green arrow Back button from the Application toolbar to return to the User Groups: Initial screen.

Viewing Existing User Groups

You can take a look at some of the predelivered R/3 user groups in R/3. R/3 delivers preconfigured user groups in the global application area. Switch to the global application area by following the menu path Environment→Application areas and selecting the Global option from the dialog box. Now that you are in the global application area, select the Possible Entries Help button for the User Groups Input field. A list of global user groups appears. The predelivered groups begin with the naming convention / SAPQUERY/, which identifies them as global, client-independent query objects in R/3.

Component 3—Functional Areas

The next component of the ABAP query is functional areas. Earlier in Chapter 3, "Reporting Database Concepts," we introduced the concept of logical databases in R/3. These were defined as a logical arrangement of R/3 database tables grouped together in a single source. The reports we create using the ABAP query tool use these logical databases (or other tables, joins, or programs) as the source of their data. Functional areas provide a special view of these logical databases. Functional areas can also be driven by tables, joins, and ABAP programming code. These types of concepts are a little more advanced than the scope of this book. Suffice it to say, however, that the functional areas based on logical databases are the most common and provide optimal performance in terms of system speed and reaction time to queries. The following figure (Figure 9-4) gives a representation of how these elements all fit together.

The figure might appear confusing at first glance, but think of it broken down into the basics:

1. A logical database is made up of a group of tables from the database.

2. A functional area is based on that logical database.

3. Application areas and language comparisons also come from the R/3 database.

4. User groups are made up of a group of users from the R/3 system.

5. All of these items meshed together give you the foundation of the ABAP query.

If you find this concept confusing, just give up now. (Of course, we are only kidding—we needed to make sure that you were still paying attention.) As we progress and actually take a

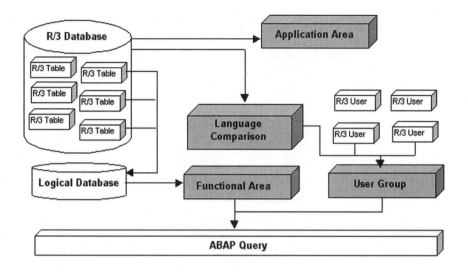

Figure 9-4 *The four components of the ABAP query display are shaded.*

look at some of these items, you will gain a better understanding of how they relate to each other, and the behind-the-scenes portion of the ABAP query will make more sense to you. Functional areas are created on the Functional Areas: Initial screen.

Create a New Functional Area

As we mentioned at the beginning of this chapter, you will need the appropriate authorizations to create a new functional area. Follow these steps to create a new functional area in the standard application area:

1. Start at the Functional Areas: Initial screen, which you can navigate to using the transaction code /nSQ02 or the menu path Tools→ABAP Workbench→Utilities→ABAP Query→ Functional areas.

2. The Functional Areas: Initial screen should appear similar to the one shown in Figure 9-5.

3. Make sure that you are in the standard application area by following the menu path Environment→Application areas and selecting the Standard option from the dialog box.

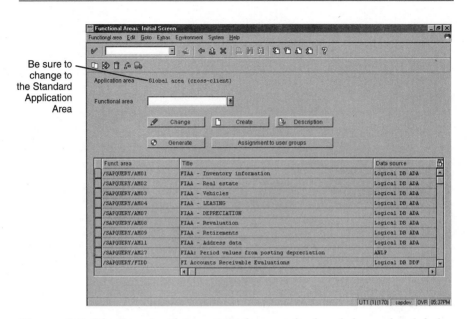

Be sure to change to the Standard Application Area

Figure 9-5 *The Functional Area: Initial screen displayed shows the global application area.*

4. Your company might have its own naming convention for objects, which you might need to follow. In our example, we will name our functional area Z_FlightData. Enter the name for the functional area that you would like to create into the Functional Area Input field, and select the Create button to proceed.

5. On the Title and Database dialog box that appears, enter a description for your functional area in the Name Input field. For our example, we will enter the Z_FlightData functional area.

6. Next, we need to enter a logical database into the logical data base field. The Possible Entries Help can be used, or you can manually enter F1S, as in Figure 9-6.

7. There are additional, more advanced options available on this screen, but at this level, we are only interested in the basics. Select the green check mark Enter key to proceed to the Change Functional Area screen.

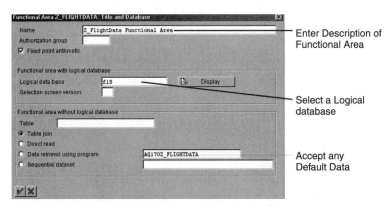

Figure 9-6 *F1S represents the test system, BC: Planned Flights, flights, and bookings that we have used in previous examples.*

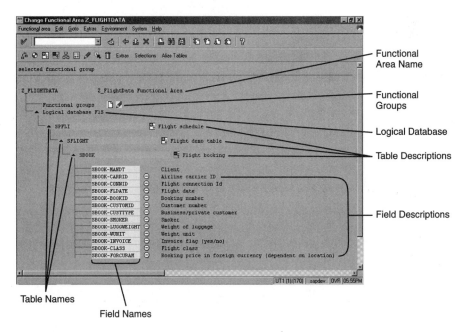

Figure 9-7 *Each level within the functional area represents a different type of object.*

8. This screen will display the functional area in a tree-structure format. Use the Expand sub-node button to the right of the SBOOK Flight Booking node to display its contents. The screen should appear similar to the one shown in Figure 9-7.

The functional area lists each of the tables that are in the logical database. Only three tables are in the F1S logical database: SPFLI (flight-schedule table), SFLIGHT (flight-demo table), and SBOOK (flight-booking table). The fields within each of these tables are listed beneath the table and can be viewed by selecting the Expand sub-node button to the right of the table name. Above the tables is something called functional groups.

Functional Groups

Functional groups enable you to place the fields from these tables into a single area for selection on your reports. The functional groups are what will appear later when we create reports using the ABAP query. We will see a list of all the functional groups, and we will use them for field selection. By default, in this functional area, no functional groups exist. In other functional areas (for example, Human Resources), functional groups are already created for you. For this example, we need to create our own group. Follow these steps to create functional groups within your functional area:

1. On your Change Functional Area screen, select the white Create button to the right of the word "Functional Groups."

2. A Create Functional Groups dialog box will appear. Enter a two-digit functional group name, followed by a description of the functional group (see Figure 9-8).

3. Select the green check mark Enter key on the dialog box to return to the Change Functional Areas screen, and your new functional group will be displayed at the top of the screen under the Functional Group heading.

4. Next, we need to add fields from the tables into our functional groups. These are the fields that will be available to us later when we create reports using ABAP Query. The fields listed under each of the tables all have an indicator icon between the field name and description. For all fields in this functional area, they appear as a minus sign inside a circle. Select the indicator icon for the SBOOK-CARRID Airline Carrier ID field, as in Figure 9-9.

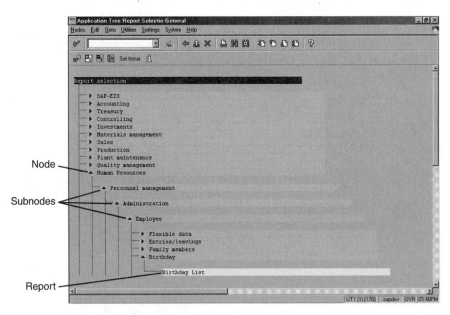

Figure 9-8 *If your company has a naming convention for objects in R/3, please use it when creating your functional group.*

Figure 9-9 *Depending on the functional area, fields might or might not appear as selected by default.*

When selecting fields, if the field for selection appears in multiple tables within the functional area, select it from the highest-level table in the hierarchy of the functional area.

Tip

5. Selecting the indicator marks the field as assigned to your functional group. This field will now be available for you to report in your ABAP queries. Select a few more fields from the SBOOK table to be added to your functional group, using the same method.

6. All selected fields will display a plus sign (+) in the indicator (circle) and display the two-digit functional group name. After adding a few fields, let's create another functional group.

7. Follow steps one through three (above) to create a new functional group. Your new functional group should appear beneath the original (see Figure 9-10).

Now that you have two functional groups, when you go to select fields (using the indicator) to assign them to a functional group, you will need to specify in which functional group to place them. At any point in time, only one functional group can be the *selected* group. The selected group appears at the top of your window, as in Figure 9-10.

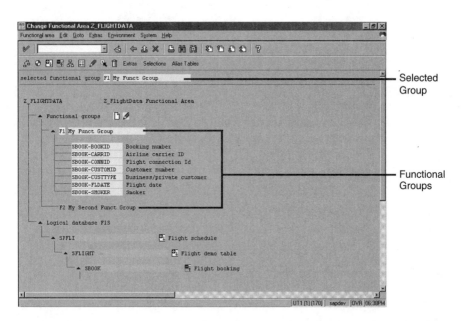

Figure 9-10 *You can create multiple functional groups to organize the data in your functional area.*

If you want to change your new functional group to be the selected group, you can double click the Functional Group name, or select it and then follow the menu path Edit→Functional group→Select functional group. Change your new functional group to be the selected group, and add a few fields from the SPFLI table. Choose different fields than selected for the original functional group (see Figure 9-11 for an example).

You are not required to segregate the data from different tables into different functional groups; although, for organizational purposes, sometimes it is helpful to do so. Expand the subnodes for your two functional groups to view the fields, as in Figure 9-12.

Saving and Generating Functional Areas

Save your functional area by selecting the open folder Save button from the Standard toolbar. Because we created new objects in R/3, we need to generate our functional area. Select the red beach ball Generate button from the Application toolbar.

The system will pause and will display an hourglass while the functional area is being generated. If there are no problems, you

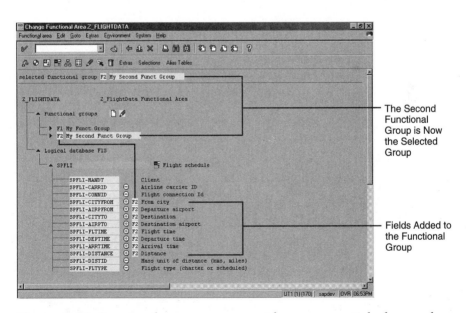

Figure 9-11 *Functional group management becomes essential when working with large, logical databases to better organize your data.*

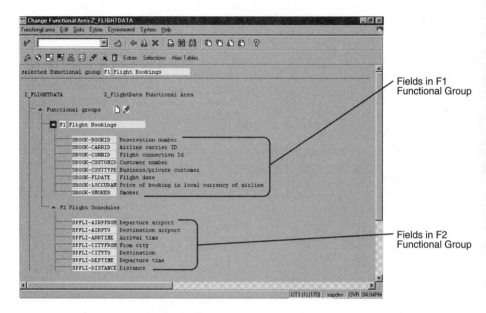

Figure 9-12 *Unlike our example, which was done for instructional purposes, when giving descriptions for your functional groups, try to use a name that adequately describes its contents.*

will view a message in your Status bar saying that the functional area is generated. After generation, if any warnings or errors arise, a dialog box will appear with the results of your generation and a list of warnings and error messages. Use the green arrow Back button to return to the Functional Areas: Initial screen.

Assign the Functional Area to a User Group

We have gone through the steps of creating a user group and creating a functional area. Next, we need to assign our new functional area to the user group we already created. Keep in mind that when you create queries in R/3, these queries are built upon the association between user groups and functional areas. Therefore, we need to create a relationship between these two items. Follow these steps to assign a functional area to a user group:

1. From the Functional Areas: Initial screen (transaction code /nSQ02), enter your functional area name into the functional

area input field, and select the Assignment to User Groups button in the center of the R/3 screen.

2. A Functional Area: Assign to User Groups screen will appear, listing all of the available user groups in your client. Select the appropriate user group using the small gray box to the left of its name, then select the Open Folder Save button on the Standard toolbar.

3. A message will appear in the R/3 Status bar that says, "Assignment of Functional Area saved."

4. Use the green arrow Back button to return to the Functional Areas: Initial screen.

Predelivered Logical Databases

There are several logical databases that come predelivered with your R/3 system. The F1S database that we used to create our functional area is an example of one of those databases. Sample logical databases available in R/3 are listed in Table 9.1.

Table 9.1 *Sample installed logical databases*

Name	Description
AAV	Logical Database Rv: Sales Documents
ACS	Example Database for Reading Archives
ADA	Assets Database
AFI	Logical Database for Orders
AGF	Accruals/Deferrals
AKV	Logical Database Rv: Sales Documents
ALV	Archiving Deliveries
ARV	Logical Database Rv: Sales Documents
ASV	Request Screen for Summary Information
AUK	Settlement Documents
AUW	Allocation Table

Table 9.1 *Sample installed logical databases (Continued)*

Name	Description
AVV	Archive Shipping Units
B1L	Transfer Requirements by Number
BAF	BAV-Data Collector
BAM	Purchase Requisitions (General)
BBM	Archiving of Purchase Requisitions
BCD	BC Log.Database: Business Partner Fax Locations
BJF	Loans Flow Records with Date Restriction
BKK	Base Planning Objects
BKM	Purchase Requisitions Per Account Assignment
BMM	Documents for Number
BPF	Treasury Business Partner
BRF	Document Database
BRM	Financial Accounting Documents
BTF	Loan Portfolios and Flows
BTM	Process Order; Print
BUD	LDB for Loans Master Data, Conditions, Documents
C1F	Cash Budget Management
CDC	Document Structure
CEC	Equipment BOM
CEK	Cost Centers—Line Items
CFK	Data Pool for SAP EIS
CIK	Cost Centers—Actual Data
CKC	Sales Order BOM
CKM	Material Master

Name	Description
CMC	Material BOM
CPK	Cost Centers—Plan Data
CRC	Work Centers
CRK	Cost Centers—Total
CSC	Standard BOM
CSR	Logical Database for Archiving BOMs
CTC	Functional Location BOM
D$I	Processing without Database
DBM	MRP Documents
DDF	Customer Database
DPM	Planned Orders
DSF	Loan Debit Position
DVS	Logical Database for Archiving DMS Data
DWF	Loan Resubmission
EBM	Purchasing Activities Per Requirement Tracking No.
ECM	Purchasing Documents Per Material Class
EKM	Purchasing Documents Per Account Assignment
ELM	Purchasing Documents Per Vendor
EMM	Purchasing Documents for Material
ENM	Purchasing Documents for Document Number
EQI	Logical Database (Equipment)
ERM	Archiving of Purchasing Documents
ESM	Purchasing Documents Per Collective Number
EWM	Purchasing Documents Per Supplying Plant
F1F	Funds Management: Funds and Funds Centers

Table 9.1 *Sample installed logical databases (Continued)*

Name	Description
F1S	BC: Planned Flights, Flights, and Bookings
FDF	Cash Management and Forecast
FEF	Cash Management—Memo Records
FRF	Drill-Down Selection Screen
FSF	Cash Management—Summary Records
GLG	FI-SL Summary and Line Items
GLU3	Flexible G/L
I1L	Inventory Data for Storage Bin
I2L	Warehouse Quantities for Storage Bin
I3L	Inventory Documents
IBF	Real Estate Logical Database (Rental Agreement)
IDF	Real Estate Logical Database
IFM	General Purchasing Info Records
ILM	Archiving Purchasing Info Records
IMA	Logical Database for Capital Investment Programs
IMC	IM Summarization (Not Usable Operationally)
IMM	Inventory Documents for Material
INM	Inventory Documents
IOC	Shop Floor Control—Order Info System
IRM	Reorganization of Inventory Documents
K1V	Generating Conditions
KDF	Vendor Database
KIV	Customer Material Information
KKF	Balance Audit Trail of Open Items

Name	Description
KLF	Historical Balance Audit Trail
KMV	SD Documents for Credit Limit
KOV	Selection of Condition Records
L1M	Stock Movements for Material
LMM	Stock Movements for Material
LNM	Stock Movements
MAF	Dataset for Dunning Notices
MIV	BC: Planned Flights, Flights, and Bookings
MRM	Reorganization of Material Documents
MSM	Material Master
NTI	Logical Database Object Networking
ODC	Shop Floor Control—Orders Per MRP Controller
ODK	Orders
OFC	Shop Floor Control—Orders Per Prod. Scheduler
OHC	Shop Floor Control—Orders by Numbers
OPC	Shop Floor Control—Orders by Material
PAK	CO-PA Segment Level and Line Items
PAP	Applicant Master Data
PCH	PD
PGQ	QM: Specs and Results of the Quality Inspection
PMI	Structure Database (Plant Maintenance)
PNI	PM Planning Database
PNM	Planning Database
PNP	Human Resources Master Data
POH	Production Orders Database—Header

Table 9.1 *Sample installed logical databases (Continued)*

Name	Description
PSJ	Project System
PYF	Database for Payment Medium-Print Programs
QAM	Inspection Catalogs: Selected Sets
QAQ	Inspection Catalogs: Selected Sets
QCM	Inspection Catalogs: Codes
QCQ	Inspection Catalogs: Codes
QEM	Result Entry
QMI	Logical Database (PM Notifications)
QMQ	Inspection Characteristics
QNQ	Quality Notifications
QTQ	Logical Database for Inspection Methods
R0F	Archiving: Bank Master Data
R0L	Archive Selection: Transfer Orders (MM-WM)
R1F	Archiving: FI Transaction Figures
R1L	Archive Selection: Transfer Requirements (MM-WM)
R2L	Archive Selection: Posting Change Notices (MM-WM)
R3L	Archive Selection: Inventory Documents (MM-WM)
R4L	Archive Selection: Inventory Histories (MM-WM)
RBL	Archiving of Transfer Requests
RHL	Archiving of Inventory History
RIL	Archiving of Inventory Documents
RKM	Reservations for Account Assignment
RMM	Reservations for Material
RNM	Reservations

Name	Description
RTL	Archiving of Transfer Orders
RUL	Archiving of Transfer Requests
S1L	Stock by Storage Bins
S2L	Warehouse Quantities for Material
S3L	Stocks
SAK	Completely Cancelled Allocation Documents
SDF	G/L Account Database
SMI	Serial Number Management
T1L	Transfer Orders by Number
T2L	Transfer Orders for Material
T3L	Transfer Orders for Storage Type
T4L	Transfer Order for TO Printing
T5L	Transfer Orders for Reference Number
TAF	Treasury
TIF	Treasury Information System
TPI	Functional Location Logical Database
U1S	User Master Reorganization: Password Changes
U2S	User Master Reorganization: Password Changes
U3S	User Master Reorganization: Password Changes
U4S	User Master Reorganization: Password Changes
V12L	Pricing Reports
VAV	Logical Database RV: Sales Documents
VC1	List of Sales Activities
VC2	Generate Address List
VDF	Customer Database with View of Document Index

Table 9.1 *Sample installed logical databases (Continued)*

Name	Description
VFV	Logical Database RV: Billing Documents
VLV	Logical Database for Deliveries
VPF	Interest/Repayment Condition Items
VXV	SD: Billing Document—Export
WAF	Securities Position Plus Additional Master Data
WOI	Maintenance Item
WPI	Preventive Maintenance Plans
WTF	Securities Positions and Flows
WUF	Securities Determ. Master Data for Positions

Component 4—Language Comparisons

The fourth and last component of our behind-the-scenes look at ABAP Query is language comparison. Many SAP customers maintain multiple languages in their R/3 systems. You can use your SAP system for several different languages. Defining queries, functional areas, and user groups involves entering a lot of text. Some of this process contributes to the internal organization of ABAP Query. A language-comparison facility exists for all of these text elements, including the column heading for reports. If you log on in English, your headings (text elements) will appear in English, and if you log on in German, they will appear in German. In other words, for each text, there is an equivalent text in one (or more) other languages. The texts you see in your R/3 system are usually displayed in the logon language. You can use this language-translation tool to perform language comparison. The way in which query objects are stored in the global area has changed since earlier versions of R/3—such that all objects are stored in their own text tables. This feature makes it possible to translate the objects using the SAP translation tool. In functional areas, a series of texts are used for which standard proposals are taken from the dictionary (long texts and headers for fields, long texts for tables, and so on). The language-comparison utility enables you to copy target texts from the dictionary and use them as defaults for the comparison. To access the ABAP Query language-comparison tool, use transaction code SQ07. A screen capture from the language comparison utility is shown in Figure 9-13.

Chapter Wrap-Up

This chapter was designed to give an overall configuration view of the behind-the-scenes, essential components for ABAP Query reporting. Again, we emphasize that regular SAP users do not need to perform the tasks outlined in this chapter, because they

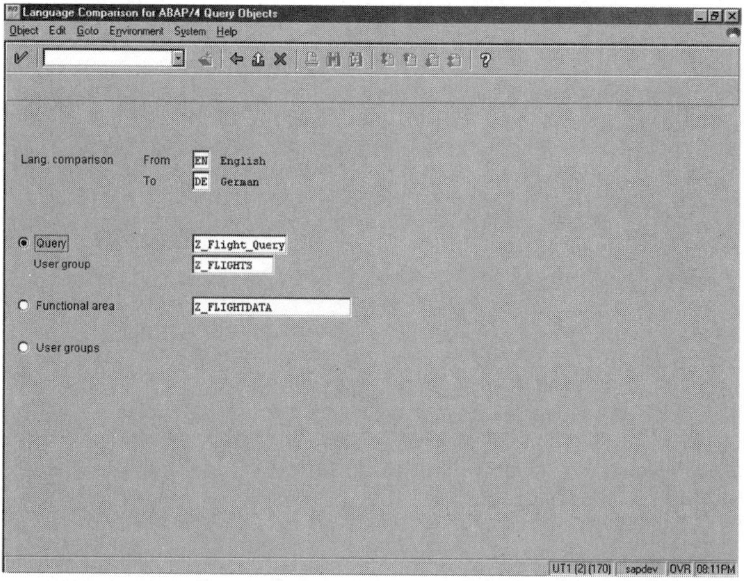

Figure 9-13 *Version 4.X and higher of R/3 contains new features in language comparison, including standard texts for functional areas.*

are commonly a function of the technical team. As an end user of ABAP Query, it is helpful to have the information about what is going on behind the scenes to help you produce your output using ABAP Query. This chapter will also help you communicate requests to your technical team when you feel that changes need to be made. In the next chapter, we begin to create custom reports using ABAP Query.

ABAP Query
Reporting Basics

ABAP Query is designed with a simple, user-friendly format where you can select fields and arrange them in the order and format you choose for your reports. In ABAP Query, reports are called queries and are generated in the form of ABAP programs.

What Is the Source of the Data?

The source of the data for your reports comes from a functional area. Functional areas provide a special view of a logical database (or table, join, or programming statements). By creating functional areas and assigning them to user groups, your system administrator determines the range of reports that individual application departments or end users can generate using the ABAP Query tool. Any fields included in functional groups within your functional area will be available for selection in your ABAP queries.

ABAP Queries

ABAP queries can be used to generate three different types of output: basic lists (which we discuss in detail in this chapter) and statistical and ranked lists. Statistical lists are used to perform mathematical calculations of data including averages and percentages. Ranked lists are generated based on numeric fields (currency or quantity). Both statistical and ranked lists might appear multiple times within a single ABAP query, as opposed to a basic list—which might only appear once.

ABAP Query Essentials

Before you can create a new query (report), you need to know which application area, user group, and functional area with which you will be working. These concepts were discussed in Chapter 9, "ABAP Query Behind the Scenes." Contact your system administrator to determine which application area, user group, and functional area with which you will be working. For our example, we will use the application area, user group, and functional area (created in Chapter 9) that is displayed in Table 10.1.

ABAP Query has a lot of screens that you can use to design and customize your report. In this chapter, we will take a look at the seven basic screens that you will encounter while creating your query. These seven screens each offer a different step in the creation process, as seen in Table 10.2.

These seven screens simply and logically segregate the steps you need to go through to create a report without any programming. See Figure 10-1 for an example.

Table 10.1 *ABAP query basics used in this section*

Name	Description
Application Area	Standard (client-specific)
User Group	Z_Flights (created in Chapter 9)
Functional Area	Z_FlightData (created in Chapter 9)

Table 10.2 *ABAP Query's seven basic screens*

Screen Number	Name	Use
Screen 1	Title, Format Screen	Stores the basic data for your report, including the report name, format, and notes
Screen 2	Select Functional Group	Where you select the names of the functional groups that contain the fields that you want to output in your report
Screen 3	Select Field	Where you select the names of the fields in the selected functional groups that you want to output in your report
Screen 4	Selections	Where you can add additional fields to appear on the selection screen of your report
Screen 5	Basic List Line Structure	Where you identify on which line and in which order you want your data to appear
Screen 6	Selection Screen	Where you specify exactly what data you want on your report (selection screens are covered in Chapter 4)
Screen 7	List Screen	Screen that contains the output of your data (the report)

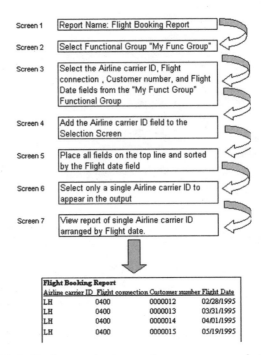

Figure 10-1 *Each step shown on the seven screens builds on the previous step, until finally the output is presented in Screen 7.*

1-2-3 Basics to Create a New Query

We will examine each of these seven screens individually. For starters, let's navigate to the ABAP Queries main screen. For each new query you create, you need to perform the following three steps:

1. Use transaction code /nSQ01 or the menu path Tools→ABAP Workbench→Utilities→ABAP Query→Queries to access the main ABAP Query screen.

2. To ensure that you are in the correct application area, follow the menu path Environment→Application areas and select the appropriate application area.

3. To ensure that you are in the correct user group (which is displayed in the Title bar), follow the menu path Edit→Other user group and select your user group from the list.

For each new query, you need to make sure that you follow these three basics. You can also ask your system administrator to set parameters for your application area and user group so that they always default to the correct information.

Create a Custom Report Using ABAP Query

Now that you are ready to go, let's create a new custom report. Follow these steps to create an ABAP query:

1. Follow the 1-2-3 basics outlined earlier in the chapter.

2. Enter a report name (using your company's naming conventions) in the Query Input field and select the Create button, as in Figure 10-2.

3. You will be prompted next to select the functional area that you will use as the source of the data for your report. From the dialog box, select the appropriate functional area and then the green check mark Choose button (see Figure 10-3).

What follows is a description of how to enter data on the seven basic screens of ABAP Query.

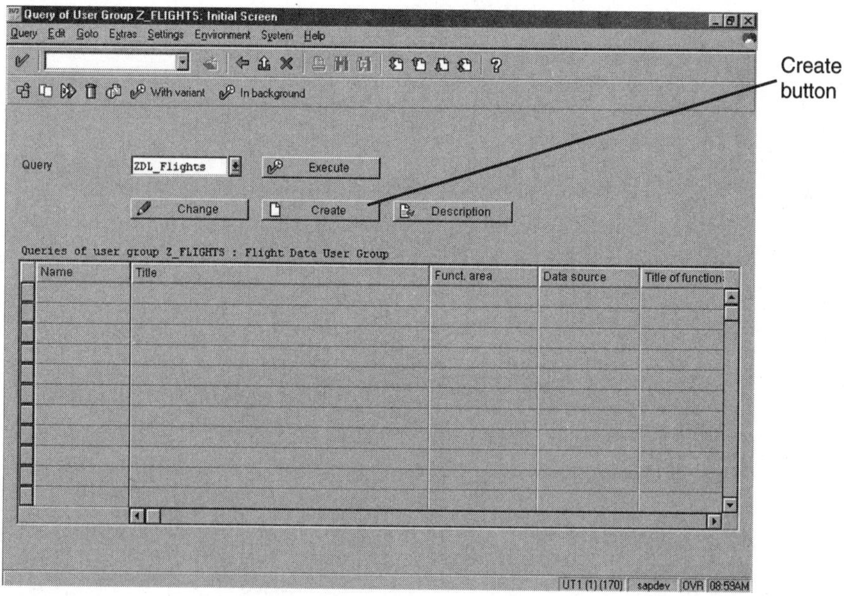

Figure 10-2 *For organizational purposes in the report name, it is a good idea to include the initials of the user who is creating the report.*

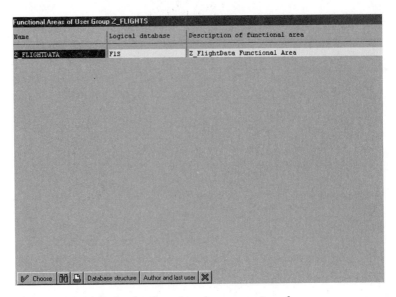

Figure 10-3 *Only the functional areas assigned to your user group will appear on this screen.*

Screen 1—Title, Format Screen

The Title Format screen is where you insert the basic data relating to your report. This data includes the title of your report and the format in which you want your report displayed. Screen 1 is displayed in Figure 10-4.

The Title, Format Screen stores the title, notes, and basic report-processing options for your report. Options available on this screen are detailed as follows.

List Format

The list format options available on this screen enable you to designate the line and column width of your report. The Line Input field specifies the number of lines to be outputted on one page for a list generated by the query. The default is blank, which outputs a continuous list on a single page. You can use the Line Input field to enter the number of lines to be outputted on a single page. If you do not want page breaks, leave this field empty. The Column Input field stores the number of columns per line. This field determines the maximum number of characters that can

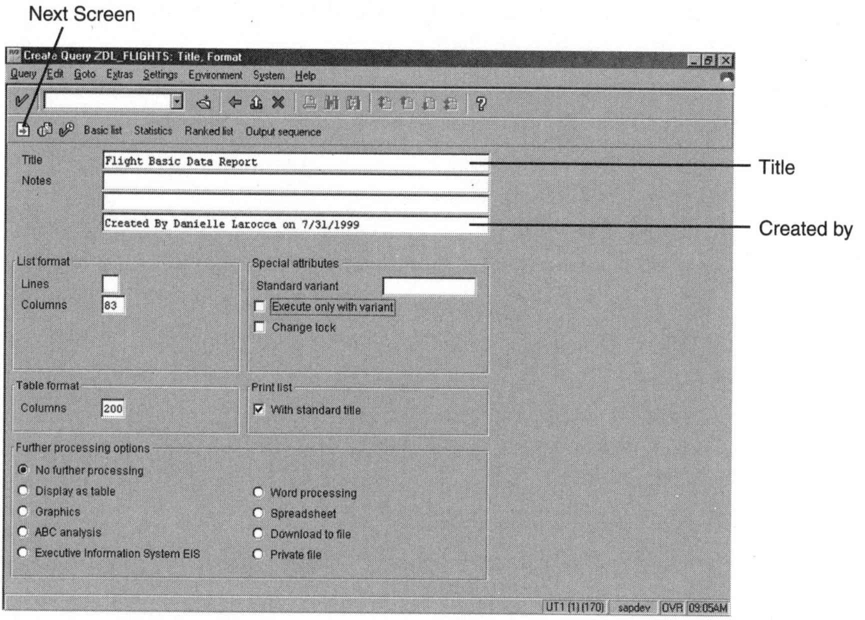

Next Screen

Figure 10-4 *For organizational purposes, it is a good idea to enter the username of the person who created the report in the Notes section of this screen.*

be displayed on one line of the list created by the query. Lines exceeding this length cause line breaks. The maximum number permitted is 255. The number entered here should be the closest estimation possible, because this number helps determine the printed layout of the report. For example, if you set all reports to be 255 so that all of your columns fit on a single line, your printed report might contain small fonts to accommodate the 255 column length. Trial and error is the best method of receiving the results you want.

Special Attributes

The Special Attributes section enables you to specify whether you want the ABAP query to run with a variant. Variants were introduced in Chapter 5, "Executing and Maintaining SAP R/3 Repforts." We go into detail about this option in the next chapter. The Change Lock check box enables you to indicate whether or not you want other users to be able to make changes to your query. By default, this check box is unmarked—indicating that any other user in your user group with the appropriate authorizations can make changes to your report. To prevent this situation, select this check box for each new query you create.

Table Format

The Columns Input field in the Table Format box determines the maximum number of characters for the width of a table view control (if you select your data to be viewed as a table, instead of as a basic list). This option exists in the next section, "Further Processing Options." You can use table-view controls to display the data of single-line basic lists, statistics, and rankings in a special format. This specification only affects the visible width, and the table control might contain more data columns than are visible in a single R/3 window.

Further Processing Options

Further processing options enable you to have the data outputted in different formats. The default setting is for "No further processing." This selection indicates that your report will display on the List screen (Screen 7) as a basic list. The other processing options are displayed in Table 10.3.

Table 10.3 *ABAP Query further-processing options*

Option	Function
No further processing	The report will display on the List screen (Screen 7) as a basic list.
Display as table	The report will appear in SAP in a spreadsheet-type table. This setting is ideal if you will be conducting any further processing of your data.
Graphics	This function enables you to display the information from your list using SAP Business Graphics. In contrast

Option	Function
	to the other functions described in this section, the graphics function can only handle an extract from one column of your sublist, and the column must contain numeric values.
ABC Analysis	The ABC Analysis function can be used for any single-line basic list, all statistics, and any ranked list that contains at least one numeric field.
Executive Information System (EIS)	This function provides a link to the *Executive Information System* (EIS) and transfers the data in your query to the EIS database via an interface so that you can perform more analyses. When you activate the function, you specify various options for storing the data in a dialog box.
Word processing	The word processing functions can be called from the list display and from the table display. This option can be used to create Microsoft Word form letters.
Spreadsheet	The spreadsheet functions can be called from the list display and from the table display. This option can be used to create Microsoft Excel spreadsheets.
Download to file	The download to file function enables you to download the data retrieved by the query to a local file on your PC. When you activate the function, you see a dialog box where you can specify the filename, location, and data format.

Table 10.3 *ABAP Query further-processing options (Continued)*

Option	Function
Private file	If you select this field, the list is not displayed on the screen when you execute the query, but the sublist is passed directly to a function module. This SAP enhancement must be implemented by the customer.

Print List

This last option displaying the With Standard Title check box indicates that you want your output to include the standard title appearing at the top of the screen in the Title Input field. By default, this box is selected.

Our Example

Use Figure 10-4 as a reference, and enter the appropriate data into the ABAP Query Title, Format Screen (Screen 1).

1. Enter the title of your report on this screen into the Title Input field.

2. For organizational purposes, it is a good idea to enter the name of the user who created the report and the date then the report was originally created in the Notes Input field.

3. Once you have entered this data, select the open folder Save button from the Standard toolbar.

4. To proceed to Screen 2, select the white arrow Next Screen button from the Application toolbar.

These directional arrow buttons are available on the Application toolbar on all of the ABAP Query screens for navigation.

Screen 2—Select Functional Group

The Select Functional Group screen is where you select the functional groups that contain the fields you want to output on your report. Only the functional groups set up in your selected functional area will appear on this screen. If you performed the steps in Chapter 9, "ABAP Query Behind the Scenes,"(for creating your own functional groups), then this concept should be even more familiar. An example of Screen 2 is displayed in Figure 10-5.

Our Example

Use Figure 10-5 as a reference, and enter the appropriate data into the Select Functional Groups screen (Screen 2).

1. Place a check mark next to each functional group that contains fields that you want to include on your report. If more functional groups were available, you could use the page navigational buttons on the bottom-right of the screen to view them.

2. Select the white arrow Next screen button on the Application toolbar to proceed to Screen 3.

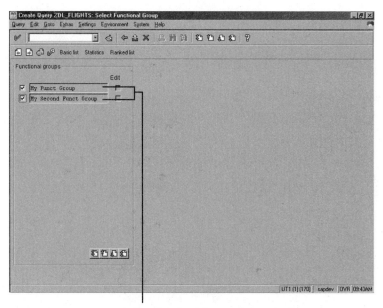

Two Functional Groups Created in the
Functional Area in Chapter 9. *(See Figure 9-10)*

Figure 10-5 *If you think there should be other functional groups added, contact your system administrator to review the functional area together.*

Screen 3—Select Field

The Select Field screen is where you select the fields within the functional groups that you want to output on your report. Only the fields set up within the functional groups in your selected functional area will appear on this screen. If you performed the steps in Chapter 9 (to create your own functional groups), then this concept should be even more familiar. A sample of Screen 3 is displayed in Figure 10-6.

Our Example

Use Figure 10-6 as a reference, and enter the appropriate data into the Select Field screen (Screen 3).

1. Place a check mark next to each field that you want to display on your report. If more fields were available, you could use the page navigational buttons on the bottom-right of the screen to view them.

2. Select the white arrow Next Screen button to proceed to Screen 4.

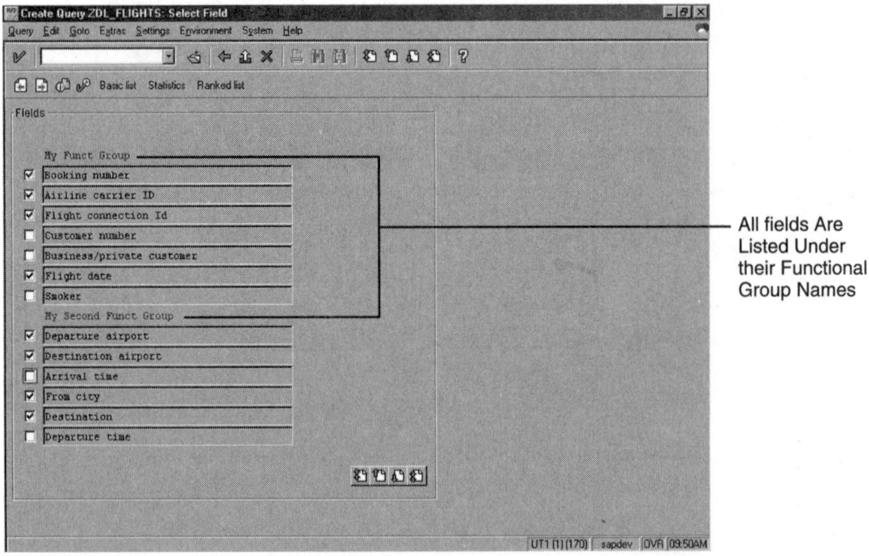

Figure 10-6 *If you think that there should be other field added, contact your system administrator to review the functional area together.*

Screen 4—Selections

The selections screen is where you can select fields to appear on the selection screen of your report. You will remember from earlier chapters that a selection screen always appears first when you execute a report to enable you to specify exactly which data you want to output. This selection screen enables you to add more fields to that selection screen to further specify your output. Screen 4 is displayed in Figure 10-7.

Our Example

Use Figure 10-7 as a reference, and enter the appropriate data into the selections screen (Screen 4).

1. Place a check mark next to each field that you want to add to the selection screen on your report. If more fields were available, you could use the page navigational buttons on the bottom-right of the screen to view them.

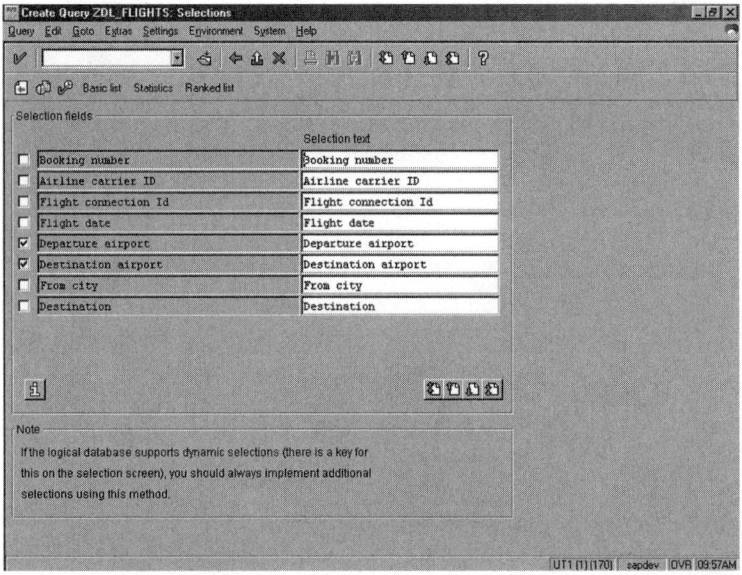

Figure 10-7 *By default, some fields might already be included on the selection screen, but you can add additional fields on this screen.*

2. Select the open folder Save button on the Standard toolbar.

3. Select the Basic List button on the Application toolbar to proceed to Screen 5.

Screen 5—Basic List Line Structure

The Basic List Line Structure screen is where you specify the layout and sort order of the fields to be displayed on your report. Screen 5 is displayed in Figure 10-8.

By default, only the first few selected fields will appear on this screen. They are all there, but with the default view, they are not all visible. You can use the page navigation buttons on the right-hand side of the screen to navigate between them, or you can select the Without Explanation button (displayed in Figure 10-8) to view more fields on a single screen. The Basic List Line Structure screen lists all of the fields you want to include in your output.

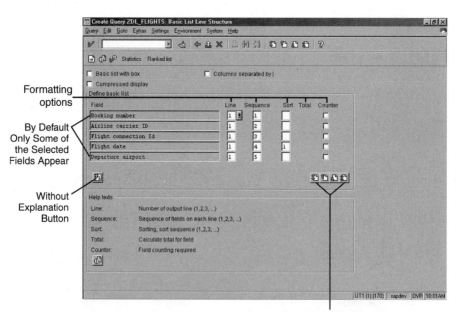

Figure 10-8 *You can specify the line and sequence number for each of your output fields on the Basic List Line Structure screen.*

Line

The Line column listed immediately to the right of the field names is where you specify the line number on which you want your output to appear.

Specifying Line 1 for all fields will make them all appear as columns next to each other in the form of a standard report. Keep in mind that if you have too many fields, regardless of the line number, they might wrap to the next line.

Sequence

The Sequence column listed immediately to the right of the Line column is used to identify the sequence you want your data to appear in with the line. For example, if all of your fields are on Line 1, you can specify that you want the Booking Number field to appear first, followed by the Airline Carrier ID, etc.

Sort

Now that you have set up your fields display with the Line and Sequence settings, you can now specify the sort order for the fields. The Sort column is listed immediately to the right of the Sequence column. You can assign sequence numbers between one and 10.

Total

The Total column is listed immediately to the right of the Sort column. Check boxes for the Total column only appear for numeric fields that can be totaled. You can place a check mark for each numeric field that you want to output the total at the end of the basic list. Also, if sort criteria exist, you can output subtotals at the end of each control level. We will talk more about control levels and subtotaling in the next chapter.

Counter

The Counter column is listed immediately to the right of the Total column. Check boxes for the Counter column can be marked for each field you want to count. The total is displayed at the end of the list. If you have specified sort criteria, you can also display how often a field has been read within a group if you are sorting and subtotaling in your report. We talk about this concept in the next chapter.

Basic List with Box

This check box appears at the top of the screen and is used for basic lists. If you select this field, the basic list is displayed in a box. The box is used as a formatting preference only, and it is designed so that it encloses only the filled part of the basic list.

Columns Separated by a Vertical Bar (|)

This check box is only available if the Basic List with Box check box is marked. Selecting this box will insert a vertical bar after each field on a line (except the last). An underscore is outputted before and after each control-level text (if sorting and subtotaling is used) and is inserted before and after each total. In addition, the individual columns in the standard header are separated by vertical bars.

Compressed Display

If you select the Compressed Display check box, the basic list is displayed in compressed format—provided that a compressed display is possible.

Our Example

Use Figure 10-9 as a reference, and enter the appropriate data into the Basic List Line Structure screen (Screen 5).

1. After entering Line, Column, and Sort values, select the green check mark Enter key to check your sequence specifications. If there is a problem with your order, a message will appear in the Status bar saying, "Check your sequence specifications." Take a look at our entries in Figure 10-9.

2. After checking your specifications, select the open folder Save button from the Standard toolbar to save your query.

3. Now that you have identified which fields to include and how you would like them arranged, the next task is to execute the query to be presented with the selection screen. Select the Execute button from the Application toolbar.

Screen 6—Selection Screen

You are now familiar with the concept of selection screens, which appear upon the execution of all reports in R/3. The selection screen gives you the opportunity to specify exactly which

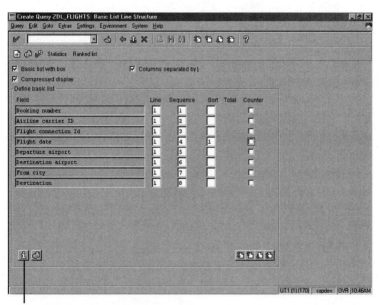

To Return the Screen to Its Original Partial
Field View, Select the With Explanations Button

Figure 10-9 *We selected the Without Explanation button to view all of our fields on a single screen.*

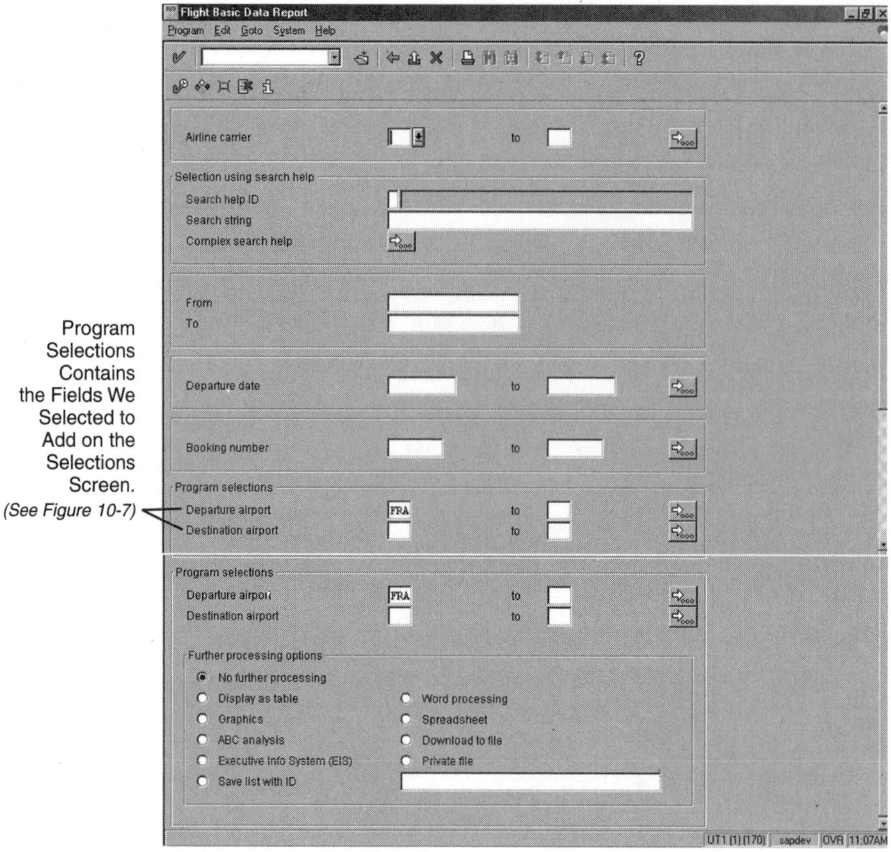

Figure 10-10 *Selection screens are helpful for specifying data for output and are viewed before the output of report data.*

data in the selected fields will be outputted on your report. A sample of the selection screen is shown in Figure 10-10.

If you want your report to include all of the data stored in the fields that you selected (without specification), you can select the Execute button from the Application toolbar. If you want to specify only certain data, however, you can enter the appropriate values on the selection screen. You might find it helpful to review Chapter 4 to see all of the different ways to use a selection screen to specify data.

Further Processing Options on the Selection Screen

You will notice that the further processing options that were available on the Title, Format Screen (Screen 1) also appear on the selection screen. Here is the distinction: If you set a further processing option on the Title, Format Screen (such as Display as Table), the default setting will always appear on the selection screen. This setting can be overridden on the selection screen. If you make a selection for a further processing option on the selection screen only and not on the Title, Format Screen, then it is not saved with the query and will need to be manually changed each time the selection screen appears (unless the selection screen was saved as a variant).

Our Example

Use Figure 10-10 as a reference, and enter the appropriate data into the selection screen (Screen 6).

1. On our selection screen, we specified that we wanted to include only flight data from the Frankfurt, Germany airport (FRA).

2. To execute the report and proceed with the finished result List screen (Screen 7), select the Execute button from the Application toolbar.

Screen 7—List Screen

Screen 7, the List screen, contains your report. The title that you specified on the Title, Format Screen (Screen 1) appears in the R/3 Title bar. A sample of the List screen is shown in Figure 10-11.

You can compare your output with the specifications added on the Basic List Line Structure screen to see how your entries resulted in your output (see Figure 10-12).

Modifying Your Query

Once your query has been created and you want to navigate between the different seven screens to make changes and modifications, you can use the Next and Previous screen white arrow buttons on the Application toolbar. These buttons are available to you on screens one through five of the ABAP query. You can also

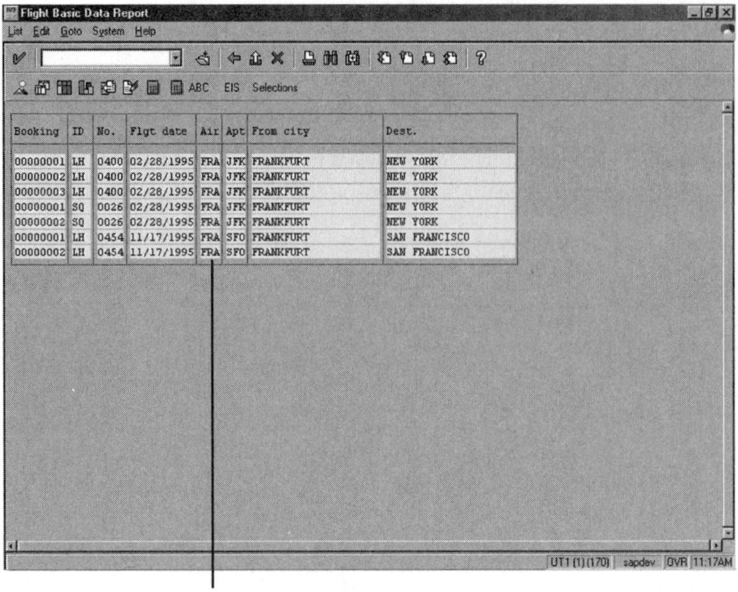

My output only includes flight data from the
Frankfurt (FRA) Airport as I specified on my
selection screen.

Figure 10-11 *Depending on the data in your R/3 system, your
output might vary.*

use the Basic List button to jump to the Basic List Line Structure
screen (Screen 5) or the Execute button to navigate to the selection screen or list of your report. Using the green arrow Back key
on the Standard toolbar from the List screen (Screen 7) will bring
you to the selection screen.

Save Your Query

From any screen in the ABAP query, except the selection screen
(Screen 6) or the List screen (Screen 7), you can select the open
folder Save button to save your query. This action logically makes
sense when you fully think about it. If you select the Save button
on the selection screen, the system will think that you want to
save the entries as a variant. And, if you select the Save button on
the List screen (Screen 7), then the system will think that you
want to save your output as a list.

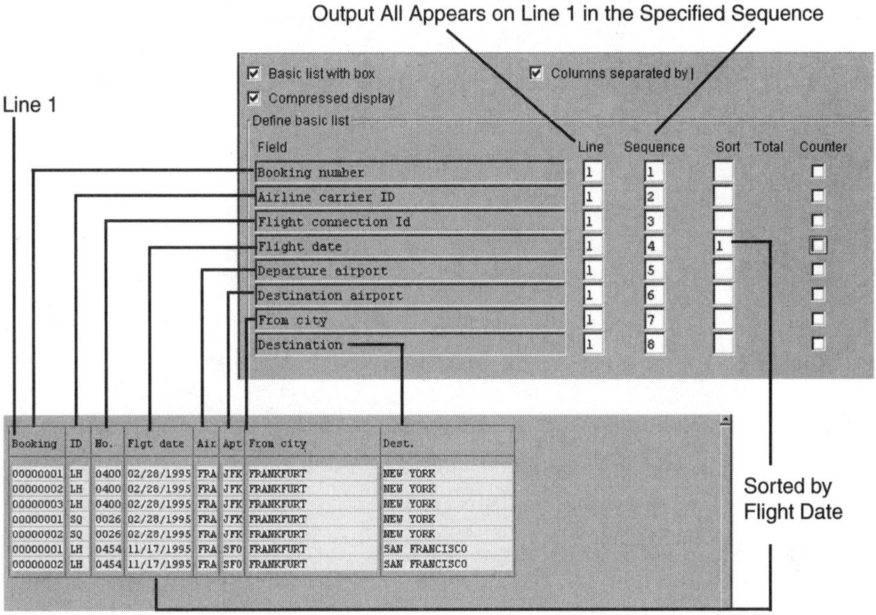

Figure 10-12 *You can vary your entries on the Basic List Line Structure screen to see the impact they will have on your output.*

Query Maintenance

Queries can be maintained and executed from the main ABAP Query screen. You can navigate to this screen using the menu path Tools→ABAP Workbench→Utilities→ABAP Query→ Queries or through transaction code /nSQ01. From this screen, which is displayed in Figure 10-13, you can perform maintenance on your queries.

Using the buttons at the top of the screen, you can execute, change, create new, or view descriptions of queries in R/3. From the Application toolbar, you can also copy, delete, or rename your queries.

Chapter Wrap-Up

When looking at the seven basic screens of ABAP Query, you can see how it would be easy to create your own reports in R/3. Part of the process is identifying where the data is in R/3 so that you

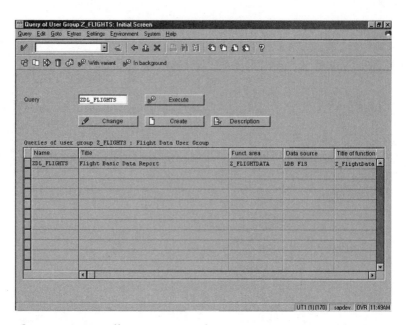

Figure 10-13 *All queries created in your user group will be displayed in the ABAP Query Initial screen.*

can select the appropriate functional area that contains the data you need. Working closely with your system administration team, which manages the logical databases and functional areas, would be to your advantage. Also, ABAP programmers have the capability to create new logical databases if there is data that you are looking for that is not in an existing logical database. Functional areas can also be created without logical databases, based on table joins, direct reads, data-retrieval programs, and sequential data sets. These are all technical topics that are maintained by ABAP programming personnel and are outside the scope of this book. The best way of determining whether the ABAP query will satisfy your report requirements is to start working with the query to see whether it produces the results you need. In some cases, some custom reports written in ABAP code might still be necessary for your organization. The ABAP Query 13 screen reference in the appendix of this book is good to use as a handy reference when working in ABAP Query. Version 4.5 of SAP contains enhanced functionality and a new look for ABAP Query.

ABAP Query Maintenance and Variants

As introduced in Chapter 10, ABAP Query is designed to be a basic, user-friendly tool to extract and output data in your R/3 system. The basic seven screens discussed in the ABAP Query introduction in Chapter 10 provide you with the basic skills for report writing in R/3. This chapter discusses some of the advanced options available in working with the query. You should become familiar with the basics and create a few queries before starting on these advanced topics.

Our Example

The example used in the chapter will involve making changes to a copy of the query created in Chapter 10. This chapter will help familiarize you with getting around the seven basic screens of the query, in addition to making copies and changes and seeing how modifications affect the final output.

Copying an Existing Query

Instead of starting from scratch, you can make a copy of an existing query. This copy will come in handy when you have queries that contain data that is similar to the output you wish to create. Instead of starting from scratch, you can begin by using a copy of an existing query. Follow these steps to make a copy of an ABAP query:

1. To make a copy of a query, begin at the ABAP Query Initial screen. Navigate to this screen using the menu path Tools→ ABAP Workbench→Utilities→ABAP Query→Queries, or use the transaction code /nSQ01.

2. Select the query you want to copy by placing your mouse in the gray square box to the left of its name (so that the line appears highlighted), and then select the Copy button from the Application toolbar.

3. The Copy a Query dialog box will appear similar to the one in Figure 11-1. You need to enter the name of your new query and then select the green check mark.

4. Your new query will appear in the ABAP Query window.

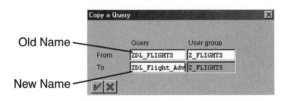

Figure 11-1 *Be sure to use your company's naming convention when naming new objects in R/3.*

Modifying an Existing Query

Select your new query from the ABAP Query window and select the Change button. Again, we will walk through the seven basic screens that were introduced in Chapter 10, except that now we only need to modify the selections and input that exist from the old query (instead of starting from scratch).

Screen 1—Title, Format Screen

The first screen that appears is the Title, Format screen (Screen 1). You need to modify the information on the Title, Format screen because it currently contains the Title and creation date of the old query. Change the Title of your query and the date it was created, as in Figure 11-2.

As you did in Chapter 10, select the open folder Save button from the Standard toolbar, then select the white arrow Next screen button from the Application toolbar.

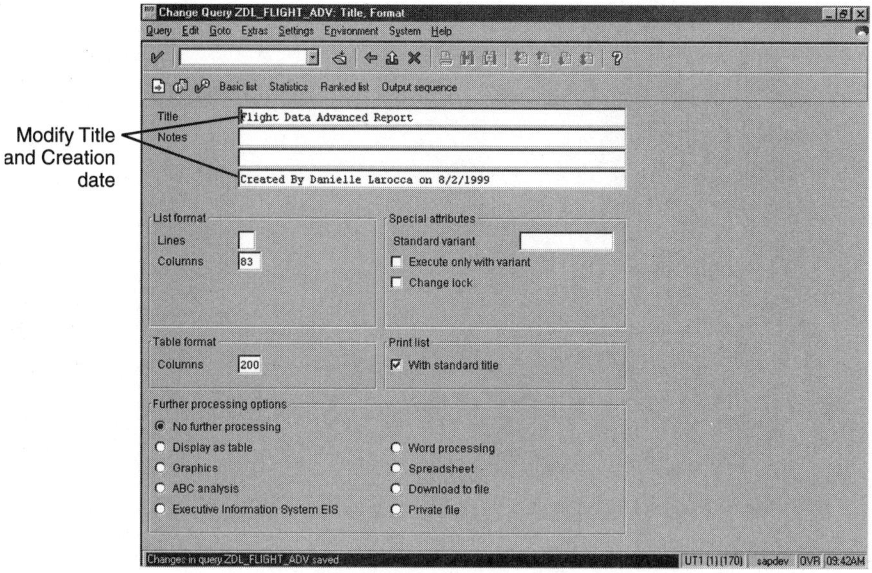

Figure 11-2 *Proper management and organization of your query titles will be beneficial as the number of queries in your user group increases.*

Screen 2—Select Functional Group

The Select Functional Group screen lists the functional groups available. The functional groups that are already used in the query contain a dimmed gray check mark in the Edit column to the right of the functional group name. These selected functional groups are already used in the query, and their fields will be available on the next screen. If you wanted to select new functional groups to be available in the query, they would be listed on this screen without a check mark in the Edit column (see Figure 11-3).

1. Select the open folder Save button from the Standard toolbar.

2. Select the white arrow Next Screen button from the Application toolbar to proceed to field selection.

Screen 3—Select Field

The Select Field screen will display a list of all available fields in your functional group that are available for inclusion in your

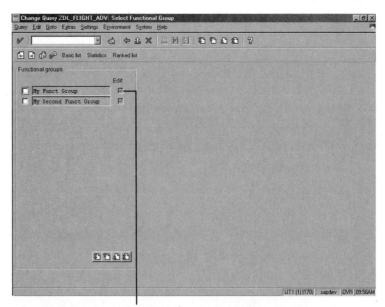

Shows that Selection of Functional Group is already chosen.

Figure 11-3 *If other functional groups were available to be added, they would appear in the list—and you could select them from this screen.*

report. Fields that are already included in the report contain a check mark. To modify the selections, mark new fields by placing a check mark next to their name, and deselect others by removing their check marks (as in Figure 11-4).

If you deselect a field that was added to the selection screen (from Screen 4 selections) in the previous query, you will be prompted with a small dialog box asking whether you also want to remove the field from the selection screen. Selecting "Yes" will remove the field from the selection screen. Selecting "No" enables you to use a field as a selection criteria without having to output it in your report. If you select the Save button on this screen, it will ask whether you want to remove the deselected fields from the list (to which you would reply "Yes").

1. Deselect the Flight Connection Id field, and select the Price of Booking field (see Figure 11-4).

2. Select the white arrow Next Screen button from the Application toolbar to proceed to the next screen.

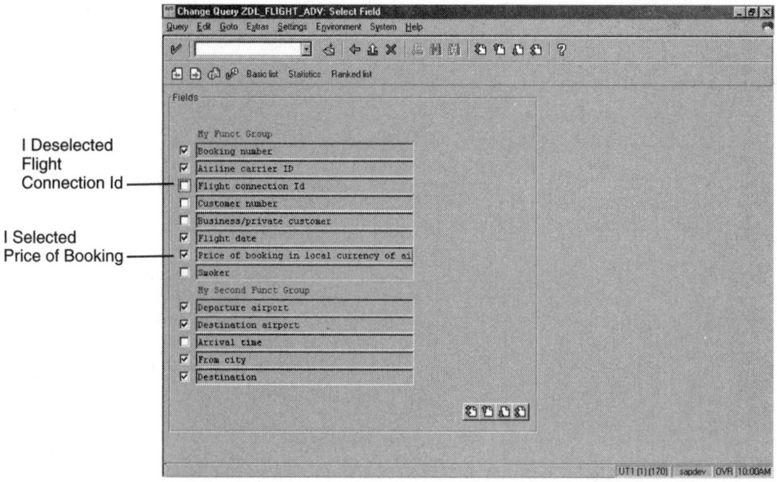

Figure 11-4 *You can modify your fields for output on the Select Field screen.*

Screen 4—Selections

On the selection screen, you can modify the fields that you want to include on your selection screen. For our example, we will add two more fields to appear in the Program Selections portion of the Selection Screen, as in Figure 11-5.

1. Select the check boxes for the Airline Carrier ID and Flight Date fields, as in Figure 11-5.

2. Select the Basic List Screen button to proceed.

Screen 5—Basic List Line Structure

The Basic List Line Structure screen is where you specify the layout and sort order of the fields to be displayed on your report. Because we added new fields and removed existing fields, it is imperative that we modify the Line, Sequence and Sort columns for our output on this screen (see Figure 11-6).

Now that a numeric field (price of booking airline in local currency) is included, we can use the Total check box. Selecting this box will produce a total at the end of the report for this field.

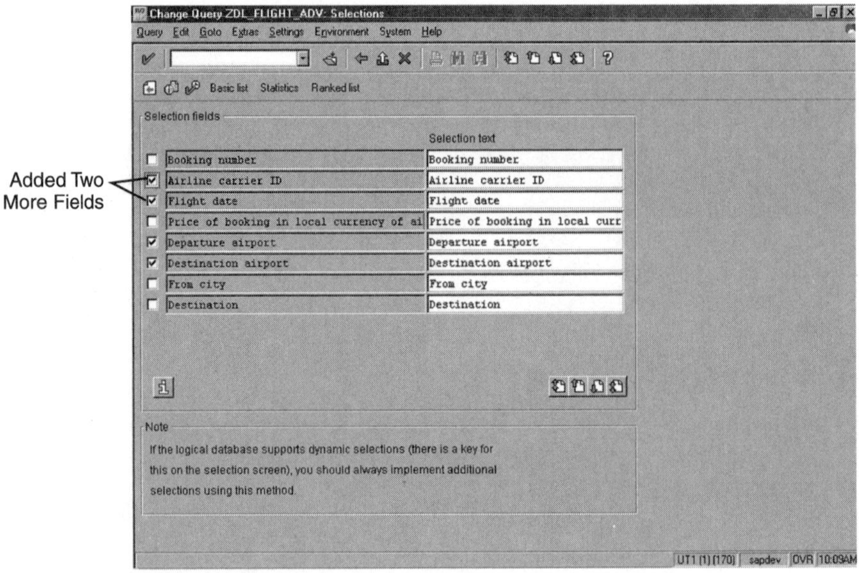

Figure 11-5 *Fields added to the Selection Screen can be used for further delineation of your output data.*

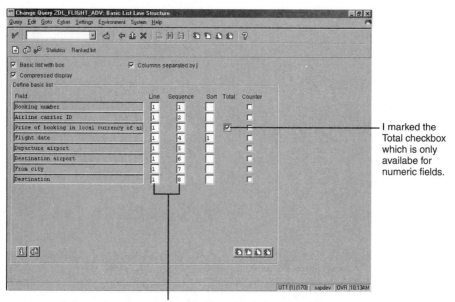

I changed my sequence specifications to include my new field.

Figure 11-6 *You must check your sequence specifications when modifying existing queries.*

1. Enter new line and sequence values, using Figure 11-6 as a reference.

2. Select the Total check box for the Price of booking field.

3. Select the open folder Save button from the Standard toolbar, then select the Execute button from the Application toolbar to view the selection screen for your report.

Screen 6—Selection Screen and Screen 7—List Screen

Without entering any specifications into the selection screen, select the Execute button to preview your report. Your new output should appear similar to Figure 11-7.

Correcting Report Output

Sometimes you will find it difficult to anticipate what imperfections your output might have. In many cases, you will have to

Destination
field wraps
to the
next line

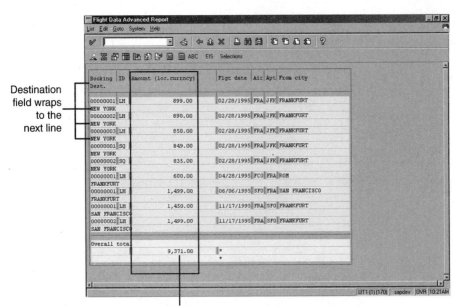

Total for Price of booking in local currency of airline

Figure 11-7 *The total for the Price of Booking field is displayed at the bottom of the report.*

create the report and view the list output before determining that there are imperfections that require correction.

Wrapping to The Next Line

From looking at the output in Figure 11-7, it appears that the report is wrapping to the second line. The Destination field appears on the second line. There are two different ways we can modify this report. The first way is to modify the column width of the report. This setting is located on the Title, Format screen (Screen 1). Follow these steps to modify the column width:

1. Navigate to the Title, Format screen (Screen 1) using the green Back arrow on the Standard toolbar.

2. As you may recall from Chapter 10, the Column field on this screen determines the maximum number of characters that can

be displayed on one line of the list created by the query. The setting we used for this report was the default value of 83. If we modify this entry from 83 to 150 and select the Save button from the Standard toolbar, we can see whether this value fixed our problem (see Figure 11-8).

3. After saving the change, select the Execute button from the Application Toolbar to see if this value fixed our problem.

4. When presented with the selection screen, select the Execute button to produce the list screen (Screen 7), as in Figure 11-9.

There are several other methods of troubleshooting the format of your output that are introduced in the next chapter.

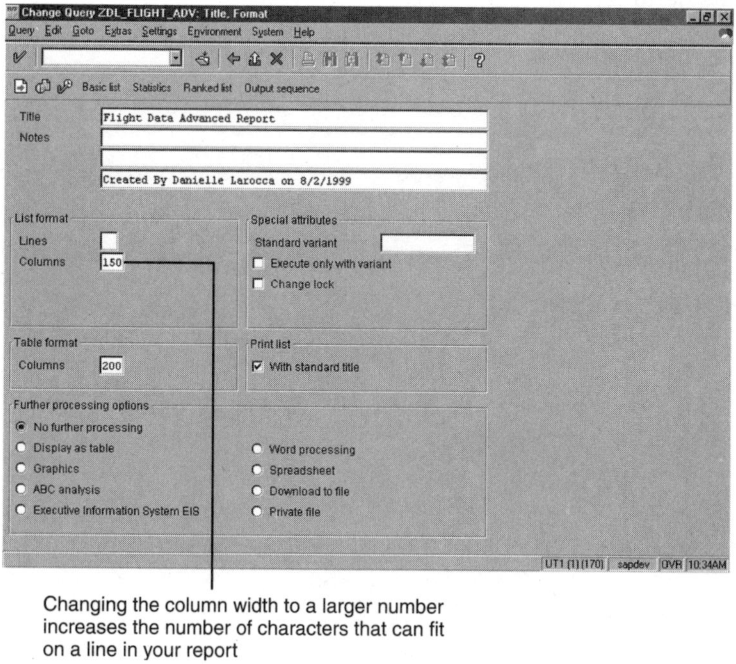

Changing the column width to a larger number
increases the number of characters that can fit
on a line in your report

Figure 11-8 *The largest value that is acceptabled in the Column field is 255.*

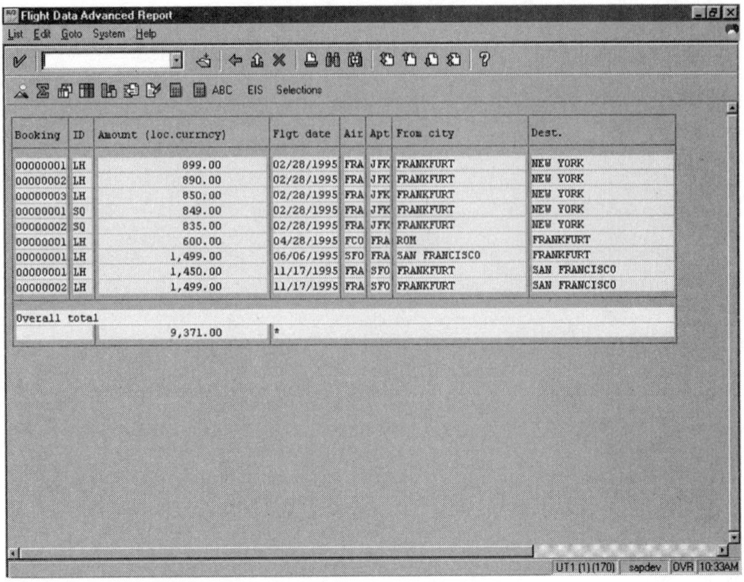

Figure 11-9 *The modification of the column width has corrected the wrapping problem.*

Selection Screens and Variants

In Chapter 4, we took a look at how entries on selection screens could be used to modify your output. We also saw how to create variants that save your entries on selection screens. To become reacquainted with the function of selection screens, let's modify the selections for this sample report.

1. Use the green arrow Back button from the Standard toolbar to return to the selection screen for your report.

2. There are several fields that we can specify data on. For this example, let's change the Destination airport to *John F. Kennedy International Airport* (JFK). This will reduce our output to display only flights where JFK is the destination airport.

3. Select the Execute button from the Application toolbar to view the list screen, as in Figure 11-10.

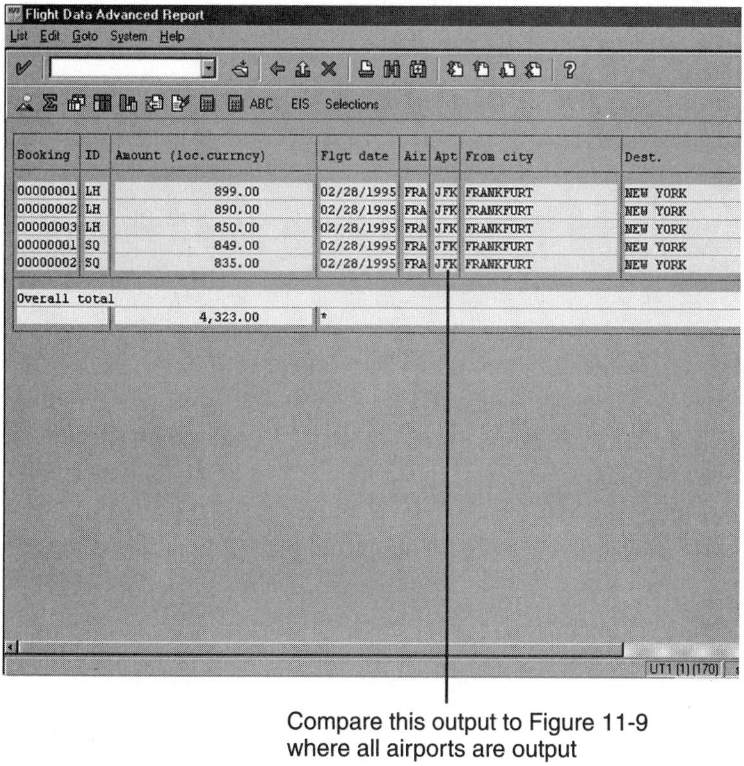

Compare this output to Figure 11-9
where all airports are output

Figure 11-10 *In some cases, Possible Entries Help is available for entries on the selection screen. In this example, we manually typed* JFK *in the Destination airport field.*

4. We can take the specification one step further by changing our selection criteria on the selection screen to say that we only want to view flights were JFK is the destination airport and Airline Carrier ID equals SQ. Use the green arrow Back button on the Standard Toolbar to return to the selection screen, and add an SQ into the Airline Carrier ID field. Execute your report again using the Execute button from the Application toolbar, and see the list screen (Screen 7) in Figure 11-11.

5. In Chapter 4, we explained that you can also use selection options to modify the data on our selection screen. Let's make

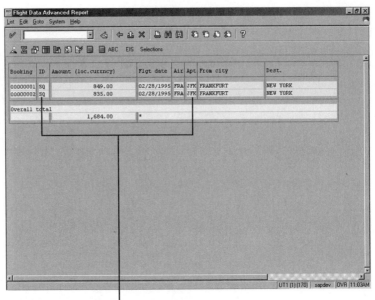

Output now includes only two fields
based on entries on the selection screen

Figure 11-11 *Using the selection screen, we can modify our output to include only the exact data that we wish to output.*

one more change to our entries on the selection screen. Use the green arrow Back button from the Standard toolbar to return to the selection screen.

6. This time, we want to select only flights where JFK is the destination airport and the Airline Carrier ID is anything except SQ. To make this change, you need to use the use Selection Options button on the Application toolbar (see Figure 11-12).

7. Position your cursor in the Airline Carrier ID field, then select the Selection Options button on the Application toolbar. Select the "not equal to" option (see Figure 11-12).

8. With your new selection criteria entered, select the Execute button on the Application toolbar to view your output, as in Figure 11-13.

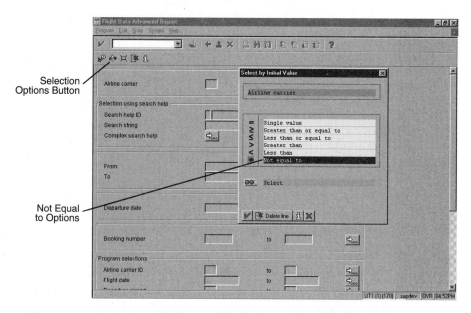

Figure 11-12 *Various advanced-selection alternatives are available on the Selection Options dialog box.*

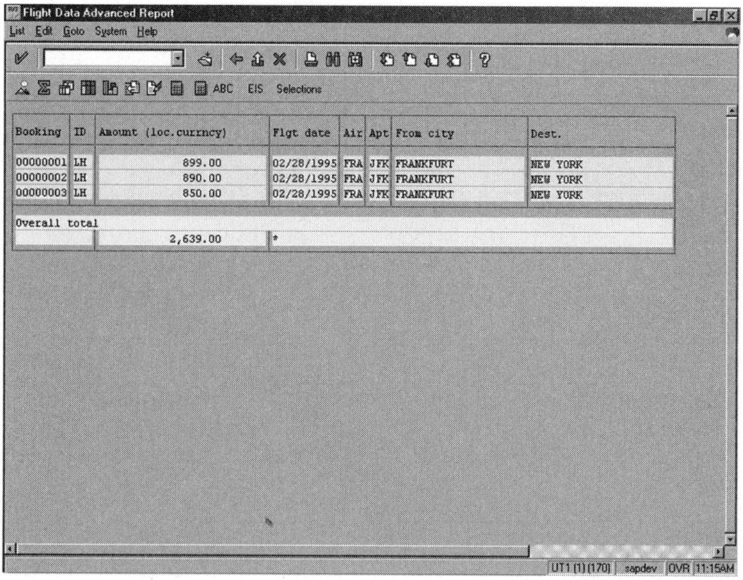

Figure 11-13 *Keep in mind that the output might vary between your screen and mine, but the fundamental concept will be the same.*

Now that we have the output exactly as we want it for this report, let's save these selection screen entries as a variant that will automatically run each time we execute this report. Be sure to save changes to your query (from any screen 1–5) before proceeding.

Creating a Variant for Your Report

In Chapter 5, we outlined in great detail the steps for creating variants from your selection screen. Here, we are only going to do a quick review step by step. If you want more detail than what is provided as follows, return to Chapter 5 for a thorough review.

1. Return to the ABAP Query main screen using the transaction code /nSQ01.

2. Select the query that you have been working with from the list by placing your cursor on the small gray box to left of the query name so that the line appears highlighted.

3. Follow the menu path Goto→Maintain variants, as in Figure 11-14.

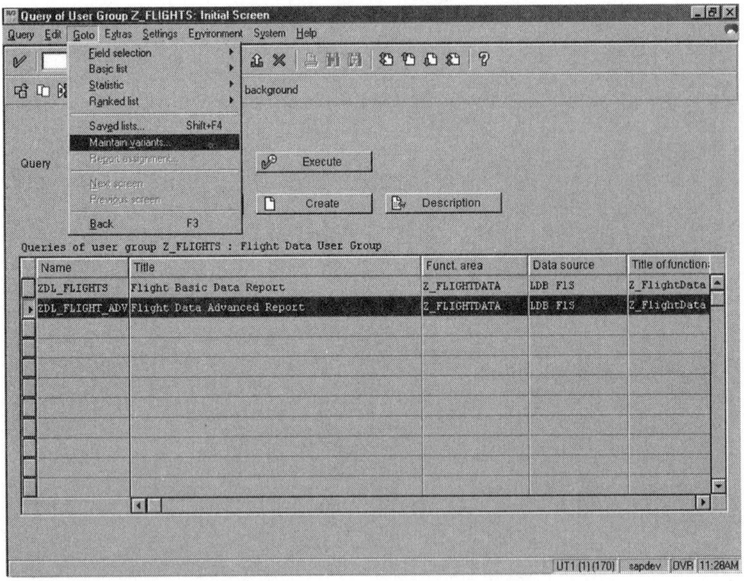

Figure 11-14 *Variants can be saved to be available for all reports or specific reports.*

4. On the initial screen, enter a name for the variant (using your company's naming convention). For our example, we will use ZFlight1. Select the Create button. A Variants Change Screen Assignment dialog box will appear similar to the one shown in Figure 11-15.

5. This dialog box enables you to specify whether you want this variant to be available for all reports or for this report only. Unmark the Variant for All Selection Screens option, and select the screen listed on the bottom of the box (in this case, screen number 1000). Select the Continue button to proceed.

6. The selection screen for the selected ABAP query will appear next. Fill in all of the appropriate values that we entered earlier to select only flights where JFK is the destination airport (and where the Airline Carrier ID is anything except SQ).

7. Select the Continue button on the Application toolbar to proceed to the ABAP: Save Attributes as Variant screen, similar to the one shown in Figure 11-16.

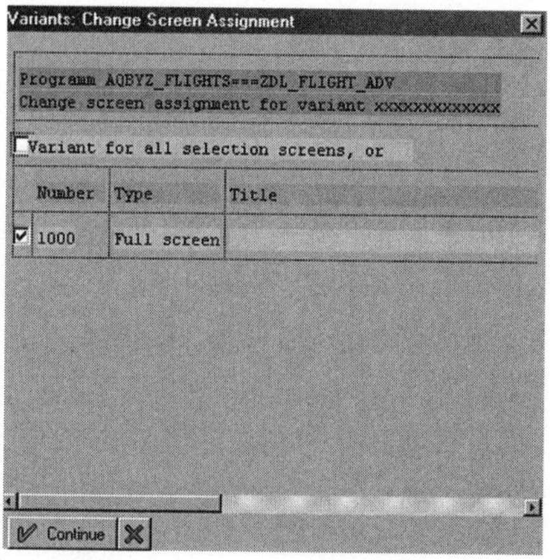

Figure 11-15 *The default entry will select the variant that will be available for all selection screens.*

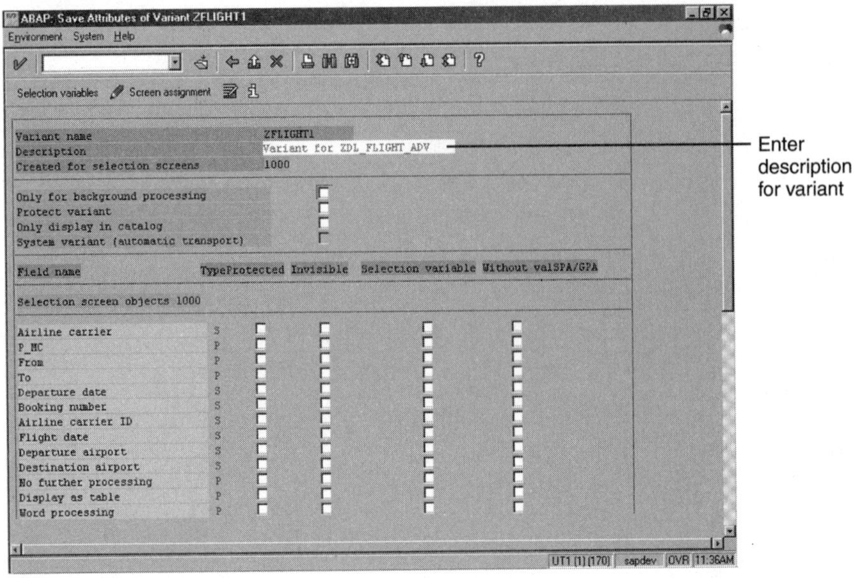

Figure 11-16 *Enter a description for your Variant on the ABAP: Save Attributes as Variant screen.*

8. Enter a description for your variant, then select the open folder Save button from the Standard toolbar to complete the creation of the variant.

9. You will be returned to the selection screen. Select the green arrow Back button two times to return to the ABAP Queries main screen.

Selecting Your Variant upon Report Execution from the Selection Screen

As mentioned in Chapter 5, you have a couple of options for using your variants to work with reporting. One way is to create a single report and save multiple variants for that report. Then, upon execution, you would select the variant that you would like to use for the report. Follow these steps to select your variant upon report execution from the selection screen:

1. On the selection screen of your report, use the menu path Goto→Variants→Get to display a list of variants that are

available for the report (a Get Variant button is also available on the Application toolbar on the selection screen).

2. Select your variant from the list, then execute your report.

Selecting Your Variant upon Execution from the ABAP Query Main Screen

Follow these steps to select your variant upon report execution from the ABAP Query main screen:

1. From the ABAP Queries main screen (transaction code /nSQ01), select your query and then select the Execute with Variant button on the Application toolbar.

2. Select your Variant from the Possible Entries Help box, and the selection screen will appear with your variant data filled in. Select the Execute button on the Application toolbar to execute your report.

Save Your Variant to Automatically Run with the Report

You can also save your variant to always run with your report. Remember that on the Title, Format screen (Screen 1) there was a place where you could fill in a variant name to be saved with the report (see Figure 11-17).

1. On the Title, Format screen (Screen 1) enter the variant name and select the Execute Only with Variant check box.

2. Upon execution, the selection screen will automatically contain the variant data.

Scheduling Your Report to Run at Preset Times

For some reports, you might want to schedule them to run at preset intervals (daily, weekly, or automatically following an R/3 event via workflow). This type of scheduling needs to be discussed and set up by your system administrator. Only reports that have variants, however, can be run using this method. If a report was scheduled to run every night at midnight, then at midnight when the report was executed, there would be no user around to fill in entries on the selection screen of the report (hence the need for a variant).

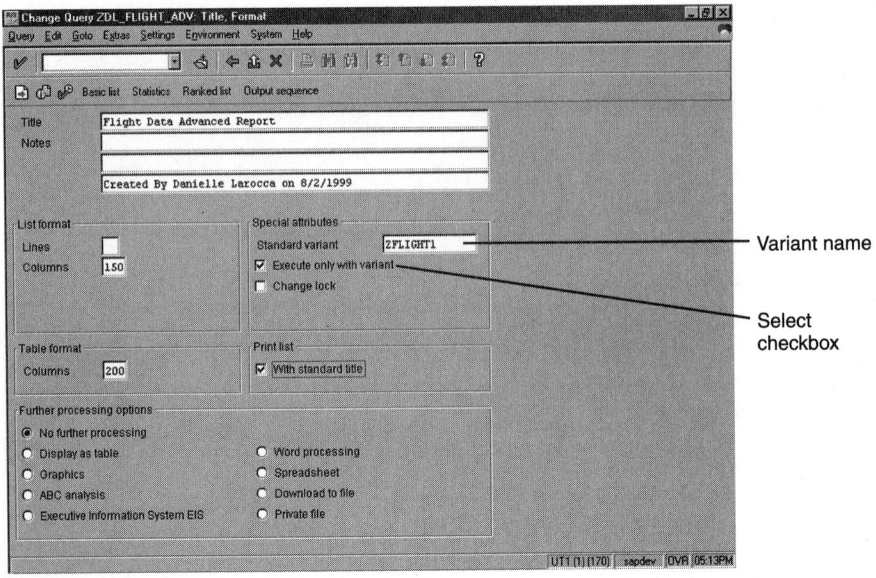

Figure 11.17 *Once saved with the query, the variant will run each time the report is executed, and the reports selection screen will contain the data from the variant.*

Chapter Wrap-Up

You should now be accustomed to navigating within your query and copying and modifying existing queries. The skills learned in this chapter are perhaps the most valuable in terms of maintaining your queries in R/3. Now that you have mastered the basic seven screens of the ABAP Query, we will move on to an additional six ABAP Query screens that deal with advanced topics such as sorting, subtotaling, and creating custom headers for your R/3 reports. The ABAP Query 13 screen reference in the appendix of this book is good to use as a handy reference when working in ABAP Query.

ABAP Query Advanced Topic—Report Customization

In the previous two chapters, you became
familiar with the seven basic screens of the
ABAP Query. The ABAP Query actually contains a total of 13 standard screens. This chapter examines these additional screens and the
further customization options they offer when
creating your own R/3 reports.

Our Example

To get started, we want to work with the query we created in
Chapter 11, "ABAP Query Maintenance and Variants." We want
to make a copy of that query, which we learned how to do at the
beginning of Chapter 11. Once a copy is made, do not forget to
change the title and date created on the Title, Format screen
(Screen 1). In addition, remove the variant and deselect the
Execute Only with Variant check box, as seen in Figure 12-1.

Navigation from Screen 5—Basic
List Line Structure

Follow these steps to jump to the Basic List Line Structure
(Screen 5) from the Title, Format screen (Screen 1), and make the
appropriate changes.

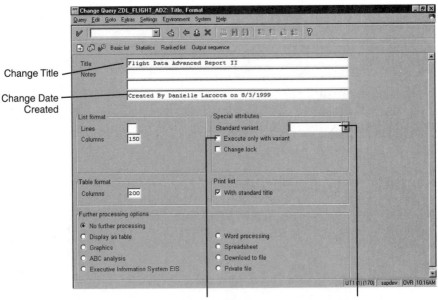

Figure 12-1 *Using the copy feature precludes you from having to create a
similar query from scratch.*

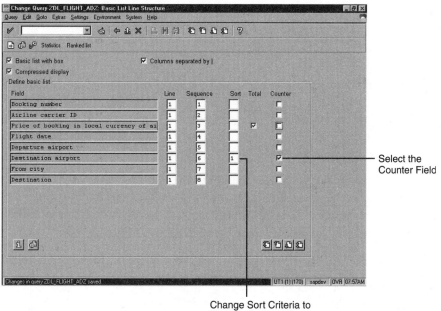

Figure 12-2 *The query will now sort by the Destination Airport field, instead of by the Flight Date field.*

1. From your Title, Format screen of your new query, select the Basic List button.

2. On this screen, change the Sort field to sort by the destination airport (instead of the flight date), and mark the Counter check box for this field as well (see Figure 12-2).

3. Save your changes by selecting the open folder Save button from the Standard toolbar.

ABAP Query Advanced Screens

The ABAP Query has six additional screens that can be used to further customize your report. Each of these six screens can be navigated to from the Basic List Line Structure screen (Screen 5). We will take a look at each of these advanced screens individually.

Screen 8—Control Levels

The Control Levels screen can be accessed by selecting the white arrow Next Screen button from the Basic List Line Structure screen (Screen 5). Screen 8 introduces the concept of control levels. A control level is a separation point in your report. Essentially, a control level is similar to a subtotal line in your report. Screen 8 enables you to put control levels or subtotals into your report on the Basic List screen for any field by which you indicated that you wanted to sort. This point is important, so we will repeat it. You can only subtotal (create control levels for) fields that you specified for sorting on the Basic List Line Structure screen (Screen 5). If you look back at Figure 12-2, you will see that we specified sorting by the Destination Airport field. This Destination Airport field is the only field available for control-level processing on Screen 8 (see Figure 12-3).

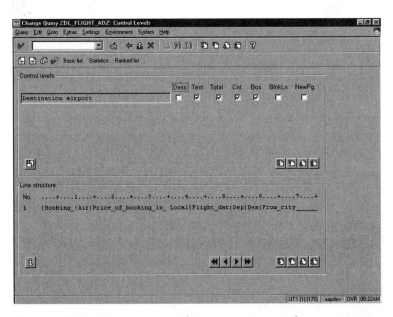

Figure 12-3 *When you specify a sort sequence, the next screen in the sequence of query screens enables you to define the sort order and the output options for control levels.*

There are several available options for your control levels on this screen. Each of the available check boxes are defined in the following table:

Table 12.1 *Available control level options*

Desc	Descending Sort	If you select this field, sorting is performed in descending order. Unless selected, the sort will appear in ascending order.
Text	Text Description	If you select this field, a text description of the control level is outputted at the beginning of the control level.
Total	Total	If you select this field, then subtotals are outputted for all fields summarized at each control level.
Cnt.	Counter	If you select this field, the system outputs a subtotal count for each field that you are counting at the end of each control level.
Box	Box	If you select this field, the system outputs a box around subtotals for each field that you are counting at the end of each control level.
BlnkLn	Blank Line	If you select this field, the system outputs a blank line under each subtotal for each field that you are counting at the end of each control level.
NewPg	New Page	If you select this field, a page break is inserted before each new control level.

Based on our entries in the Control Levels screen shown in Figure 12-3, our executed report appears in Figure 12-4.

From the Control Levels screen, you can execute your query by selecting the Execute button, or you can navigate to other ABAP Query screens by using the white arrow Navigational Screen arrows on the Application toolbar. You can also jump back to the Basic List Line Structure screen (Screen 5) by selecting the Basic List button from the Application toolbar.

Screen 9—Control-Level Texts

The next advanced ABAP Query screen can be accessed by selecting the white arrow Next button from the Control Levels screen (Screen 8). In the previous screen, the control level and subtotal texts are always the standard texts provided by ABAP Query, as in Figure 12-5.

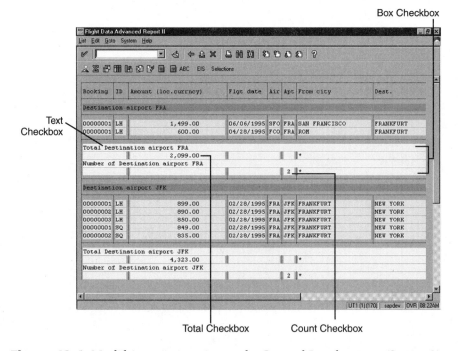

Figure 12-4 *Modifying your entries on the Control Levels screen (Screen 8) will have a direct result on your report's output.*

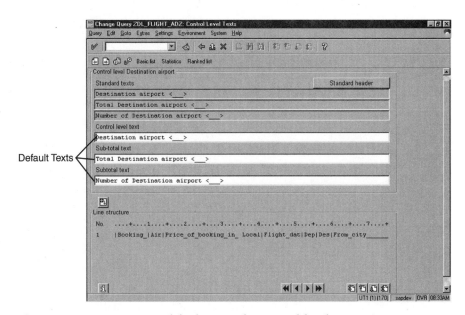

Figure 12-5 *You can modify the way the control-level texts appear on your report from the Control Level Texts screen (Screen 9).*

Take a look at Figure 12-4 to see where these texts appear in the report. These texts are modifiable from the Control Level Texts screen. You can replace the existing text with your own, but be careful not to modify the characters placed to the right of the description. We will modify the control-level texts, as seen in Figure 12-6.

After modifying our control-level texts, we executed our report to view the changes (see Figure 12-7).

From the Control Level Texts screen, you can execute your query by selecting the Execute button, or you can navigate to other ABAP Query screens by using the white arrow Navigational Screen arrows on the Application toolbar. You can also jump back to the Basic List Line Structure screen (Screen 5) by selecting the Basic List button from the Application toolbar.

Screen 10—List Line Output Options

The next advanced ABAP Query screen can be accessed by selecting the white arrow Next button from the Control Level

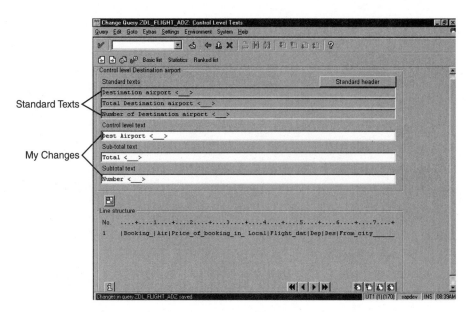

Figure 12-6 *The templates in the texts (with < and > as delimiters) are placeholders for the contents of the Control Level field.*

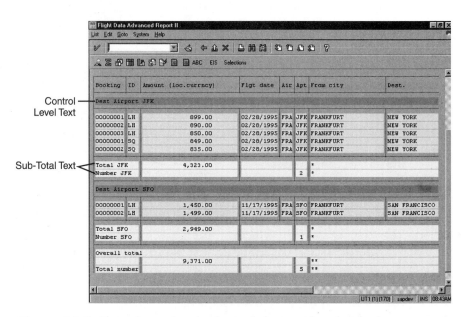

Figure 12-7 *If you have already changed the texts but decide that you want to use the standard texts after all, you can reinstate them by selecting the Standard Header button.*

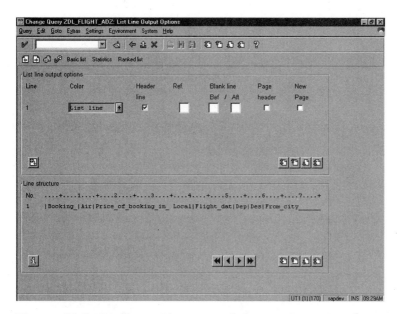

Figure 12-8 *On Screen 11, you can define output options for individual fields.*

Texts screen (Screen 9). On the List Line Output Options screen, you can define output options for each line (see Figure 12-8).

The list line refers to the data in your report that is considered to be the list (in other words, the actual line items). There are several available selections on the List Line Output Options screen. Each of the available options is defined in Table 12.2.

Table 12.2 *List line output options*

Color	Color	Color enables you to modify the color in which the output appears in your report. There are 15 available colors to select from, using the Possible Entries Help button in the Color field.
Header line	Header line	If you select this field, column headers are presented for the fields in this line.

Table 12.2 *List line output options (Continued)*

Ref.	Reference line	This field is used to specify dependencies between different lines of the list. If you enter the number of another line here, the line is only outputted if the line you enter here is also displayed. This feature is helpful for mailing labels, for example, if name data is on Line 1 and address data is on Line 2. The name data should only appear if an address exists. In this case, you must enter 1 in the column Ref. for Line 2.
Bef.	Blank line before	This field determines how many blank lines should be inserted before the output of the line.
Aft	Blank line after	This field determines how many blank lines should be inserted after the output of the line.
Page header	Page header	If you select this field, the relevant line is outputted in the page header when you start a new page, and one of the following lines results in a new page.
New page	New page	If you select this field, a new page is started before the line is outputted on the report.

We will modify the selections on this screen (see Figure 12-9). Our modifications are evident in the output on the Report List screen (Screen 7), as shown in Figure 12-10.

From the List Line Output Options screen, you can execute your query by selecting the Execute button—or you can navigate to other ABAP Query screens using the white arrow Navigational Screen arrows on the Application toolbar. You can also jump back to the basic List Line Structure screen (Screen 5) by selecting the Basic List button from the Application toolbar.

Our Example

For the remaining two advanced ABAP Query screens, we want to use a different query as an example. Save any changes to your open query, and return to the ABAP Query main screen (transaction

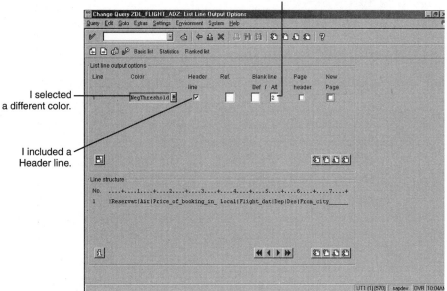

Figure 12-9 *On the List Line Output Options screen, you can define output options for each line.*

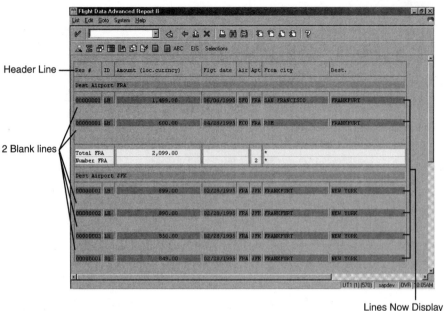

Header Line

2 Blank lines

Lines Now Display
in Selected Color

Figure 12-10 *Changing the colors of the list items does not have an effect on a printed report, unless you set the system for color printing of lists in R/3.*

code /nSQ01). As we did at the start of this chapter, we would like to work with the query we created in Chapter 11. We want to make a copy of that query (which we learned how to do at the beginning of Chapter 11). Once a copy is made, do not forget to change the title and date created on the Title, Format screen (Screen 1). In addition, remove the variant and deselect the Execute Only with Variant check box. We will work with this query for the last two advanced screens in ABAP Query. Execute your query to ensure that the format appears similar to the one shown in Figure 12-11.

Screen 11—Field Output Options

Using the Field Output Options screen, you can place fields in a particular place on the screen and insert text at desired points in your list. You can access the Field Output Options screen from the Basic List Line Structure screen (Screen 5) by selecting the

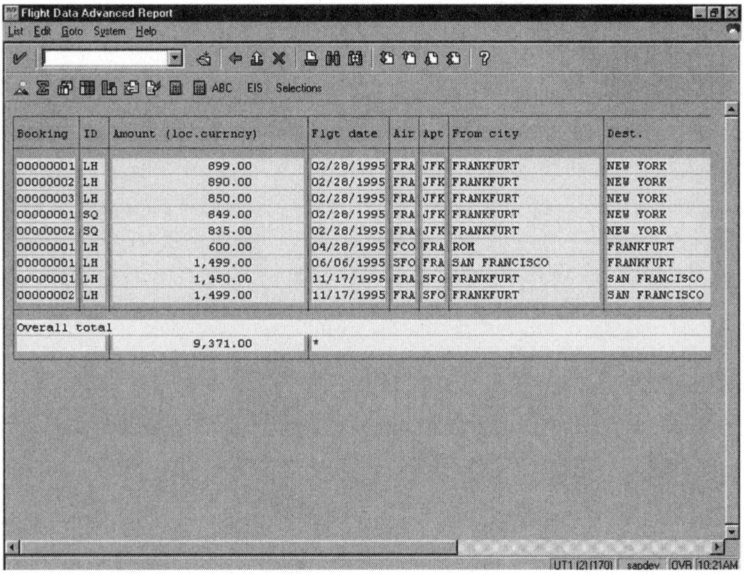

Booking	ID	Amount (loc.currncy)	Flgt date	Air	Apt	From city	Dest.
00000001	LH	899.00	02/28/1995	FRA	JFK	FRANKFURT	NEW YORK
00000002	LH	890.00	02/28/1995	FRA	JFK	FRANKFURT	NEW YORK
00000003	LH	850.00	02/28/1995	FRA	JFK	FRANKFURT	NEW YORK
00000001	SQ	849.00	02/28/1995	FRA	JFK	FRANKFURT	NEW YORK
00000002	SQ	835.00	02/28/1995	FRA	JFK	FRANKFURT	NEW YORK
00000001	LH	600.00	04/28/1995	FCO	FRA	ROM	FRANKFURT
00000001	LH	1,499.00	06/06/1995	SFO	FRA	SAN FRANCISCO	FRANKFURT
00000001	LH	1,450.00	11/17/1995	FRA	SFO	FRANKFURT	SAN FRANCISCO
00000002	LH	1,499.00	11/17/1995	FRA	SFO	FRANKFURT	SAN FRANCISCO
Overall total							
		9,371.00	*				

Figure 12-11 *Keep in mind that the format should be the same, but the data might differ.*

white arrow Next Screen button four times. All of the ABAP Query screens are in order from one to 13. The white arrow Navigational buttons can be used to navigate between the different screens. On this screen, you can also modify the column width of data in your output (see Figure 12-12).

Length

The first two columns listed to the left of the fields are for column length. These columns actually represent the standard (std) and new column widths for the fields in your output. Take a look at the length for the price of airline booking in local currency width that is set to 20. Now, take a look at your output in Figure 12-11. That column is pretty wide for the data. You can modify the displayed width of this field by changing the number in the New column. We will change the 20 to a 10 and will examine the resulting change in our output (see Figure 12-13).

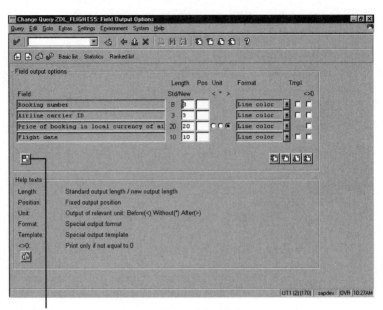

As on the Basic List Line Structure Screen (Screen 5), the
w/out explanation button can be used to display more fields.

Figure 12-12 *On the Field Output Options screen, you can
define output options for individual fields.*

Pos. (Position)

The Position column determines the position of the field in the
output line. The first character in the line has position 1. If this
field is left blank, the field is always outputted following the preceding field or from position 1 (if it is the first field of the line). If
you want to modify exactly which position your data appears in
a list, you can change this setting. A ruler is also available at the
bottom of the screen to help you specify the correct position.
Selecting the Line Structure button on the bottom left-hand side
of the screen will display the ruler. Modifying a field position on
a report can be helpful if you need to create an extract file to be
used electronically for another source. This concept is discussed
in Chapter 14, "Creating Extract (Interface) Files Using ABAP
Query"). This feature is used, for example, if you were given a
flat-file layout specification of fields and their positions, because

Width 20

Booking	ID	Amount (loc.currncy)	Flgt date	Air	Apt	From city	Dest.
00000001	LH	899.00	02/28/1995	FRA	JFK	FRANKFURT	NEW YORK
00000002	LH	890.00	02/28/1995	FRA	JFK	FRANKFURT	NEW YORK
00000003	LH	850.00	02/28/1995	FRA	JFK	FRANKFURT	NEW YORK
00000001	SQ	849.00	02/28/1995	FRA	JFK	FRANKFURT	NEW YORK
00000002	SQ	835.00	02/28/1995	FRA	JFK	FRANKFURT	NEW YORK
00000001	LH	600.00	04/28/1995	FCO	FRA	ROM	FRANKFURT
00000001	LH	1,499.00	06/06/1995	SFO	FRA	SAN FRANCISCO	FRANKFURT
00000001	LH	1,450.00	11/17/1995	FRA	SFO	FRANKFURT	SAN FRANCISCO
00000002	LH	1,499.00	11/17/1995	FRA	SFO	FRANKFURT	SAN FRANCISCO
Overall total							
		9,371.00	*				

Field output options

Field	Length Std/New
Booking number	8 8
Airline carrier ID	3 3
Price of booking in local currency of ai	20 10
Flight date	10 10

Booking	ID	Amount (lo	Flgt date	Air	Apt	From city	Dest.
00000001	LH	899.00	02/28/1995	FRA	JFK	FRANKFURT	NEW YORK
00000002	LH	890.00	02/28/1995	FRA	JFK	FRANKFURT	NEW YORK
00000003	LH	850.00	02/28/1995	FRA	JFK	FRANKFURT	NEW YORK
00000001	SQ	849.00	02/28/1995	FRA	JFK	FRANKFURT	NEW YORK
00000002	SQ	835.00	02/28/1995	FRA	JFK	FRANKFURT	NEW YORK
00000001	LH	600.00	04/28/1995	FCO	FRA	ROM	FRANKFURT
00000001	LH	1,499.00	06/06/1995	SFO	FRA	SAN FRANCISCO	FRANKFURT
00000001	LH	1,450.00	11/17/1995	FRA	SFO	FRANKFURT	SAN FRANCISCO
00000002	LH	1,499.00	11/17/1995	FRA	SFO	FRANKFURT	SAN FRANCISCO
Overall total							
		9,371.00	*				

Width 10

Figure 12-13 *Be particularly careful when modifying column widths for numeric fields. Upon later executions of the report, as values increase, so will the necessary column width.*

you would be able to create a file based on those specifications. See Figure 12-14 for an example of how to modify the position of a field.

Unit (Currency)

This three radio-button selection enables you to specify whether you want any currency amounts displayed with their currency descriptor (i.e., USD for the U.S. dollar). The three possible selections are described in Table 12.3.

Field Begins at Position 1   Field Immediately Follows Previous Field

Booking	ID	Amount (loc.currncy)	Flgt date	Air	Apt	From city	Dest.
00000001	LH	899.00	02/28/1995	FRA	JFK	FRANKFURT	NEW YORK
00000002	LH	890.00	02/28/1995	FRA	JFK	FRANKFURT	NEW YORK
00000003	LH	850.00	02/28/1995	FRA	JFK	FRANKFURT	NEW YORK
00000001	SQ	849.00	02/28/1995	FRA	JFK	FRANKFURT	NEW YORK
00000002	SQ	835.00	02/28/1995	FRA	JFK	FRANKFURT	NEW YORK
00000001	LH	600.00	04/28/1995	FCO	FRA	ROM	FRANKFURT
00000001	LH	1,499.00	06/06/1995	SFO	FRA	SAN FRANCISCO	FRANKFURT
00000001	LH	1,450.00	11/17/1995	FRA	SFO	FRANKFURT	SAN FRANCISCO
00000002	LH	1,499.00	11/17/1995	FRA	SFO	FRANKFURT	SAN FRANCISCO

Overall total

9,371.00 *

Field output options

Field	Length Std/New	Pos
Booking number	8	8	10
Airline carrier ID	3	3	30
Price of booking in local currency of ai	20	10	
Flight date	10	10	

Booking	ID	Amount (lo	Flgt date	Air	Apt	From city	Dest.
00000001	LH	899.00	02/28/1995	FRA	JFK	FRANKFURT	NEW Y
00000002	LH	890.00	02/28/1995	FRA	JFK	FRANKFURT	NEW Y
00000003	LH	850.00	02/28/1995	FRA	JFK	FRANKFURT	NEW Y
00000001	SQ	849.00	02/28/1995	FRA	JFK	FRANKFURT	NEW Y
00000002	SQ	835.00	02/28/1995	FRA	JFK	FRANKFURT	NEW Y
00000001	LH	600.00	04/28/1995	FCO	FRA	ROM	FRANK
00000001	LH	1,499.00	06/06/1995	SFO	FRA	SAN FRANCISCO	FRANK
00000001	LH	1,450.00	11/17/1995	FRA	SFO	FRANKFURT	SAN F
00000002	LH	1,499.00	11/17/1995	FRA	SFO	FRANKFURT	SAN F

Overall total

9,371.00 *

Field Begins at   Field Begins at
Position 10   Position 30

Figure 12-14 *The modifying report output field positions feature is used primarily in the creation of extract files.*

Table 12.3 *Unit currency display options*

Button	Description	Sample
Radio Button 1	If you select this field, the relevant currency or unit is outputted in the report list before the currency amount or quantity.	USD 1500.00
Radio Button 2	If you select this field, the relevant currency or unit is not outputted in the report list.	1500.00

Button	Description	Sample
Radio Button 3	If you select this field, the relevant currency or unit is outputted in the report list after the currency amount or quantity.	1500.00 USD

Format

The Format field enables you to modify the color of the field (column) displayed in your report. Using the Format box, you can modify the color of each individual field. There are 15 available colors to select from, using the Possible Entries Help button in the Color field.

Tmpl. (Template)

The template option enables you to include formatting characters in a field. By selecting this option, you can make your specifications for the template on the next screen (Screen 12). For example, you can insert a text or enter separator before a field, such as the word "Date," before a date is outputted. The output length of the field is subsequently increased by the number of formatting characters. After selecting the template option for a field, return to the Field Output Options screen to see the modified output length in the column New. For our example, we will select the template option for the Flight Date and City fields, and we will see how this information comes together when we view Screen 12.

< >0 (Ignore Zero Indicator)

If you select this check box, a value of the field is only outputted if it is not equal to zero. This formatting option prevents your report from being cluttered with 0.00 entries for any field where no value exists.

From the Field Output Options screen, you can execute your query by selecting the Execute button, or you can navigate to other ABAP Query screens using the white arrow Navigational Screen arrows on the Application toolbar. You can also jump

back to the Basic List Line Structure screen (Screen 5) by selecting
the Basic List button from the Application toolbar.

Screen 12—Field Templates

You can access the Field Templates screen by selecting the white
arrow Next Screen button from the Field Output Options screen.
The Field Templates screen (Screen 12) only emerges if you previously selected the Template option for fields on the Field Output
Options screen (Screen 11). In our example in Screen 11, we
selected the Flight Date and City fields so that they now appear on
the Field Templates screen (Screen 12), as in Figure 12-15.

We want words to appear in the columns next to each of these
two fields, so we will add them to Screen 12 (see Figure 12-16).

From the Field Templates screen, you can execute your query
by selecting the Execute button, or you can navigate to other
ABAP Query screens using the white arrow Navigational Screen
arrows on the Application toolbar. You can also jump back to the

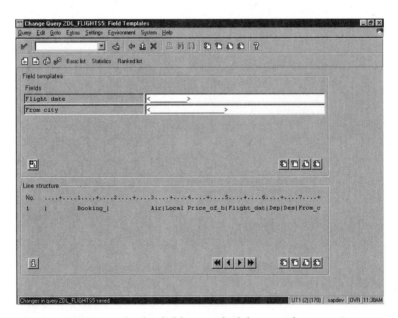

Figure 12-15 *Only the fields specified for templates on Screen*
11 will appear for entry on Screen 12.

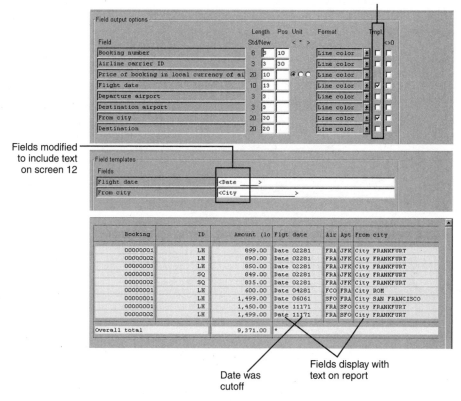

Fields selected on screen 11

Fields modified to include text on screen 12

Date was cutoff

Fields display with text on report

Figure 12-16 *Because text was added to these fields, we will have to return to the Field Output Options screen (Screen 11) to modify the Length New Fields entry to allow for the expanded output of the data.*

Basic List Line Structure screen (Screen 5) by selecting the Basic List button from the Application toolbar.

Screen 13—Basic List Header

You can access the Basic List Header screen by selecting the white arrow Next Screen button from the Field Output Options screen (Screen 11) if no templates were selected. Otherwise, the screen will appear sequentially after the Field Templates screen (Screen 12). On the Basic List Header screen, you can define a page header and footer for the pages of the report on the Basic List Header screen (see Figure 12-17).

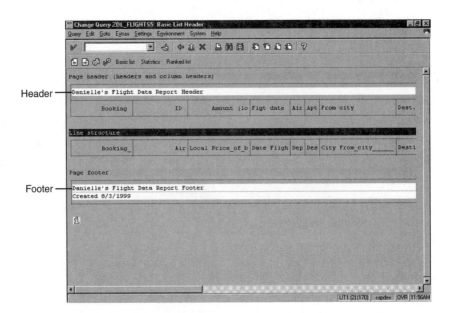

Figure 12-17 *You can have multiple line headers or footers by following the menu path Edit→Line→Insert.*

Your custom header and footer will appear on the displayed view of your report in addition to the printed copy, as in Figure 12-18.

Inserting Variables into Header and Footers

You can also insert variables—such as the page number, date, and time—into your report headers and footers. A sample of variable insert options are displayed in Table 12.4.

Table 12.4 *Header and footer variable examples*

Text	Description
&%Page	Inserts the current page number into the header or footer
&%Date	Inserts the current date into the header or footer
&%Time	Inserts the current time into the header or footer

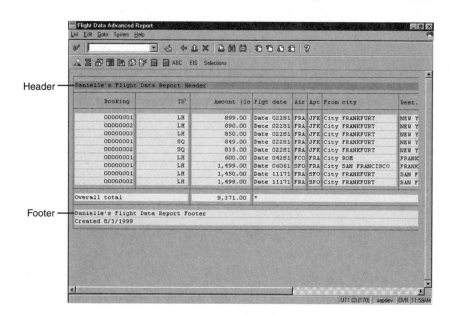

Header

Footer

Figure 12-18 *Custom headers and footers personalize reports created in ABAP Query.*

From the Basic List Header screen, you can execute your query by selecting the Execute button, or you can navigate to other ABAP Query screens by using the white arrow Navigational Screen arrows on the Application toolbar. You can also jump back to the Basic List Line Structure screen (Screen 5) by selecting the Basic List button from the Application toolbar.

Graphics Screen

In ABAP Query, an additional screen exists after the Basic List Header screen that is used to define graphic layouts. One-line basic lists, statistics, and ranked lists can be displayed in graphical format in R/3. On the Graphics screen, you can define graphical output depending on the values you choose to display and the graphic type you use (see Figure 12-19).

Chapter Wrap-Up

Reporting in R/3 with the ABAP Query can be done easily and efficiently. The skills learned in this chapter should enable you to

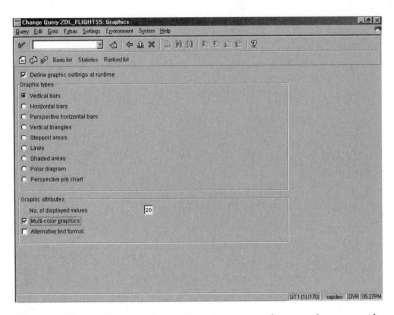

Figure 12-19 *SAP Business Graphics provides a wide range of graphics options and data interfaces, as well as various commands for manipulating data.*

begin creating advanced reports for your R/3 data. The best method of working with the ABAP Query tool to unleash its possibilities is trial and error. Manipulating values and selections on the 13 screens and viewing the resulting changes in your output is the best way of becoming an R/3 ABAP Query-reporting professional. The ABAP Query 13-screen reference in the appendix of this book is good to use as a handy reference when working in the ABAP Query.

ABAP Query Advanced Topic—Functional Area Customization

In previous chapters, we became familiar with the seven basic and six advanced screens of the ABAP Query. In Chapter 9, we introduced the technical, behind-the-scenes configuration of how functional areas are established. This chapter is a technical chapter intended for an audience of individuals who will be maintaining functional areas—or for an advanced ABAP Query user with ABAP programming skills. If this description does not represent you, read through the chapter to gain a better understanding of how new functional areas are managed and modified, so that you will be better able to provide appropriate requests to the functional area administrator regarding proposed modifications.

Functional Area Modifications

As introduced in Chapter 9, the fields within the functional groups in the functional areas are what appear for selection on the Select Fields screen of your ABAP queries. You can perform modifications on these fields within the functional area to affect the way they display in the ABAP Query.

Our Example

For the examples in this chapter, we will use the functional area (Z_FLIGHTDATA) that we created in Chapter 9. Follow these steps to open your functional area for modifications:

1. Navigate to the Functional Areas: Initial screen using the transaction code /nSQ02 or the menu path Tools→ABAP Workbench→Utilities→ABAP Query→Functional areas.

2. Select the functional area created in Chapter 9 (or its equivalent), then select the Change button. The functional area should be similar in format to the one shown in Figure 13-1.

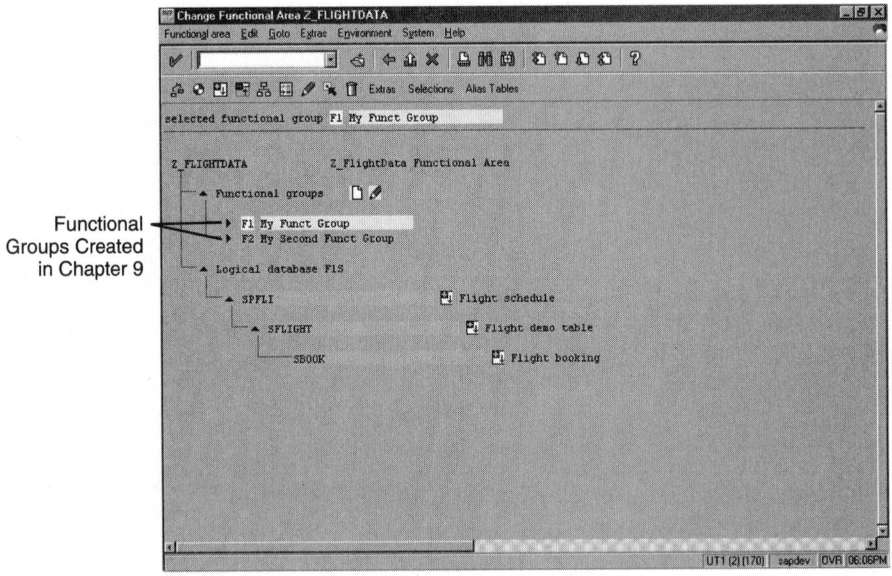

Figure 13-1 *Our sample functional area contains three R/3 sample tables: SPFLI, SFLIGHT, and SBOOK.*

Renaming Objects in the Functional Area

You can rename objects in your functional area to provide more meaningful descriptions. In some instances, the names provided by R/3 are a bad German-to-English translation. In other cases, you might want to change the names of fields to be consistent with your company's naming conventions.

Renaming Functional Groups

For starters, the two functional group names (created for examples in Chapter 9) do not provide a good description of the data they contain. Follow these steps to rename a functional group:

1. Place your cursor on the functional group you wish to rename, and follow the menu path Edit→Functional group→Change functional group.

2. A Change Functional Groups window will appear, from which you can rename the descriptions of your functional groups (see Figure 13-2).

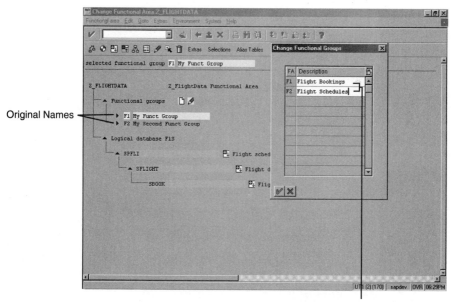

Figure 13-2 *Your new functional group names will now be available on the Select Functional Group screen (Screen 2) in the ABAP Query.*

Renaming Fields

You might also need to rename fields in R/3. For example, some companies prefer to use their own terms for certain fields. Follow these steps to rename a field in your functional area:

1. Place your cursor on the field, and follow the menu path Edit→Change field.

2. A Change the Text of a Field and Functional Group Assignment dialog box will appear, similar to the one shown in Figure 13-3.

3. Modify the field name in the Long Text Input field, and select the green check mark Enter key to complete the change.

Renaming Column Headings

In addition to renaming fields in R/3, you might want to modify the column headings that appear on the top line of the report for the field. For example, some companies prefer to use their own terms for certain fields. Follow these steps to rename a column heading for a field in your functional area:

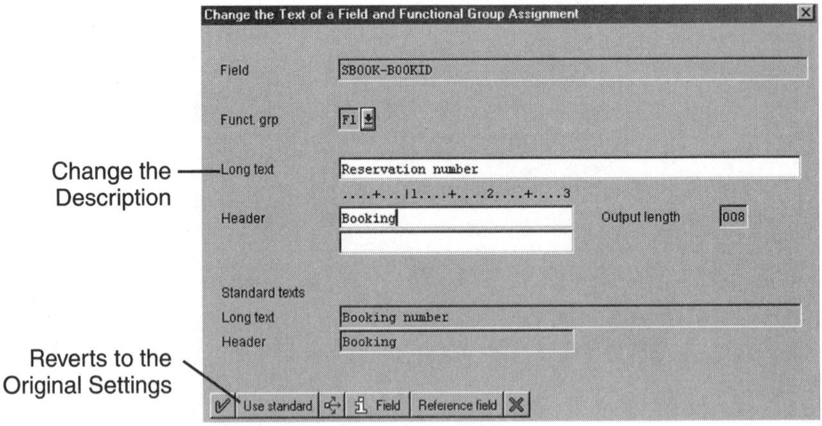

Figure 13-3 *Your new field names will be available on the Select Field screen (Screen 3) in the ABAP Query.*

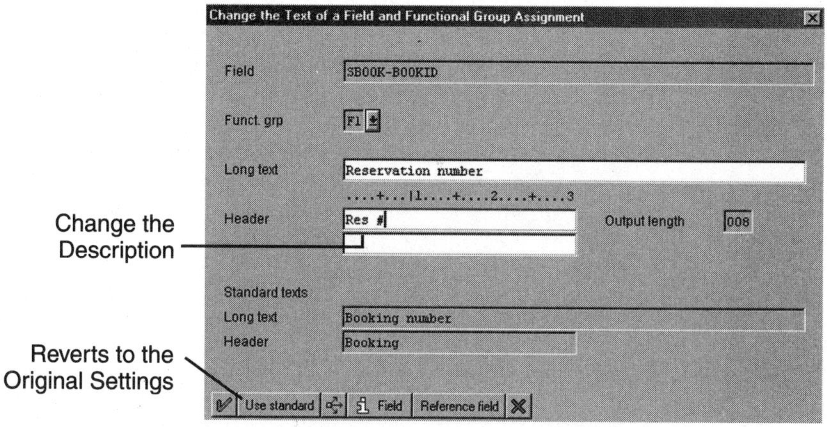

Figure 13-4 *Your new column heading will be available on the Reports Output List screen (Screen 7) in ABAP Query.*

1. Place your cursor on the field, and follow the menu path Edit→Change field. A Change the Text of a Filed and Functional Group Assignment dialog box will appear, similar to the one shown in Figure 13-4.

2. Modify the column heading in the Header Input field and select the green check mark Enter key to complete the change.

   When list reports are created using ABAP Query, the column heading for the field will now reflect the new name.

Adding Calculated Fields to a Functional Area

In some cases, you might want to add new fields to be available for selection for your ABAP queries. These fields are called calculated fields. Using our Flight Reservation System used in the functional area as an example, let's say that you wanted to manipulate numbers. Let's add a new field that stores the price of a booking plus 10 percent (your markup), which would be the cost that you would be offered to clients. You can create a calculated field to store this value. The creation of calculated fields in R/3 functional areas requires you to be familiar with the ABAP language. If you are not familiar with the language of ABAP, you can view how the samples are explained here and try them in your own functional areas using your own field names. Follow these steps to create a new calculated field:

1. Locate a field displayed in the table (or another table) that is the same format of the field you want to create. For example, the new field will be a currency field similar to the Price of Booking field. Look to the left of the Price of Booking field to see its technical name. This name is displayed as SBOOK-LOCCURAM. Make a note of the name, because we will use it in a minute.

2. Place your cursor on a table in the functional area that will contain the new field (you should place the field in the same table as any fields that you will use for reference in your calculated field). For our example, we are adding a field to the SBOOK flight-booking table.

3. Follow the menu path Goto→Extras, or select the Extras button from the Application toolbar. A Database Table Enhancements dialog box will appear. Select the white Create button.

4. A Create Additional Information dialog box will appear. Enter a name for your new field (using your company's naming conventions), and select the Additional field radio button (see Figure 13-5). Select the green check mark Enter button to proceed.

5. Next, you will be presented with an Additional Field dialog box. In this box, you need to enter a description of the field and a header that you want to appear as a column heading on your reports (see Figure 13-6).

6. Next, you next need to enter a format for your new field. For example, is it a field that will store text, numbers, or dates? Instead of manually entering the type of field, you can specify that you want the new field to be in the same format as an existing field. At this point, you would enter the price of booking table and field name copied from the SBOOK table (see Figure 13-6).

7. Select the red pencil Editor button at the bottom of the dialog box to launch the ABAP Editor. The ABAP Editor screen is

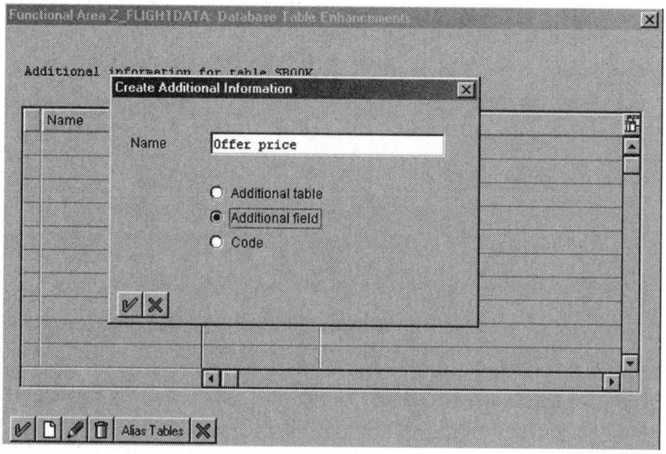

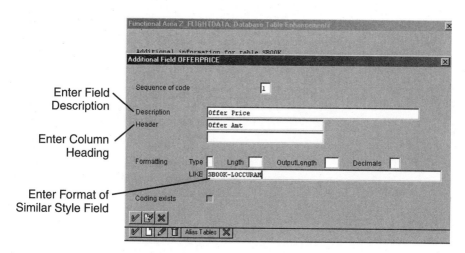

Figure 13-5 *The additional tables and code radio buttons offer more advanced options available on this dialog box.*

Figure 13-6 *The format of your new field can be entered manually, or you can specify that you want the new field to be in the same format as an existing field.*

where ABAP programmers write code in the R/3 system. We will enter a basic line of code to create our calculated field (see Figure 13-7).

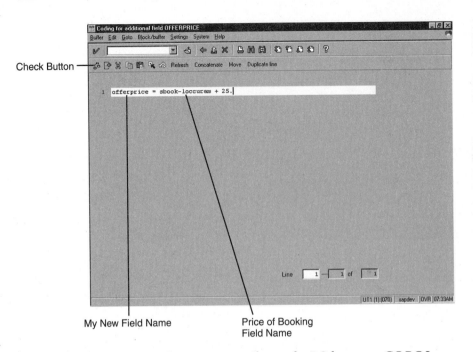

Check Button

My New Field Name   Price of Booking
                         Field Name

Figure 13-7 *The ABAP language is similar to the PC language COBOL.*

8. Interpreting the line of code shown in Figure 13-7, you can translate it to say, "Make the value of the OfferPrice field equal to the Price of the Booking field (SBOOK_LOCCURAM) plus $25." After typing the code, select the Check button from the Application toolbar to validate your code (the Check button is shown in Figure 13-7).

9. If no error messages are displayed in the Status bar, select the Save button from the Standard toolbar. Next, select the green arrow Back button to return to the previous dialog box, then select the green check mark Enter key on both dialog boxes to return to the Change Functional Area screen.

10. Now that you created a new field, you need to add that field to one of your functional groups. Expand the SBOOK flight-booking table and look for the new field, Offer Price. Once

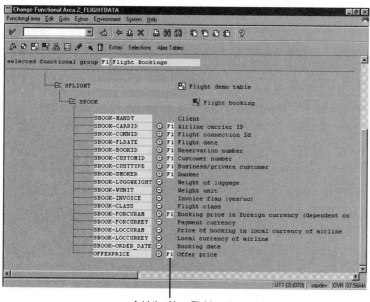

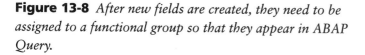

Add the New Field to the
F1 Functional Group

Figure 13-8 *After new fields are created, they need to be assigned to a functional group so that they appear in ABAP Query.*

you locate this field, turn its indicator on for the appropriate functional group (see Figure 13-8).

11. Save and generate your functional area.

Create a New Query and Include Calculated Fields

By now, you should be an expert at creating queries in R/3. Create a new query using the specifications in Table 13.1.

Your query output should appear similar in format to the output shown in Figure 13-9.

Additional Technical Topics for Modifying Functional Areas

These technical topics are introduced here only to provide you with an overall understanding of the possibilities of working with

Table 13.1 *Specifications for a new ABAP Query report*

Functional Group	Field Name	Line	Sequence	Sort
Flight bookings	Offer Price	1	6	
Flight bookings	Reservation Number	1	1	1
Flight bookings	Airline Carrier ID	1	2	
Flight bookings	Booking Price in Foreign Currency	1	5	
Flight schedules	Departure Airport	1	3	
Flight schedules	Destination Airport	1	4	

the ABAP Query and the functions behind the scenes that make it work.

Assigning Additional Tables

In addition to creating additional fields, you can also add additional tables to your functional area. This task is an advanced technical topic and can only be managed by your functional area administrator. This task requires ABAP programming skills and an in-depth knowledge of the workings and relationships between the data in your R/3 database.

Multiple Additional Table Assignments (Alias Tables)

The addition of multiple table assignments enables you to link a table to a functional area as an additional table (exactly once).

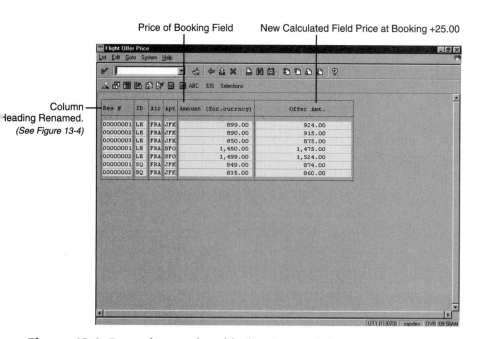

Figure 13-9 *Depending on the table data in your R/3 system, your output might appear different—but the format of the report should be the same.*

Whenever you attempt to link the table a second time as an additional table, you will receive an error message informing you that the table can only be used once. The use of alias tables provides you with the capability to link the same table more than once. This task is an advanced technical topic and can only be managed by your functional area administrator—and requires ABAP programming skills and an in-depth knowledge of the workings and relationships between the data in your R/3 database.

Functional Areas without Logical Databases

Functional areas can also be created without logical databases. These functional areas can be based on table joins, direct reads, data-retrieval programs, and sequential data sets. From the descriptions alone, you can probably guess that advanced ABAP programming skills are required for this type of functional-area creation.

Creating Extra Selection Fields

As you know, all queries in R/3 have a selection screen that is presented before the query is run. Within the ABAP Query, you can use the Selections screen (Screen 4) to add additional fields to your selection screen. Part of the selection possibilities that appear on the screen are determined by the logical database. You can also define additional selection fields (parameters and selection criteria) from within the functional area. These selection fields appear on the selection screens of all queries created using the functional area and form a set of standard selection fields for these queries. As you might presume, this task is an advanced technical topic that can only be managed by your functional area administrator and requires ABAP programming skills and an in-depth knowledge of the workings and relationships between the data in your R/3 database.

Special Features for Functional Areas for the Human Resources Module

Unlike the other modules, Human Resources has a concept called infotypes. Infotypes store information about an employee in the Human Resources module. For example, infotype 0002 stores an employee's personal data (see Figure 13-10).

Behind the scenes, the Human Resources data is stored in tables—similar to all other R/3 data—but it is presented to the user through infotypes. When creating a functional area for the Human Resources module, you will find that the setup procedure is slightly different than the standard discussed in Chapter 9. Functional areas based on Human Resources logical databases (PNP and PCH) will prompt you with a screen for the entry of infotype numbers during the creation of the functional area. Depending on which logical database you select (PNP or PCH), a different range of infotypes is available. Logical Database PNP (Human Resources master data) is used to create a functional area containing only Human Resources master data, infotypes 0000 through 0999, and infotypes 2,000 through 2,999. The PCH (Personnel Development) Logical Database is used to create functional areas containing only *Personnel Development* (PD) infotypes 1,000 through 1,999. To create a functional area containing data from both master data (PA) and PD, use Logical

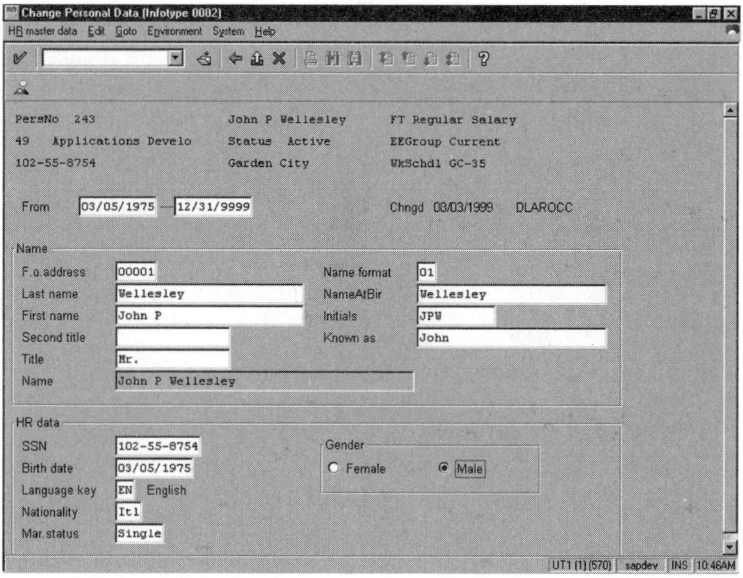

Figure 13-10 *More than 4,000 infotypes exist in the human resources module.*

Database PCH, because this database can refer to the PNP database. After entering a range of infotypes for your functional area, your functional areas screen will display all of the selected tables that store the data, in addition to a series of functional groups based on the infotypes. Functional areas for the Human Resources module already contain functional groups segregated by infotype (see Figure 13-11 for an example).

You will learn how to create a functional area using a Human Resources logical database in Chapter 15, "The Human Resources Information System."

Chapter Wrap-Up

An ABAP-trained system administrator manages your R/3 functional area. If you are not utilizing the full potential of the functional area, your ABAP Query reports are probably coming up short. In turn, your company might be compensating by having several reports custom written in ABAP code, bypassing the

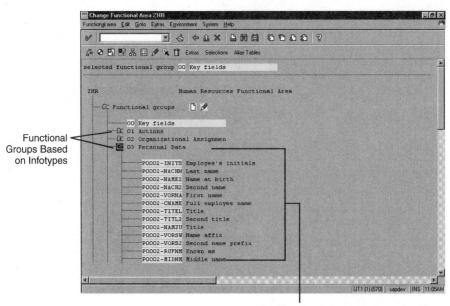

Functional Groups Based on Infotypes

This Functional Group corresponds with Infotype 0002, compare the fields listed to the Infotype shown in Figure 13-10.

Figure 13-11 *You can also create additional functional groups in a human resources functional area.*

ABAP Query tool altogether. This situation is to your company's disadvantage. Requiring an ABAP programmer to write several custom reports for users has three drawbacks. First, this situation places heavy reliance on the programmer and his or her skills. The company will spend much money in order to keep the programmer's services available for a task that could just as easily be transferred to the user, who has a well-designed functional area with which to work. Secondly, this situation prevents the user from being empowered with the skills to create his or her own reports and encourages the user's dependence on programmers for assistance with using the data. Last, custom reports might require additional customization in the future as needs and release versions change. All in all, creating good functional areas is a must for all R/3 implementations. The better designed the functional area, the more superior user reports will be.

14

ABAP Query Advanced Topic—Creating Extract (Interface) Files Using ABAP Query

In previous chapters, we became familiar with the reporting tools available in R/3. You learned how to create your own reports, and later we will explain how to work with the report output in other external applications. A time might come when it will be necessary for you to create extracts of your SAP information that will be provided to outside sources. An example of an extract in the Human Resources module is an extract of a payroll to be transmitted to a bank for the purposes of direct deposit. These types of files are referred to as interfaces or extracts in R/3.

These interfaces or extracts take your SAP R/3 data and save it as a file to be sent on disk, via EDI, via electronic transmission, etc., to a third party. There are two main cautions when working with downloaded data in R/3. The most important caution is that the security restrictions inherent in SAP no longer protect the document once it is outside the R/3 system. The second caution is that the downloaded data is no longer representing real-time R/3 data. The moment that the data leaves the SAP system, it becomes a frozen snapshot of that data.

Our Example

We will use the following specification for the example used in this section. The fields listed are from functional groups in the Z_FLIGHTDATA functional area, created in Chapter 9.

The Specification

The first step is obtaining a specification of how you want your data to appear. This specification is provided by the source that will be receiving the file. The specification is defined as a layout of how the source wants the data presented. Specifications, sometimes referred to as "flat-file layouts," include a list of fields, their format, and the positions that they should appear in on the report. Based on the specification, you can create an ABAP Query extract file to satisfy the output requirements (see Table 14.1).

Table 14.1 *Specifications for the extract file* `flightdata.txt`

Field Name	Start Position	End Position
Reservation Number	1	8
Airline Carrier ID	9	11
Flight Connection ID	12	15
Flight Date	16	25
Departure Airport	26	28

Field Name	Start Position	End Position
Destination Airport	29	31
Destination	32	47
From City	48	63

Creating an Extract Using the ABAP Query

The first step is to make sure that all of the requested fields in the specification are available in your functional area. Keep in mind that the functional area will contain fields that were modified as part of a lesson in Chapter 13. For example, the Booking Number field was renamed to the Reservation Number field. Next, you need to create the query. Follow the same steps for creating the query, as outlined in Chapter 10. As a hint, we have created this query already in Chapter 10. Refer to our example where we created the ZDL_FLIGHTS query. If available, make a copy of this query and use that one for this chapter. If you are using a copy, be sure to change the information entered on the Title, Format screen to reflect the new query. After creating a basic query of the data, execute the query to view its output screen. The format should be similar in format to Figure 14-1.

Screen 5—Basic List Line Structure

Upon query execution, the presentation of the data appears on the screen. If we downloaded the list to a file, it would not necessarily be in the positional format defined in the specification (and would not meet our needs). First, we need to check the field entry on the Basic List Line Structure screen (Screen 5). See Figure 14-2 to ensure that the sequence matches the specification. Also, be sure to unmark each of the three check boxes at the top of the Basic List Line Structure screen if selected (see Figure 14-2).

Screen 8—Field Output Options

Once the sequence is verified, you need to modify the positional information for the fields. This modification is done on the

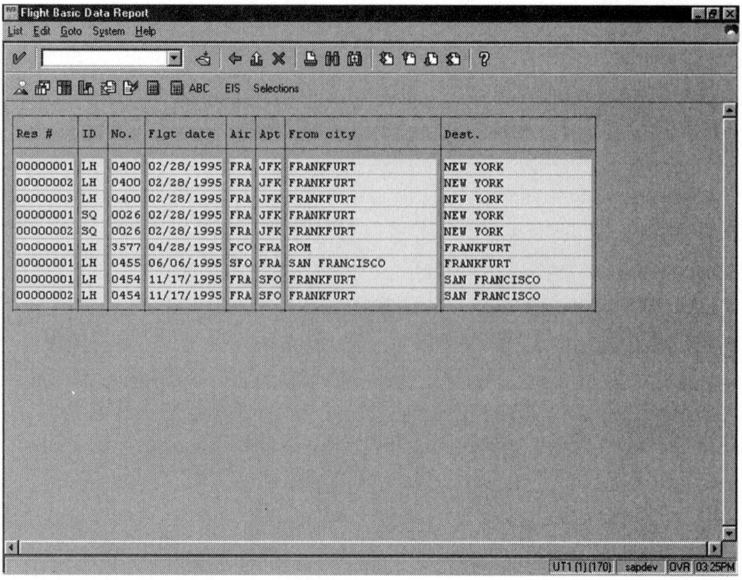

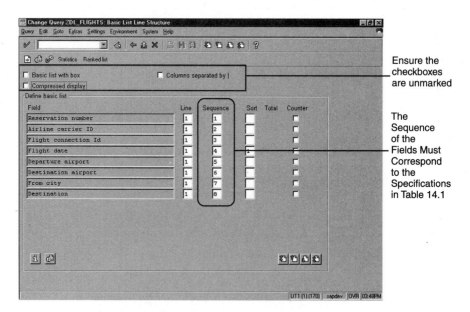

Figure 14-1 *The format of your query should appear similar to the one shown here, although the data within the query might be different.*

Figure 14-2 *The Basic List Line Structure screen defines the layout, format, and order in which the fields are presented on the List screen (Screen 7).*

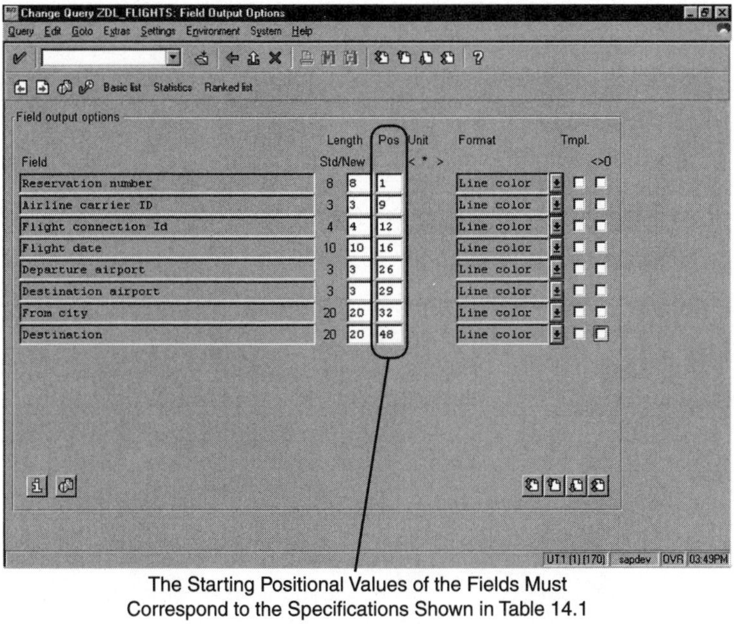

The Starting Positional Values of the Fields Must
Correspond to the Specifications Shown in Table 14.1

Figure 14-3 *If the Pos. field is left blank, the field will position itself behind the preceding field.*

Field Output Options screen (Screen 8) of the ABAP Query. Each field in the query is listed along with its width and a column to manually enter the starting position of the field in the output line. This information was supplied in the specification. Make the appropriate changes in the Pos. column for each field based on the specification in Table 14.1, as shown in Figure 14-3.

After making the necessary modifications to the Pos. column, execute the report to view the results (see Figure 14-4).

Screen 1—Title, Format Screen

Now that the output is as it should be (positionally), we need to create the file. This task can be done using the processing options on the Title, Format screen (Screen 1). Navigate to the Title, Format screen (Screen 1) of your query. On the bottom of Screen 1, further processing options are displayed. By default, the No Further Processing radio button is selected, which outputs the

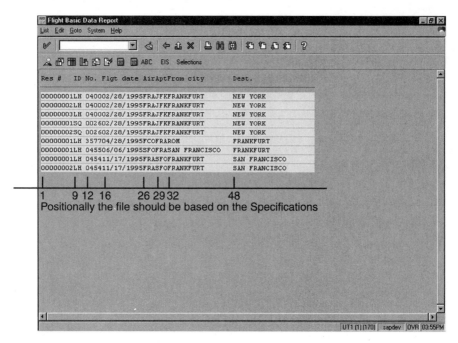

Figure 14-4 *The resulting view of the list might appear garbled and unfriendly when viewed in the ABAP Query, but it should be in the appropriate format.*

data onto a List screen (Screen 7). Change the selection to the Download to File radio button, and select the open folder Save button from the Standard toolbar (see Figure 14-5).

Screen 6—Selection Screen (Enter Parameter)

Select the Execute button from the Application toolbar on the Title, Format screen to proceed to the selection screen for the query. Because we changed the Further Processing option, when you select the Execute button on the selection screen, you will be prompted not with an output screen but with a parameter dialog box asking for the path, filename, and format for your output (see Figure 14-6).

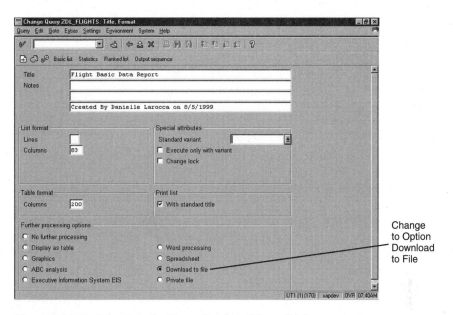

Figure 14-5 *Selecting the Download to File radio button passes the output to the download interface and stores it as a file.*

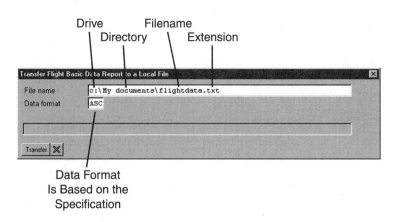

Figure 14-6 *The data format can be modified based on the information provided in the specification.*

After entering a path and filename for the output, select a data format for the output. Usually, the specification provided to you will instruct you on which data format to use. In our example, we are creating a standard text file, so we used an ASC format. The available formats are listed in Table 14.2.

Table 14.2 *R/3 data formats for downloading files*

Format	Description
ASC	ASCII format
BIN	Binary format
DBF	Database format
IBM	ASCII with IBM code-page conversion (DOS)
WK1	Spreadsheet format
DAT	ASCII data table with column tab

If you are unsure of which format to use for your file, try varying the format and viewing the results to see what works best for the particular extract file. Select the green check mark Enter key on the Transfer to a Local File dialog box, and a message will appear in your Status bar saying, "Bytes Transferred."

Verifying the Format of Your Output

Once the file is saved to a location on your computer, you should check the output against your specification. There are positional editing software applications available that can be used to do this task, or you can use the DOS editor that comes with Windows 95. The DOS editor is similar to a positional version of the Windows Notepad, which enables you to view the positional numbers of your data.

Using the DOS Editor for Positional Validation

Follow these instructions to view your new file using the DOS Editor to validate its positional accuracy:

1. Follow the menu path Start→Programs→MS_DOS Prompt to launch DOS.

2. At the first prompt you receive, type the word `edit` and hit Enter (see Figure 14-7).

3. An MS-DOS Prompt EDIT screen will appear. Use the menu path File→Open to open the query that you saved to your PC (see Figure 14-8).

4. After selecting your file, select the Open button. Your file will be presented in DOS Editor's window. ·

5. Using the arrow navigational keys on your keyboard, move through the data and watch the Col: number in the bottom right-hand side of the window change. This number corresponds to the position in the file (see Figure 14-9).

6. Compare the positions to your specifications, and return to the query to modify your output if necessary. Then, check your output again.

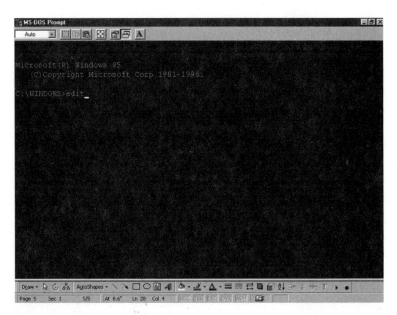

Figure 14-7 *The DOS Editor comes preinstalled with Windows 95 systems.*

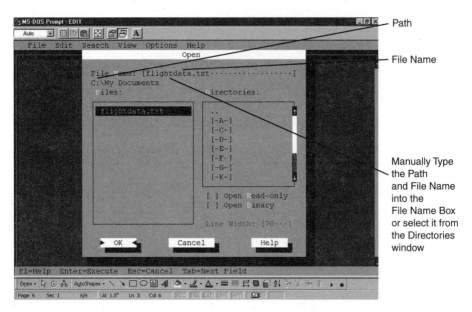

Figure 14-8 *Enter the path and filename used to save your file in ABAP Query.*

Figure 14-9 *Check the starting and ending position numbers of your file against the specification provided.*

Specifications that Include Constants

Sometimes extract files need to include constant values. These values might represent account or processing numbers. In either case, these values need to be included for each line item of data created in the file. This section explains how to create an extract file that includes constants, without having to perform any programming.

Our Example

For this next section, make a copy of the query used in the previous example. Be sure to modify its title and created-by date on the Title, Format screen (Screen 1).

The Specification

The specification in Table 14.3 is provided by the source that will be receiving the file. The fields listed are from functional groups in the Z_FLIGHTDATA functional area created in Chapter 9.

Table 14.3 *Specifications for the extract file* `flightdata2.txt`

Field Name	Value	Start Position	End Position
File Number	0001234	1	7
Reservation Number		8	15
Airline Carrier ID		16	18
Flight Connection ID		19	22
Flight Date		23	32
Departure Airport		33	35
Destination Airport		36	38

Table 14.3 *Specifications for the extract file* flightdata2.txt *(Continued)*

Field Name	Value	Start Position	End Position
Destination		39	53
From City		54	68
Account Designator	WELLESLEY	69	77

Adding Constants to a Query

If this extract were being created by an ABAP programmer, code would need to be written that would retrieve the necessary data from the database and insert the constant values where necessary. Because we are creating the extract using the ABAP Query tool (and because we are assuming that you do not have any ABAP programming skills), we are going to trick the ABAP query into providing us with the data we need. For starters, we need to add two dummy fields to our query that we will use as the file number (0001234) and the account designator (WELLESLEY) fields that will store the constant values.

Screen 3—Field Selection

In Chapter 11, we took a look at modifying our existing queries. Here we will put those skills to work by modifying this existing query. Start by adding two more fields to the query. Additional fields can be added using the Field Selection screen (Screen 3). Because we will place our own values (the constants) into these fields, it does not matter which two fields are used. For our example, we will add the Customer Number and the Business/Private Customer fields from the flight bookings functional group (see Figure 14-10). After adding the fields, select the Save button on the Standard toolbar.

Screen 5—Basic List Line Structure

Now that we have added two new fields, we need to modify the layout and sequence in which these fields are displayed in the

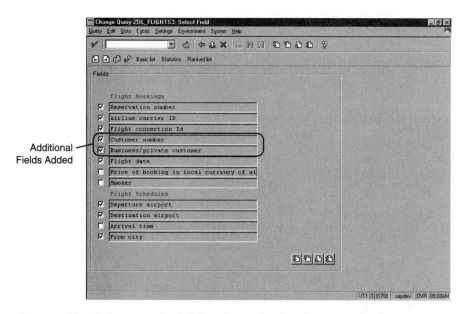

Figure 14-10 *Because the fields will not display their actual values, any fields can be selected for use as constants.*

report. This characteristic is modified on the Basic List Line Structure screen (Screen 5), which can be accessed by selecting the Basic List button on the Application toolbar. Change the sequence of the fields to correspond to the specification provided. In our example, we will use the Business/Private Customer field as the File Number field and the Customer Number field as the Account Designator field from the specification. Make the appropriate sequence specifications so that the numbers match up to the sequence shown in the specification (see Figure 14-11). After making the necessary modifications, select the Save button on the Standard toolbar.

Screen 8—Field Output Options

Earlier in the chapter, we took a look at the Field Output options screen that enables us to specify the positional assignment of our fields. As we did earlier in the chapter, modify the Pos. column with the starting numbers of the fields provided in the specification—keeping in mind what the two dummy fields represent (see Figure 14-12).

Order of Fields
Must Match
Specification
in Table 14.3

Being Used
for the File
Number Constant

Being Used
for the Account
Designator
Constant

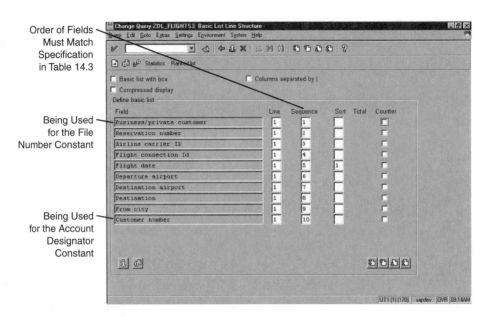

Figure 14-11 *The order of the fields must match the order in the specification. Be sure to check your sequence specifications.*

Dummy Field

Dummy Field

Enter Starting
Number From
Specification
in Table 14.3
From Here

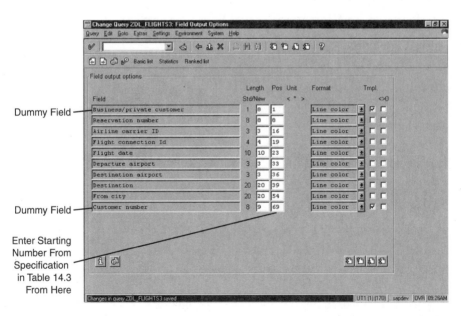

Figure 14-12 *The width and position numbers of the fields must match the layout provided in the specification.*

Back in Chapter 12, we learned how to use the Tmpl. (template) check box listed to the right of the fields to add text before the output of our data. We will use the template function to fill in our constants and use the Pos. (position) column-width selection to make only that text appear in the box. This trick will display the data entered as the template as the only text in the field. If you are still confused, then read on—because this process will make more sense as we walk through it. Mark the Tmpl. (template) check box for our two constant dummy fields (see Figure 14-12). Select the white arrow Next Screen button to proceed to the Field Templates screen, where we will enter our constants.

Screen 9—Field Templates

You might recall from Chapter 12 that we used this field earlier to output a word before our data. In one of the examples, we added the text "Date" before the output of our data—so that in our output, each date field was proceeded by the text "Date" (refer to Figure 12-16 in Chapter 12). On the Field Templates screen, enter the constants for each of the fields (see Figure 14-13). Select the open folder Save button on the Standard toolbar.

Screen 8—Field Output Options

The last task we need to do is modify the column widths of our two dummy fields to display only the value of the constant (see Figure 14-14).

Screen 6—Selection Screen

Select the Execute button from the Application toolbar on the Field Templates screen to proceed to the selection screen for the query. To preview the output in ABAP Query, be sure to change the further processing option at the bottom of the selection screen to "No further processing." When you select the Execute button on the selection screen, preview your output to see how the constants appear in lieu of the field data for the Business/Private Customer field (file number in the specification) and for the Customer Number (account designator in the specification). Also make sure that all other fields appear in their appropriate positions (see Figure 14-15).

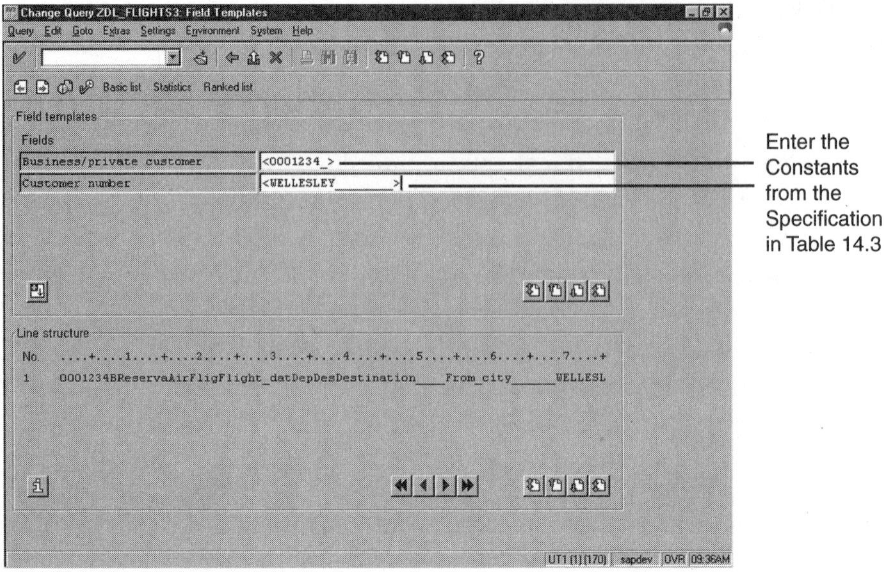

Figure 14-13 *We are using the Template field to enter the value of our constant, and we will adjust the width of the field so that only the constant is displayed.*

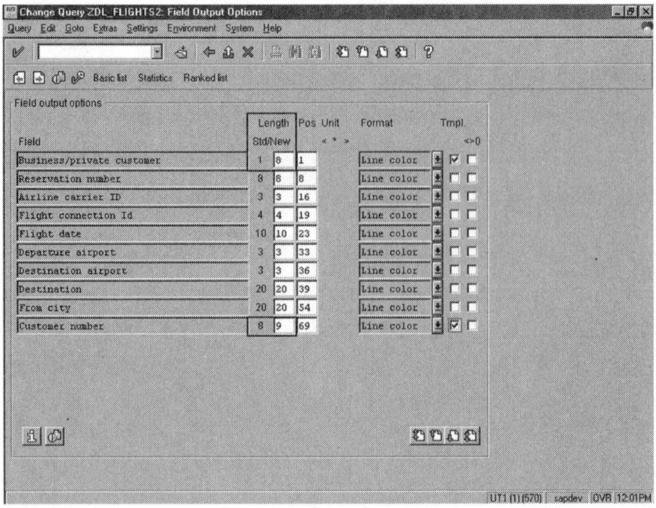

Figure 14-14 *The Business/Private Customer field was enlarged to eight positions to fit the 0001234 file number, and the Customer Number field was enlarged to nine positions to fit the WELLESLEY account designator.*

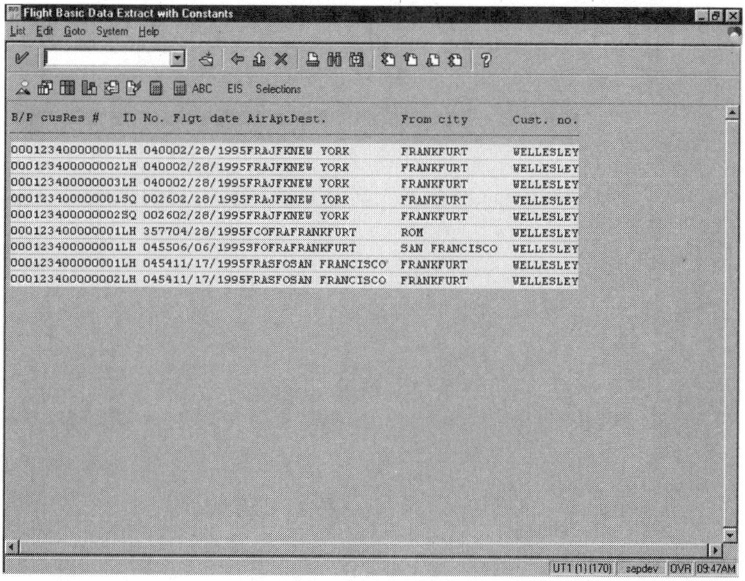

Figure 14-15 *The resulting view of the list might appear garbled and unfriendly when viewed in ABAP Query, but the view should be in the appropriate format.*

Use the method outlined earlier in the chapter for verifying the positional data using the DOS Editor tool, and then change the Further Processing option back to "Download to file." The creation of an extract file that includes constants is complete.

Chapter Wrap-Up

Hopefully, you were happy to learn that it does not require the skills of an ABAP programmer to create extract fields in R/3. Using ABAP Query, you can create custom extracts (including the use of constants) in several different formats. The skills learned in this chapter should empower you to think of other ways in which the conventional methods of using ABAP Query can be tricked ever so slightly. This knowledge will help you produce the output you need in R/3.

15

The Human Resources
Information System

The R/3 Human Resources module is unique
compared to the other R/3 modules, because
the Human Resources module uses infotypes
for the presentation of data in R/3.

Infotypes

The master data for the Human Resources system is displayed to the user in the form of infotypes. Each infotype logically segregates a portion of the Human Resources information. Sample infotypes include Personal Data (0002), which stores an employee's name, birth date, gender, etc., or basic pay (0008), which stores an employee's annual salary, pay-scale group, level, grade, etc. Table 15.1 gives a description of some of the infotypes in the R/3 Human Resources module.

Table 15.1 *Sample infotypes from the R/3 Human Resources module*

0000 Actions	0161 IRS Limits USA
0001 Organizational Assignment	0162 Ins. Y.E.T.A. Data JP
0002 Personal Data	0165 Deduction Limits
0003 Payroll Status	0167 Health Plans
0004 Challenge	0168 Insurance Plans
0005 Leave Entitlement	0169 Savings Plans
0006 Addresses	0170 Spending Accounts
0007 Planned Working Time	0171 Gen. Benefits Data
0008 Basic Pay	0172 Spending account payments
0009 Bank Details	0177 Registration of Country of Birth NL
0010 Capital Formation	0179 Tax SG
0011 Ext. Bank Transfers	0181 Additional Funds SG
0012 Fiscal Data D	0182 Alternat. Names Asia
0013 Social Insurance D	0183 Awards
0014 Recur. Payments/Deds.	0184 Resume Texts

0015 Additional Payments	0185 ID Data
0016 Contract Elements	0186 CPF
0017 Travel Privileges	0188 Tax Australia
0019 Monitoring of Dates	0189 C.Pay: Funds Procedure
0020 DEUEV	0190 C.Pay: Previous ER
0021 Family/Related Person	0191 C.Pay: Expenses
0022 Education	0192 C.Pay: Assignment
0023 Other/Previous ERs	0194 Garnishment Document
0024 Qualifications	0195 Garnishment Order
0025 Appraisals	0196 Employees Provident Fund
0026 Company Insurance	0197 Employees' Social Security
0027 Cost Distribution	0198 Schedular Deduction Tax
0028 Int. Medical Service	0199 Addl. tax deduction
0029 Workers' Compensation	0200 Garnishments DK
0030 Powers of Attorney	0204 DA/DS Statistics DK
0031 Reference Pers. Nos.	0207 Residence Tax Area
0032 Internal Control	0208 Work Tax Area
0033 Statistics	0209 Unemployment State
0034 Corporate Function	0210 Withh. Info. W4/W5 US
0035 Company Instructions	0211 COBRA
0036 Social Insurance CH	0212 COBRA Health Plans
0037 Insurance	0213 additional family info
0038 Fiscal Data CH	0215 CP: Transaction Data
0039 Add. Org. Assign. CH	0216 Garnish. Adjustment

Table 15.1 *Sample infotypes from the R/3 Human Resources module (Continued)*

0040 Objects on Loan	0217 Code INSEE F
0041 Date Specifications	0218 Pensioner Fund No. F
0042 Fiscal Data A	0219 Ext. Organizations
0043 Family Allowance A	0220 Superannuation Aust.
0044 Social Insurance A	0221 Manual Check
0045 Company Loans	0222 Company Cars GB
0046 Company Pension Fund	0224 Canadian Taxation
0048 Residence Status	0225 Comp. Car Unavail. GB
0049 Red. Hrs/Bad Weather	0227 TFN Australia
0050 Time Recording Info.	0230 Supp. to P0008 PSG
0051 ASB/SPI Data	0231 Supp. to P0001 PSG
0052 Wage Maintenance	0232 Child Allowance D
0053 Company Pension	0233 Social Economic Bal.
0054 Works Councils	0234 Add. Withh. Info. US
0055 Previous Employer A	0235 Other Taxes US
0056 Sickness Certs. A	0236 Credit Plans
0057 Membership Fees	0237 Supp. to P0052 PSG
0058 Commuter Rate A	0241 Tax Data Indonesia
0059 Social Insurance NL	0242 Jamsostek Insurance Indonesia
0060 Fiscal Data NL	0261 Loading Leave Aust.
0061 Social Insurance E	0264 Family NL
0062 Fiscal Data E	0265 Special Regulations
0063 Social Ins. Funds NL	0266 Supp. to P0027 PSG
0064 Social Insurance F	0267 One Time Pay. Off-Cy.

0065 Tax Data GB	0268 Company Loans JP
0066 Garnishment Order CA	0269 ADP File Number
0067 Garnishment Debt CA	0270 COBRA Payments
0068 Garnishment Adjustment CA	0272 Garnishment (F)
0069 National Ins. GB	0273 Taxes—SE
0070 Court Orders GB	0274 Pension Insurances—SE
0071 Pension Funds GB	0275 Garnishments—SE
0072 Fiscal Data DK	0276 OPIS—SE
0073 Private Pension DK	0277 Exceptions—SE
0074 Leave Processing DK	0278 Basic data PF (CH)
0075 ATP Pension DK	0279 Individual Values PF (CH)
0076 Worker's Comp. NA	0280 Contractual Elements
0077 Additional Pers. Data	0281 Beneficial Loans
0078 Loan Payments	0283 Archived Objects
0079 SI Additional Ins. D	0288 Family CH
0080 Maternity Protection/ Parental Leave	0302 Additional Actions
0081 Military Service	0303 Premium Reduction NL
0082 Additional Abs. Data	0304 Addl. Basic Pay
0083 Leave Compensation	0309 IRD Nbr New Zealand
0084 SSP Control GB	0310 Superannuation NZ
0085 SSP SSP(1)L Form Data GB	0311 Leave Balance Adj
0086 SSP/SMP Exclusions GB	0312 Leave History Adj
0088 SMP Record GB	0313 Tax New Zealand

Table 15.1 *Sample infotypes from the R/3 Human Resources module (Continued)*

0090 Additional Income E	0315 Time Sheet Defaults
0092 Seniority E	0317 Spec. Provisions NL
0093 Previous Employers D	0318 Family view Indonesia
0094 Residence Status	0319 Private Insurances Indonesia
0098 Profit Sharing F	0341 Start of DEUEV
0100 Social Insurance B	0352 Additional Family Information (TW)
0101 Fiscal Data B	0353 Income Tax (TW)
0102 Grievances NA	0354 Labor Insurance (TW)
0103 Bond Purchases	0355 National Health Insurance (TW)
0104 Bond Denominations	0356 Empl. Stab. Fund (TW)
0105 Communication	0357 Saving Plan (TW)
0106 Family/Rel. Person B	0358 EE Welfare Fund (TW)
0107 Working Time B	0362 Membership view Indonesia
0108 Personal Data B	0367 SI Notification Supplements A
0109 Contract Elements B	0369 Social security data
0110 Pensions NL	0370 INFONAVIT loan
0111 Garnishmt/Cession D	0371 Other Employment Wages
0112 Garnishment Claim D	0373 Loan Repayment JP
0113 Garnish. Interest D	0374 General Eligibility
0114 Garnishment Amount D	0375 HCE Information

0115 Garnishment Wages D	0376 Medical Service Data
0116 Garn. Transfer D	0377 Miscellaneous Plans
0117 Garn. Compensation D	0378 Event: permissions
0118 Child Allowance D	0380 Compensation History
0119 Child Allowance Amount D	0381 Compensation: employee eligibility
0120 Company Pension CH	0382 Compensation stock plan
0121 RefPerNo Priority	0388 Union due Ded. JP
0122 CA Bonus	0395 External Org. assignment
0125 Garnishment B	0396 Expatriate attributes
0126 Supplem. Pension D	0402 Payroll Results
0127 Commuter Traffic NL	0403 Payroll Results
0128 Notifications	0404 Military Service (TW)
0130 Test Procedures	0405 Absence Event
0131 Garnishment/Cession	0408 CBS NL
0132 Garnishment Claim A	0409 External Agencies NL
0133 Garn. Interest A	0412 Family data view for SG
0134 Garnishment Amount A	0416 Time Quota Compensation
0135 Spec. Garn. Cond. A	0467 Addt'l SI Notif.Data f.Comp.Agts A
0136 Garn. Transfer A	0506 Tip Indicators
0137 Garn. Compensation A	0512 Exemption Certificate: Part-Time EE
0138 Family/Rel. Person B	0546 Termination Data
0139 EE's Applicant No.	0547 BIK(TAX) Infotype for Malaysia
0140 SI Basic Data JP	0900 Sales Data

Table 15.1 *Sample infotypes from the R/3 Human Resources module (Continued)*

0141 SI Premium Data JP	0901 Purchasing Data
0142 Residence Tax JP	2001 Absences
0143 Life Ins. Ded. JP	2002 Attendances
0144 PropertyAccum.Sav. JP	2003 Substitutions
0145 Personnel Tax Sta. JP	2004 Availability
0146 Y.E.A. Data JP	2005 Overtime
0147 Pers. Appraisals JP	2006 Absence Quotas
0148 Family JP	2007 Attendance Quotas
0149 Taxes SA	2010 EE Remuneration Info
0150 Social Insurance SA	2011 Time Events
0151 External Ins. SA	2012 Time Transfer Specifications

There are more than 4,000 infotypes in the R/3 Human Resources module. A sample infotype from the Human Resources module is infotype 0077 (Additional Personal Data), as shown in Figure 15-1.

Because of this unique aspect of the Human Resources module, it contains a unique tool that can be used for reporting in R/3.

The Human Resources Information System

In R/3, each of the modules contains an information system used for reporting. The most unique and newest information system is in the Human Resources module. The Human Resources Information System, referred to as HRIS, contains four reporting and query components—each offering special functions to satisfy specific reporting requirements in R/3. The four components of the HRIS are listed as follows, and a picture of the main screen of the HRIS is shown in Figure 15-2:

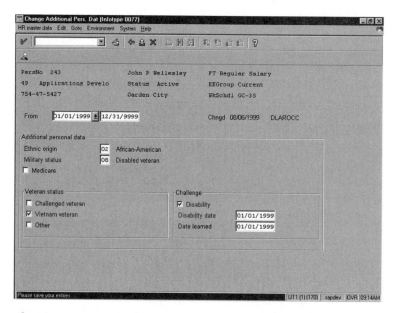

Figure 15-1 *Each infotype in the Human Resources module stores distinct information regarding an employee.*

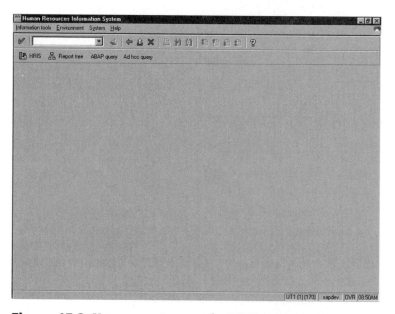

Figure 15-2 *You can navigate to the HRIS using transaction code* /nPIMN *or by using the menu path Human resources→ Information system.*

- Ad-Hoc Query

- ABAP Query

- Report Tree

- HRIS

Ad-Hoc Query

The Ad-Hoc Query is a tool designed with the same philosophy as the ABAP Query tool discussed earlier in several chapters of this book. The Ad-Hoc Query enables you to create queries using user groups, functional areas, and functional groups. The focus of the Ad-Hoc Query, however, is more on posing questions to the database than on reporting. We take a look at the Ad-Hoc Query next in Chapter 16, "Ad-Hoc Query Reporting Tool (Human Resources Module)," where you will see the distinction between this tool and the ABAP Query.

ABAP Query

The ABAP Query is a powerful tool that you can use to create your own SAP reports without any programming experience whatsoever. At this point, you are probably already an expert in working with ABAP Query, which is a useful tool for reporting in the Human Resources module. ABAP Query reporting in the Human Resources module also has one distinct advantage: No functional groups need to be created in a Human Resources functional area, because they are already created based on the infotypes.

Report Tree

Report trees were discussed in Chapter 7. The R/3 General Report Selection Trees contain a node for Human Resources reports. Selecting the Report Tree button from the HRIS provides you with a view of the report tree, displaying only the Human Resources reports (see Figure 15-3).

Standard Reports in the R/3 Human Resources Module

A sample of approximately 500 available reports in the Human Resources module are listed in Table 15.2.

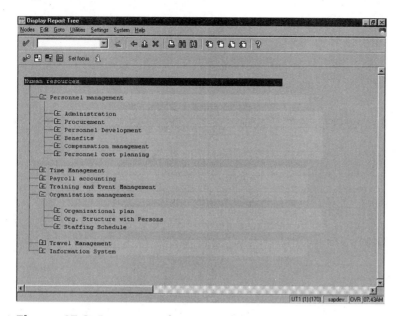

Figure 15-3 *Reports can be executed from a report tree by double-clicking the report name.*

Table 15.2 *Sample Human Resources reports*

Al Eight Prebookings Pertaining to an Attendee	Group Attendee Bookings
AAP: Movement Analysis Report USA	Group Value for Appraisal Evaluation
AAP: Turnover Analysis Report USA	Hard Copy of Room Reservations Data Screen
AAP: Workforce Distribution Report USA	Head Count per Company Code/Plant I Cost Center Person Subgroup
Absences per Employee	History of Appraisal Point Total
Absences per Organizational Unit	HR—Generate Reconciliation Report

Table 15.2 *Sample Human Resources reports (Continued)*

Act Promoting Proportional Labor Participation of Foreigners	HR System Documentation
Add Directory for Payroll Accounting Results (Cluster Rd)	HR Time—Time Evaluation
Address List of Employees (Japan)	HR—Na: OSHA—101 Report
Administration of HR Plan Scenarios	HR—Na: OSHA—200 Report
Analysis of Customizing for Planning Table	HR: Connection to Third-Party Payroll—Online Documentation
Anniversaries	HR: Loan Account for Employer Loans
Annual Compensation Limit for Health Insurance: Evaluation of Infotypes	HR: OED: Batch Input for Christmas Bonus
Annual Municipal Payroll Tax—Explanation	Import of Test Data from T535q
Annual Payment Limit for HI: Evaluation of Accounting Results Annual Planning	Income Statistics for Employers' Association in the Chemical Industry
Applicant Selection	Income Statistics for Employers' Association in the Metal Industry
Applicant Statistics	Income Tax Return—Model July 1994
Application from Employee Income Tax and Family Dependent Tax	Income-Related Expenses Statement

Appraisals	Infotype Statistics
Approval of Trips	Infotype and Subtypes
Attendance and Sales Statistics	Insert Personnel Qualifications
Attendance Statistics	Insurance Deduction Application Form
Attendee Appraisals	Interface for HR Travel Expense→Financial Accounting Fl
Attendee List	Interface Payroll Accounting/Accounting
Attendee's Qualifications	Internal Cost Allocation for Business Events
Attendees to be Rebooked	Internal Employee List
Attendee's Training History	Job and/or Position Description
Authorities and Resources	Job Assignment List
Authorization Conversions (Personnel Area)	Job Assignment Notice
Automatic Pay Increase—Pay Scale Level Update	Job Assignment Notice (Hiring)
Automatic Special Payments: Recalculation Indicators	Job Description
Available Reserved Resources	Job Index
Bank Connections for Payments to Employees	Key Plan for Education Types (Poo22)
Bank Details	Label Printout with Country-Specific Address Editing
Batch Input for Creating New Tax Records at Beginning of Year	Labor Strength Statistics Report

Table 15.2 *Sample Human Resources reports (Continued)*

Batch Input for Retrieval of Confirmations	Leave and Quota Deduction Check
Batch Input Session for Sickness Certificates (A)	Leave Obligation Report
Batch Input to Incentive Wages	Leave Reconciliation Lists (Leave Overview)
Batch Input: Annual Leave	Letter to Employee
Benefit Enrollment (Groups)	Letter to Health Insurer Concerning Changes to Pensions/Related Benefits
Benefits—Cost Summary	Life/Non-Life Insurance Deduction List (Payroll)
Benefits Administration: Change of Benefit Election	List All Possible Tables (Generically)
Benefits Administration: Eligibility—Directory	List Data Medium Exchange for Health Insurance Funds
Benefits Administration: Participant Date Directory	List Dates for Pay Period/ Subunit
Benefits Administration: Premium Reports Health Plans	List of All HR Terms Objects
Benefits Administration: Premium Reports— Insurance Plans	List of Alternative Qualifications
Benefits Administration: Premium Reports— Savings Plans	List of Applicants by Actions
Benefits Administration: Vesting Reports for Savings	List of Applicants by Event

Benefits Administration: Premium Reports— Spending Accounts	List of Applicants by Name
Benefits Dependents List	List of Applications
Birthday List	List of Assignment Notice (Hiring)
Bonus and Other Payments for Health Insurance	List of Cancellations
Booking for Group Attendee	List of Employees Who Lose Qualification for Health Insurance at Age 65
Bookings of Attendee	List of Employees (Employee Entry and Leaving, or the Employee Directory)
Bookings Pertaining to an Attendee	List of Employees (Sorted by Entered Year)
Business Event Appraisals	List of Employees (Sorted by Job)
Business Event Brochure	List of Employees (Sorted by Personal Group and Organization)
Business Event Cost Calculation and Cost Transfer to Company	List of Employees (Sorted by Personal Group and Title)
Business Event Dates	List of Employees Who Are Exempt from Employment Insurance
Business Event Demand	List of Liable Amount for Fixed Liable Insurance Fee
Business Event Hierarchy by Group and Type	List of Maternity Data

Table 15.2 *Sample Human Resources reports (Continued)*

Business Event Hierarchy Sorted by Group and Type	List of Mutual Indemnity Societies (Wage Statement)
Business Event Prices	List of Permanent and Tax Residence (for Check)
Business Event Schedule	List of Planned Actions for Personnel Officer
Calculate Business Event Prices and Transfer to Infotype 1021, "Price"	List of Retirees
Calculate Present Value: Employee Loans with Lowest Interest Rates	List of Tax Cards Not Submitted
Canadian EEA Report	List of Vacancy Assignments
Cancellation List per Attendee	List Personnel Calculation Rules
Cancellation List per Business Event	Listing of Customizing Tables
Capital Formation Overview	Load State Tax Authorities Into Reciprocity Table
Car Search List Catalog	Load Tax Areas and Tax Authorities per Tax Area
Change Attributes for Schemas and Cycles	Load Tax Authorities into SSI Mapping Table
Change Authorization Groups	Load Tax Types and Tax Types per Tax Authority
Change of Basic Pay List	Load ZIP Codes for Tax Areas
Change of General Benefits Data	Logged Changes in Infotype Data
Change of Pay Scale Assignment List	Maintain Job Description

Change of Title List	Maintain Log
Character of Single Tasks	Maintain Position Description
Character of Tasks in Organizational Structure	Maintain Vacancy Assignments
Check Cost Center Assignment	Maintain Wage Types According to Assignments to Human Resources Creditors
Check Cycles (Check Report)	Maintaining Standard Accounts for Travel Expense Accounting
Check for Payday on Holiday or Weekend	Master Data Headers
COBRA Reports	Material Requirements per Business Event
Compa-Ratio Analysis	Messages for the Supplementary Pension Fund
Compare BSI Mapping Table with BSI Tax Authority Table	Model Blank Letter to Employees
Compare Cycles	Model for Standard Letter
Compare Schemas	Model Report for Travel Expense Statistics
Comparison of Text Elements	Module for Tax Calculation
Compensation of Admin. Batch Input	Name, Address, Salary (in Microsoft Office)
Compensation Administration	New Valuation of Absence Records Using Batch Input
Compensation Administration—Call Up Matrix	New Year Tax Update Utility— Infotype 0224 (Canada)

Table 15.2 *Sample Human Resources reports (Continued)*

Compensation Administration—Matrix	NIC Metal and Engineering Industries Education and Training Fund Levy Return
Compensation Administration—Matrix List	Non-Lapsable Company Pension Entitlement
Connection with Word-Processing System	Notification of Pay Rate Increases
Contribution Statement for Supplementary Benefits	Notifications of Sickness
Conversion of Compensation Administration	Off-Cycle Batch Processes—Start Process
Conversion of Health Insurance Fund Tables for Validation Tables Creation	Off-Cycle Payroll—Print Payroll Results
Conversion of Health Insurance Fund Tables for Nursing Insurance	Organigram with Persons
Copy Custom Tax Authorities	Organigram without Persons (Position-to-Position Reporting Structure without Persons)
Copy Employee Groups	Organization of Interface Results
Copy Formulas for Employee Overrides	Organizational Structure
Copy Program for Experience Rates	Organizational Structure with Persons
Copy Tax Companies	Organizational Structure with Positions
Cost Element Reports: Enter Selection Criteria	Organizational Structure with Work Centers

Cost Element Reports: Execute Selection; Generate Temporary Set	Output Business-Event Notifications
Country Version—Deletion Program	Overview of Absence and Attendance Data
Create "Interests and Preference" for Employees	Overview of Daily Work Schedules
Create a Number Range for Terms Objects from Human Resources	Overview of Employer Loans
Create and Edit Career Model	Overview of Trips
Create Copy of Wage Type(s)	Overview of Trips with Fine Selection
Create Data Carrier for Labor Union IGM	Overview: Income Threshold (Health Insurance Fund)
Create Number Range for Features	Pay Date Calendar Display
Cumulated Time Evaluation Results: Time Balances/ Wage Types	Pay Increase Due to Personnel Promotion (Japan)
Current and Annual Income Survey for Trade and Commerce	Pay Scale Increase (Indirect and Direct Wage Types) with Batch Input
Daily Work Schedule	Pay Scale Increase for Indirectly Valued Wage Types
Data Medium Exchange (Travel Expenses)	Pay Scale Reclassification by Age Or Seniority with Batch Input
Data Medium Exchange: Travel Expense Accounting	Payment Report (Total Number of Payments); Japan

Table 15.2 *Sample Human Resources reports (Continued)*

Data Medium Exchange: Travel Expense Accounting (USA)	Payments and Deductions
Data Selection	Payroll Accounting with Company Tax Office
Data Selection for Personnel Cost Planning	Payroll Accounts
Date Monitoring	Payroll Calendar
Day Programs and Time Models	Payroll Driver (USA)
Defaults for Pay Scale Reclassification	Payroll Journal (Canada)
Delete an Existing Planning Group	Payroll Journal (USA)
Delete Off-Cycle Batch Entries	Payroll Master Data Listing
Delete/Restore Travel Accounting Areas	Payroll Overtime Report
Details of Trip	Payroll Period-End Totals
Directory of Personnel Calculation Rules	Payroll Reconciliation
Display/Change/Delete/ Firmly Book Room Reservation	Payroll Results for Cluster Rx
Display an Existing Planning Group	Payroll Statement Report— Remuneration Statement (Canada)
Display and Maintain Infotypes	PD Database Statistics

Display and/or Print List of Attendees for Room Reservation	PD Order List
Display and/or Print Name Tags for Attendees	DC Time Management—PAttendance Check
Display Attendance List	POC Time Management—Time Statement Forms
Display Attendance List per Organizational Unit	Pensionable and Insurable Earnings Review Report (Canada)
Display Career Model Structure	Personal Work Schedule
Display Employee's "Interests and Preferences"	Personnel Appraisal List (Japan)
Display Infotypes for an Object	Personnel History List (All Events); Japan
Display Infotypes with Data Dictionary Structures	Personnel History List (Org./Position/Job); Japan
Display Log of Report Starts	Personnel Master Data Listing
Display Lunch of Kitchen Facility	Personnel Master Data Sheet A Sheet (for Employees)
Display of Organizational Assignment	Personnel Number Selection for Fast Data Entry (Japan)
Display of Qualifications Catalogue (T77qa and T77qb)	Personnel Number Selection for Fast Data Entry
Display Organizational Assignment for Persons	Personnel Record List
Display Pay Scale Groups	Persons with Disability—Overview

Table 15.2 *Sample Human Resources reports (Continued)*

Display PC Cluster: Personal Calendar	Plan Business Event
Display PD Database	Planned Labor Costs
Display Personal Timetable	Position Description
Display Personal Shift Plan	Prebookings per Attendee
Display Room Reservation Data for Rmail Processing	Prebookings per Business Event Type
Display Room Reservation	Prebookings Pertaining to an Attendee
Display Room Reservation of Attendee	Preliminary Program—Data Medium Exchange for Several Payment Runs; France Only
Display Room Reservation Pertaining to an Organizer	Preliminary Program—Data Medium Exchange for Several Payment Runs
Display Room to be Supplied by Kitchen Facility	Preliminary Program—Data Medium Exchange for Several Payment Runs; Denmark
Display Short and Long-Term Documents from Infotype Log	Preprogramming Data Medium Exchange (E-Version) for Separate Payment Run
Display Staff Functions	Prerequisites for Attendance
Display Target Requirement in Daily Overview	Preselection of Business Event Group and Type
Display Target Requirement in Weekly Overview Display Time Balances	Print Notifications (Layout Set)
Documentation Conversion Form Osys→Hypertext	Print Program for Sickness Certificates

Employees by Nationalities	Printing of Reports for the Supplementary Pension Fund
Employees by Salary, Seniority, and Organizational Unit (Total and Average Salaries According to Seniority)	Printout of Loan Results
Employees Sorted by Employee Groups and Subgroups	Profile Matchup Persons→ Position/Job
Employees Sorted by Pay Level (Employee Numbers and Percentages by Pay Scale Groups)	Project Interest Calculation
Employees who have Power of Attorney	Promotion Notice (Japan)
Download Absence Reasons to Dass	Qualification Profiles for Applicants
Download Human Resources Mini-Master Record to SAP-Dass	Qualifications and Tasks
Download Mini-Master to Sequential File	Recalculate Cumulations for Group and Individual Incentive Wages
Edit Payroll Results (USA)/ Payroll Statement Report/ Remuneration Statement	Recalculate Cumulations for Individual Incentive Wages
Edit Position Requirements	Reclassification In Incentive Wages
Education/Further Training of Employees	Recurring Benefits/Deductions: Link Between IT 001 4 and IT 001 5 via T588z

Table 15.2 *Sample Human Resources reports (Continued)*

Eligibility Change	Recurring Tasks: Complete Actions After Data Transfer
Eeo-1 (Equal Opportunity) Report USA	Recurring Tasks: Complete Actions After Printout
Employee Who Has Social and Employment Insurance	Recurring Tasks: Direct Transfer of Applicant Data
Employee Absences	Recurring Tasks: Print Letters (SAPscript)
Employee Data as Mail Merge Fields in Microsoft Word	Recurring Tasks: Print Letters (Winword)
Employee Demographics	Recurring Tasks: Transfer Applicant Data to Master Data File
Employee Entries/ Withdrawals	Reevaluate (Day Programs)
Employee History Report	Reference Personnel Numbers
Employee List	Relate Positions to Organizational Units
Employees According to Seniority and Age	Relationship Display
Employees and Their Family Members (Family Members)	Remuneration Statements
Employees and Their Family Members	Reorganization for Cluster B2-Time Evaluation Results
End-of-Year Report Driver/ Interface	String Search in Reports
End-of-Year Reporting: Add Subtotals and Append to Export File	Structure of Leave Deduction Cluster PC—Leave and Quota Deduction

End-of-Year Reporting: Append End of Data to Export File	Submit Report for Mail Processing
End-of-Year Reporting: Exit Include	Suggestion List for Advancement of Case Groups; Germany Only
Environment Analyzer: Function, Operations, Schemas, and Cycles	Suitable Evaluation Paths
Err List of Addresses of Employees	Summarized Form 1 for Travel Expense Accounting
Establish Position Hierarchy	Summarized Form 2 for Travel Expense Accounting
Establish Retroactive Accounting Date by Retroactive Elimination of a Public Holiday	Supply Third-Party Payroll Accounting System
Evaluation Letter for Child Allowance Bonus	Survey of Employment Payrolls and Hours (Canada)
Evaluation of Appraisals	Survey of Employment Payrolls and Learning Institution (Canada)
Evaluation of Garnishment Results	Statistics; Germany Only
Evaluation of Job Advertisement	Table Fields from Data Dictionary
Evaluation of Recruitment Instrument	Task Catalog
Evaluation of Vacancies	Task Description
Example of Report Structure for Evaluation of Applicant Data	Task Description for Jobs

Table 15.2 *Sample Human Resources reports (Continued)*

Existing Jobs	Task Description for Positions
Existing Objects	Task (Activity) Profile for Positions Along Organizational Structure
Existing Organizational Units	Tax Form Generator (Filing of Tax Interface . . .)
Existing Positions	Tax Form Pd7a
Existing Tasks	Tax Infotype Summary
Existing Work Centers	Tax Reconciliation
Explode Schemas and Personnel Calculation Rules	Tax Statement (Canada)
Extend Positions	Tax Type Statement (US)
External Employee List	Telephone Directory
External Routines for Loans	Test Number Procedure of the Supplementary Pension Funds
Feature Structure	Time Accounts
Features and Their Subfeatures and Predecessors	Time Management: Error Processing
Features Directory	Time Recording Overview List
Firmly Book/Cancel/Lock/ Unlock Business Event	Time Spent in Each Pay Scale Area/Type/C-Group/Level
Flexible Employee Data Reporting	Time Spent in Pay Scale Group (Japan)
Follow-Up Business Event	Time-Related Statistical Evaluations for Verified Capital
Formation Contracts	Transaction Overview
Formulas for Employee Overrides	Transfer Acknowledgment

Frequency of Attendance and Absences	Transfer Reconciliation Report
Function Library: Generated Test Report	Transfer Withholdings for Third Parties
Further HR-PD Selection Criteria (Further Selection Criteria)	Travel Expense Evaluation by Periods (Trip Cost Reporting by Periods)
Further Training Plan for Persons	Travel Expense Accounting: Create Batch Input Session for Post Document
Garnishment: Display Answer Letters	Trip Data Accounting
Garnishment: Display Notice Letters	Undo Transfer Steps
Garnishment History	Union Dues List. Data Carrier; Germany Only
Garnishment: Print Notice Letters	Update of Reconciles Cluster GP by Dynamic Measure
Garnishment Statistics	Update of Remittance Tables from Temse Object (Written by Evaluation)
General: Setup Qualification and Requirement Profiles	Update Routine for Insert/ Delete in Table T535p
Generate Calendars	Update Utility for PIS Change Indicator of Infotype 0147 (Appraisal)
Generate Data Include for Conversions (Explode Include Structure)	Upload Time Events from Sequential File
Generate Master Data Header After Transport	Use of Wage Types in Payroll Accounting

Table 15.2 *Sample Human Resources reports (Continued)*

Generate Monthly Work Schedules	Vacant/Obsolete Positions
Generating a Cycle Check	Vehicle List
Generating Features	Vets-100 Report USA
Generating Reduced Meals Rates	Wage Type Catalog
Generating Reduced Meals Rates According to Times	Wage Type Certificate After Payroll Accounting Period (France)
Generation/Checking of Schemas	Wage Type Distribution
Generation of Catalog Index File	Wage Type Statement (Employee Payroll Wt Payments/Deductions)
Generation of Free Format Conversion (Main Program)	Wage Type Statement by Payroll Periods (International Version)
Generation of Payroll Periods	Wage Types from Table T51 I or T512t
Generation of Qualifications Catalog	Wage Type Listing (Payroll Accounts)
Generation of Reports for Selection of Specific Persons and Applicants	Widow/Widower List (Japan)
Generation of Views According to Client	Work Centers per Organizational Unit
Generation Report for Schema Check	Work Centers Requiring Health Examinations Along Organizational Structure

Generation I Checking of Schemas	Work Centers with Restrictions
GL Account Assignment	Work Centers with Restrictions on Organizational Structure
Graphic Overview of Attendance/Absences	Workers Compensation Assessable Earnings Report (Canada)
Graphical Resource Reservation	Working Time from Time and Incentive Wage Earners

Keep in mind that the enhanced report tree for Version 4.0B contains an additional 100 Human Resources reports to the standard General Report Selection Tree (see Chapter 7 for more information).

Tip

Human Resources Information System (HRIS)

The HRIS component provides a straight-forward method of requesting reports in R/3 and enables you to request reports from inside Structural Graphics.

Structural Graphics

Structural Graphics is a tool in the Organizational Management application component that enables you to display and edit the structures and objects in your R/3 organizational plan. This tool has a great advantage, because Structural Graphics enables you to view objects and structures and perform a variety of maintenance activities for the objects in graphical format (see Figure 15-4 for an example).

As Figure 15-4 displayed, there are two windows that are viewable in the HRIS. The left window displays the organizational structure, which can display organizational units (with persons or positions), and the right-side window displays a report list. On the HRIS screen, you can select an object in the Graphics window and select a report for the object in the Reporting

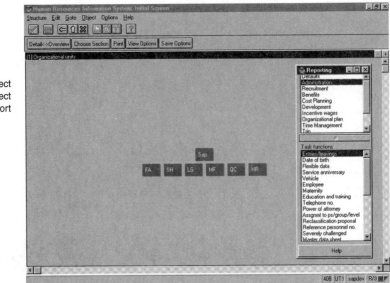

Select an Object
and then select
a report

Figure 15-4   *You can work with the structure of your company's organization using Structural Graphics.*

window. Using this method of selection described, you do not
need to enter data into a selection screen. Another advantage is
the availability of reports from all areas of the Human Resources
module, both PA and PD, in a single spot.

Business Graphics

R/3 also has a component called Business Graphics. Using
Business Graphics, you can ask the system to display information
using three or four-dimensional graphs. An example would be in
the Personnel Cost Planning component of Human Resources.
Within this component, you can request a report that segregates
personnel costs based on organizational units. The Business
Graphics component displays costs for selected organizational
units in a three-dimensional bar graph.

Chapter Wrap-Up

There are some exceptional aspects to reporting in the Human Resources module of R/3. The design of the HRIS and its use of Structural Graphics provides you with a single source to satisfy your reporting needs, based on the organizational objects configured in your Human Resources module. This use of infotypes also provides a clear advantage to the ABAP Query and Ad-Hoc Query reporting, in that functional groups are preassigned based on these infotypes. This idea becomes more evident in the next chapter, when we explain how to use the Ad-Hoc Query tool to create reports in R/3.

Ad-Hoc Query Reporting Tool (Human Resources Module)

An additional reporting tool is available for the Human Resources module that is based on the same premise as the ABAP Query tool. The Ad-Hoc Query tool is also built upon the same user group and functional area foundation as the ABAP Query and can be used to report from infotypes from the R/3 Human Resources module. The tool is user friendly and is designed to pose queries to your R/3 database with regard to your R/3 Human Resources data. Using the Ad-Hoc Query tool, you can select fields from different infotypes to be included on reports. As you will recall, infotypes store individual data about an employee. As a review, a sample info-type from the Human Resources module, infotype 0006 (Employee address), is shown in Figure 16-1.

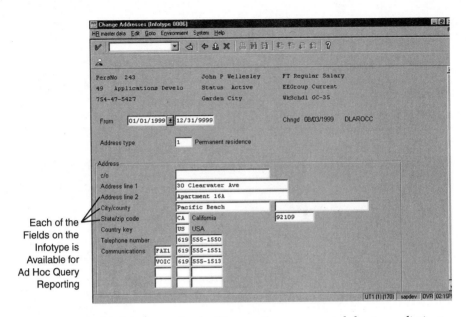

Figure 16-1 *Each infotype in the Human Resources module stores distinct information regarding an employee.*

Our Example

For this chapter, we need to create a functional area based on the Human Resources logical database, PNP. We introduced the topic of creating functional areas earlier in Chapter 9, and we discussed the special considerations in the creation of functional areas for the Human Resources module in Chapter 13. In this example, we will walk through the steps of the creation of a functional area for the Human Resources module.

Creating a Functional Area for Use
with the Ad-Hoc Query

Follow these steps to create a new functional area using the Human Resources logical database PNP:

1. Begin with the transaction code /nSQ02 or the menu path
   Tools→ABAP Workbench→Utilities→ABAP Query→
   Functional area.

2. Follow the menu path Environment→Application area, and select the standard area (client specific) to ensure that you are processing in the correct environment. (For more information about the different application areas, see Chapter 9).

3. Enter a name (using your company's standard naming convention, if available) for your functional area in the Functional Area Input field, and select the Create button.

4. A Title and Database dialog box will appear, asking you to provide a description of the functional area in the Name Input field and to select a logical database from the Possible Entries Help in the Logical Database field.

5. When selecting a logical database for Human Resources, keep the following point in mind. Depending on which logical database you select (PNP or PCH), a different range of infotypes is available. Logical database PNP (Human Resources master data) is used to create a functional area containing only Human Resources master data (infotypes 0000 through 0999 and 2,000 through 2,999). The PCH (Personnel Development) logical database is used to create functional areas containing only *Personnel Development* (PD) infotypes 1,000 through 1,999. To create a functional area containing data from both Master Data (PA) and PD, use logical database PCH. This database can refer to the PNP database (this last method requires the skills of an ABAP programmer).

6. Enter the logical database PNP, then select the green check mark Continue button (see Figure 16-2).

7. An infotype selection screen with the Title bar HR Query: Functional Area Generator will appear next. Enter a range of infotype numbers (consistent with the logical database selected, as in Step 5), or use the Multiple Selection button to select individual infotypes (as explained in Chapter 4). For our example, we will enter a range of 0000 through 0030 (see Figure 16-3).

8. Select the Execute button from the Application toolbar to display the functional area (see Figure 16-4).

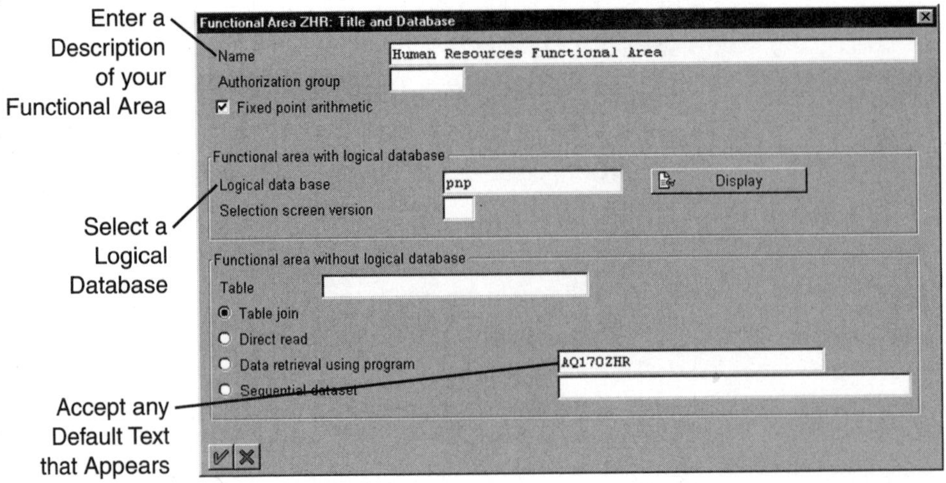

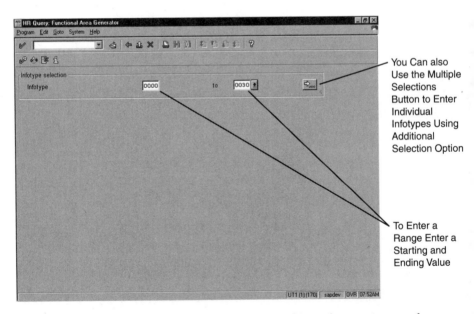

Enter a
Description
of your
Functional Area

Select a
Logical
Database

Accept any
Default Text
that Appears

Figure 16-2 *We will use the logical database* PNP, *which provides us with the appropriate master data infotypes for the Personal Administration (PA) of employees.*

You Can also
Use the Multiple
Selections
Button to Enter
Individual
Infotypes Using
Additional
Selection Option

To Enter a
Range Enter a
Starting and
Ending Value

Figure 16-3 *You can select up to a maximum of 95 infotypes in your functional area.*

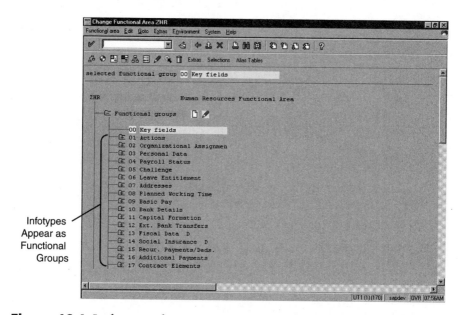

Figure 16-4 *In functional areas using Human Resources logical databases, functional groups are created for you.*

9. You can see that each of the selected infotypes, 0000 through 0030 (use Figure 16-1 as a reference), appear as functional groups in your functional area. The functional group numbers, however, do not correspond to the infotype numbers. Use the (+) Expand Node button to view the fields listed under the 07 Addresses Functional Group. You will see that the fields listed correspond to the fields on the address infotype (see Figure 16-5).

10. As mentioned in Chapter 13, you can also add your own functional groups or add fields to the key fields functional group listed at the top. SAP recommends adding the Personnel Number field to the key fields functional group. In our example, we have taken the personnel number from the Actions table (P000), as in Figure 16-6, and added it to the 00 Key Fields Functional Group. For a review of how to add fields to the functional groups, see Chapter 13.

11. Save the functional area by selecting the open folder Save button from the Standard toolbar, and generate the functional area by selecting the Generate button from the Application toolbar.

12. After a message appears in the Status bar saying that your functional area has been generated, use the green arrow Back button to return to the main Functional Area screen.

13. Next, the functional area needs to be assigned to our user group (review Chapter 9 for additional information) by selecting the Assignment to User Groups button on the main screen.

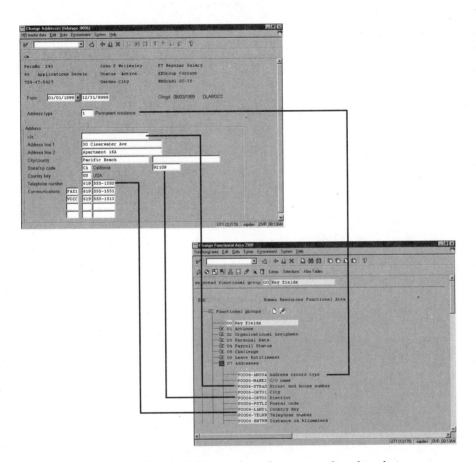

Figure 16-5 *The fields available on the infotypes are listed in their corresponding functional groups.*

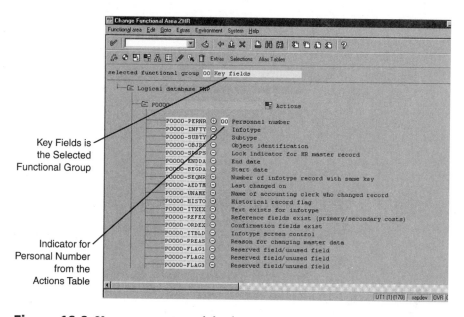

Figure 16-6 *Upon generation of the functional area, if you do not add any fields to the key fields functional group, then you will receive a warning message saying that a functional group contains no fields.*

14. Select your appropriate user group from the list, then select the Save button on the Standard toolbar.

15. Your functional area is ready to go. Use the green arrow Back button to return to the main R/3 window (or use transaction code /nS000).

Ad-Hoc Query Introduction

Unlike the consecutive screen format of ABAP Query, the Ad-Hoc Query is a simple, two-tab display. With the reduction of screens comes a loss of customization capability. The two-tab display does provide you with a basic capability to extract data from your Human Resources infotypes, however, SAP promotes the Ad-Hoc Query as an ideal tool used to pose one-time queries to your R/3 system. These types of questions include the following:

- How many employees are female?

- Which employees in the accounting department have a birthday in February?

- How many employees in the San Diego, California office earn more than $500,000 annually?

- Which employees in the New Jersey office earn less than $75,000 annually and received an annual bonus in 1999?

- How many employees are male and are younger than age 50, excluding employees earning $100,000 a year or more?

The Ad-Hoc Query was designed for these types of questions. You can navigate to the Ad-Hoc Query main screen by using the menu path Human Resources→Information System and by selecting the Ad-Hoc Query button from the Application toolbar (or by using the transaction code /nPQAH). An example of the main Ad-Hoc Query screen is shown in Figure 16-7. Keep in mind that on the initial launch of the Ad-Hoc Query, you might need to select your functional area from a list.

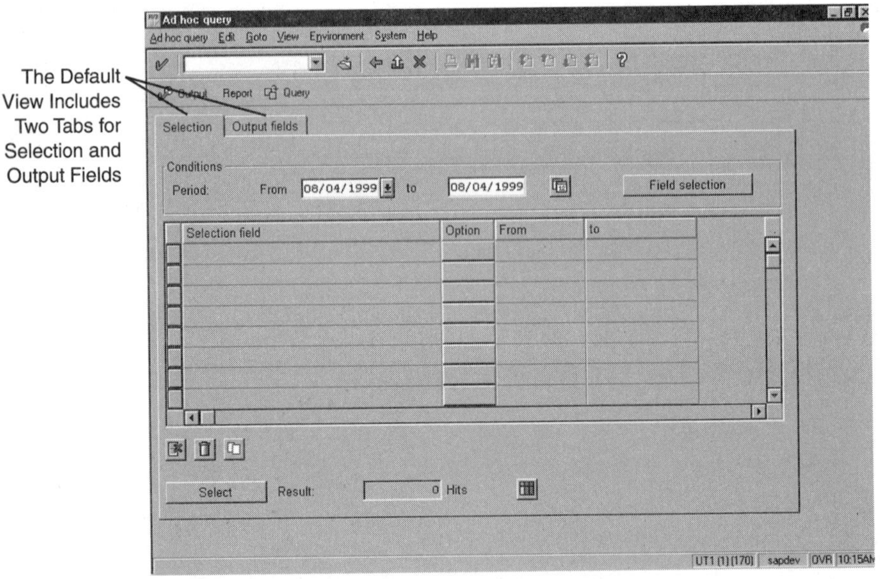

Figure 16-7 *The standard view of the Ad-Hoc Query tool displays two tabs, and the Expert view displays three tabs.*

Create an Ad-Hoc Query

Follow these steps to create an Ad-Hoc Query using the functional area you just created:

1. From the Ad-Hoc Query main screen displayed in Figure 16-7, ensure that you are in the correct application area (use the menu path Environment→Other work area), user group (use the menu path Environment→Other user group), and functional group (use the menu path Environment→Other functional area). This step is similar to the 1-2-3 basics used to create ABAP queries.

2. Use the Field Selection button on the right-hand side of the main screen to begin field selection for your query. A dialog box will appear, listing each of the fields in the functional groups of your functional area (see Figure 16-8).

3. Expand a few nodes to view the fields listed within the functional groups, and note that two columns exist next to each field name. The two columns correspond to the two tabs of the ABAP query (see Figure 16-9).

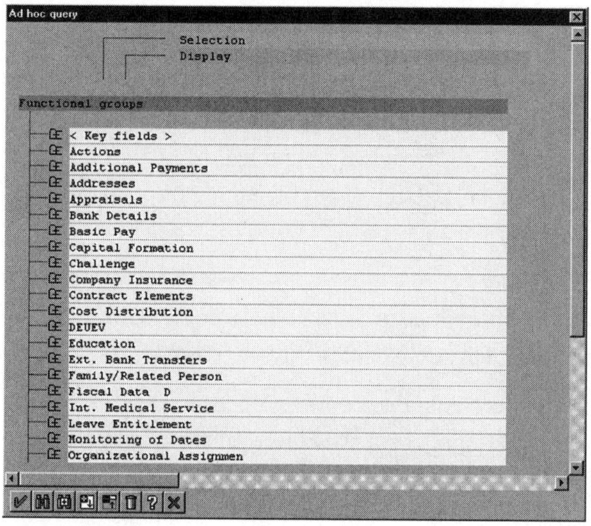

Figure 16-8 *The names of each of your functional groups appear to the right of an Expand Node button (+).*

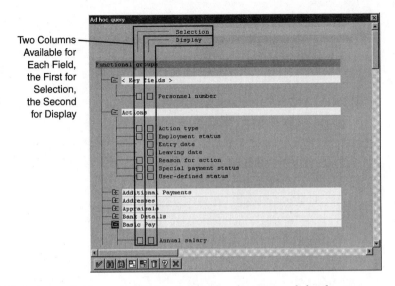

Two Columns
Available for
Each Field,
the First for
Selection,
the Second
for Display

Figure 16-9 *Some fields are available for both selection and display in your Ad-Hoc query.*

4. Marking a check box for selection makes the field available for selection and places that field on the Selection tab of the Ad-Hoc Query screen.

5. Marking a check box for display includes the field in the output of the report and places that field on the Output Fields tab of the Ad-Hoc Query screen.

6. If you are looking for additional information about a field, you can display a description of the field by placing your cursor on the field name and selecting the F1 key on your keyboard (see Figure 16-10).

7. In the Ad-Hoc Query dialog box (shown in Figure 16-9), we are selecting the following fields to be used for a sample in this chapter (see Table 16.1):

8. Based on these selections, the Personnel Number and Annual Salary fields should appear on the Selection tab of the Ad-Hoc Query screen, as in Figure 16-11.

9. Based on the earlier selections, the Annual Salary, First Name and Surname, and Job Title fields should appear on the Output Fields tab of the Ad-Hoc Query screen (see Figure 16-12).

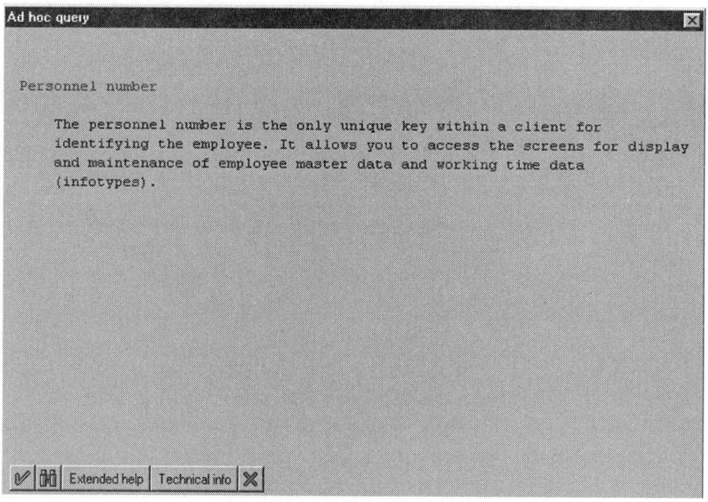

Figure 16-10 *The Personnel Number field and the F1 key on the keyboard were selected to display a description of the field's contents.*

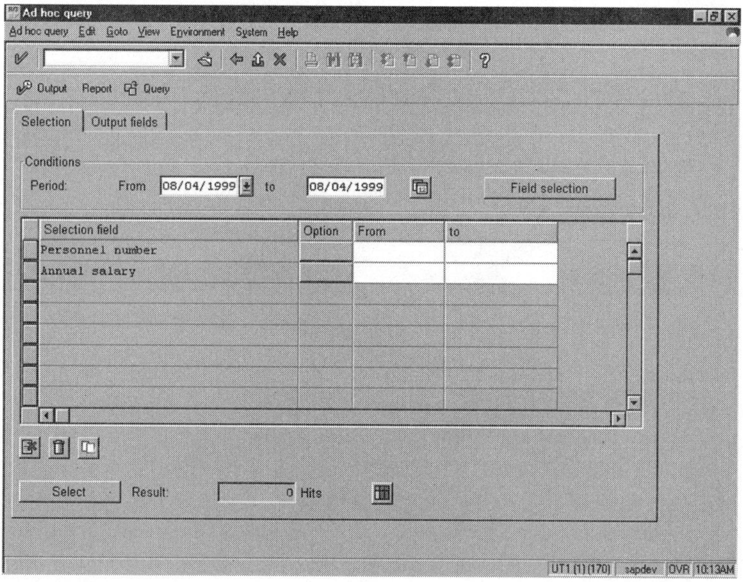

Figure 16-11 *Fields available on the Selection tab can be used just like they are used in selection screens for reports. See Chapter 4 for additional information about selection screens in R/3.*

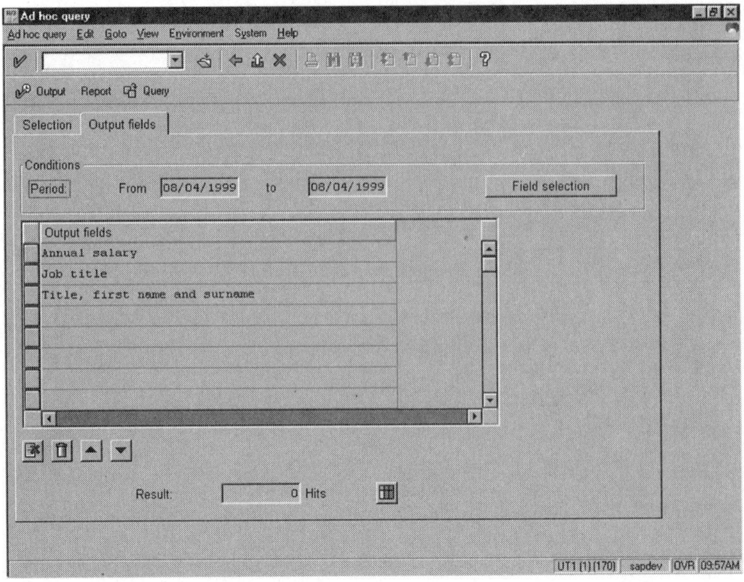

Figure 16-12 *Fields appearing on the Output Fields tab of the Ad-Hoc Query will be displayed in the report's output.*

Table 16.1 *Selections used for our sample Ad-Hoc Query report*

Functional Group	Selection	Display	Field Name
Key fields	X		Personnel number
Basic pay	X	X	Annual salary
Personal data		X	Title, first name, and surname
Organizational assignment		X	Job title

10. For a preview of the report, select the Execute button on the Application toolbar. Your output will appear similar in format to the output displayed in Figure 16-13.

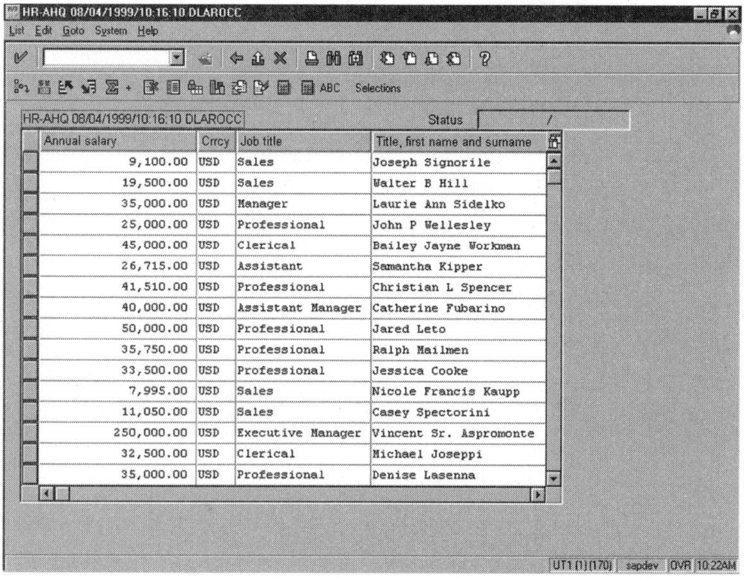

Figure 16-13 *Fields appear in the sequence in which they are listed on the Output Fields tab (see Figure 16-12).*

Working with the Selection Tab of the Ad-Hoc Query

The Selection tab is used as a selection screen for your Ad-Hoc query. This tab includes the same functions as available on selection screens in regular R/3 reporting. The first and most important component is period indicators.

Period Indicators

You will recall that all selection screens in R/3 display a Period Date Range option at the top of the screen, which enables you to specify the point in time within which you want your query to be valid. The Ad-Hoc Query displays these period boxes at the top of the screen, just beneath the tab markers. A calendar-shaped Reporting Period button is also available to the right of the period fields, and you can use this button to indicate whether the query should be run for the following:

- Today
- Current month

- Current year

- All

- Past

- Future

Selection Options

After entering the desired period into the Period Input fields, you need to specify which type of data you want to see. Because the Selection tab works like a selection screen, you can enter values directly into the input fields to specify your output. For example, the query displayed in Figure 16-13 contains all 16 employees in our sample Human Resources module. We can modify the entries on our Selection tab to specify that a specific group will be included in our output. For example, we can indicate that we only want to view employees whose annual salary is $35,000. In the input field for annual salary, we will enter the amount 35,000 (see Figure 16-14).

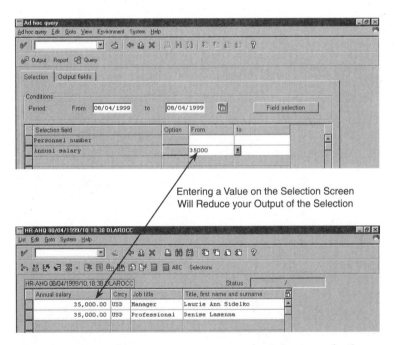

Figure 16-14 *After entering criteria on the Selection tab, the output becomes restricted from its original list (shown in Figure 16-13) to include only the specified data.*

Maintain Selection Options

In Chapter 4, we introduced the Maintain Selections box, which is used for additional flexibility on your R/3 selection screens. This box is available on the Selection tab of the Ad-Hoc Query to assist you with specifying output. This box can be accessed by selecting the gray Option button that appears between the Selection field name and the From box in the selection grid (see Figure 16-15).

By using the ([ ]) Interval option on the Maintain Selection Options dialog box, we will specify a range of values for our output so that the report only includes employees whose annual salary is between $30,000 and $40,000 (see Figure 16-16).

Retrieving a Figure Instead of Output

At the start of this chapter, we gave you some sample questions that could be answered using Ad-Hoc Query. For example, one question asked the number of employees who were of a certain gender. You can create an Ad-Hoc query to display a list of all employees who are male, for example, or you can just receive the number of employees who are male. The Select button that appears at the bottom-left of the screen can be used to count the number of employees fitting the criteria entered on the Selection tab (see Figure 16-17).

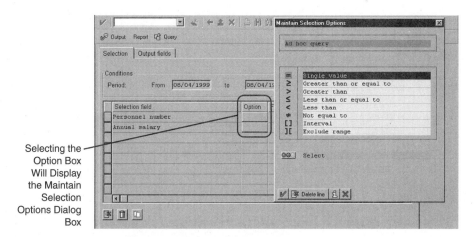

Figure 16-15 *Eight advanced-selection options are available on the Maintain Selection Options dialog box.*

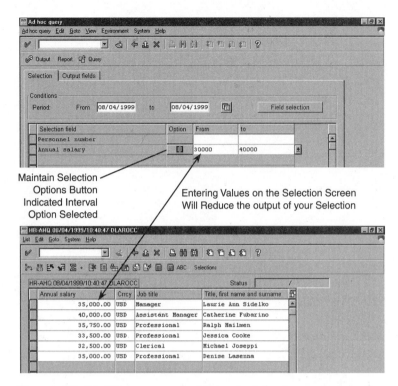

Figure 16-16 *You can use the Maintain Selection options to further specify your selection criteria.*

A small blue grid button (List of Personnel Numbers) is displayed immediately to the right of the Number of Hits field and can be used to see a list of employee personnel numbers and names of employees who fit this criteria (see Figure 16-17).

Working with the Output Fields Tab of the Ad-Hoc Query

The Output Fields tab is used to manipulate the format of the output that will display your Ad-Hoc Query. Unlike ABAP Query, no advanced options exist that can be used on this screen to change the format of your data—but the Ad-Hoc Query does provide you with some capabilities.

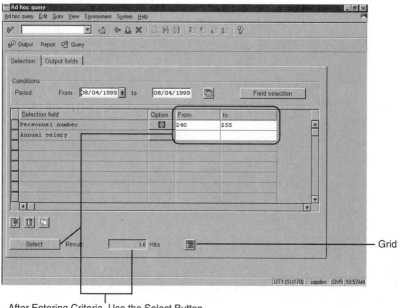

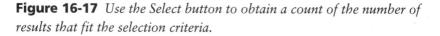

After Entering Criteria, Use the Select Button
to Obtain a Count of the Number of Employees
Who Hit the Criteria

Figure 16-17 *Use the Select button to obtain a count of the number of results that fit the selection criteria.*

Field Sequence in Your Report

Any fields selected for display will appear listed in the Output Fields tab. You can vary the order that they will appear in your Ad-Hoc query by selecting a field (using the gray Selection button to the left of the field name), and then using the navigational arrows on the bottom of the window (see Figure 16-18).

Saving Ad-Hoc Queries and Lists

Once your Ad-Hoc query is executed and your data is displayed, the same toolbar options available for most R/3 reports for sorting and exporting the file are available. The Application toolbar buttons and their uses for further processing are outlined in Table 16.2.

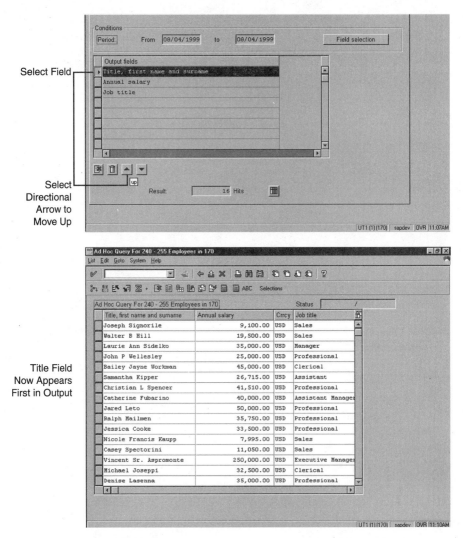

Figure 16-18 *Field sequence output can be manipulated using the directional up and down arrows on the bottom of the Output Fields tab.*

Table 16.2 *The Application toolbar Ad-Hoc Query output*

Button	Name	Function
	Display Initial	Restores table display to its original format (assuming that you made changes)

Button	Name	Function
	Convert Currency	Converts the currency of a currency field (if multiple currencies are used in your configuration)
	Sort Ascending	Sorts the selected column in ascending order
	Sort Descending	Sorts the selected column in descending order
	Sum	Summarizes the selected numeric column
	Hide Lines/ Columns	Hides selected lines or columns from the display
	Deselect All	Deselects any selections in the table view
	Fix Columns	Freezes the selected column
	Unfreeze Columns	Unfreezes the selected column
	Graphic	Generates a business graphic of the output (when available)
	Download to File	Downloads the output to a file
	Word Processor	Launches Microsoft Word and readies the data for insertion into a merged Word document
	Table Calculation	Launches Microsoft Excel and presents the data in spreadsheet format
	ABC Analysis	Presents the data in an alphabetical analysis format, based on specifications entered

Table 16.2 *The Application toolbar Ad-Hoc Query output*

Button	Name	Function
EIS	EIS	Transfers data to the EIS
Selections	Selections	Displays the entries made on the selection screen for the report in a dialog window

Saving Lists

To save your Ad-Hoc Query output list (remember the important distinction between lists and queries), you can follow the same procedures as with the ABAP Query and most standard R/3 report lists.

Saving Queries

To save your Ad-Hoc query, first ensure that you are on either the Selection or Output Fields tabs. Then, select the menu path Ad-Hoc Query→Save. A dialog box will appear, in which you need to provide a query name and description. Be sure to use your company's naming convention if applicable when saving the report (see Figure 16-19).

Later in Chapter 22, "Customizing Report Trees in R/3" you will learn how to add custom-made ABAP Query and Ad-Hoc Query reports to R/3 report trees.

Ad-Hoc Query Expert Mode

An additional tab called Complex Operations can be added to the Ad-Hoc query. The options available on this tab are used for the Ad-Hoc query in what is known as Expert mode. From either the Selection or Output Fields tabs, follow the menu path View→Expert mode (see Figure 16-20).

Complex reporting is available using Expert mode, but this type of report creation requires advanced SAP skills and an in-depth knowledge of the structure and relationships between the

Figure 16-19 *Similar to ABAP queries, saved Ad-Hoc queries can be added to R/3 report trees.*

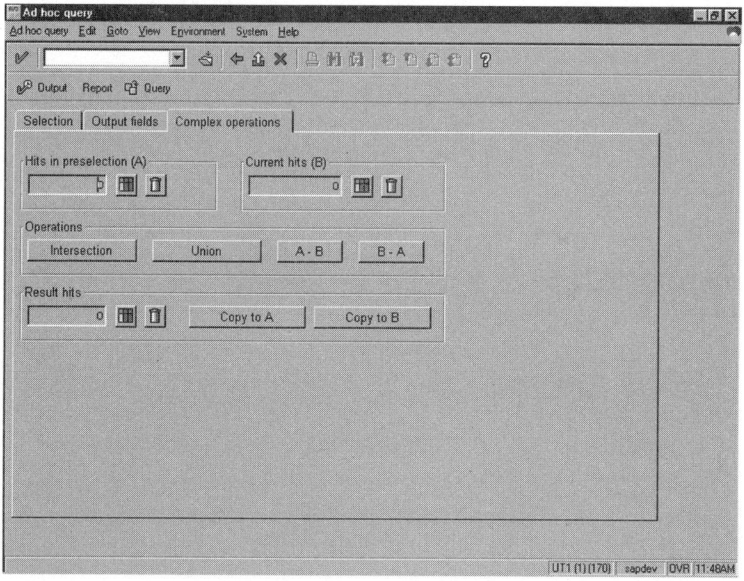

Figure 16-20 *The Expert mode options require advanced skills for processing, which are not generally used by standard users in Ad-Hoc Query reporting.*

R/3 Human Resources tables. Expert mode is not designed for regular users.

Chapter Wrap-Up

The Ad-Hoc Query tool is a great utility when you want to pose questions to your R/3 system. In terms of day-to-day reporting, we prefer the more advanced functionality of ABAP Query for Human Resources reporting. The Ad-Hoc Query tool is perfect for assisting you with retrieving immediate answers to perhaps complicated questions (i.e., how many full-time employees are U.S. citizens, work in the London office, earn more than $100,000 a year, and are older than age 50?) in your Human Resources module.

R/3 Reporting in Microsoft Excel

After examining some standard R/3 reports and
creating some of your own custom reports, you
can see that the format and printed output are
both extremely basic. Further processing of
your R/3 report output is available via an integration between SAP R/3 and Microsoft Excel.
This integration permits you to view your R/3
output in a Microsoft Excel worksheet at the
simple click of a button. Many advantages exist
in working with your SAP R/3 data in
Microsoft Excel. A sample of the advantages
are listed as follows:

- The capability to change output format (fonts, graphics, page settings, and print options)

- The capacity to manipulate the data (use of calculations for further analysis)

- The opportunity to create charts and graphs (for a visual representation of the data)

- Better sizing and spacing for printing (Microsoft Excel enables you to manually adjust how the printed page will appear)

OLE Architecture

The capability to work with your SAP data in Microsoft products is possible using OLE technology. OLE architecture represents object linking and embedding. This OLE technology is used for the cooperative sharing of information among different applications. This integration permits the format and integrity of data to remain consistent across applications, including SAP R/3 and Microsoft products.

Our Example

For you to perform the tasks in this chapter, you need to have Microsoft Excel installed on your PC.

Note

If you begin to follow along and you realize that a connection is not available between SAP and Microsoft Excel, contact your system administrator. He or she can verify that this option is installed (it is usually installed as part of the default for SAPGUI 4.0 and later).

The query that we will be using as our example in this chapter is a copy of a query created in Chapter 12. The basic information for the query appears in Figures 17-1 and 17-2. If you do not have an existing query available to copy, create a new query based on the information presented in the figures.

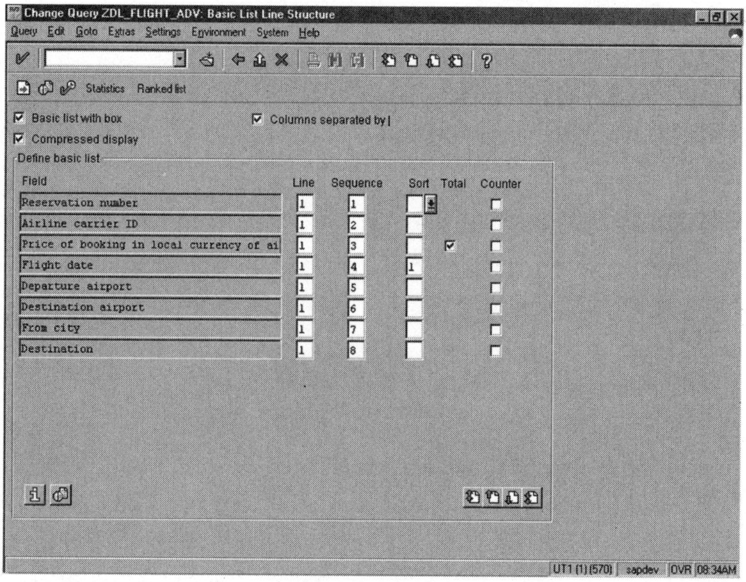

Figure 17-1 *The Basic List Line Structure screen provides you with the necessary information for setting up the query.*

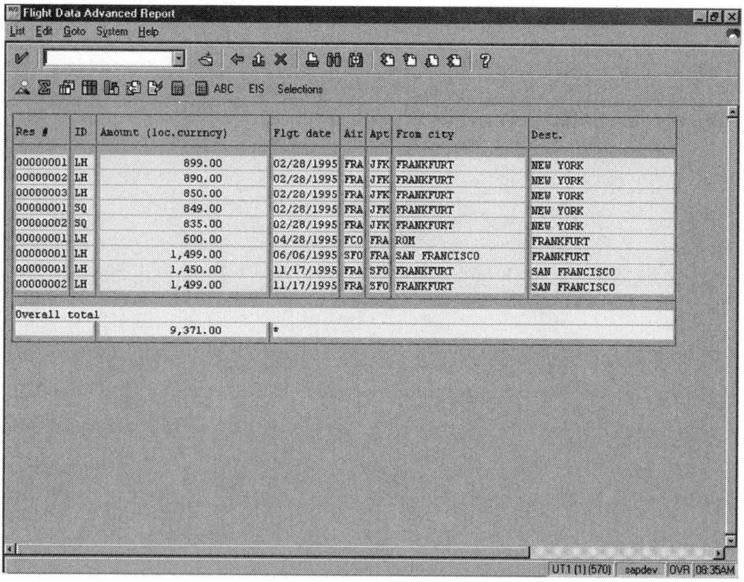

Figure 17-2 *Your report output should appear similar in format to the output shown in this figure.*

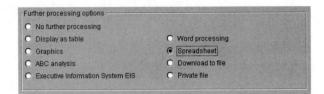

Figure 17-3 *Specifying a further processing option on the Title, Format screen (Screen 1) will save the option with the query.*

Further Processing Options

You will recall from earlier chapters that the Further Processing Options area is available from within ABAP Query on the Title, Format screen (Screen 1) and on the selection screen (Screen 6) for reports. These further processing options, among others, enables you to specify that you would like your data outputted to a spreadsheet (see Figure 17-3).

If a further processing option is specified on the Title, Format screen (Screen 1), then it is saved with the query and will be the format for the output of the query upon execution. If you want to be able to make the decision on the further processing of the query at run time, however, you can instead fill in the selection on the Queries selection screen (Screen 6). This change is not saved with the query if it is only entered on the selection screen (unless you save the selection screen as a variant, and then save the variant as part of the query).

Output Data to Spreadsheet

For our example, we will select the Spreadsheet radio button option (as shown in Figure 17-3) from the further processing options on the Queries selection screen. Next, we will execute our query by selecting the Execute button from the Application toolbar on the selection screen. An Export dialog box will appear, presenting several options for the processing mode for our data. We will select the Excel Display radio button and the green check mark Enter key, as in Figure 17-4.

My report output will now appear in Microsoft Excel (see Figure 17-5).

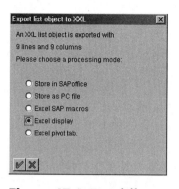

Figure 17-4 *Five different processing options are available for saving the file in a spreadsheet.*

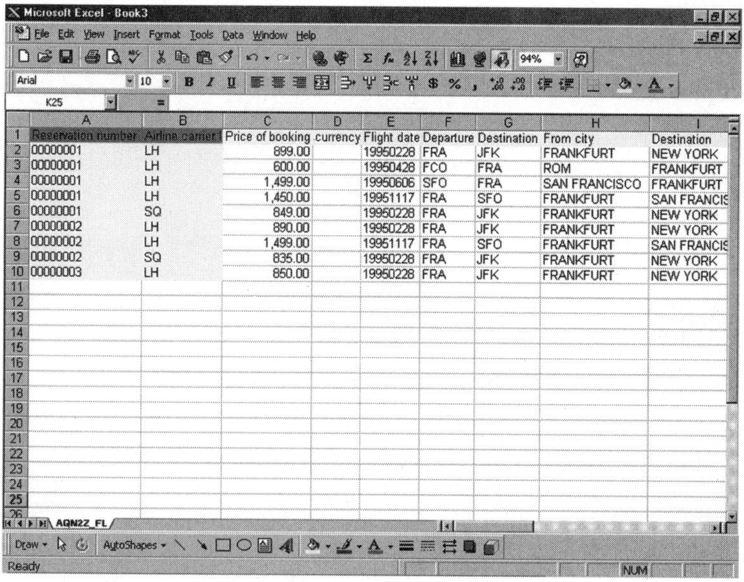

	A	B	C	D	E	F	G	H	I
1	Reservation number	Airline carrier	Price of booking	currency	Flight date	Departure	Destination	From city	Destination
2	00000001	LH	899.00		19950228	FRA	JFK	FRANKFURT	NEW YORK
3	00000001	LH	600.00		19950428	FCO	FRA	ROM	FRANKFURT
4	00000001	LH	1,499.00		19950606	SFO	FRA	SAN FRANCISCO	FRANKFURT
5	00000001	LH	1,450.00		19951117	FRA	SFO	FRANKFURT	SAN FRANCIS
6	00000001	SQ	849.00		19950228	FRA	JFK	FRANKFURT	NEW YORK
7	00000002	LH	890.00		19950228	FRA	JFK	FRANKFURT	NEW YORK
8	00000002	LH	1,499.00		19951117	FRA	SFO	FRANKFURT	SAN FRANCIS
9	00000002	SQ	835.00		19950228	FRA	JFK	FRANKFURT	NEW YORK
10	00000003	LH	850.00		19950228	FRA	JFK	FRANKFURT	NEW YORK

Figure 17-5 *Compare the output in Figure 17-2 with the output presented in Microsoft Excel.*

This output was quick and easy, but take a closer look at the data in Column E of Figure 17-5. Using this method can sometimes produce quirky results. For example, the flight dates that appear in Column E of Microsoft Excel now appear as numbers (in the order of year, month, and day), rather than dates. Also, any totals or subtotals do not appear for the data when exported to Microsoft Excel. You will recall the list screen for the report (as shown in Figure 17-2) produced a total at the end. The data, when presented in Microsoft Excel, does not. There are ways around some of these quirky nuances, which we explore later in this chapter. For the most part, however, your data appears relatively seamless in Microsoft Excel. From here, you can perform further processing of your data.

Output Data to Display as Table

Another way to work with your data in Microsoft Excel is to select the Display as table further processing option on the queries selection screen. Make this change for your report, then select the Execute button from the Application toolbar on the selection screen. Your R/3 data will now appear on the List screen (Screen 7) in table form, as in Figure 17-6.

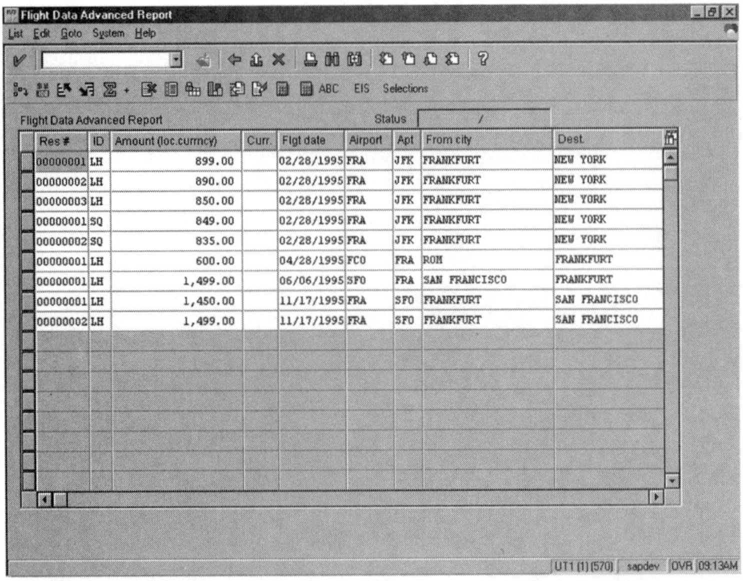

Figure 17-6 *Compare the output in Figure 17-2 with the output presented in this figure.*

Using this method also removes the totals and subtotals from the report output. When you choose to display your output in the form of a table, however, you are provided with a new Application toolbar that contains additional functional options. These options were introduced in Chapter 16 and are detailed in Table 17.1.

Table 17.1 *Application toolbar for display as table output*

Button	Name	Function
	Display Initial	Restores table display to its original format (assuming that you made changes)
	Convert Currency	Converts the currency of a currency field (if multiple currencies are used in your configuration)
	Sort Ascending	Sorts the selected column in ascending order
	Sort Descending	Sorts the selected column in descending order
	Sum	Summarizes the selected numeric column
	Hide Lines/ Columns	Hides selected lines or columns from the display
	Deselect All	Deselects any selections in the table view
	Fix Columns	Freezes the selected column
	Unfreeze Columns	Unfreezes the selected column
	Graphic	Generates a business graphic of the output (when available)

Table 17.1 *The Application toolbar for display as table output* *(Continued)*

Button	Name	Function
	Download to File	Downloads the output to a file
	Word Processor	Launches Microsoft Word and readies the data for insertion into a merged Word document
	Table Calculation	Launches Microsoft Excel and presents the data in spreadsheet format
	ABC Analysis	Presents the data in an alphabetical analysis format, based on specifications entered
	EIS	Transfers data to the EIS
	Selections	Displays the entries made on the selection screen for the report in a dialog window

From the List Output screen displayed in Figure 17-6, select the Table Calculation button. The Export List dialog box shown in Figure 17-4 will appear. Select the Excel Display option and the green check mark Enter key. Your data will appear in Microsoft Excel just as it did when you selected the Spreadsheet further processing option on the selection screen in the previous section (see Figure 17-5).

The same quirks apply when using this method for downloading to Microsoft Excel. Let's try another method.

Output Data to Download to File

The option to download the data to a file can be made on the further processing options on the Title, Format screen (Screen 1), on the selection screen (Screen 6), or by selecting the Download to file button on the Application toolbar. Or, you can use the menu path List→Download to file, which is what we will use for our example. Whichever method you choose, a Transfer to Local File dialog box will appear, and you must enter a path, filename, and format for your file (see Figure 17-7).

Table 17.2 outlines the several options for formatting the saved file.

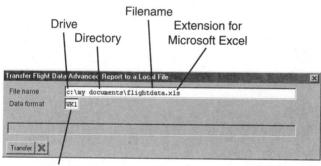

Figure 17-7 *Be sure to end the filename with an extension that is appropriate for the application you will use to open the file.*

Table 17.2 *Data format options available for downloading*

Format	Description
ASC	ASCII
BIN	Binary
DBF	Database format
IBM	ASCII with IBM code-page conversion (DOS)
WK1	Spreadsheet format
DAT	ASCII data table with Column tab

Spreadsheet (WK1) Data Format

Selecting the WK1 spreadsheet format as outlined in Table 17.2 will bring the data into the spreadsheet and remove its formatting and column headings. Select the Transfer button to download the file. Launch Microsoft Excel, and open your file from the directory that you specified to see the output. See Figure 17-8 for an example. Using this method apparently still loses the formatting of the Flight Date field.

ASCII (DAT) Data Format

This time, let's begin from the List screen (Screen 7), as shown in Figure 17-6, and select the Download to File button from the Application toolbar. This time, select a new file location, name, and path, and select the DAT format on the Transfer to Local File dialog box (see Figure 17-9). This selection will produce different results and will remedy the flight date problem.

Launch Microsoft Excel, and open your file from the directory that you specified to see the output. Because the file was saved in

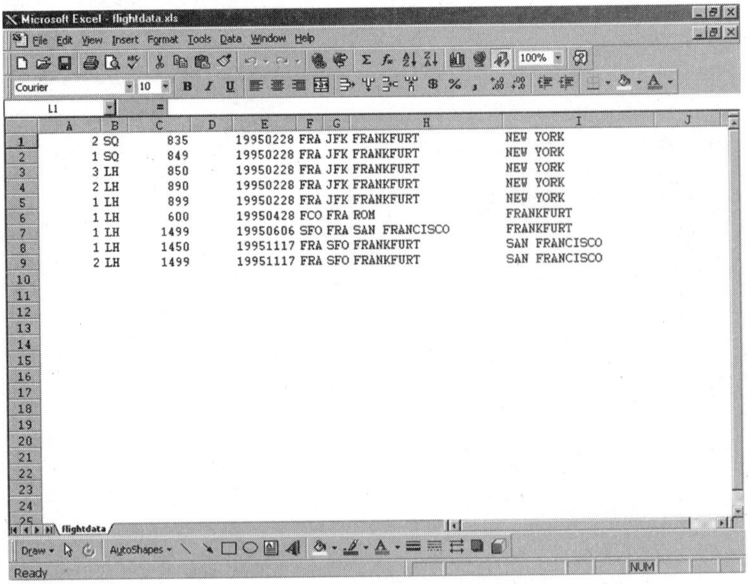

Figure 17-8 *Compared to Figure 17-5, using this method removes formatting of data and does not translate R/3 dates as dates in Microsoft Excel.*

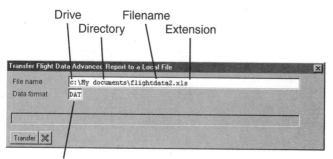

Figure 17-9 *ASCII-formatted files are saved in a standard format until translated by the application that is used to open them.*

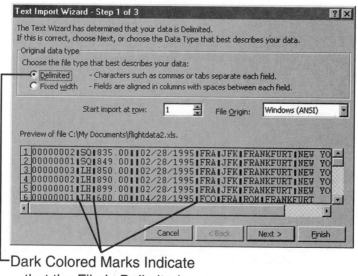

Figure 17-10 *The Microsoft Excel Text Import Wizard enables you to enter formatting criteria for your file before opening it.*

DAT format and not the WK1 spreadsheet format, Microsoft Excel enables you to specify the formatting options for your data. Upon selecting your file for opening, you are presented with a Text Import Wizard dialog box similar to the one shown in Figure 17-10.

This file has been saved in a delimited format, meaning that small, delimiting characters appear between each column segregating the data. Microsoft Excel recognizes this fact and selects the Delimited radio button on the Text Import Wizard. The three-step wizard will enable you to enter formatting criteria for your data. Select the Next button on the Text Import Wizard. Again, Microsoft Excel recognizes the type of delimiter that was placed in the file and displays your segregated columns (see Figure 17-11). Select the Next button to continue.

Remember the flight date problem mentioned earlier? Using the Text Import Wizard, you can specify the format of each individual column of data. On the third and final window of the Text Import Wizard, you can select columns and specify their format(s) (see Figure 17-12).

Without this specification of the date field, the field would appear as a general number in Excel—as it did in the other examples. Select the Finish button to complete the import into Microsoft Excel (see Figure 17-13).

Each Column Is Now Separated

Figure 17-11 *The Microsoft Excel Text Import Wizard is a three-screen, step-by-step application designed to assist you with producing your desired output.*

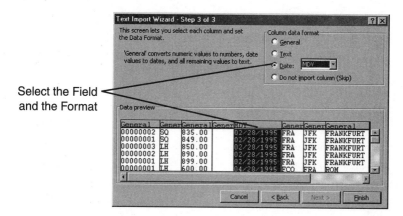

Figure 17-12 *Specifying the format of the data ensures that the data is presented in Microsoft Excel in the same format as it appears in SAP R/3.*

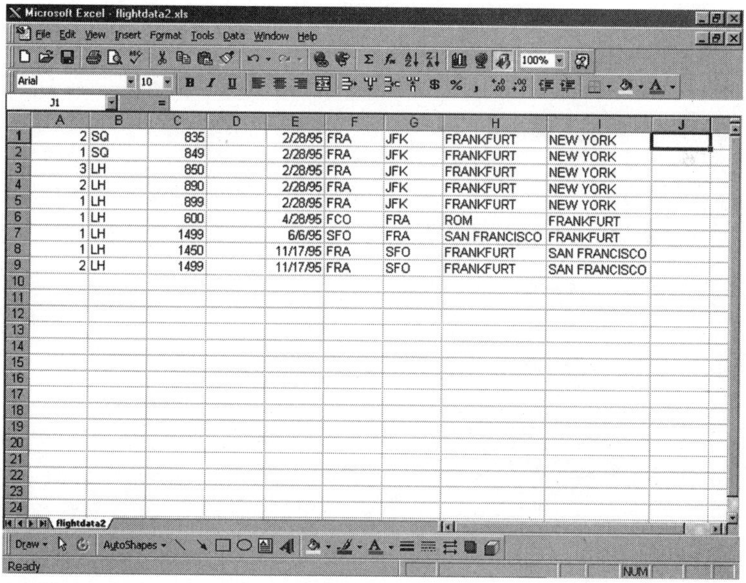

Figure 17-13 *This figure appears similar to Figure 17-8, except that now the dates are formatted appropriately and are recognized as dates in Microsoft Excel.*

Performing Further Analysis of Your R/3 Data

One of the main benefits of working with your SAP R/3 data in Microsoft Excel is that you can produce charts and graphs of your R/3 data. For example, let's use the spreadsheet we created in the first exercise in this chapter, which is displayed in Figure 17-5. Use your mouse to select (highlight) the Airline Carrier ID and Price of Booking fields (Columns B and C). Column D is used to store the currency code for the Price of Booking. Because the data used in our example is universal, it does not contain a three-digit currency code (in other words, USD for the U.S. dollar). Select the Microsoft Excel menu path Insert→Chart. A Microsoft Excel Chart Wizard dialog appears, in which you can select from options on four different screens to produce a chart of your SAP data. Select a graph option, and then proceed through the four screens (accepting the default selections is OK). Then, view your output (see Figure 17-14).

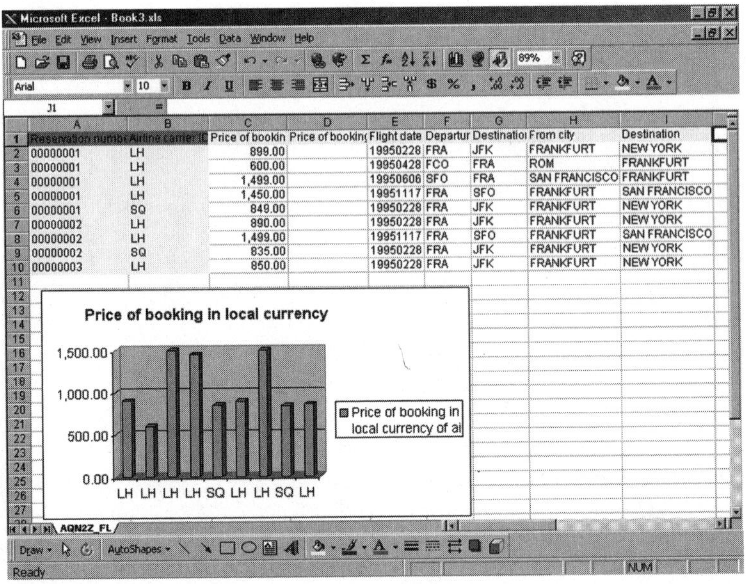

Figure 17-14 *One of the advantages to working with your R/3 data in Microsoft Excel is the capability to create charts and graphs easily using the Microsoft Excel Chart Wizard tool.*

Working within Microsoft Excel has endless possibilities. Using the Help application and the Microsoft Assistant (the annoying little character in the dialog box window), you can seek assistance to help you perform a variety of manipulations of your R/3 data. For example, you can create a report that includes graphics in the headers, and you can manipulate your report to fit on a certain number of pages. In addition, you can also vary the texts, formats, fonts, and colors of your output.

Downloading SAP Objects to Microsoft Excel

You are not limited to downloading ABAP and Ad-Hoc queries into Microsoft Excel. You can download even standard and custom reports created in ABAP code into Microsoft products. In R/3, you can also download standard reports, queries, and report tree structures into Microsoft Excel. For example, from the main SAP R/3 window, use the menu path Information systems→General report selection to view the standard report tree. This object can be downloaded to Microsoft Excel, as well. From this screen, you can use the menu path System→List→Save→Local file (see Figure 17-15).

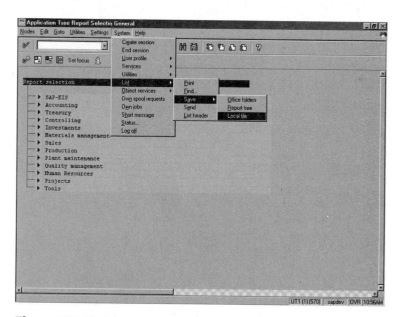

Figure 17-15 *The menu path System→List→Save→Local file is available from many SAP screens.*

Using this method, a Save List in File dialog box will appear, from which you can select one of three options for your file (see Figure 17-16).

A Transfer List to a Local File dialog box will appear. As you did in earlier examples, enter a location, filename, and extension for your file (see Figure 17-17). Select the green check mark Enter key to proceed.

Launch Microsoft Excel, and open your file. You will see the Import Text Wizard introduced earlier in the chapter. Proceed through the three-screen wizard and view your results (see Figure 17-18).

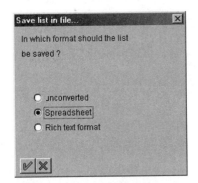

Figure 17-16 *The three options available here are consistent with options outlined earlier in the chapter.*

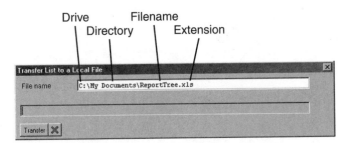

Figure 17-17 *You should always enter a unique name for a file when downloading from R/3.*

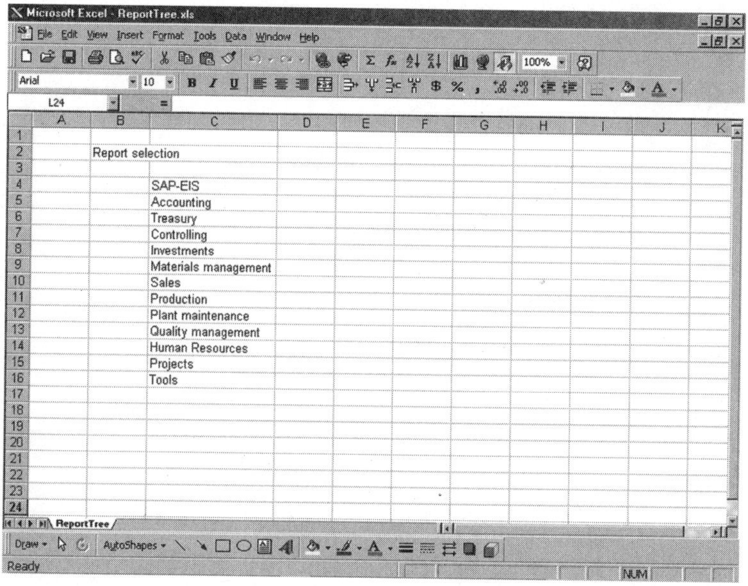

Figure 17-18 *The R/3 General Report Selection Tree now appears in a Microsoft Excel spreadsheet.*

Chapter Wrap-Up

For users who are familiar with the workings of Microsoft Excel, its uses as an external reporting tool for R/3 data are endless and well known. Some companies have even written programs that download their data to Excel files on a scheduled basis to generate reports. This functionality is all made possible through the use of ABAP programming in R/3 and the use of macros or Visual Basic in Microsoft Excel. Trial and error is the best method of learning how to work with your SAP R/3 data in Microsoft Excel. Once you master these skills, they will be essential for producing better-looking and more valuable reports of your R/3 data.

R/3 Reporting
in Microsoft Access

Many companies use Microsoft Access as their
main reporting tool. Microsoft Access is a database program that stores data in tables and produces output in reports. On a basic level, SAP is
essentially based on the same concept. Your R/3
system also stores information in a database
(this concept was discussed in Chapter 3), and
you can use tools to create your own reports.

In Microsoft Access, the capability to create reports is enhanced through the use of wizards and standard reports that require no user skills whatsoever. Many companies use a standard program written in ABAP code that extracts information from the R/3 database at regularly scheduled intervals and populates that data into a Microsoft Access database used for reporting. There are advantages and disadvantages to using this method. The main advantage is the ease of use and user-friendly format of the reporting tool in Microsoft Access. The main disadvantage is that data downloaded to Microsoft Access is no longer real-time data in the system and only represents the data as of the point in time in which it was downloaded. Keeping all these points in mind, you will find that this chapter focuses on teaching a user how to download data to Microsoft Access for the purpose of creating basic reports.

Our Example

The example we will use for this chapter will be from the same ABAP query used in the previous chapter. The basic information for the query appears in Figures 18-1 and 18-2. If you do not have an existing query available, create a new query based on the information presented in Figures 18-1 and 18-2.

Output Data to the Database

The first step is to collect the data for your report. For our example, we want to create a report of the data displayed in Figure 18-2 in Microsoft Access. We have a handful of options for exporting the data (these options were introduced in the previous chapter). Typically, downloading the data to a file in DAT format works best. In many cases, however, using the trial-and-error system will suit you well.

Creating the Export File for Microsoft Access

The creation of an export file was discussed in the previous chapter. The steps to create an export file for Microsoft Access are the same and are reviewed here. The option to download the data to a file can be made by using the further processing options on the Title, Format screen (Screen 1), by using the selection

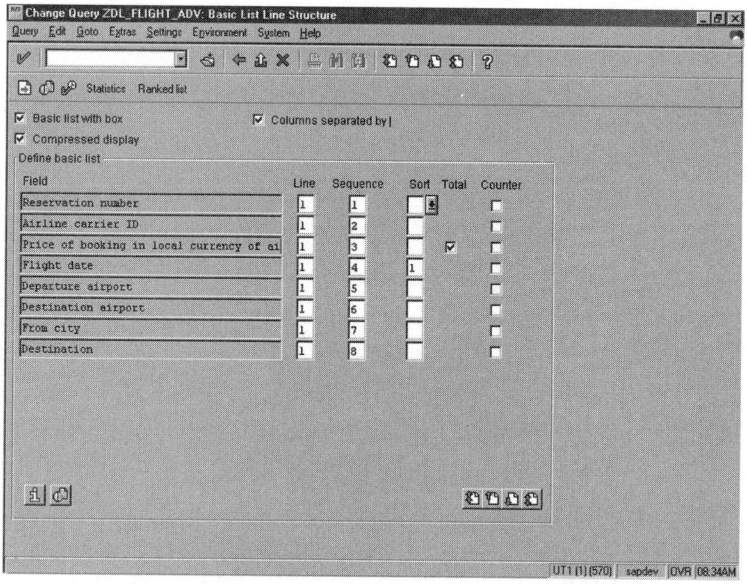

Figure 18-1 *The Basic List Line Structure screen provides you with the necessary information for setting up the query.*

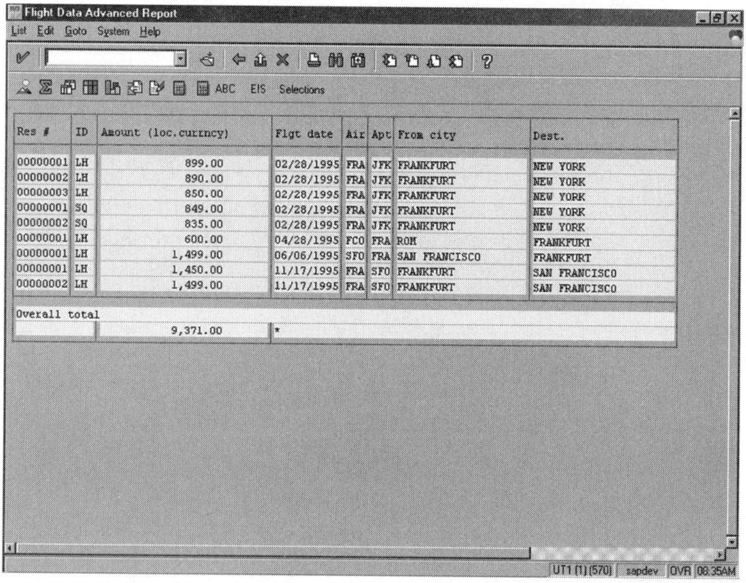

Figure 18-2 *Your report output should appear similar in format to the output shown in this figure.*

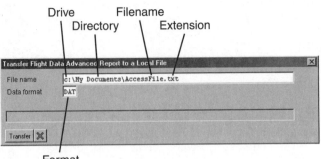

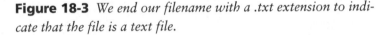

Figure 18-3 *We end our filename with a .txt extension to indicate that the file is a text file.*

screen (Screen 6), or by selecting the Download to file button on the Application toolbar when the report output is displayed. Also, you can use the menu path List→Download to file, which is what we will use for our example. Follow these steps to create an export file of your R/3 data for use in Microsoft Access:

1. Start from the List screen (Screen 7) of your report, similar to the one shown in Figure 18-2, and follow the menu path List→Download to file.

2. A Transfer to Local File dialog box will appear, and you must enter a path, filename, and format for your file (see Figure 18-3).

3. The format that works best is DAT. Select the Transfer button to download the file. A message will appear in the Status bar, indicating that the bytes were successfully transferred to the file.

Working in Microsoft Access

Microsoft Access is a user-friendly database management tool. Microsoft Access has several help applications and step-through wizards that provide instructions on how to use the database to its potential. This chapter will cover only the basic functions of creating a table and a report in Microsoft Access. If at the end of this chapter you feel that Microsoft Access is a suitable tool for your use, you might want to invest in an instructional book on Microsoft Access to assist you with maximizing your results.

Creating a New Database in Microsoft Access

Follow these steps to create a new database in Microsoft Access:

1. The first step is to launch Microsoft Access on your PC and select the Blank Database option from the dialog box (see Figure 18-4), then click the OK button to proceed.

2. Next, you need to select the location where you want the file stored on your PC and the name of the database (see Figure 18-5).

Figure 18-4 *You will only need to create a database one time, and this database can be used for multiple purposes.*

Figure 18-5 *The extension for your Microsoft Access database will be .mdb.*

3. After entering the location and name, select the Create button. A new (empty) Microsoft Access database will appear.

4. The Access Database is separated into six tabs. We will only concentrate on two of these tabs in this chapter (see Figure 18-6).

Importing SAP R/3 Data into Microsoft Access

The next step would be to import the file we created earlier into a table in Microsoft Access. Follow these steps to import the SAP file into Microsoft Access:

1. From the main screen of Microsoft Access, displayed in Figure 18-6, use the menu path File→Get External Data→Import.

2. An Import dialog box will appear, and you must select the location and filename of the file saved earlier (refer to Figure 18-3) in SAP R/3 (see Figure 18-7).

3. After entering the appropriate information, select the Import button, and the Import Text Wizard dialog box (introduced in Chapter 17) will appear.

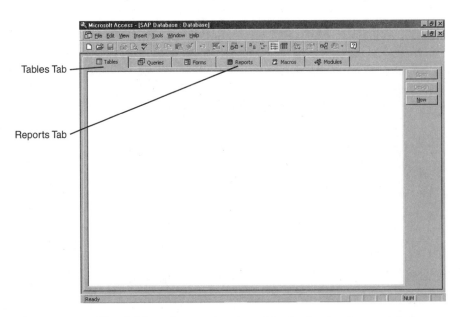

Figure 18-6 *The Tables tab contains the tables in the database, and the Reports tab contains all of the reports in the database.*

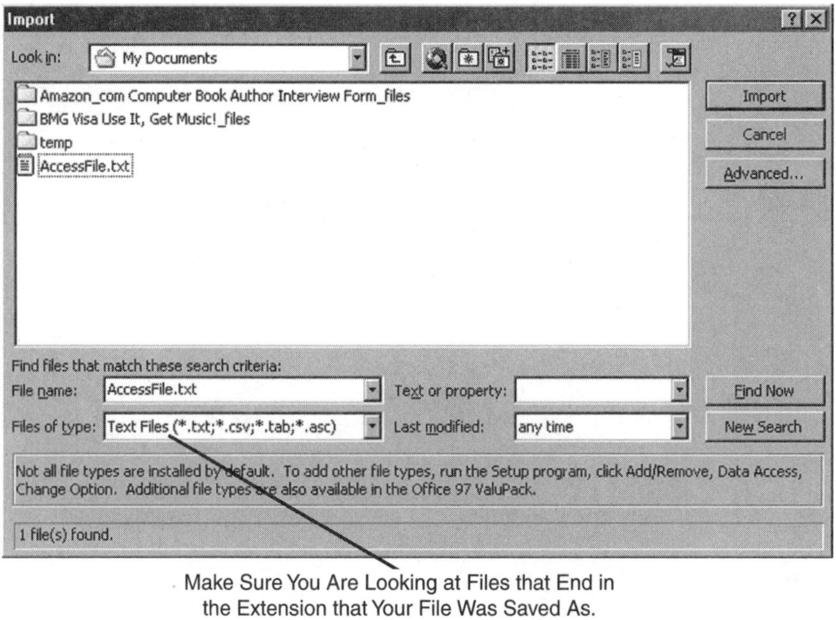

Make Sure You Are Looking at Files that End in
the Extension that Your File Was Saved As.

Figure 18-7 *The SAP file is associated as a text file, because it was saved in an ASCII (DAT) format.*

The standard installation of Microsoft Access on your PC might not include all of the import file types necessary to complete the next step of the import. If you do not have text files as a Files of Type option in your Import dialog box, then you need to reinstall Microsoft Access and modify the install options to include the full set of options.

Tip

4. Step through the Import Text Wizard using the Next button, accepting the default selections until you reach the third screen. At this point, you are asked to provide column headings for your data. On this screen, select each column and type in a new name for each column (see Figure 18-8).

5. After renaming the fields appropriately, make sure that the columns are of the correct data type (as we did earlier in Chapter 17). Specifically, the Flight Date field should be changed to the date format.

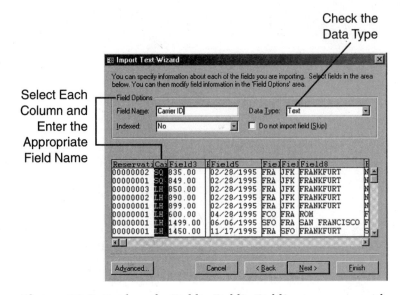

Figure 18-8 *Replace the Field1, Field2, Field3, etc., names with the appropriate headings for the fields.*

6. Select the Next button to proceed to the final screen, again accepting the default entries until you reach the last screen in the dialog box that contains the Finish button. Select the Finish button to complete the import.

7. A new, small dialog box will appear, saying that your data was successfully imported. Select the OK button on this dialog box.

Viewing Your Microsoft Access Table

To view the data in your Microsoft Access database table, select the table with your mouse. Then, select the Open button on the right-hand side of the Microsoft Access window. Your Microsoft Access Database table will appear much like a spreadsheet, with the fields listed in columns with the data presented in each column (see Figure 18-9). Use the menu path File→Close to close the open table.

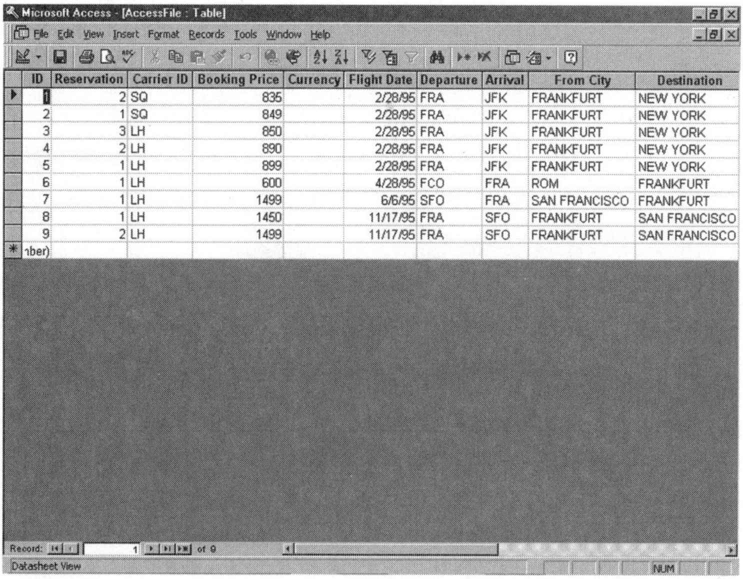

ID	Reservation	Carrier ID	Booking Price	Currency	Flight Date	Departure	Arrival	From City	Destination
1	2	SQ	835		2/28/95	FRA	JFK	FRANKFURT	NEW YORK
2	1	SQ	849		2/28/95	FRA	JFK	FRANKFURT	NEW YORK
3	3	LH	850		2/28/95	FRA	JFK	FRANKFURT	NEW YORK
4	2	LH	890		2/28/95	FRA	JFK	FRANKFURT	NEW YORK
5	1	LH	899		2/28/95	FRA	JFK	FRANKFURT	NEW YORK
6	1	LH	600		4/28/95	FCO	FRA	ROM	FRANKFURT
7	1	LH	1499		6/6/95	SFO	FRA	SAN FRANCISCO	FRANKFURT
8	1	LH	1450		11/17/95	FRA	SFO	FRANKFURT	SAN FRANCISCO
9	2	LH	1499		11/17/95	FRA	SFO	FRANKFURT	SAN FRANCISCO

Figure 18-9 *Microsoft Access database tables look similar to Microsoft Excel worksheets when displayed.*

Using the Microsoft Access Report Wizard

Now that your R/3 data is in a table in your Microsoft Access database, you can create reports from it. Creating reports in Microsoft Access is easy, especially with the assistance of the Report Wizard. Follow these steps to create a report of your SAP R/3 data in Microsoft Access.

Creating a New Report of Your SAP Data in Microsoft Access

1. From the main screen of Microsoft Access, which is displayed in Figure 18-6, select the Reports tab. Next, select the New button from the right-hand side of the screen.
2. You will be prompted with a New Report dialog box similar to the one shown in Figure 18-10.
3. Select the Report Wizard Option and then your table name from the dialog box, then select the OK button to proceed.

Select the
Report Wizard

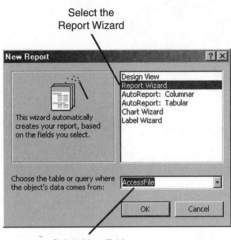

Select Your Table

Figure 18-10 *In addition to the Report Wizard, you can create reports from scratch in Microsoft Access, or you can have Microsoft Access create an AutoReport for you.*

4. The first screen of the report wizard enables you to select the fields from your table that you want to include in your report. Fields are selected using the small gray > buttons in the center of the report wizard. In our example, we will include all fields with the exception of the ID field, which is automatically assigned by Microsoft Access (see Figure 18-11).

5. After selecting the fields you want to include in the report, select the Next button to proceed to the second screen of the report wizard.

6. This screen enables you to add grouping levels to your report. This concept is similar to the control level concept introduced with the ABAP Query. For our example, we will group based on flight date (see Figure 18-12).

7. After selecting the grouping levels, select the Next button to proceed to the third screen of the report wizard.

8. This screen enables you to enter sort criteria for your report. For our example, we will sort by Flight Date and Carrier ID.

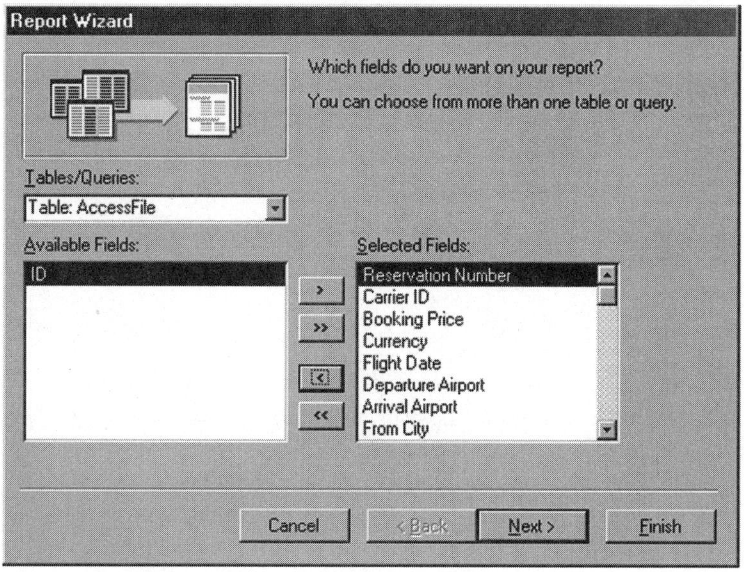

Figure 18-11 *The ID field is a counter assigned by Microsoft Access to provide a unique index for the table.*

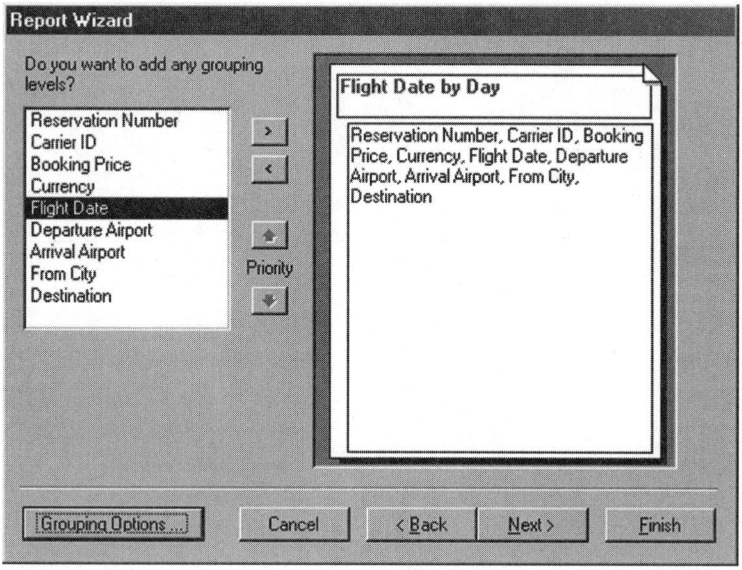

Figure 18-12 *Grouping levels enable you to provide subtotals for your data.*

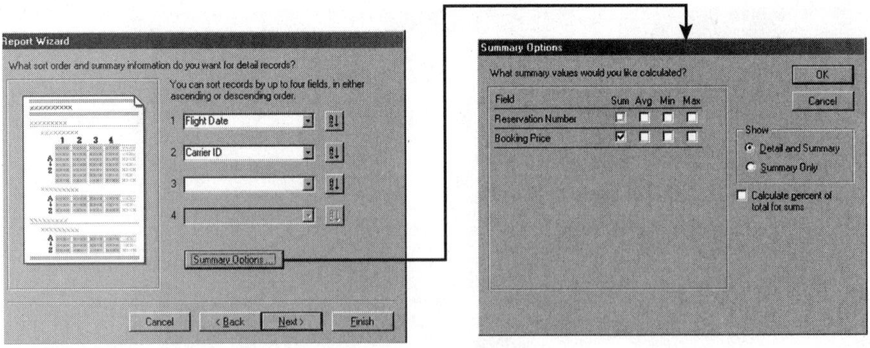

Figure 18-13 *Summary options are available for any sorted field and include options for displaying totals, averages, minimums, and maximums for detail and summaries of data.*

A button on this screen also enables you to specify summary options for your data (see Figure 18-13).

9. After selecting the sort criteria and summary options, select the Next button to proceed to the fourth screen of the report wizard.

10. On this next screen, you can select a layout and orientation for the report (see Figure 18-14).

11. After selecting the layout and orientation, select the Next button to proceed to the fifth screen of the report wizard.

12. On the fifth screen, you can select from one of six predefined styles for the report. Select a style, and then select the Next button to proceed to the final screen of the report wizard.

13. On the last screen of the report wizard, enter a title for your report. Then, select the Finish button.

14. Microsoft Access will pause for a moment while it creates your report, and then your report will be displayed on the screen (see Figure 18-15).

The final output includes all of the formatting, sorting, and options that you select on the wizard screens.

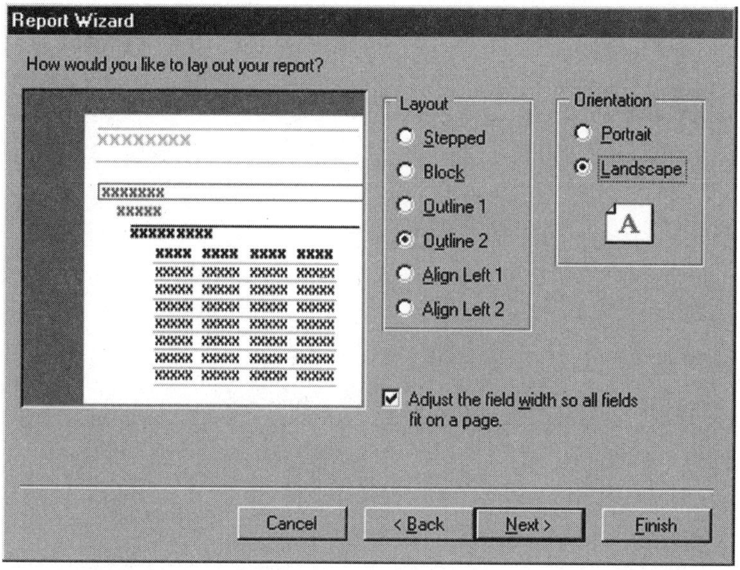

Figure 18-14 *Trial and error will help you determine which layout works best with each report.*

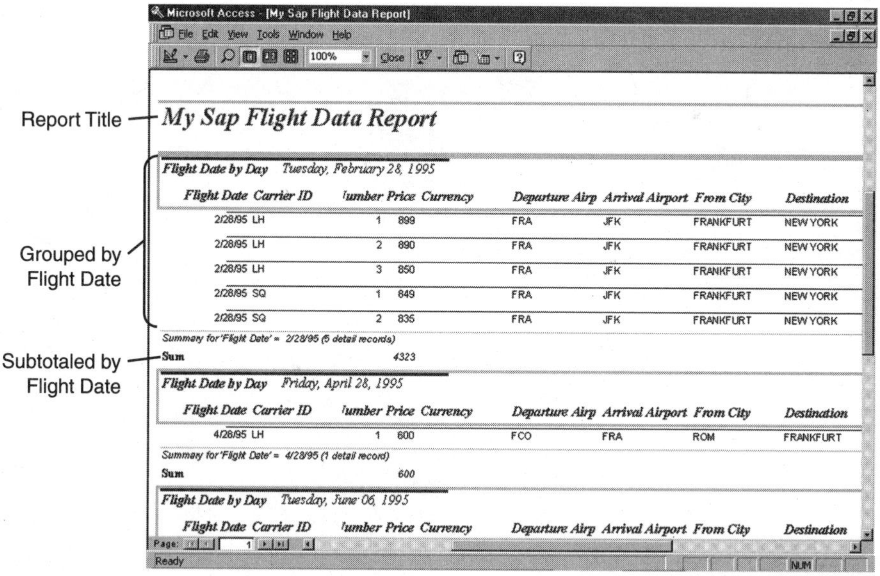

Figure 18-15 *The finished report includes all of the specifications entered on the Report Wizard screens.*

Creating Labels for Your SAP Data
in Microsoft Access

Report Wizard can also be used to create labels from your SAP R/3 data in Microsoft Access. Labels can also be created via a mail merge with Microsoft Word, and this concept is discussed in Chapter 19, "Creating Form Letters in Microsoft Word." For this example, we will create luggage tag labels using the data in the flight data table that we already imported into Microsoft Access. Follow these steps to use the report wizard to create labels from your R/3 data in Microsoft Access:

1. From the main screen of Microsoft Access, which is displayed in Figure 18-6, select the Reports tab. Next, select the New button from the right-hand side of the screen.

2. You will be prompted with a New Report dialog box similar to the one shown earlier in Figure 18-10. This time, select the Label Wizard option and then your table name. Select the Next button to proceed to the next screen in the report wizard.

3. You will be prompted to select the size of the label you want to create. Microsoft Access has a large assortment of preset labels, so select the appropriate label size and type (see Figure 18-16). Then, select the Next button to proceed.

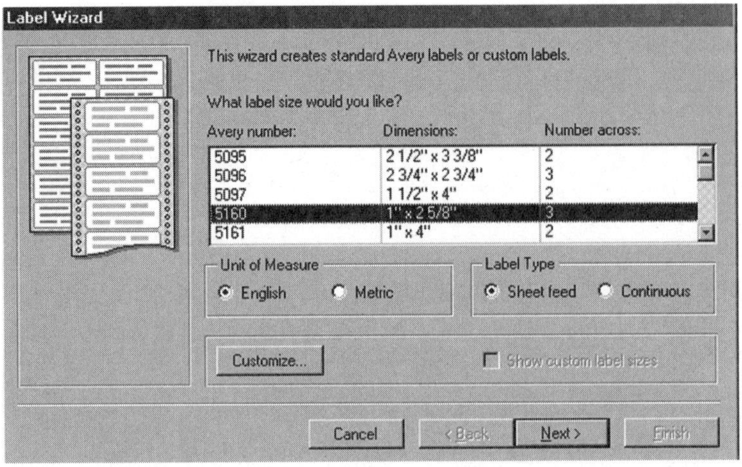

Figure 18-16 *Most store-bought labels display the standard four-digit identification code of the label or its dimensions on the outside packaging.*

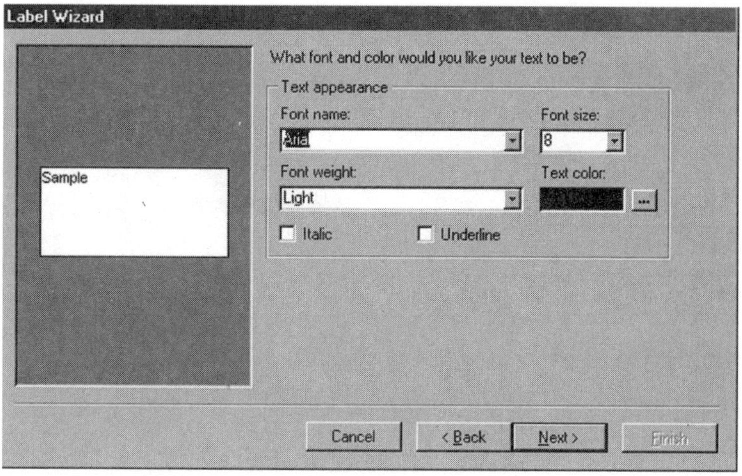

Figure 18-17 *Make the font size appropriate to the size of the printed label.*

4. On the next screen, select the font name, weight, size, and color for the printed text for your labels (see Figure 18-17). Then, select the Next button to proceed.

5. Select the fields that you want to appear on the label using the small gray > selection button in the center of the wizard screen. Type any other text (see Figure 18-18), then select the Next button to proceed.

6. Next, select the fields that you wish to sort by, then select the Next button to proceed.

7. For the last step, enter a name for your report, and then select the Finish button to view a sample of your luggage tag labels (see Figure 18-19).

Creating a Graph of Your SAP Data in Microsoft Access

In Chapter 17, we took a look at how to create a graph of your R/3 data in Microsoft Excel. Microsoft Access has a report wizard that will walk you through the creation of a graph in Microsoft Access. Follow these steps to create a graph of your R/3 data in Microsoft Access:

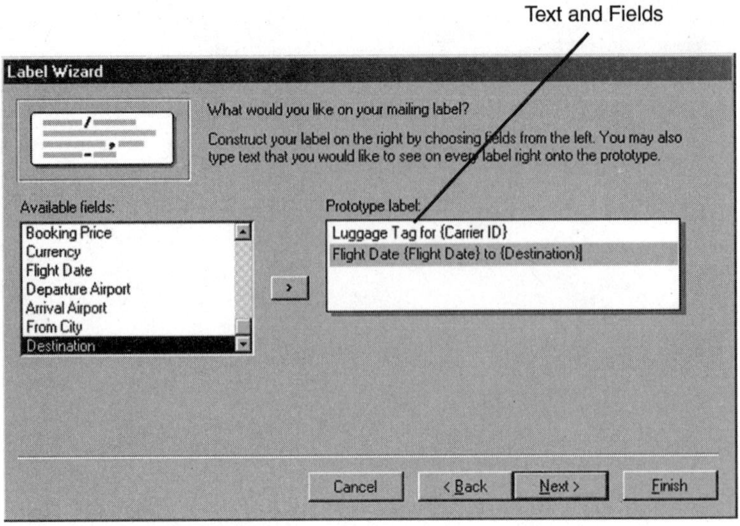

Text and Fields

Figure 18-18 *You can intersperse text with fields on your labels.*

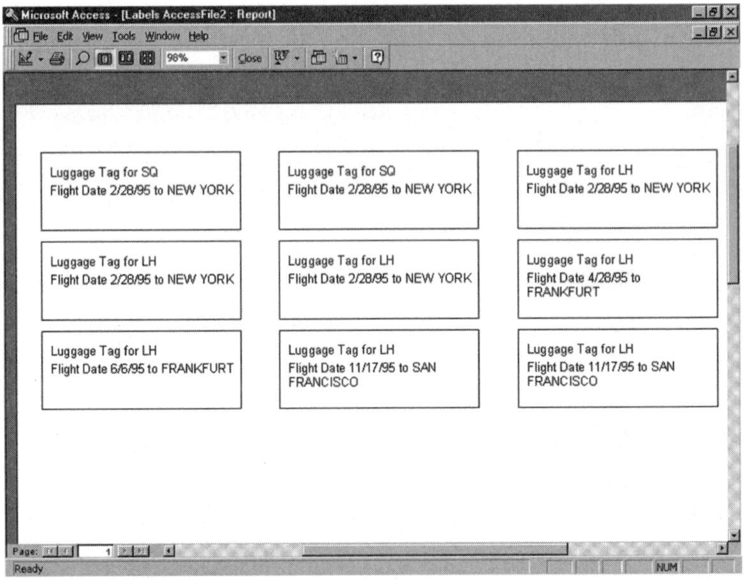

Figure 18-19 *You can add additional formatting to the labels, including pictures and special fonts.*

1. From the main screen of Microsoft Access, displayed in Figure 18-6, select the Reports tab. Next, select the New button from the right-hand side of the screen.

2. You will be prompted with a New Report dialog box similar to the one shown earlier in Figure 18-10. This time, select the Chart Wizard option and your table name. Select the Next button to proceed to the next screen in Report Wizard.

3. On the first screen, select the fields that you want to include in your chart. For our example, we will select the Flight Date and Booking Price fields. Select the Next button to proceed.

4. The next screen enables you to select a format for your chart (see Figure 18-20). Select a format, and then select the Next button to proceed.

5. On the next screen, select which fields appear on which axis of the graph. You can double-click a field to display additional options (see Figure 18-21). Select the Next button to proceed to the last screen in the report wizard.

6. For the last step, enter a name for your report. Then, select the Finish button to view a sample of the chart (see Figure 18-22).

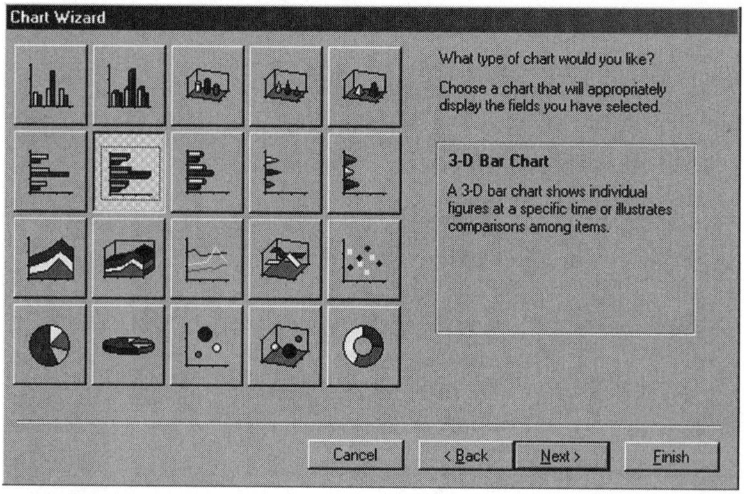

Figure 18-20 *Select a graph that is appropriate for displaying your data.*

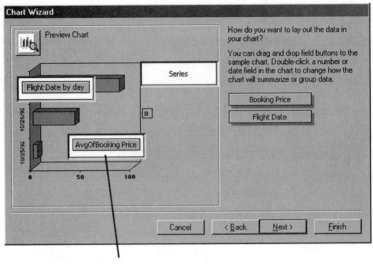

Double-Click to Display Grouping
and Summarizing Options

Figure 18-21 *You can modify the grouping or summarization of how the data is presented on an axis by double-clicking the field name.*

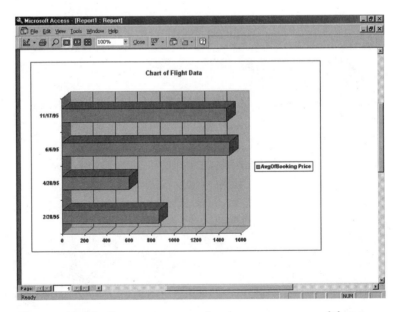

Figure 18-22 *Once you create the chart, you can modify it in Microsoft Access.*

AutoReporting in Microsoft Access

Microsoft Access also has options for creating AutoReports. An AutoReport does not walk you through a wizard to create a report; rather, once it is selected, it automatically creates a report for you in either columnar or tabular format. This quick, two-step process does not enable you to select any formatting options, but it does create a quick report of your data. To take a look at AutoReports, follow these steps:

1. Select the Reports tab and then the New button from the right-hand side of the window.

2. In the New Report dialog box, select an AutoReport option and your table name (see Figure 18-23). Then, select the OK button.

3. There are no screens for you to fill in and no user intervention. Your new report output will be displayed, as in Figure 18-24.

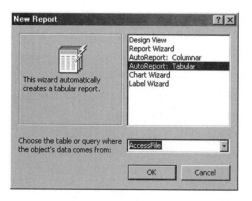

Figure 18-23 *AutoReports are created in Microsoft Access with no user intervention.*

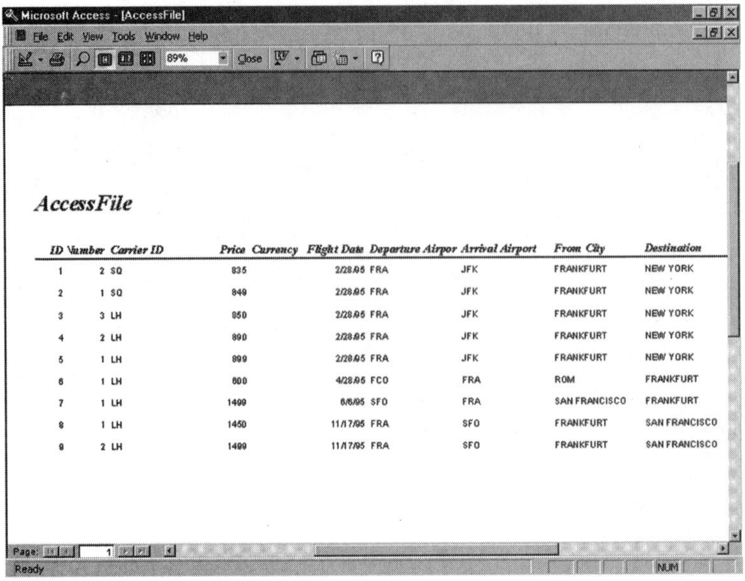

ID	Number	Carrier ID	Price	Currency	Flight Date	Departure Airpor	Arrival Airport	From City	Destination
1	2	SQ	835		2/28/95	FRA	JFK	FRANKFURT	NEW YORK
2	1	SQ	849		2/28/95	FRA	JFK	FRANKFURT	NEW YORK
3	3	LH	850		2/28/95	FRA	JFK	FRANKFURT	NEW YORK
4	2	LH	890		2/28/95	FRA	JFK	FRANKFURT	NEW YORK
5	1	LH	899		2/28/95	FRA	JFK	FRANKFURT	NEW YORK
6	1	LH	800		4/28/95	FCO	FRA	ROM	FRANKFURT
7	1	LH	1499		6/6/95	SFO	FRA	SAN FRANCISCO	FRANKFURT
8	1	LH	1450		11/17/95	FRA	SFO	FRANKFURT	SAN FRANCISCO
9	2	LH	1499		11/17/95	FRA	SFO	FRANKFURT	SAN FRANCISCO

Figure 18-24 *AutoReports are helpful for creating quick, simple reports of your SAP R/3 data.*

Chapter Wrap-Up

All in all, Microsoft Access has a great deal of wizard applications to assist you with creating reports, labels, and charts of your R/3 data. The most popular method of working with SAP R/3 data and Microsoft Access is through automated processes, including the automatic scheduled extraction of data from the R/3 system and the automatic population of that data into Microsoft Access. This functionality considerably cuts down the effort required, because there is no longer a need for the import and export procedures detailed in the chapter. Also, this functionality enables a more focused approach on the creation of reports, labels, and charts of your R/3 data. Another advantage is that once created, the reports in R/3 can be used over and over with each new download of SAP data.

Creating Form Letters in Microsoft Word

One of the most significant capabilities of the SAP R/3 reporting, ABAP, and Ad-Hoc Query tools is the capacity to create form letters from SAP data. A form letter enables you to create a standard letter, envelope, or label, then merge data from a data source to appear precisely at a certain spot in the document. You can also use existing letters and documents and customize them to include merge fields from your data source. An overview of form letters is shown in Figure 19-1.

Data

First	Last	Company	Adress 1	City	State	Zip
John	Wellesley	Aspro Mechanical	16 Hope Avenue	Massapequa	NY	11758
Pat	Smith	Innovative Travel Promotions	41 Pacific Street	Brooklyn	NY	11209
Bruce	Carpenter	Amity Travel	1906 Walter Way	Amity Harbor	WA	63552
Kent	Arlington	Much Financials	11 101st Street W	Wantagh	OH	96358

Form Letters

<<First>> <<Last>> > <<Company>> <<Address>> <<City>>, <<State>> <<Zip>> Dear <<First>>, Greetings. This letter is a promotional advertisement to offer <<Company>> a discount on the purchase of bulk office supplies.	John Wellesley Aspro Mechanical 16 Hope Avenue Massapequa, NY 11758 Dear John, Greetings. This letter is a promotional advertisement to offer Aspro Mechanical a discount on the purchase of bulk office supplies.

Envelopes

123 Office Deals
500 Park Ave
NY, NT 11011

John Wellesley
Aspro Mechanical
16 Hope Avenue
Massapequa, NY 11758

Labels

John Wellesley
Aspro Mechanical
16 Hope Avenue
Massapequa, NY 11758

Pat Smith
Innovative Travel Promotions
41 Pacific Street
Brooklyn, NY 11209

Figure 19-1 *Form letters save enormous amounts of time and energy.*

Our Example

The example we will use for this chapter will be from the same ABAP query used in the two previous chapters. The basic information for the query appears in Figures 19-2 and 19-3. If you do not have an existing query available to copy, create a new query based on the information presented in Figures 19-2 and 19-3.

Output Data to the Database

The first step is to collect the data you want to report. ABAP Query's selection screen (Screen 6) is a handy tool for delineating precise outputs. For example, a popular use of form letters from

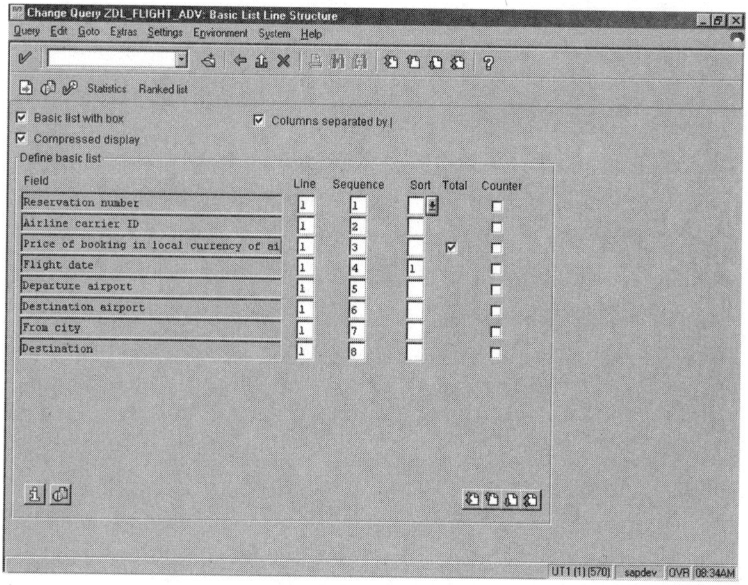

Figure 19-2 *The Basic List Line Structure screen provides you with the necessary information for setting up the query.*

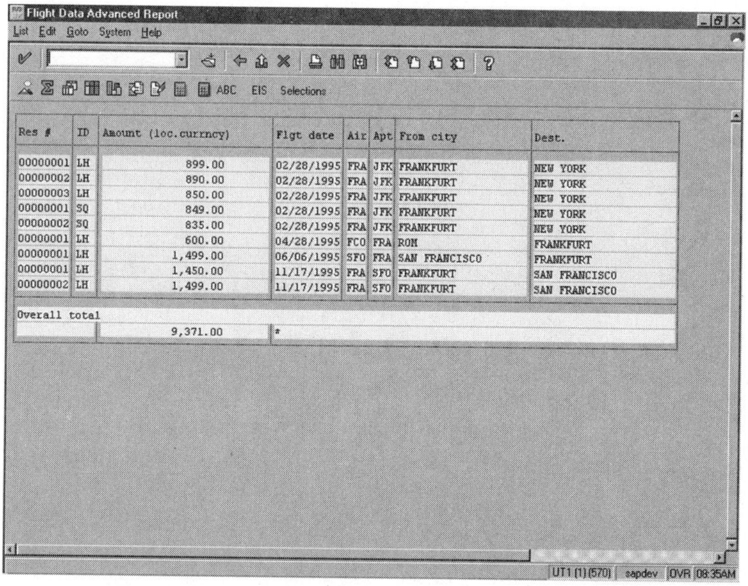

Figure 19-3 *Your report output should appear similar in format to the output shown in this figure.*

R/3 data is for mass mailings to employees in the Human Resources module. Let's say that a health insurance provider's coverage levels are changing, and this change affects 2,500 or so of your 50,000 employees. Using the selection screen of ABAP Query, you can select only the 2,500 individuals who participate in that particular plan and generate a form letter notifying them of the change. Form letters are also popular for delivering mass mailings to customers to notify them of new products—or to vendors to notify them of policy changes. The uses of this option are infinite. For our example, the data we want to use as our data source for a form letter in Microsoft Word is displayed in Figure 19-3.

Creating the Data Source for Microsoft Word

The creation of an export file was discussed in the two previous chapters. Creating an export file for a Microsoft Word form letter is even simpler, because SAP R/3 does all of the work for you. Follow these steps to download your R/3 data as the data source for a Microsoft Word form letter:

1. From the List screen (Screen 7) of your standard report (similar to the one shown in Figure 19-3), select the menu path List→Word processing, or select the Word Processing button on the Application toolbar.

2. A Word Processor Settings dialog box will appear, similar to the one shown in Figure 19-4. In this box, you can specify

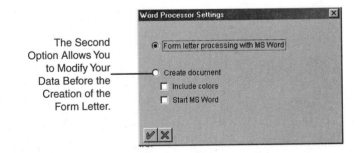

The Second Option Allows You to Modify Your Data Before the Creation of the Form Letter.

Figure 19-4 *Selecting the second radio button will save the report data into a text file that you can use as a data source for a mail merge.*

whether to launch Microsoft Word automatically with the report data as the data source or to create a *Rich-Text Format* (RTF) file that you can associate later as a data source for a form letter.

3. Select the Form Letter Processing in Microsoft Word radio button, then select the green check mark Enter key to proceed.

4. An MS Word Settings dialog box will appear next, where you can specify merge and password options that are explained in Tables 19.1 and 19.2.

Table 19.1 *Mail merge fields options*

Option	Description
New Word document	This selection will launch Microsoft Word and produce a new, blank document that is ready for insertion of fields from SAP and manually typed text.
Current Word document	This selection assumes that you have a Word document already open on your PC that will be ready for the insertion of fields from SAP.
Existing Word document	This selection will launch Microsoft Word and present a dialog box enabling you to select an existing Word document ready for the insertion of fields from SAP.

Table 19.2 *Password options*

Option	Description
Own password	This selection will enable you to create a Microsoft Word password that will be required to open the Word document.

Table 19.2 *Password options (Continued)*

Option	Description
Generate password	The selection of this option will protect the PC file with a password that is only known at run time. Access to the document at a later time is not possible. You should use this function only if you want to edit the document at once (and then no longer require the document).
No password	This selection will create the document and will not require a password.

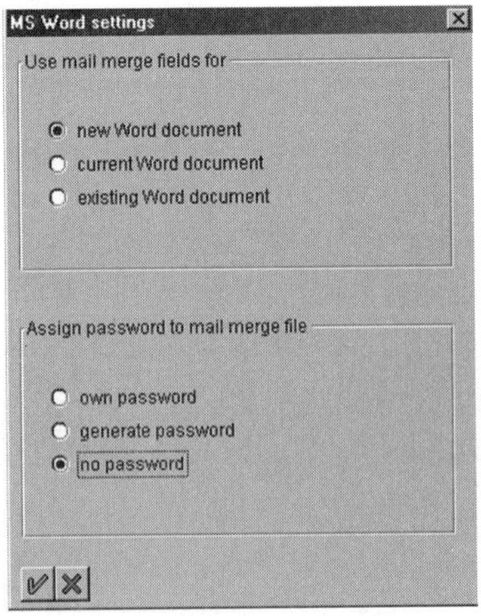

Figure 19-5 *Instead of using an existing document, we have decided to create a new Word document from scratch to use for our form letter.*

5. After making the appropriate selections, see our example in Figure 19-5. Select the green check mark Enter key to proceed.

6. Microsoft Word will launch and display a new, blank Word document with a button on the Application toolbar called

Insert Merge Field. This button is used to insert SAP fields into your Microsoft Word form letter.

Working in Microsoft Word

You should understand that once the export of data from SAP into Microsoft Word is complete, the data no longer reflects real-time data in SAP, and the data is only valid as of the time it was exported. In fact, that data is no longer attached to your R/3 system. Changes made to the data in Microsoft Word will have no effect on your SAP R/3 data.

Creating a Form Letter for Your SAP Data

Now that the SAP data is downloaded to Word, you can create a new letter and use your SAP data as inserted fields in the letter. Your Microsoft Word document appears virtually blank and includes a button on the Application toolbar that will be used for the insertion of your SAP fields. Follow these steps to create your Microsoft Word form letter from your SAP data:

1. Delete the "insert the mail merge fields" line that automatically appears at the top of the Microsoft document, and replace it with the text you want to include in your form letter. In our example in Figure 19-6, we created a reservation document.

2. After adding any picture (optional) and typing some text, add an SAP field by selecting it from the Insert Merge Field button on the Application toolbar (see Figure 19-7).

3. Add more text and insert a few more SAP fields. Then, be sure to save your Microsoft Word document by selecting the Save button on the Standard toolbar.

The merge fields will appear within brackets inside your document. These placeholders will be located where the downloaded SAP data will be inserted.

Viewing Your Form Letter Output

Once your form letter has been created, you can view the output of the document by selecting the <<ABC>>, View Merged

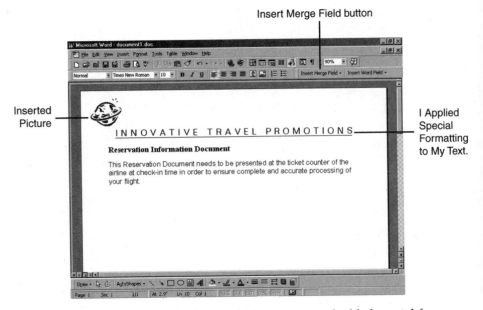

Figure 19-6 *In our example, we inserted a picture and added special formatting to make the document look unique.*

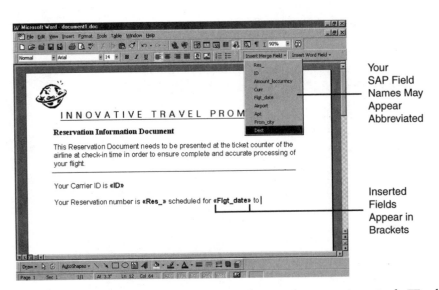

Figure 19-7 *Merge fields can be inserted more than once in a single Word document.*

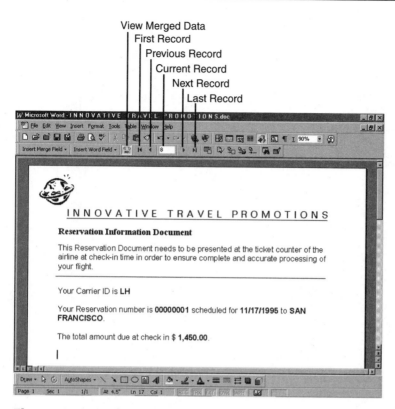

Figure 19-8 *Each record can be previewed using the <<ABC>> and arrow navigational buttons.*

Data button from the Application toolbar. This view will enable you to preview each individual form letter with the actual data inserted by using the navigational buttons on the Application toolbar (see Figure 19-8).

Edit Data Source Options

Let's say that when you're viewing your individual output, you notice a field value that you want to change for a particular record. Understand that the change made in the data source of the form letter will have no impact on your SAP data in your R/3 system. To edit the data source, select the Edit Data Source button from the far right of the Application toolbar. A form will appear, listing each individual record and navigational buttons that you can use to navigate between the records (see Figure 19-9).

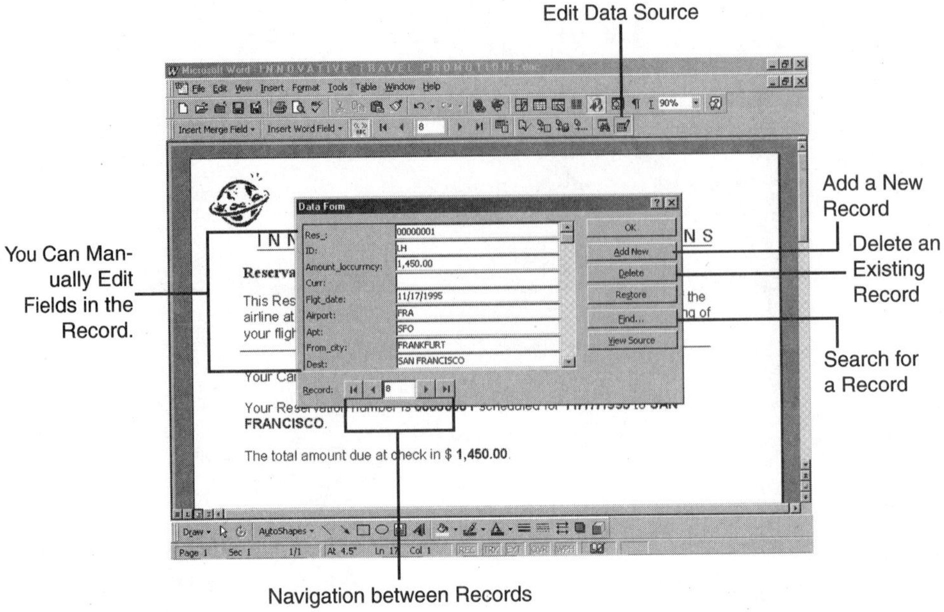

Edit Data Source

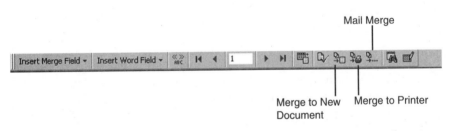

Add a New
Record

You Can Man-
ually Edit
Fields in the
Record.

Delete an
Existing
Record

Search for
a Record

Navigation between Records

Figure 19-9 *Editing the data source in Microsoft Word will have no effect on the data stored in your SAP system.*

Mail Merge

Merge to New
Document

Merge to Printer

Figure 19-10 *The Mail Merge Application toolbar contains several options for processing your form letter.*

Processing Output Options

Once your form letter document is complete, you can choose to merge the document into a new document or send it to the printer. The toolbar buttons for these options are shown in Figure 19-10.

Merge to a New Word Document

You can select the Merge to New Document button on the Application toolbar, which will create a new Microsoft Word document of your output. This new document is no longer a merge document with insert fields; rather, it is an actual output of your data. This new document is no longer connected to a data source.

Merge to Printer

You can select the Merge to Printer button on the Application toolbar, which will send your output to your selected Microsoft Word printer. The output appears as it did when you selected the viewed Merged Data button from the Application toolbar.

Creating Mailing Labels from Your SAP Data

In Chapter 18, we examined how to create mailing labels from our SAP R/3 data. That same capability is available using Microsoft Word. For this example, we will create luggage tags similar to the ones created in Chapter 18. Follow these steps to create labels from your R/3 data in Microsoft Word:

1. Launch Microsoft Word. On a new, blank document, select the menu path Tools→Envelopes and Labels.

2. An Envelopes and Labels dialog box opens, and you can use the Options button to select which type of labels you want to create (see Figure 19-11).

3. Select the New Document button to create a new document full of labels.

4. Use the Save button on the Standard toolbar to save your labels to a desired location, then exit Microsoft Word.

5. In SAP, from the List screen (Screen 7) of your report (similar to the one shown in Figure 19-3), select the menu path List→Word processing or select the Word Processing button on the Application toolbar.

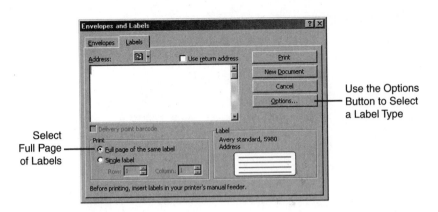

Figure 19-11 *Envelopes or labels can both be created using the steps outlined in this section.*

6. A Word Processor Settings dialog box will open, similar to the one shown in Figure 19-4. Select the Form Letter Processing with MS Word option, then select the green check mark Enter button.

7. On the MS Word Settings dialog box, select the Existing Word Document radio button and then the green check mark Enter button.

8. An Open MS Word dialog box opens, asking you for the name and location of your file. Enter the name and location of the file saved in Step 4, and select the Open button.

9. Microsoft Word launches, displaying your labels document and the Mail Merge toolbar containing the options to insert your SAP fields.

10. Fields are inserted in the same way as before, with one exception. With labels, you are placing multiple records on a single page, so you need to use the Word Field <<Next Record>> to separate the records (see Figure 19-12).

11. You can use the <<ABC>> View Merged Data button to preview your labels (see Figure 19-13) and the Merge to New Document or Merge to Printer buttons on the Application toolbar to output your data.

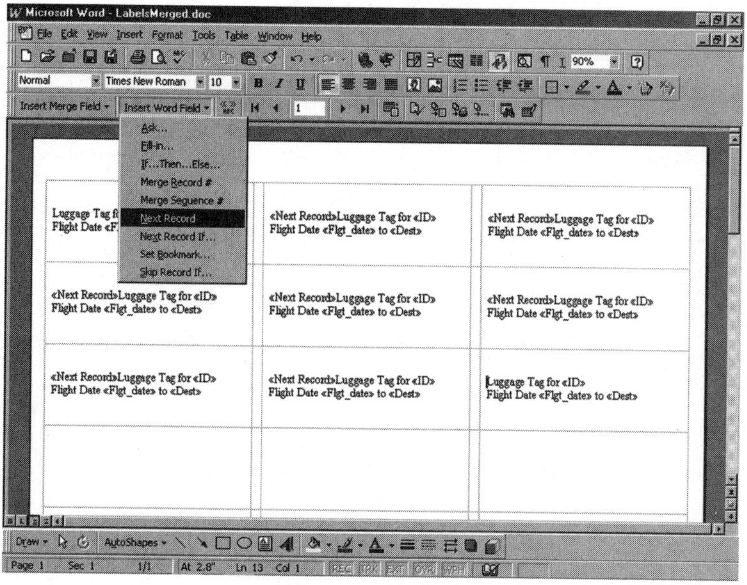

Figure 19-12 *The <<Next Record>> field can be selected from the Insert Word Field button on the Application toolbar.*

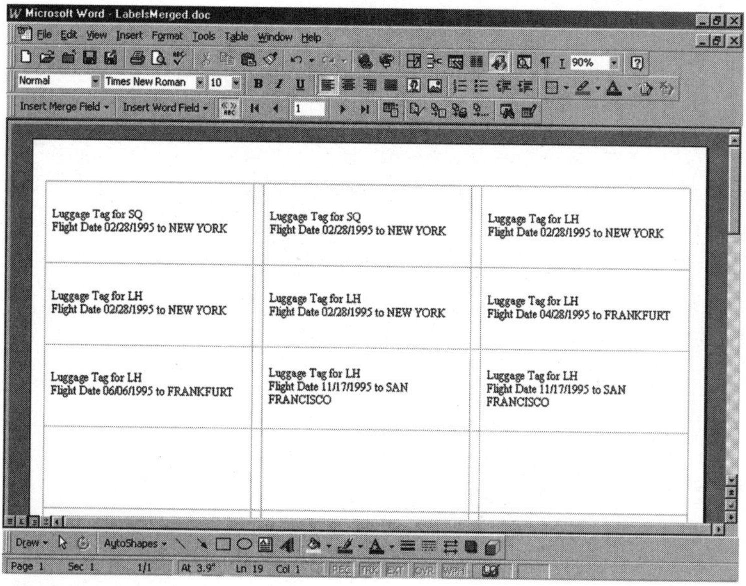

Figure 19-13 *You can add graphics and special formatting to labels in Microsoft Word.*

Creating Labels in Microsoft Word
Versus Microsoft Access

Some users might prefer using Microsoft Word to create labels, while others might prefer using Microsoft Access to accomplish this task. In this book, we prefer to create labels in Microsoft Access, because you only need to create a single label design for all labels—as opposed to Microsoft Word, where you need to format each label on the page. As always, using the trial-and-error method of working with the two tools and gaining an increased familiarity with Microsoft products will help you decide which tool works best for you.

Form-Letter Maintenance

Each time a form letter is created in Microsoft Word, it contains the data from SAP that is only current as of the time that data was downloaded. You can reuse created form letters each time you create a new export from your SAP system by selecting the Use Existing Word Document radio button during the download.

Chapter Wrap-Up

Working with your data in Microsoft Word to create form letters and labels will save you valuable time and resources. The most popular method of working with SAP R/3 data and Microsoft Word is through automated processes, including the automatic scheduled extraction of data from the R/3 system and the automatic population of that data into a Microsoft Word data source. This process would considerably reduce the efforts required, because there would no longer be a need for the import and export procedures detailed in this chapter. Also, this functionality would enable a more focused approach toward creating form letters, labels, and other documents from your R/3 data.

Third-Party Reporting Tools For Sap R/3

As this book has shown, there are plenty of
tools that you can utilize to create and manage
your own reports in R/3. Some companies
decide to use external or third-party tools for
their reporting needs. This chapter gives an
overview of some of the tools available that can
be used to assist you in creating your own
reports in SAP R/3.

Seagate Software

Seagate Software's EIM solutions for SAP help organizations opti-
mize their investments in the SAP R/3 system by enabling R/3
data to be better used for decision support. Through a standardized interface, EIM solutions provide the tools for non-technical
users to access, share, and analyze R/3 data within a flexible
infrastructure designed to reliably deliver queries, reports, multi-
dimensional OLAP cubes, and other critical business information.
EIM solutions economically access data across SAP modules that
can be easily combined with other non-SAP data sources.

Organizations can use EIM solutions to access R/3 data in a
variety of direct and indirect ways—each of which honors R/3
system security, meta layer, and data integrity without degrading
system performance. Seagate Software's EIM solutions are certified for the SAP Business Warehouse, which is a member of the
SAP complementary partner program and is a certified BAPI
partner.

Seagate ABAP Query Driver for R/3

The Seagate QuickStart for R/3 package is designed to give SAP
R/3 users access to the underlying business intelligence that is
within their R/3 system through Seagate Info, Seagate Crystal
Reports, and Seagate Holos. The ABAP Query driver contained in
the Seagate QuickStart for R/3 package accesses R/3 data by running existing ABAP queries on the R/3 server. Communication with
the R/3 server is accomplished through SAP's standard *Remote
Function Call* (RFC) interface, thus honoring R/3 server security.

The ABAP Query driver contained in the Seagate QuickStart
for R/3 package works with R/3 Versions 3.1g and later. The
query driver retrieves R/3 data by running the pre-existing ABAP
Queries that are stored on the R/3 system. Using these queries
enables users to take the query data and turn it into presentation-
quality output with Seagate Crystal Reports, without having to
worry about which tables the data is coming from or the relationships between those tables.

Seagate Crystal Reports

Seagate Crystal Reports 7 is the market-leading database access and analysis tool that will be available in seven languages, including English, French, German, Japanese, Italian, Brazilian Portuguese, and Spanish. For presentation-quality reports from virtually any database, flexible analysis and formatting capabilities, or advanced interactive reporting over the Web, Seagate Crystal Reports 7 is the only tool you need. Benefits and features of Crystal Reports are shown as follows:

- New reports are a snap, because Report Experts guide you through the process of connecting to your data, selecting fields and records, sorting, and using comprehensive formatting and layout features.

- You can create subreports, conditional reports, summary reports, cross-tabs, form reports, multiple details, mailing labels, and more.

- You can examine trends, expose relationships or zero in on important facts with features including charting, geographic mapping, field highlighting and an interactive analysis window. Use subreports, formulas, and customizable cross-tabs to perform further analyses. You can interactively zoom in, drill down, or alter graphs and maps to examine items of interest.

- You can use advanced features such as grouping, sorting, subreports, and cross-tabs to create the report to meet your precise needs.

- Users with compatible browsers can view live, presentation-quality reports using either Java or ActiveX-based Smart Viewers with full navigation and local export capabilities. True multi-platform client support is provided with additional plain- and frames-based HTML viewers.

- The Java-based Crystal Query tool enables your browser to perform ad-hoc querying and analysis over the Web. Selection criteria and sort orders can then be changed dynamically while viewing for true interactive data analysis.

- You can export your report to popular formats including Microsoft Word and Excel, HTML, or even e-mail. You can compile reports into stand-alone applications for interactive viewing, distribute reports via the Web, or just print them out as hard copies.

Seagate Analysis

Leveraging technology from Seagate Crystal Reports, Seagate Analysis provides users with the capability to quickly design and format reports based on query results and OLAP cube navigation. You can also edit existing Crystal Reports. Users can easily transform their analysis into presentation-quality reports complete with formatted text, colorful charts, and highlighted data. Embracing the worldwide popularity of Microsoft® Excel as a tool for basic data analysis, Seagate Analysis enables users to easily transition data from the query or OLAP view directly into familiar columns and rows for further analysis, formatting, and graphing.

Seagate Analysis is designed to seamlessly integrate with Seagate Info, an enterprise-scaleable system used by thousands of companies worldwide to access, analyze, report, and share information with people across the organization. Now in its fourth generation, Seagate Info provides more than a million people in thousands of companies worldwide with a proven, scaleable system for linking people and information. By connecting all the users of Seagate Analysis into a collaborative system that streamlines the decision-making process, Seagate Info adds a secure, manageable, information-sharing infrastructure to your organization.

Comparing Seagate Analysis with Seagate Crystal Reports

Seagate Analysis offers all of the business intelligence basics: ad hoc query and multidimensional (OLAP) analysis and reporting, with export to Microsoft Excel. Seagate Crystal Reports enables you to create powerful, presentation-quality reports. Take advantage of its flexible analysis and formatting capabilities, including mapping, customized graphing, cross-tabs, and subreports. From stand-alone reports to integration in applications,

Figure 20-1 *Visit the Seagate Software home page at*
www.seagatesoftware.com.

Seagate Crystal Reports meets all of your reporting needs. A look
at Seagate Software's Web site is shown in Figure 20-1. The contact information for Seagate Software appears as follows.

Seagate Software

840 Cambie Street

Vancouver, BC, V6B 4J2

Web site: http://www.fetchseagate.com/SAP

Telephone: 1-800-877-2340

E-mail: sales@img.seagatesoftware.com

Sterling Software

With more than 10,000 tables in a typical SAP R/3 database, delivering a robust reporting solution is no simple task. SAP provides a
number of options when it comes to extracting information from

the database. While Sterling Software's long-term strategy already includes efforts towards ODBC compliance with BW and will possibly include SAP's BAPIs, Sterling has had proven success in helping R/3 customers who have reporting problems today. For many organizations with implementations of SAP R/3, the issue of reporting is taking center stage as users realize the inadequacies of the standard reporting capabilities of this popular ERP package. Some of the more critical issues include ease of use, performance, backlogs, and the exorbitant cost of ABAP programming.

MyEureka!

According to Sterling Software, Sterling provides the market's only guaranteed solution for reporting against real-time, transaction-level SAP data. This solution, including the industry's first BI Web Portal, enables all levels of users to create cross-module and cross-application reports and to easily deploy them over the Web or desktop. Sterling Software's solution offers many features that are of particular benefit to R/3 customers, including the following:

• Default SAP R/3 MyEureka! metadata to provide instantaneous access to the most commonly used information in the R/3 database

• Automatic mapping of easy-to-understand table and column descriptions from the SAP data dictionary

• The flexibility to make changes and/or additions to that metadata quickly, without having to redo all of the work done previously

• A server-based Enterprise architecture for UNIX and NT Servers to handle a large number of users, large amounts of data, and the scheduling production reports

• The capability to create complex, sophisticated reports with unsurpassed ease of use

• The capability to combine and relate cross-module information

• The capability to combine and relate SAP and non-SAP data

- The capability to disseminate information automatically to corporate intranets/extranets/Web sites, printers, to central servers via e-mail, or to the desktop

- The market's first Business Intelligence Portal, which enables users to view and execute reports or any other business content from an Intranet or Internet Portal

- Experienced consulting staff to help implement a complete enterprise reporting solution against SAP R/3

- The combination of a sophisticated Report Designer tool with a server-based Report Server for UNIX and/or NT servers, providing a highly scaleable, three-tier, server-based solution ready for the demands of SAP R/3's enterprise-wide applications. Sterling Software's multi-tier architecture combines the flexibility of empowering end users to write reports with the administrative control required by large-scale implementations.

MyEureka! Cube Explorer

The MyEureka! Cube Explorer takes advantage of the three-tier architecture to provide multi-dimensional analysis capabilities. This program is ideal for business analysts, managers, and executives to use in performing "what-if" analyses to review performance of business operations and help forecast future results. The MyEureka! Cube Explorer is designed to maximize ease-of-use as analysts review data for trends and critical success factors over a certain period of time. The MyEureka! Cube Explorer is simple, intuitive, and easy for end users at all skill levels, providing a full set of interactive analysis capabilities. Users can also view predefined data slices in live briefing books that support the entire range of interactive analysis capabilities. The MyEureka! Cube Explorer provides a perfect, easy-to-use, slice-and-dice interface for analyzing the data within BW using matrices, charts, traffic lighting for key indicators, unlimited dimension nesting, graphical drill-down facilities, and more. Sterling Software's solution is proven and is based upon the proper foundation. Having conducted extensive research to determine the true needs of R/3 customers, Sterling

Software has acquired substantial R/3 knowledge, has made product enhancements specific to R/3, and has created a proven methodology for implementing R/3 reporting solutions. A look at Sterling Software's Web site is shown in Figure 20-2. Contact information for Sterling Software is provided as follows.

Sterling Software

SAP Solutions Team

3295 River Exchange Drive

Norcross, GA 30092 USA

Telephone: 1-800-458-0386

Fax: 1-770-409-8953

E-mail: Sapteam@infoadvan.com

Web site: www.sterling.com

Figure 20-2 *Visit the Sterling Software home page at* www.sterling.com.

GETPAID

GETPAID Software, the leading supplier of collection and deduction-management software, announced its latest SAP interface certification for SAP's R/3 system. GETPAID works in tandem with the R/3 and R/2 *Financial Information* (FI) and *Sales and Distribution* (SD) modules to give financial personnel a powerful tool to implement their deduction resolution, credit, and collection processes.

The integration between the products is achieved through a series of *Remote Function Calls* (RFCs), which enable rapid transfer of data from R/3 to GETPAID without ever writing information back into R/3. The integration enables R/3 and GETPAID to seamlessly provide time-critical information to credit managers, collectors, and customer service personnel. The transfer of data from A/R to the GETPAID interface takes place via a download process. R/3 shares invoice, debit, credit, and adjustment detail information with GETPAID. Transaction information is transferred daily in order to calculate daily open balances and aging. In addition, R/3 will share master file information with GETPAID.

GETPAID and R/3 share a single set of customer data for order entry, receivables, and collection transactions. New customer, address, and contact information is entered and maintained in R/3. All customer inserts and updates entered in R/3 are transferred to GETPAID using a set of RFCs to ensure that both customer databases mirror one another. GETPAID takes the A/R and customer-specific data within R/3 and presents the information in a user-friendly format. Driven by its powerful strategic engine, GETPAID benefits include dramatic increases in productivity and improvements in cash flow and customer satisfaction. GETPAID also implements best practices reporting for management of *Accounts Receivable* (A/R) deduction resolution (residual transactions) and collection activities. GETPAID is a registered trademark of GETPAID Software. For a look at GETPAID's Web site, see Figure 20-3. Contact information for GETPAID appears as follows.

Figure 20-3 *Visit the GETPAID Software home page at* www.getpaid.com.

GETPAID Software
959 Route 46 East
Parsippany, NJ 07054
1-800-395-9996
E-mail: info@getpaid.com
Web site: www.getpaid.com

Spectrum Logic

Reporting in SAP is not only about creating list reports. Users also need to think of forms, invoices, purchase orders, etc. Spectrum Logic Corporation develops the tools that make Jetform work better with SAP R/3. Take a look at the sample invoice and bill of lading shown as follows in Figures 20-4 and 20-5.

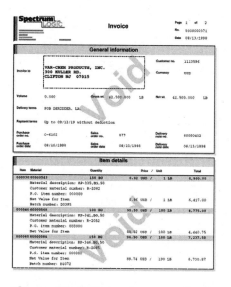

Figure 20-4 *Using Spectrum Logic products, you can include graphics, logos, and colors in your SAP form.*

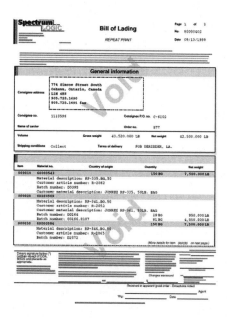

Figure 20-5 *Unlike SAPScript, FormVision enables you to present your output in a graphical format.*

FormVision

Forms Toolbox, a Spectrum Logic product, comes with a form-conversion and form-building utility as well as a host of other form-development time savers. FormVision is a must-have for companies considering (or who currently own) Jetform, an industry leader in the *What-You-See-Is-What-You-Get* (WYSIWYG) forms design tool arena and the leading forms product for SAP R/3. Features of FormVision include the following:

- FormVision Writer: Automatically transforms existing SAP layout sets into Jetform-compatible layout sets

- FormVision Editor: Inserts and deletes fields within SAP with the click of a button. For the first time ever, non-programmers can actually add fields onto SAP documents without having to search the SAP data dictionary.

- FormVision Integrator: Seamlessly integrates the components of the Jetform form solution into the SAP architecture

- FormVision Redirector: Gathers and redirects information between SAP and Jetform components. This feature enables job tracking and makes a Jetform solution transparent to the user.

Additional features of FormVision include the following:

- FormVision Smartboxes: Intelligent fields that only print if there is related data present. This feature makes the form more aesthetically pleasing while saving paper by using the maximum amount of usable space.

- Forty-eight Dynamic Forms: FormVision comes with 48 Dynamic Forms. Additional forms can be converted as needed with FormVision Writer, then edited using the FormVision Editor—easily creating vibrant, attention-grabbing documents.

- Development Safe: Watermarks such as "Void" appear automatically when printing test documents (no more inadvertent mailings of test documents to important clients).

- Fax and Print cover pages

Spectrum Logic has helped some large companies get the most out of their Jetform investment. To learn more about Spectrum Logic's products and services, you can contact them using the contact information that appears as follows. A look at its Web site is shown in Figure 20-6.

Spectrum Logic Corporation

774 Simcoe Street South

Oshawa, ON

CANADA L1H 4K6

Telephone: 1-877-SLC-FORM

Fax: 1-905-720-1691

Web site: http://www.sapall.com

E-mail: mailto:sales@sapall.com

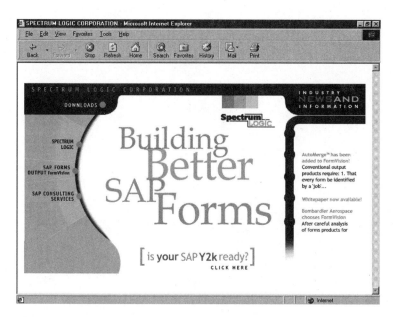

Figure 20-6 *Visit the Spectrum Logic home page at* www.sapall.com.

REVEAL for SAP

REVEAL® is an easy-to-use and highly flexible report distribution, management, and warehousing solution for output from mainframe, mid-range, and network-based applications. REVEAL offers a universal means of capturing, distributing, and storing reports and other information objects from a wide variety of sources through an economical, easy-to-maintain sever architecture and GUI. An overview of the structure of REVEAL is shown in Figure 20-7.

REVEAL for SAP® is part of the REVEAL line of e-business report-management solutions from O'PIN Systems. By implementing REVEAL for SAP, organizations gain immediate and lasting benefits, such as the following:

• Delivering desktop documents

• Increasing productivity

• Shortening cycle times

Figure 20-7 *REVEAL provides unified distribution, storage, security, viewing, version control, and advanced Microsoft Office integration for all SAP reporting outputs.*

- Eliminating report reruns
- Viewing, printing, and exporting reports
- Page and column level security
- Reducing paper costs

REVEAL sets the standard for application-linked report distribution. The following list describes even more REVEAL company benefits:

Improved Information Access

- Instantaneously capture and organize the hundreds of different SAP reports generated with any report-writing application, regardless of output format, ASCII, PCL, Postscript, PDF, Excel, Word, TIFF, and any other file type into an intuitive, easy-to-navigate online report library.

- Provide exceptionally fast, secure online viewing, searching, exporting, and downloading at your fingertips using your standard Windows desktop or the new REVEAL/JavaWeb on your Netscape or Internet Explorer browser.

Increased Information Security and Effortless Administration

- REVEAL-captured reports can be secured to the individual column of information within a page, so that users can access only the precise parts of a report they need (and only the parts of a report that they are authorized to view). Also, security is rigorously enforced across all features—from viewing, searching, and printing to downloading and exporting—so your sensitive information is totally protected.

- REVEAL's GUI administration resides with SAP's database and security tree; therefore, user definitions, report conventions, and security are automatically linked for single point of entry, automatic synchronization, and minimal maintenance.

Enhanced System Performance

- REVEAL substantially reduces the high network traffic and CPU resources consumed by database queries and report printing.

Statistics show that up to 90 percent of ERP information needs can be satisfied by REVEAL-captured reports, freeing up system resources for optimum utilization and better overall response times.

- REVEAL can provide an additional measure of performance when deployed on cost-effective PC server platforms, regardless of the SAP host platform.

Higher User Productivity

- No benefit is more dramatic than the impact on improved user productivity arising from the clear, crisp REVEAL/JavaWeb screen displays that all users can master in minutes, to an array of power features for specific departments. REVEAL SmartFinder enables you to quickly cut through your report repository with a single search to find specific information buried within multiple reports. This feature supercharges your response times to customer service and other inquiries.

Easy Extensibility

- REVEAL SmartOffice Integration provides dynamic, highly flexible, and uniquely configurable links connecting SAP output and the entire Microsoft Office suite—supporting the creation of a entirely new, tailored application extension and productivity enhancement by integrators, IS staff, and even end users.

- REVEAL for SAP can be extended to manage all of your report outputs, from mainframe and legacy to other manufacturing, sales, and support systems (anything that produces reports or viewable files).

- REVEAL for SAP is the ideal migration vehicle for organizations that are beginning to implement SAP, because it smoothes the transition from their earlier systems to advanced SAP-based output. Users can receive their new SAP reporting through the same simplified viewing framework as their older system's output, so training is compressed and adoption is accelerated.

About REVEAL Solutions Group

In the final analysis, the product is only as good as the organization that stands behind it. REVEAL has been the choice of more than 500 of the biggest and best-managed organizations throughout the world and has been recognized as a leader in customer service and support. REVEAL is devoted to delivering the highest customer value attainable.

REVEAL Solutions Group is a division of O'PIN Systems, SPC. Founded in 1985, O'PIN is a pioneer in the development of information delivery and report management solutions. REVEAL solutions capitalize on the convergence of three major factors: the spread of server-based computing, the rise of corporate networks based on TCP/IP protocols, and desktop dominance of Windows-based PCs and browsers. Businesses and institutions are adopting the strategy to put their organizations online with a PC on every desk. They realize that a major portion of the information output they need is produced by core business applications managed by their data center.

Headquartered in Minneapolis, Minnesota, O'PIN Systems delivers its solutions through direct sales and business partnerships in the United States and throughout the world. With an installed base of Fortune 500, governmental, and institutional customers, O'PIN Systems focuses on developing easy-to-use products that deliver mainframe-level power and unique functionality across computer networks. O'PIN's REVEAL software is deployed in more than 500 major organizations worldwide, including 3M, Hughes Network Systems, Health Systems International, Transamerica Financial Services, SGS-Thomson, the United States Department of Defense, and PepsiCo, Inc. O'PIN provides extensive support, implementation, and training services along with its software solutions. A sample of REVEAL's Web site is shown in Figure 20-8. Contact information for the product can be found as follows.

REVEAL Solutions Group

A division of O'PIN Systems, SPC

7900 International Dr. Suite 305

Bloomington, MN 55425

(800) 888-1804

E-mail: sales@opin.com

Web site: www.opin.com

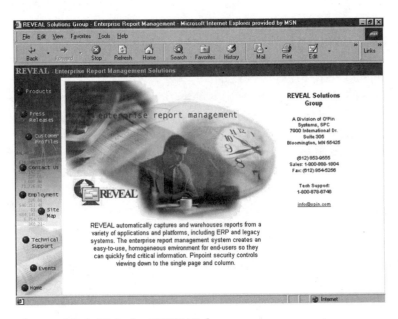

Figure 20-8 *Visit the REVEAL home page at* www.opin.com.

ARGUS

ARGUS Tools—A Higher Level of Human Resources Reporting

At more than 40 SAP-HR customer sites, the ARGUS tools have been proven to increase productivity throughout the SAP-HR implementation cycle. The Argus tools broaden the efficiency of the initial implementation and extend the productivity of the key Human Resources end users.

A combination of extensive consultant input and international experience enables Argus to provide its customers with a comprehensive reporting tool that satisfies the most complex Human Resource reporting requirements. The ARGUS HR Query Tool offers SAP-HR users a powerful tool to extract Human Resources data from the SAP R/3 system. The ARGUS Query Tool has been completely developed in the SAP ABAP development workbench. This element positions the Query tool as a further enhancement to offer the SAP-HR user an online information tool to query the SAP-HR database.

The development of the Argus HR Query Tool has taken into account a full integration with the SAP-HR module. A single environment to maintain and query data simplifies even the most complex reporting tasks for the Human Resources end user. One of the most crucial functions that this integrated Human Resources reporting tool offers its users is quick response times to any query. Benchmark measurements have shown Argus Query to process complex reporting requests efficiently, even for large employee populations. In addition to its extensive reporting functionality, the Argus Query is also a user-friendly product. The user can formulate a complex query in two easy steps. By selecting an employee population and defining a report layout, the user can query the following areas:

- Employee Master Data (Personnel Administration Infotypes)

- Applicant Master Data and Actions (PB* Infotypes)

- Organizational Management Data (HRPLAN data)

- Person related PD reporting

- Payroll and Time result data and Travel expenses (Cluster data using an extraction concept)

Query Population Settings

Reporting is possible on any user selected population. The resulting personnel data can be then be exported to any of the following:

- A standard SAP-HR report, which is launched via the report selection tree of SAP-HR. This report displays the selected population.

- ARGUS Cloud: A PC-based program that creates a two-dimensional graphic of any information in the database (e.g., basic salary versus seniority, or age versus pay scale). This feature enables the human resources user to visualize complex relationships in the company structure.

- Pre-defined MS Excel Macros (e.g., Age Pyramid): This functionality enables the creation of a two-dimensional pyramid graphic in Microsoft Excel with data plotted on the horizontal and vertical axes.

Query Layout Settings

The user can extract specific personnel data from the SAP-HR database for the selected employee population. With the report layout settings, the user can define which fields he or she wants to incorporate in the generated employee reports. The report layout options include the following:

- Query-field selection (Master Data fields, Virtual fields (to group information or to give semantic values), Date fields, Complex relational fields)
- Basic mathematical operations (sum and average)

  Advanced functionality includes the following:

- Complex mathematical operators (COUNT, MAX, MIN)
- Defined sort sequence of the output report layout
- Ascending or Descending indicator for the output list
- The "All" indicator, which allows the display of infotype data, even if the infotype has not been created in SAP-HR
- The "today" and "link" indicator, which manages collision information (e.g., for overtime statistics)

The employee population and report layout settings also enable the user to filter the extracted data for maximum reporting flexibility.

As an example, the required fields are dependent type, name, and age. You want to report only those dependents who are children, however. Without filtering, the resulting list will display information about all dependents. Using the filter, you can exclusively display information about dependents who are children. A preview of the ARGUS Query is shown in Figures 20-9 and 20-10.

Variants

The Argus query tool enables the user to store predefined queries for the population and report layout settings as standard SAP program variants. Two kinds of variants exist—public and private—which enables variants to be accessed and executed by a specific user or by a group of key human resources users.

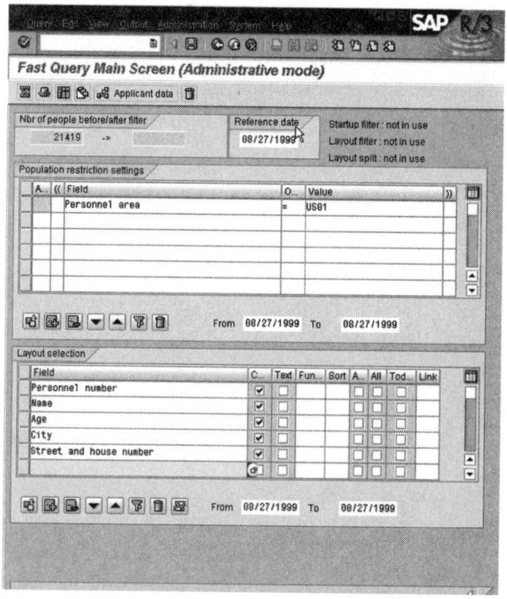

Figure 20-9 *The ARGUS Query Main screen shown here is taken from SAP's Version 4.6.*

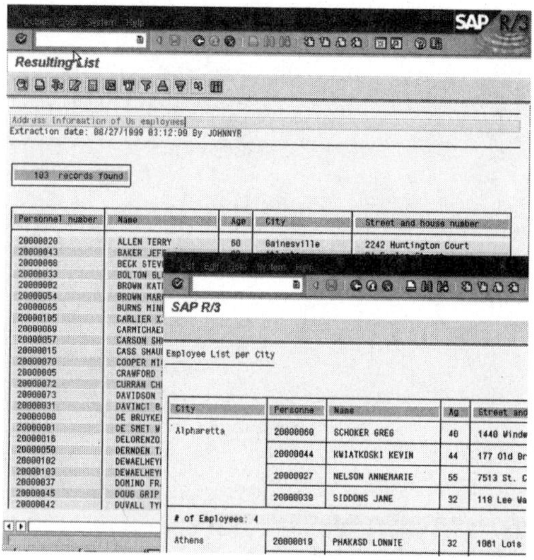

Figure 20-10 *The sample ARGUS Query output screen shown here is taken from SAP's Version 4.6.*

Query Result List

The Query result list contains the information about the selected employee population according to the defined report layout settings. The mathematical operations enable the generated list to be presented in a statistical format. For standard SAP-HR reporting, a personnel list can also be generated. With both options, drill-down functionality is available to the level of the individual employee's Master Data. The drill-down functionality is available by double-clicking the displayed employee personnel data. This capability extends to actually displaying or maintaining the employee Master Data with standard SAP transactions.

The Query result list offers a tight integration with the Microsoft Office Suite (including Microsoft Word Mail merge, Microsoft Access, and Microsoft Excel). This integration is particularly well demonstrated with Microsoft Excel. Data can be downloaded from the query result list into a Microsoft Excel pivot table. This feature enables the user to easily visualize even the most complex grouping of the employee information with a standardized layout. The definition of the pivot table (fields on line, column, and data) can even be defined in the SAP environment and be saved as a query variant.

The Argus Query tool also enables advanced filtering of the query result list. This resulting list can be filtered again by the fields of result layout for specific user-defined criteria. This functionality can be extremely useful when the user wants to limit the displayed information.

As an example, all employees' child dependents are displayed in the resulting list, but you only want to see the list of the dependent children who are older than 15. The query result list also enables the user to execute a standard SAP-HR Personnel Administration report.

Advanced Output Features

The Argus HR Query is enhanced by a powerful complementary tool called the Layout Wizard. The Layout Wizard is an add-on to the HR Query that enables the user to improve the performance of the query. The Layout Wizard also increases the output layout functionality. Each predefined type of layout that can be selected in the Layout Wizard provides the user with a number of specific settings that enable the employee data to be displayed in a customized format. The Layout Wizard add-on also provides the user with the opportunity to create his or her own mathematical formulas to format the statistical result lists in any selected report layout.

Authorization Management of the Argus HR Information

Argus Query fully supports the standard SAP-HR authorization concept. The profiles of the users are taken into account in the Argus Query reporting, which enables the user of the Query tool to have access to employee information on a controlled basis. Employee information can be restricted by the standard SAP-HR authorization profiles (objects P_ORGIN, P_ORGPD, P_NNNN, and P_ORGXX or P_APPL).

Easy Customizing

The Argus Query can be easily customized to meet the specific needs of your company's users. The administrator can change or add customization and manage the authorizations according to the company's requirements. This customization concept is integrated in the Argus Query *Implementation Guide* (IMG). The IMG concept is supported by standard SAP customizing and can be used with limited technical knowledge. The Argus Query documentation provides a concise and complete guide to customizing the Query tool.

ARGUS Summary

ARGUS Query is a powerful reporting tool with the capability to exceed the complex reporting requirements of the most demanding human resources users. The Argus Query Tool is a flexible solution to the increasingly important need for strategic human resources reporting. Specialized support groups in various parts of the world enable Argus to provide customer support to the entire corporate spectrum. The knowledgeable support staff is capable of providing world-class technical and functional support for the Argus Query tool. Continuous development of the Argus Query tool ensures that additional functionality will be provided in upgrade releases to the product. Argus's international experience has enabled the Query tool to handle multiple language formats and country-specific legal reporting requirements. The Argus Query tool provides world-class human resource reporting functionality in an integrated SAP R/3 environment. This functionality enhances the productivity of the SAP R/3 HR suite by enabling key human resources users to make effective decisions with the query tool. The contact information for ARGUS appears as follows.

Argus Integrated Solutions

15 Piedmont Center Suite 820

3575 Piedmont Road NE

Atlanta, GA 30305

Telephone: 1-404-869-2040

Chapter Wrap-Up

In excess of the more than 3,000 standard reports delivered with the R/3 system, SAP offers a handful of tools that users can utilize to create their own reports in SAP R/3. In addition, custom programs can be written by ABAP programmers to yield even more reports. On top of that, the third-party software products discussed in this chapter can also be used for reporting in R/3. Explore the different standard reports and the various reporting tools discussed in this book, then assess your company's reporting needs when deciding how your company will manage and administer reporting in R/3.

21

List Management
Using SAPoffice

SAPoffice is the R/3 system's e-mail and folder system. Lists can be saved in SAPoffice in folders for later review or can be sent via SAPoffice e-mail to internal SAP users or external e-mail addresses.

Note	Documents are sent to external users using telematic services, X.400, or the Internet. Documents are sent to SAP users in another system using SAP Comm (Version 3.0 or lower) or SAP Connect.

Documents can be accessed in the folder system, and each user can create his or her own folder structure for documents when using private folders. This concept is similar to file management in Microsoft's Windows Explorer or File Manager, where files are segregated into folders. Using shared folders, the authorization concept enables users to create folders with general information or information for specific groups that can be viewed by many groups.

Saving Lists to a Private Folder

To get started with SAPoffice, we will use the Birthday List report that we have used throughout the book as our example.
To save an R/3 list in an SAPoffice folder, follow these steps:

1. From your reports output list screen, select the menu path System→List→Save→Office folder, as in Figure 21-1.

2. A Store in SAPoffice dialog box will appear, similar to the one shown in Figure 21-2.

3. Enter a name and description for your document, and select the Move button to continue.

4. You will return to your List Output screen.

Your list has been saved in your Private folder in SAPoffice, so now, let's take a look at this application.

SAPoffice Basics

As mentioned earlier, SAPoffice is the e-mail and folder system of SAP R/3. SAPoffice is based on a hierarchical tree structure of folders. The basic element of SAPoffice is the folder. Like folders in your Windows 95 Windows Explorer, folders can contain other folders. Within each folder, subfolders can contain lists. Private and shared folders can be set up to accommodate personal and public lists and documents. You can navigate to your SAPof-

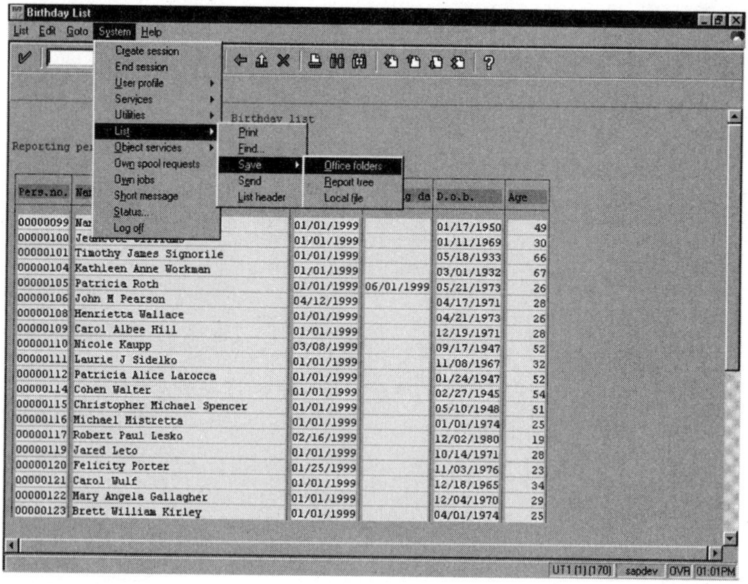

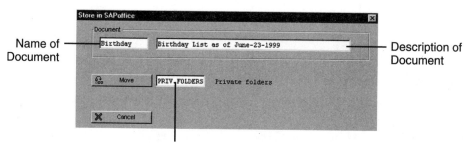

Figure 21-1 *This system menu option is available from almost all SAP R/3 screens.*

Figure 21-2 *SAPoffice is integrated into your R/3 business applications.*

fice Private folder from the main R/3 screen by following the menu path Office→Folders→Private folders. Your screen will look like the one shown in Figure 21-3.

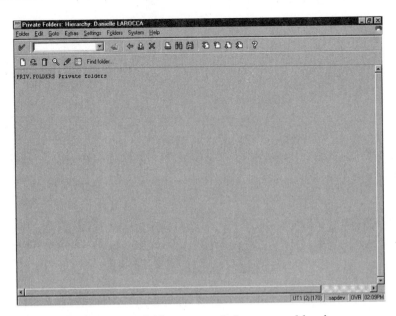

Figure 21-3 *Private folders can only be accessed by the user or by the user's designated substitute.*

You will see the SAPoffice Private Folders Application toolbar in Table 21.1.

Table 21.1 *SAPoffice Private Folders Hierarchy Application toolbar*

	Create	Creates additional folders within your private folder
	Move	Moves multiple folders or lists within your private folder
	Delete	Deletes a selected folder or list
	Choose/ Display	Views folders or lists within a selected folder

	Change	Changes an existing folder
	Key	Provides a color key or legend for your private folders
Find folder...	Find Folder	Provides search capabilities within your private folder

Table 21.1 indicates that if we want to view the list that we added to our Private folder, then we should be able to select the folder and then select the Choose/Display button from the Application toolbar. Selecting the Private folders text and then selecting the Choose/Display button brings us to a display of all lists that we have saved in this folder (see Figure 21-4).

From the SAPoffice screen, we can display our saved list by double-clicking the list. Several options are also available on the Application toolbar that we can use with the report (see Table 21.2).

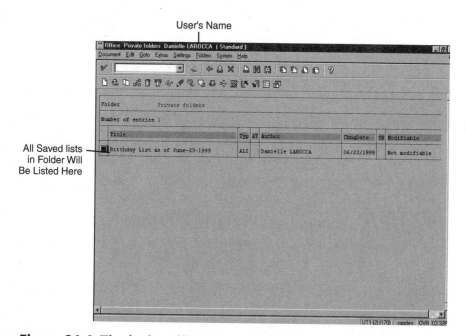

Figure 21-4 *The display of lists shows the description of our list and the date it was created.*

Table 21.2 *SAPoffice Private Folders Application toolbar*

	Create	Creates additional documents in your private folder
	Move	Moves documents between folders
	Copy	Makes a copy of a list or document in your private folder
	Link	Makes a link in another folder to a list or document
	Delete	Deletes a list or document
	Send	Transmits the list or document through SAP office e-mail
	Display	Views the selected list or document
	Change	Changes an existing document
	Attachment List	Displays a list of attachments to the selected item
	Create Attachment	Creates an attachment to the selected list or document
	General Header	Changes the list or document header
	Link List	Displays a link list of any linked items to your list or document
	Refresh	Updates the display on the screen
	Sort Ascending	Sorts all displayed lists and documents (A through Z)

	Sort Descending	Sorts all displayed lists and documents (Z through A)
	Key	Provides a color key or legend showing explanations for the different symbols used in the private folders
	Configuration	Specifies how the folder list, and thus the contents of the folder, are presented

Creating New Documents in SAPoffice

In R/3, documents are classified using different types. The document type is assigned when the document is created and defines which functions can be applied to the document. An administration table exists for defining types. An easy way to think about types in R/3 is to compare the types to other applications on your PC. For example, Microsoft Excel documents are of the type "spreadsheet" and contain a file extension of .xls. See Table 21.3 for more examples.

Table 21.3 *PC documents types reference*

Application	Document Type	Extension
Internet URL	Internet	.URL
Microsoft Access	database	.MDB
Microsoft Excel	spreadsheet	.XLS
Microsoft PowerPoint	presentation	.PPT
Microsoft Windows Notepad	text file	.TXT
Microsoft Windows Paintbrush	picture	.BMP

Table 21.3 *PC documents types reference (Continued)*

Application	Document Type	Extension
Microsoft Windows Wordpad	write file	.WRI
Microsoft Word	document	.DOC
SAP	binary file	.BIN
SAP	SAP archive	.ARC
SAP	distribution list	.DLI
SAP	SAPoffice folder	.FOL
SAP ABAP/4	lists	.ALI
SAP Business Graphics	graphic file	.GRA
SAP Business Object Repository	object file	.OBJ
SAP Editor	SAP raw file	.RAW
SAP Script	SAP script file	.SCR
WinZip	compressed file	.ZIP

The first step in creating a new document in SAPoffice is to define what type of document it will be. You can use the white Create button on the Application toolbar to create new documents in SAPoffice. From your Private Folders screen (like the one shown in Figure 21-4), select the white Create button.

The first selection in the Create Document Header dialog box applies to the type. This selection is also referred to as the document class. You specify the type as a means of classification. For our example, we will classify our sample document as a .doc type, which (as shown in Table 21.3) associates our document as a Microsoft Word Document. This type assignment of .doc enables us to create a Microsoft Word document from within our SAP R/3 application. After specifying the type, we enter a title for our

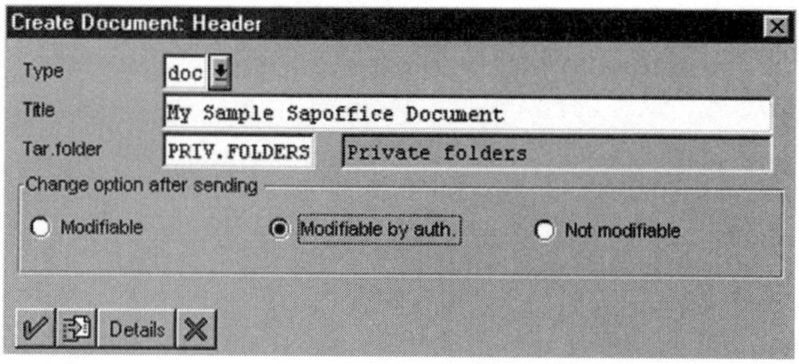

Figure 21-5 *The Create Document Header dialog box enables you to specify the format of the document.*

document and a target folder name in which we would like the file to be placed. By default, the file will move to our Private folder.

Changing Options for a Document in SAPoffice

On the Create Document Header dialog box, we can also specify the change options for our document, and three different settings exist. If our document is in a shared folder and we select the Modifiable radio button, all users with the appropriate change authorization within the shared folder can modify the document. If the document is in a private folder (as in our example) and the Modifiable radio button is selected, only the document creator (and the receiver, if the document is transported via e-mail) can modify the document. If the Modifiable by Auth. radio button is selected, only the creator of the document (or the authorized administrator, if the document is in a shared folder) can modify the document. If the document is transported via e-mail, the recipient will not have the authority to change the document. If the Not Modifiable radio button is selected, neither the author (nor the recipients, if transmitted via e-mail) can change the document after it has been sent.

Placing an Existing File into Your SAPoffice Folder

Instead of creating a new document, perhaps you have an existing file on your system that you would like to include in your shared folder in SAPoffice so that other users can view the file. This file would be added in a similar fashion. For our example, we will use a picture saved on our hard drive. Follow the steps outlined here to add an existing file to your SAPoffice folder:

1. From the main R/3 window, follow the menu path Office→ Folders→Private folders.

2. Select the Choose button from the Application toolbar to display any existing items in your Private folder.

3. Select the white Create button from the Application toolbar, and the Create Document Header dialog box—similar to the one shown in Figure 21-6—opens.

4. Enter a type, title, and change option for your document (see Figure 21-6).

5. Select the Import button to launch the Open dialog box (see Figures 21-7 and 21-8).

6. Select the path and filename for the file you want, then select the Open button. For our example, we selected a picture from our C:\Windows directory.

7. You will return to your Private folders R/3 window, and your file will be listed (see Figure 21-9).

8. To view your document, place an X in the box next to it and select the Choose button from the Application toolbar (or double-click the document name).

Figure 21-6 *Use a meaningful description in the Title field that other users of your shared folder will recognize.*

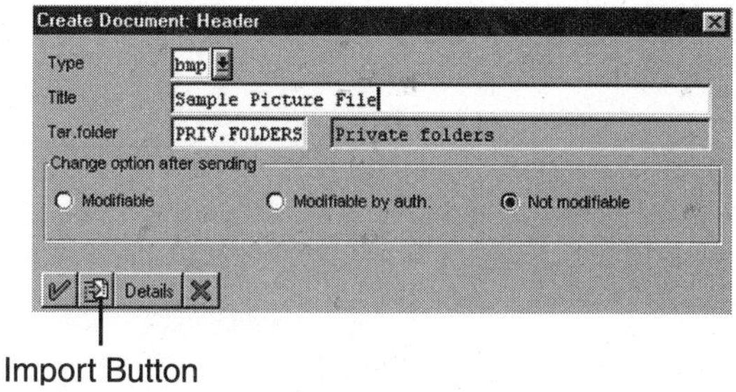

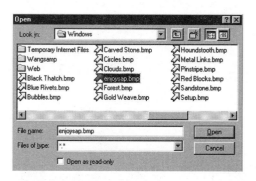

Import Button

Figure 21-7 *The Import button on the Create Document Header dialog box can be used to bring in existing documents from your PC.*

Figure 21-8 *The Open dialog box is the same as the box that appears when you open any file in Windows.*

9. The application associated with the document (in this case, Microsoft Paintbrush) will launch and display your file (see Figure 21-10).

10. When you are finished viewing your document, exit the application in which it is being displayed to return to R/3.

11. A Call PC dialog box opens and provides you with instructions for viewing your file. Select the green check mark Continue (Enter) key to return to SAPoffice (see Figure 21-11).

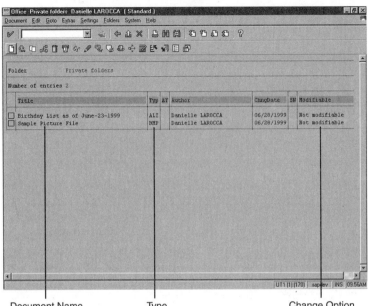

Document Name   Type   Change Option

Figure 21-9 *Your saved documents are listed in your Private folder.*

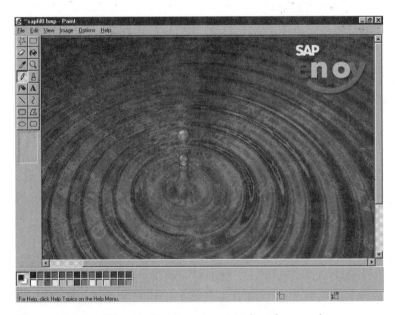

Figure 21-10 *The application associated with your document (via the type) will launch to display your file.*

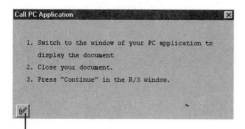

Continue

Figure 21-11 *After closing the external application you used to view your file, you will return to an R/3 dialog box.*

Folder Management

You can use multiple files to segregate and organize your documents in R/3, much like you can on your PC. For example, within Microsoft's Windows Explorer, multiple folders are used for organizing files on your PC (see Figure 21-12).

The same theory applies to SAPoffice, which is also based on a hierarchical tree structure of folders. By default, your SAPoffice will contain a Shared folder and a Private folder. In terms of document management, organization is the key. You can have hundreds of important lists and documents saved in your folders, but if they are not organized and easily accessible, then they are of little use.

Create a New Folder within Your Private Folder

From the main SAP R/3 screen, navigate to SAPoffice using the menu path Office→Folders→Private folders. Your default Private folder will be listed. Follow the steps outlined here to create a new folder within your Private folder:

1. Select the white Create button from the Application toolbar.

2. A Create Folder: Header dialog box opens, similar to the one shown in Figure 21-13.

3. Enter a name and title for your folder. The language and target folder information will be the default. The Sensitivity options are outlined in Table 21.4.

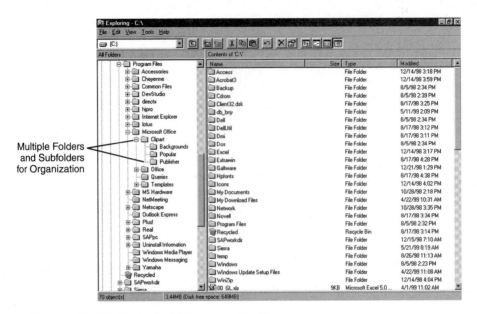

Multiple Folders
and Subfolders
for Organization

Figure 21-12 *Multiple folders provide file management.*

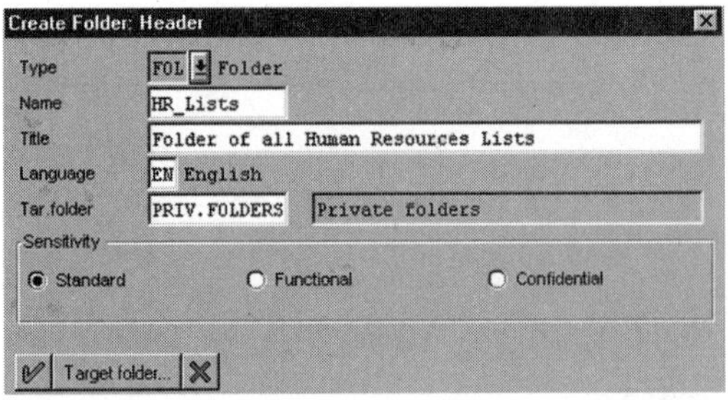

Figure 21-13 *The header applies to the name and basic data in your folder.*

Table 21.4 *Sensitivity options*

Standard	If this radio button is selected, the folder, distribution list, or document is marked as Standard. If an object is classified as Standard when a substitute logs on in your mailbox,

	the substitute will be able to access standard folders, standard distribution lists, and standard documents. If a standard document is sent and the recipient has activated automatic forwarding for all documents, the standard document is forwarded. If the recipient has set automatic forwarding for functional documents only, the document is not forwarded.
Functional	If this radio button is selected, the document is marked as Functional. A functional assignment usually means that the object contains business information. An assignment of Functional is irrelevant for folders and distribution lists, because they cannot be sent. If a substitute logs on in your mailbox, he or she can access functional documents. If a functional document is sent and the recipient has activated automatic forwarding, the document is forwarded.
Confidential	If this radio button is selected, the folder, distribution list, or document is marked as Confidential. If a substitute logs on in your mailbox, the confidential folders, distribution lists, and documents are not displayed. If a confidential document is sent and the recipient has activated automatic forwarding for all documents, the document is forwarded.

4. The Sensitivity aspect concerns the substitute function and controls the access authorization of the substitute for the folder. Select an appropriate sensitivity, then select the green check mark Enter key.

5. A Create Folder screen opens, similar to the one shown in Figure 21-14.

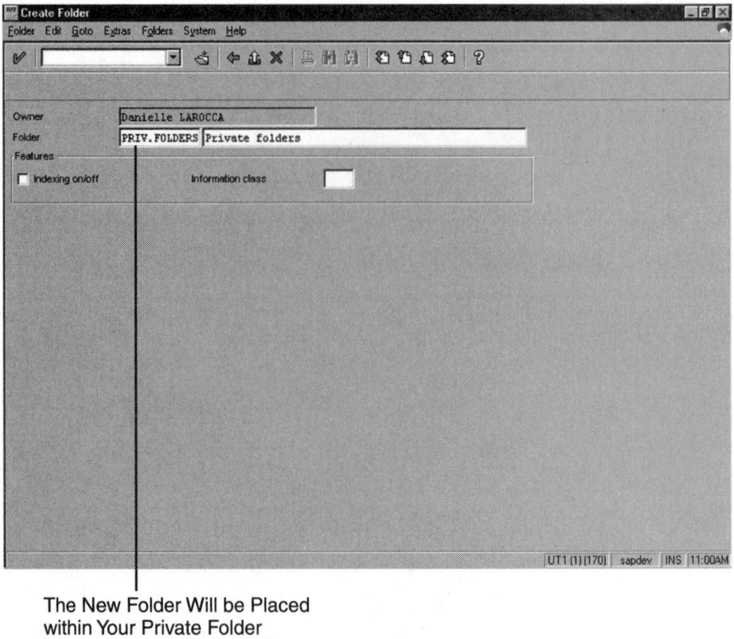

The New Folder Will be Placed
within Your Private Folder

Figure 21-14 *The Create Folder window is used to specify whether an index and information class will be assigned to your folder.*

Tip

You can activate an index for your folder, which causes the folder and all documents in the folder to be indexed and enables faster searches. You are required to assign an information class to the folder if you want to activate an index. An information class provides information about the index file and about the attributes that might have been defined for this class. The information class must be defined in Table TFIC.

6. Select the open folder Save button on the Application toolbar to complete the creation of the folder, and a message opens in your Status bar saying that the folder has been created.

7. Use the yellow arrow Exit button until you return to the main R/3 screen. Navigate to SAPoffice by using the menu path Office→Folders→Private folders.

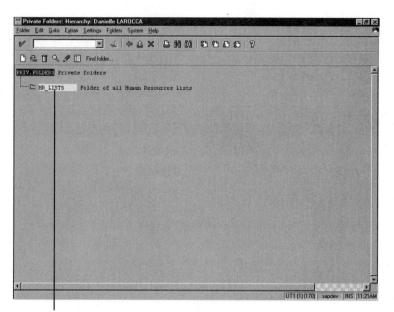

New Private Folder

Figure 21-15 *You can create multiple Private folders to orga-nize your SAP lists.*

8. Your new folder will now be listed under your Private folder (see Figure 21-15).

Moving Objects Between Folders in SAPoffice

Now we have created a new folder that does not contain any objects. Let's add our Human Resources saved Birthday list from earlier in the chapter to our new folder. From the Private folders view shown in Figure 21-14, we can take a look at all items in our Private folder. Place your cursor on the highest level of your Private folder and select the Choose button from the Application toolbar. The list will now include all objects in your Private folder, including the new folder we just created (see Figure 21-16).

The buttons on the Application toolbar (detailed in Table 21.2) can be used to move and work with objects in SAPoffice. Follow the steps outlined here to move objects between folders in SAPoffice:

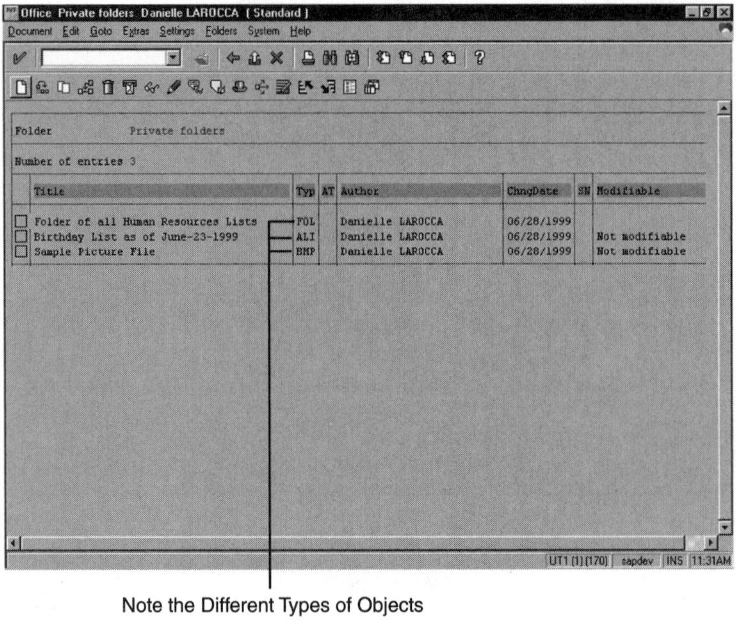

Note the Different Types of Objects

Figure 21-16 *Our Private folder shows all objects, including our newly created folder.*

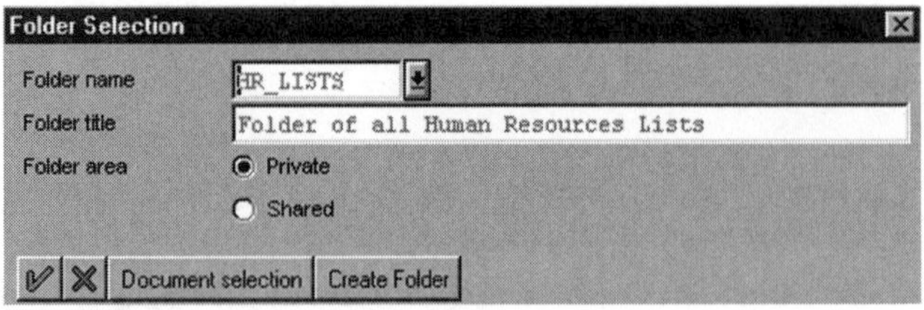

Figure 21-17 *The destination folder is indicated on the Folder Selection dialog box.*

1. Select the object you wish to move by placing an X in the box to the left of the object.

2. Select the Move button from the Application toolbar. A Folder Selection dialog box, similar to the one shown in Figure 21-17, opens.

3. Select the appropriate folder name, and the title automatically appears.

> You can also create new folders by using this method. Select the Create **Tip**
> folder button from the Folder Selection dialog box.

4. Select the green check mark Enter key on the Folder Selection dialog box.

5. This action returns you to the Private folder view, and your object will no longer be listed. Select the folder to which the object was moved, then select the Display button from the Application toolbar (or double-click the folder title). The moved object will appear within the new destination folder.

Transmitting SAPoffice Documents

Documents can be transmitted from your outbox or personal folders. In the inbox, you can forward documents to other users and reply to these documents. You can send documents that you have created, as well as forward items that you have received to other users. Using the Application toolbar, you can configure, copy, delete, and manage your SAPoffice documents. There are two distinct ways of sending documents in R/3: internally and externally. Documents are sent internally when they are sent to other SAPoffice users in the same system. Documents are transmitted externally when they are sent to non-SAPoffice users or to SAPoffice users in another SAP system.

> Authorizations are required for both the internal and external transmis- **Tip**
> sion of documents. Contact your system administrator for more infor-
> mation.

Sending a List Using SAPoffice

In R/3, you have the capability to send objects to another user through SAPoffice e-mail. Again, let's use the Birthday List report as an example. Let's say that you generate the Birthday List report and display the output. Directly from that list output screen, you can e-mail the list to another user. Follow these steps to e-mail your list output:

1. From this report's list output screen, select the menu path List→Save→Office.

2. The Create Document and Send screen will appear, similar to the one shown in Figure 21-18.

3. Enter a note (if applicable) and a recipient's name (the user who will receive the list).

4. Select the Send button from the Application toolbar, and the recipient will receive your note in his or her inbox with a link to the attached birthday list (see Figure 21-19).

Figure 21-18 *Using the mail system, you can send documents internally (to other SAP users in the same system) and externally (to non-SAP users or to SAP users in another system).*

Figure 21-19 *The list will appear as an attachment to the e-mail.*

Chapter Wrap-Up

SAPoffice is a large, detailed system used to manage your e-mail and SAP documents. This chapter has only scratched the surface of the capabilities of some of the functions within SAPoffice in your R/3 system. The focus of this chapter was to familiarize you with SAPoffice to manage lists and other files within R/3. Although we have already pointed out this fact a few times in this book, lists are objects that are frozen in time. When you run a report and save the list output as a document in SAPoffice or e-mail the list to another user, the list is only current as of the time that you ran the list. For example, if we generate a Birthday List report on June 1, 1999, and save it as an SAPoffice document, when we open that list a month later, the list will still only be current with data in the system as of June 1, 1999. The list will not include any new employees added to the system since that time. The skills learned in this chapter, including saving an e-mail list, will come in handy when working with and managing information using your R/3 system.

Customizing Report Trees in R/3

In Chapter 7, we examined the R/3 General Report Selection Tree. That tree comes prede-livered with your R/3 system; however, the tree can be customized. In addition, you can create your own reporting trees in R/3. In this chapter, we will describe how to add existing R/3 reports, ABAP and Ad-Hoc Queries (created earlier in this book), and saved lists to report trees in R/3.

The Report Tree: Initial Screen

You can take a look at a list of reports for a specific module by looking at that module's information system. For example, use the menu path Human resources→Information system and select the Report Tree button from the Application toolbar. This action will display the information system (list of reports) that are specific to the Human Resources module. Using the menu path Settings→Technical names on/off, you can view the technical names for the different nodes in the tree (see Figure 22-1).

Create a new session, and start a new transaction at the same time by using the transaction code /oSERP. This action creates a new session and brings you to the Report Tree: Initial screen, as shown in Figure 22-2.

From this screen, we can create, modify, or display existing report trees in R/3.

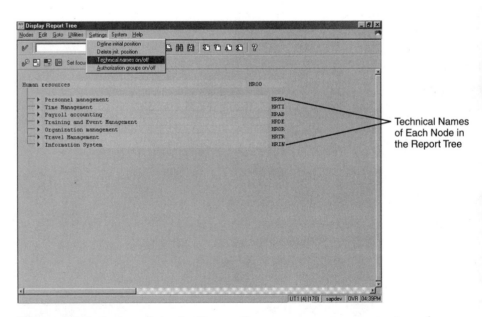

Figure 22-1 *Each node in the Human Resources report tree contains a four-character technical name.*

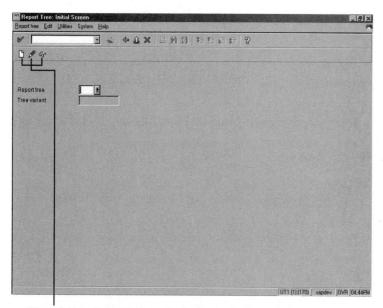

Three Options Are Available on the Application Toolbar to Create, Change, and Display Report Trees

Figure 22-2 *Transaction code* SERP *is used for customizing and creating report trees in R/3.*

Customizing an Existing Report Tree

Our first look at customizing report trees will show how to add a report to an existing report tree. Return to your original session that displays the HRIS (shown in Figure 22-1). Note that the name of the Human Resources top node of the tree is HR00. Switch to your second session, and enter the report tree node name (HR00) in the Report Tree Input field. Then, select the glasses Display button from the Application toolbar. You see that each of the seven nodes of the tree are similar to those in Figure 22-1. Use your green Back arrow to return to the Initial screen.

Creating Tree Nodes in a Report Tree

You can place reports, queries, and lists into existing nodes of a report tree, or you can create your own nodes. Follow the steps outlined here to create your own node in an existing report tree. If you have two sessions that are still open, perform these steps in your second session:

1. Use transaction Code /nSERP to access the Report Tree: Initial screen.

2. In the Report Tree Input field, type the highest-level report tree four-character node under which you would like your node to appear. For our example, we will use HR00.

3. Select the red pencil Change button from the Application toolbar. A Change Report Tree screen opens.

4. Select the node in the tree that you would like your node to appear under, then select the white Create button from the Application toolbar. For our example, we will use HR00.

5. A Create Node dialog window opens. The white boxes in the center are where you enter the four-digit name and description for your new report nodes (see Figure 22-3).

6. Select the open folder Save button on the dialog window, and a message emerges in the Status bar saying that your tree is saved. Select the green check mark Enter key on the dialog window, and the report tree now displays your node (see Figure 22-4).

7. Follow steps four through six to create three more nodes under the new node you just created (see Figure 22-5).

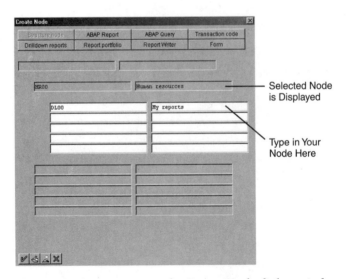

Figure 22-3 *You can use the Create Node dialog window to create nodes and add existing objects to report trees in R/3.*

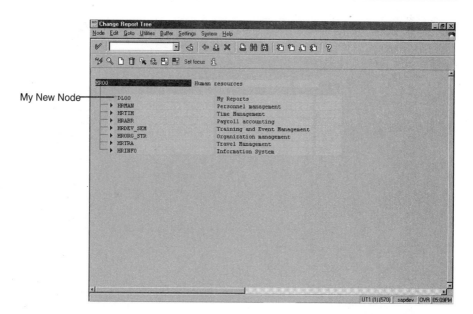

Figure 22-4 *Adding new nodes to existing trees is a good way to organize your reports and lists in your SAP system.*

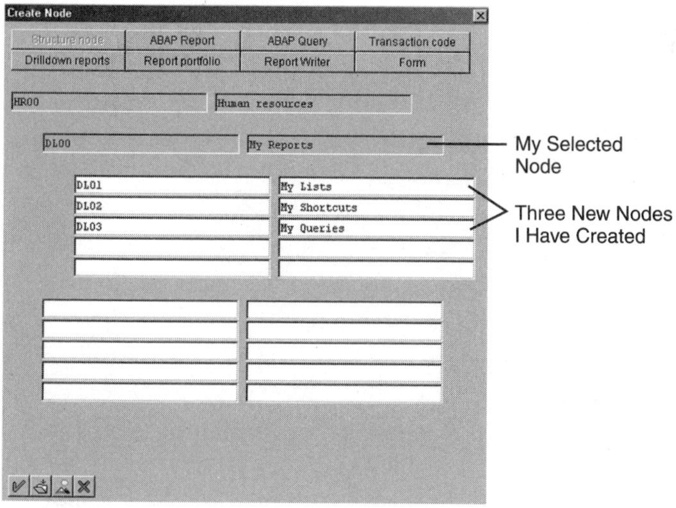

Figure 22-5 *We created three new nodes to segregate our objects from the standard Human Resources reporting tree.*

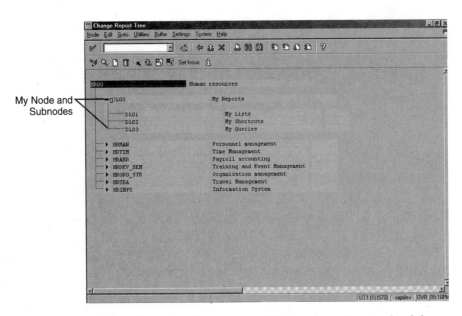

Figure 22-6 *Throughout the chapter, we will place items into each of these three newly created nodes.*

8. The Human Resources report tree now contains a new node, with three subnodes that we will use to store our information (see Figure 22-6).

Toggling between SERP and SARP

In the earlier section, we used transaction code SERP to access the Report Tree: Initial screen, which we used to make modifications to a report tree. To display report trees in their tree structure, you need the SARP transaction code. Create a new session and start a new transaction using the transaction code /oSARP. This code will bring you to a screen that looks almost identical to the one accessed using transaction code SERP, with one notable exception. The Application toolbar for this screen only provides a button for Display, and no maintenance functions can be carried out using transaction code SARP (see Figure 22-7).

When adding reports, queries, lists, and shortcuts to report trees in R/3, you need to toggle between the change (SERP) and display (SARP) views of the report tree if you want to see your

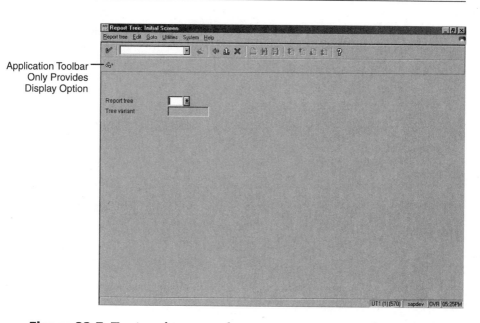

Figure 22-7 *To view changes made to report trees, you need to use transaction code* SARP.

report tree in a tree diagram. Before getting started, make sure that you have at least two sessions open: one session for SARP, and one for SERP.

Adding Reports to a Report Tree

You can add predelivered SAP system reports, ABAP, Ad-Hoc queries, or custom reports written by ABAP programmers to report trees in SAP. To accomplish this task, you need to obtain the technical name of the report. For existing, standard R/3 reports, locate the report in an existing report tree so that you can view its technical name by using the menu path Settings→ technical names on/off. If the report is custom made for your company, you can obtain the report name from the ABAP programmer who created the report. Follow these steps to add an existing report to the report tree:

1. Obtain the program name for your report. For our example, we will use the Human Resources OSHA-200 report. The technical/ program name of the report is RPSOSHU1.

2. Use transaction code /nSERP to access the Report Tree: Initial screen, and enter the report tree name into the Input field. Select the Change button from the Application toolbar. We will again use HR00.

3. Select the node in the tree under which you would like to place the report. For our example, we will select the DL00 node and then the white Create button from the Application toolbar.

4. The Create Node dialog window opens. Select the ABAP Report button from the top of the window. Enter the technical or program name of your report into the Report Input field, as in Figure 22-8

5. Select the open folder Save button, and a message opens in the Status bar saying that the report was copied into the node. Select the green check mark Enter key to proceed.

6. When you return to the screen, you will not see your report listed. Toggle to your other session (SARP), and enter your

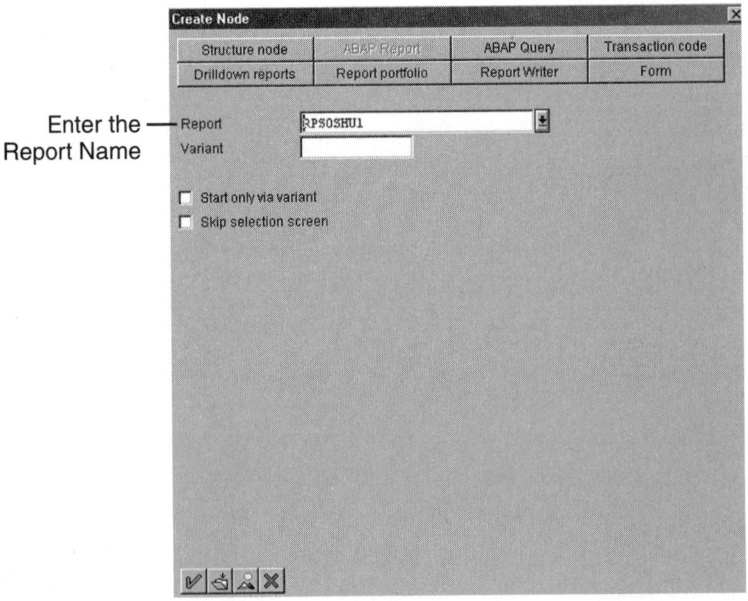

Figure 22-8 *When selected, the ABAP Report button is dimmed at the top of the window.*

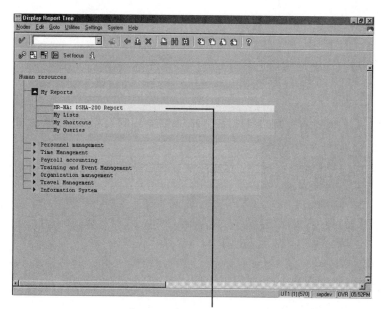

Report Added to the Report Tree

Figure 22-9 *The OSHA report is now executable directly from our node in the report tree.*

report tree name (our example is HR00). Select the Display button, then expand the node where the report was placed to view the report listing (see Figure 22-9).

Toggling between SARP and SERP is helpful for giving you a visual tree-structure view of the items in your report tree. You can view the items in report trees through transaction code SERP by double-clicking a node in the tree. This action displays a new screen listing all of the objects in the selected node. We explore this scenario later when we discuss deleting reports from report trees.

Adding ABAP and Ad-Hoc Queries to a Report Tree

Because a large portion of this book is dedicated to teaching you how to create your own ABAP queries, we can only expect that you will add these ABAP queries to report trees for fast execution and organizational maintenance of your reports. Follow these steps to add ABAP queries to an existing R/3 report tree:

1. Obtain the basic information for your query, which includes the user group (our example will be Z_FLIGHTS, which was created in Chapter 9) and the query name (our example will be ZDL_FLIGHTS, which was created in Chapter 10).

2. Use transaction code /nSERP to access the Report Tree: Initial screen, and enter the report tree name into the Input field. Select the Change button from the Application toolbar. We will again use HR00.

3. Select the node in the tree under which you would like to place the report. For our example, we will select the DL03 (our queries) node, then select the white Create button from the Application toolbar.

4. The Create Node dialog window opens. Select the ABAP Query button from the top of the window. Enter the user group name into the User Group Input field and the query name into the Query field (see Figure 22-10).

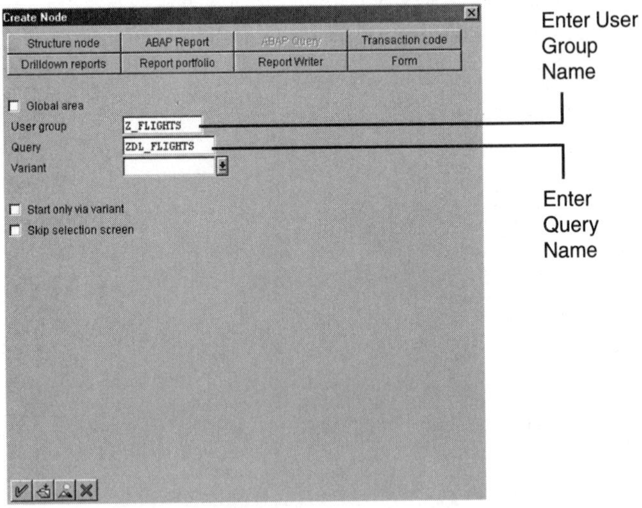

Figure 22-10 *Variants can also be entered for reports and queries in the Create Node dialog window.*

5. Select the open folder Save button, and a message emerges in the Status bar saying that the query was copied into the node. Select the green check mark Enter key to proceed.

6. When you return to the screen, you will not see your query listed. Toggle to your other session (SARP), and enter your report tree name (our example is HR00). Select the Display button. Expand the node where the query was placed to view the report listing (see Figure 22-11).

Saving Variants to Run with Reports and Queries in the Report Tree

Any added reports, queries, and lists are now executable from the report tree. If no variant is saved with the query (this concept was discussed in Chapter 10), then the report or query's selection screen is blank when you execute the report or query from the report tree. You can also save a variant with a report or query

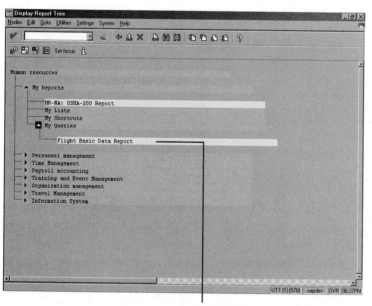

My ABAP Query

Figure 22-11 *You can view the technical names of the reports in your nodes by using the menu path Settings→Technical names on/off.*

from within the report tree. Take a look at Figures 22-8 and 22-10. Not only can you add the variant, but you can also use the two check boxes to specify that you only want the report to start via the variant and/or that you want to skip the selection screen.

Adding Transactions to a Report Tree

In SAP, transaction codes have simplified navigation. These four-character codes can be used from any screen in lieu of a menu path for quick and direct navigation to a particular screen in R/3. You can add transaction codes to the report tree for ease of use or to access custom-made screens that do not have menu paths available. Follow these steps to add a transaction code to a report tree:

1. Obtain the transaction code for the transaction you want to add to the report tree. We will use S000 for our example, which is the main SAP R/3 window.

2. Use transaction code /nSERP to access the Report Tree: Initial screen, and enter the report tree name into the Input field. Select the Change button from the Application toolbar. We will again use HR00.

3. Select the node in the tree under which you would like to place the report. For our example, we will select the DL02 (our shortcuts) node, then select the white Create button from the Application toolbar.

4. The Create Node dialog window opens. Select the Transaction Code button from the top of the window. Enter the transaction code into the appropriate input field, as seen in Figure 22-12.

5. Select the open folder Save button, and a message emerges in the Status bar saying that the transaction code was copied into the node. Select the green check mark Enter key to proceed.

6. When you return to the screen, you will not see your query listed. Toggle to your other session (SARP), and enter your report tree name (our example uses HR00), and select the Display button. Expand the node where the transaction code was placed, then use the menu path Settings→Technical names on/off to view the transaction code listing and its technical name (see Figure 22-13).

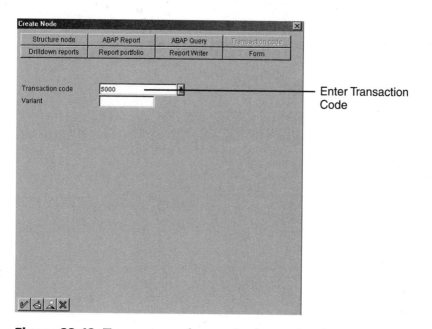

Figure 22-12 *Transaction codes can also be saved with variants so that the input fields are already filled in on the screen.*

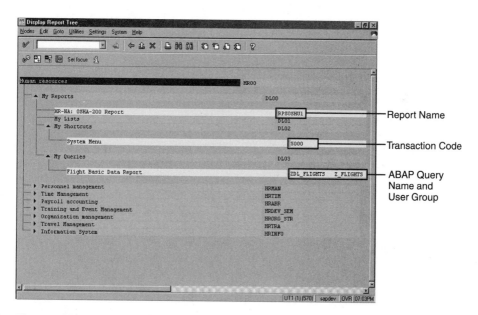

Figure 22-13 *Double-clicking the link in the report tree will bring you directly to that transaction in R/3.*

Adding Saved Lists to a Report Tree

The distinction between lists and reports has been emphasized in several chapters of this book, because the difference between the two is extremely significant. Although you have probably grown tired of hearing this statement by now, we will again note that a saved list represents the data only as of the point in time in which it was saved and is not representative of the current data in your database. For our example, we will use the Payday Calendar Display report from the first chapter. Follow these steps to add a list to a reporting tree:

1. From a list screen (the final output of a report), follow the menu path System→List→Save→Report tree (or List→Save→ Report tree, depending on the screen). See Figure 22-14 for an example.

2. A Save List dialog box opens, and you need to enter the name of the saved list (see Figure 22-15).

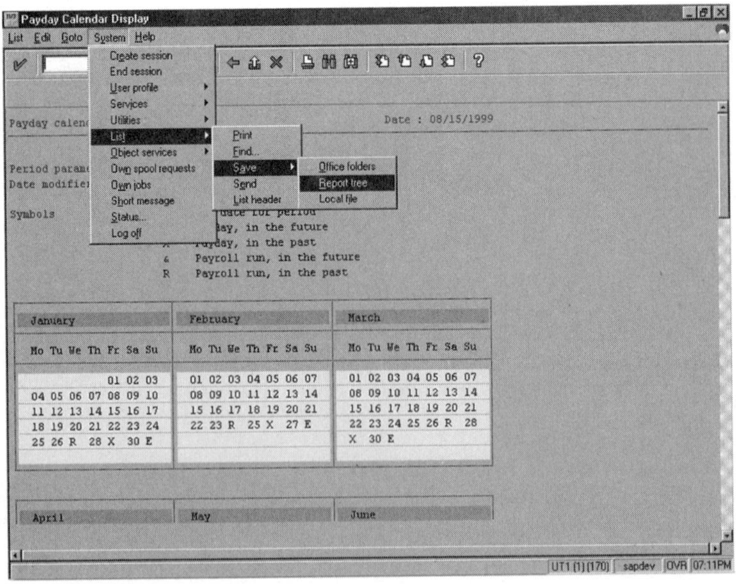

Figure 22-14 *Lists can be saved to local files, to SAPoffice, or to report trees in R/3.*

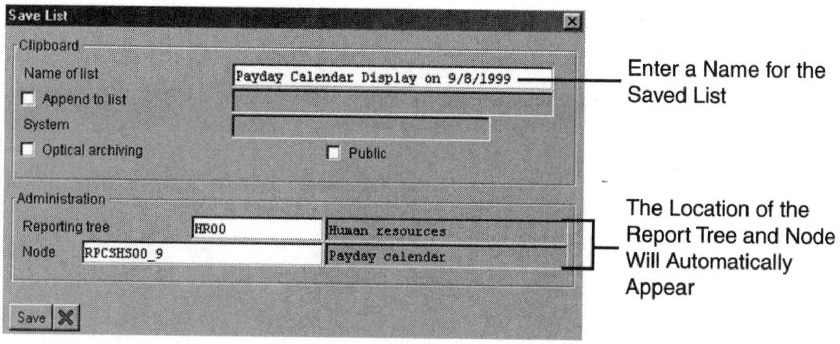

Figure 22-15 *You should include the date that the list was saved in the title of the saved list.*

3. Select the Save button on the dialog box, and a message emerges in the Status bar saying that the list was saved to the node.

4. Toggle to your other session (SARP) and enter your report tree name (our example uses HR00), and select the Display button. Expand the node where the original report was located (in our example, the report was under Payroll accounting→Payroll accounting—USA→Payday→Payday calendar) to view the saved list as a node under the report (see Figure 22-16).

Additional Options in the Create Node Dialog Box

Some advanced options are present in the Create Node dialog window, but these topics are not within the scope of this book. Please review the SAP Help application for assistance with the additional options and for more information about the functionalities available in the Create Node dialog window for drilldown reports, report portfolios, Report Writer, and form options.

Creating a New Report Tree

You might want to create your own report trees instead of adding new nodes and reports to existing report trees. You can create multiple report trees in R/3. Follow these steps to create a new report tree in R/3:

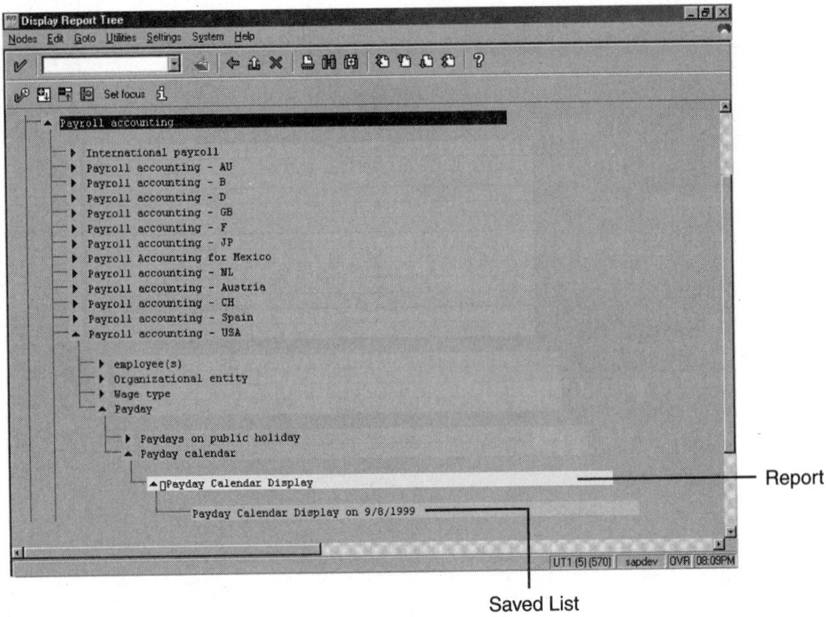

Figure 22-16 *Multiple saved lists can be included in a report tree for a single report.*

1. Use transaction code /nSERP to navigate to the Report Tree: Initial screen.

2. Enter a four-character report tree name (according to your company's standard naming conventions), and select the white Create button (see Figure 22-17).

3. A Change Report Tree window opens, displaying the highest level of the tree. By default, the description of the report tree is the same as the four-character name assigned to the tree.

4. Select the report tree name, then use the menu path Node→Change node text to access a dialog box where you can rename your report tree description (see Figure 22-18).

Customizing Your Report Tree

Any modifications made to the report tree are made in the same fashion as those outlined earlier in the chapter for adding existing objects to report trees. You can add multiple nodes,

Enter a Report Tree Name

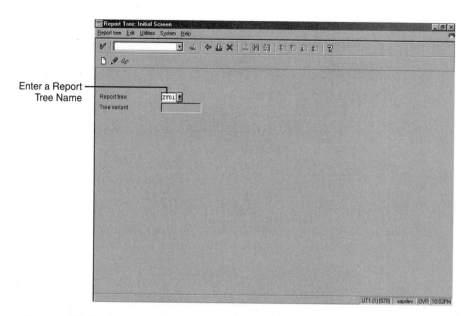

Figure 22-17 *Names of custom report trees need to begin with either Y or Z.*

Default Name

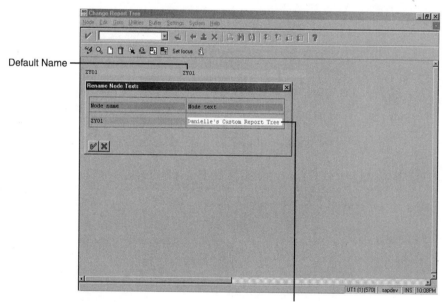

New Name

Figure 22-18 *Individual users can have their own report trees containing their own reports.*

reports, queries, transaction codes, and lists to your custom report tree using the step-by-step approach outlined earlier in this chapter.

Sample R/3 Report Trees

A sample of the report trees that are delivered with your R/3 system are outlined in Table 22.1.

Table 22.1 *Overview of report trees in R/3*

AUTH	Infosystem Authorizations
BPR1	Activity-Based Costing
COPA	Profitability Analysis
ECCS	Consolidation
EIS	Executive Information System
FIA1	Asset Accounting Infosystem
FIAA	Asset Accounting Infosystem
FIAAKIND	Asset Accounting Infosystem
FIAP	Vendors
FIAR	Customers
FIGL	General Ledger
FILC	Consolidation
FIMD	Asset Accounting Infosystem
FISL	Special Purpose Ledger
FMCA	Funds Management
FMCB	Cash Budget Management
HR00	Human Resources
HR21	Time Management
HR22	Tools

HRJP	Administration (Japan)
HRPA	Administration
IMFA	Investment Management
IMFR	Appropriation Requests
J1BR	Reporting (Brazil)
OPA1	Overhead Orders
PC	Product Cost Controlling
PC01	Product Cost Planning
PC03	Product Cost by Period
PC04	Product Cost by Sales Order
PC05	Costs for Intangible Goods
PC06	Product Cost by Order
PC07	Actual Costing/Material Ledger
PC2	Order-Related Production
PC2A	Order-Related Production
PC3	Make-to-Order Production
PC3A	Make-to-Order Production
PC4	Repetitive Manufacturing
PC5	Base Object Costing
PC8	Product Costing
PCA1	Profit Center Accounting
PCF	Cost Objects
PCI	Process Manufacturing
PCIA	Process Manufacturing
PS01	Project Information System
PS81	Individual Overviews

Table 22.1 *Overview of report trees in R/3 (Continued)*

PS90	Overview
PS91	Project Information System
PS92	Revenues
PS93	Finances
PS94	Line Items
PS95	Summarization: Overview
PS96	Summarization: Costs
PS97	Summarization: Revenues
PS98	Summarization: Finances
PSC4	Consistency Checks
RCL1	Reconciliation Ledger
RKS1	Cost Center Accounting
SAP1	Report Selection
SAP2	Report Selection
SAPF	Forms
SDAL	Sales Activity: Address/Report
TRMA	Treasury Management
TRTC	Cash Management
TRTD	Loans
TRTG	Money Market
TRTM	Market Risk Management
TRTR	Derivatives
TRTV	Foreign Exchange
TRTW	Securities
VI01	Cost Element Reports

VI02	Funds Overview
VI03	Structure Reports
VI04	Journal Entry Reports
VI05	Overviews
VI06	Master Data/Agreements
VI07	Controlling/Settlements
VI08	Real Estate Information System
VI09	Selection Versions
VI10	Master Data
VI11	Contracts
VI12	Overviews
VI13	Controlling RE Objects
VI14	Service/Heating Cost Settlement
VI15	Taxes
VI16	Co-Third-Party Management
VICP	Correspondence

Chapter Wrap-Up

Executing reports from report trees in R/3 is the easiest way to produce output in R/3, because it eliminates the need to navigate to the ABAP Query screen to run a handful of reports (and then to navigate to ABAP Workbench to execute some more reports). Report trees provide a single source (or starting point) of reference, from which you can navigate to R/3 transactions via transaction-code shortcuts in the tree or directly to reports or saved output. The report tree is an ideal way of organizing your R/3 information.

Appendix A

Screen 1—Title, Format Screen

The Title, Format screen (Screen 1) stores the basic data for your report—including the report name, format, notes, etc.

Figure APP-1 *Screen 1—Title, Format screen*

435

Screen 2—Select Functional Group Screen

The Select Functional Group screen (Screen 2) is where you select the names of the functional groups that contain the fields you want to output in your report.

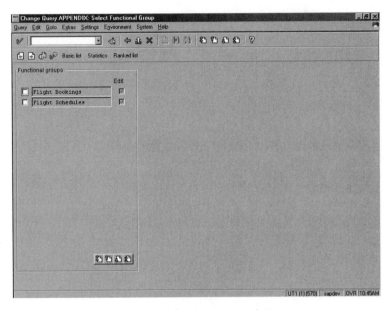

Figure APP-2 *Screen 2—Select Functional Group screen*

Screen 3—Select Field Screen

The Select Field screen (Screen 3) is where you select the names of the fields in the selected functional groups that you want to output in your report.

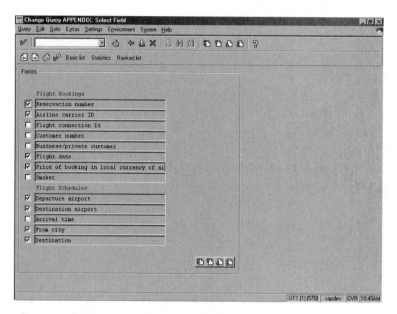

Figure APP-3 *Screen 3—Select Field screen*

Screen 4—Selections Screen

The Selections screen (Screen 4) is where you can add additional
fields to the selection screen of your report.

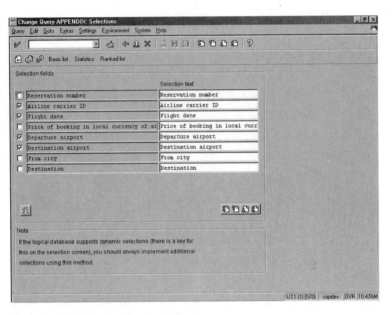

Figure APP-4 *Screen 4—Selections screen*

Screen 5—Basic List Line Structure Screen

The Basic List Line Structure screen (Screen 5) is where you identify on which line and in which order you want your data to appear in the report.

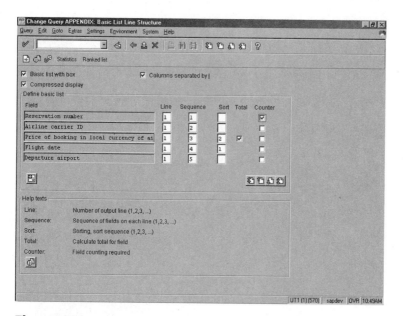

Figure APP-5 *Screen 5—Basic List Line Structure screen*

Screen 6—Selection Screen

The Selection screen (Screen 6) is where you specify exactly which data you want included on your report (selection screens are covered in Chapter 4).

Figure APP-6 *Screen 6—Selection screen*

Screen 7—List Screen

The List screen (Screen 7) is the screen containing the output of
your data, the final results, the report, etc.

Figure APP-7 *Screen 7—List screen*

Screen 8—Control Levels Screen

The Control Levels screen (Screen 8) enables you to place control
levels or subtotals into your report for any field on which you indicated that you wanted to sort on the Basic List screen (Screen 5).

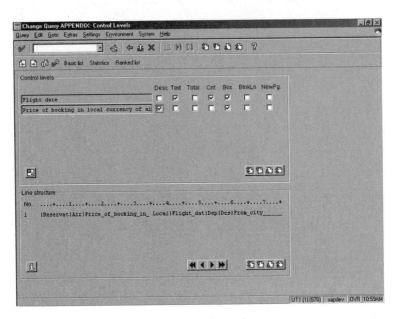

Figure APP-8 *Screen 8—Control Levels screen*

Screen 9—Control Level Texts Screen

The Control Level Texts screen (Screen 9) enables you to modify
the way the control-level texts appear on your report.

Figure APP-10 *Screen 10—List Line Output Options screen*

Screen 10—List Line Output Options Screen

The List Line Output Options screen (Screen 10) enables you to define output options for each line.

Figure APP-9 *Screen 9—Control Level Texts screen*

Screen 11—Field Output
Options Screen

The Field Output Options screen (Screen 11) makes it possible to place fields in a particular place on the screen and to insert texts at desired points in your list.

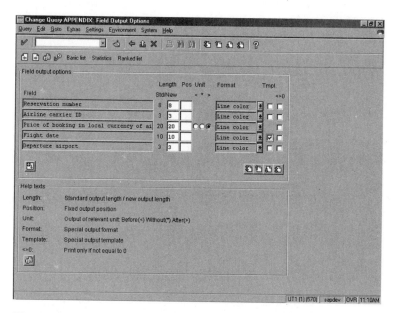

Figure APP-11 *Screen 11—Field Output Options screen*

Screen 12—Field Templates Screen

The Field Templates Screen (Screen 12) only opens if you previously selected the Template option for fields on the Field Output Options screen (Screen 11). You can use this screen to insert text into the column's proceeding fields.

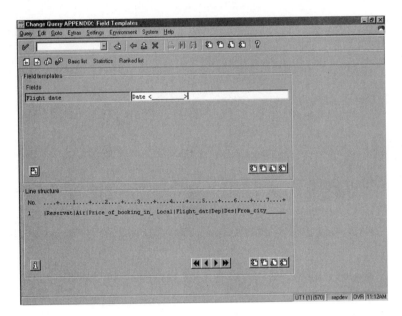

Figure APP-12 *Screen 12—Field Templates Screen*

Screen 13—Graphics Screen

The Graphics screen (Screen 13) is used to define graphical output, depending on the values and graphic type you selected.

Figure APP-13 *Screen 13—Graphics Screen*

Index

Boldface numbers indicate illustrations.

About the Author

 Danielle Larocca is a SAP analyst and author currently working in New York. Danielle holds several SAP technical certificates for topics including Basis Technology, ABAP Dictionary, ABAP List Processing, and ABAP Transaction Programming. In addition, she specializes as a SAP Project Leader and Trainer as well as a Human Resources Configuration and Functional Specialist, holding SAP certificates for components within the Human Resource module, including Payroll, Benefits, Time Management, and Compensation. Danielle has programmed, documented, and instructed multiple computer languages and applications, including SAP's ABAP, Visual Basic, *Electronic Data Interchange* (EDI), and Oracle. Danielle earned a bachelor of science degree in psychology and is an active ASUG member. She currently resides on New York's Long Island.